THE CAMBRIDGE COMPANION TC
TOCQUEVILLE

The Cambridge Companion to Tocqueville is a collection of critical interpretive essays by internationally renowned scholars of the work of Alexis de Tocqueville. The essays cover Tocqueville's principal themes – liberty, equality, democracy, despotism, civil society, religion – and his major texts (*Democracy in America, Recollections, Old Regime and the Revolution,* and other important reports, speeches, and letters).

The authors analyze both Tocqueville's contributions as a theorist of modern democracy and his craft as a writer. Collections of secondary work on Tocqueville have generally fallen into camps, either bringing together only scholars from one point of view or discipline or dealing with only one major text.

This *Companion* crosses national, ideological, disciplinary, and textual boundaries to bring together the best in recent Tocqueville scholarship. The essays not only introduce Tocqueville's major themes and texts but also put forward provocative arguments intended to advance the field of Tocqueville studies.

Cheryl B. Welch received her M.A. and Ph.D. from Columbia University. She is the author of *Liberty and Utility: The French Idéologues and the Transformation of Liberalism* and *De Tocqueville* and editor, with Murray Milgate, of *Critical Issues in Social Thought.* She has also written numerous articles in journals such as the *American Political Science Review, Political Theory, History of Political Thought,* and *History of European Ideas.* She has received research grants from the National Endowment for the Humanities and the Mellon Foundation, and she has been a Fellow at the Radcliffe Institute, at Harvard Law School, and at the Carr Center for Human Rights Policy at the Kennedy School of Government.

Continued after the Index

The Cambridge Companion to
TOCQUEVILLE

Edited by Cheryl B. Welch
Simmons College

CAMBRIDGE
UNIVERSITY PRESS

CAMBRIDGE UNIVERSITY PRESS
Cambridge, New York, Melbourne, Madrid, Cape Town, Singapore, São Paulo

Cambridge University Press
32 Avenue of the Americas, New York, NY 10013-2473, USA

www.cambridge.org
Information on this title: www.cambridge.org/9780521840644

First published 2006

Printed in the United States of America

A catalog record for this publication is available from the British Library.

Library of Congress Cataloging in Publication Data

Cambridge companion to Tocqueville / edited by Cheryl B. Welch.
   p. cm. – (Cambridge companions to philosophy)
Includes bibliographical references (p.) and index.
ISBN-13: 978-0-521-84064-4 (hardback)
ISBN-10: 0-521-84064-3 (hardback)
ISBN-13: 978-0-521-54996-7 (pbk.)
ISBN-10: 0-521-54996-5 (pbk.)
   1. Tocqueville, Alexis de, 1805–1859. 2. Political science – Philosophy
I. Welch, Cheryl B. II. Series.
JC229. T8 C36 2006
320/.092 22-dc22   2005024955

ISBN-13 978-0-521-84064-4 hardback
ISBN-10 0-521-84064-3 hardback

ISBN-13 978-0-521-54996-7 paperback
ISBN-10 0-521-54996-5 paperback

CONTENTS

vii

CONTRIBUTORS

Seymour Drescher is University Professor of History and Professor of Sociology at the University of Pittsburgh. His works include *The Mighty Experiment: Free Labor Versus Slavery in British Emancipation* (Oxford University Press, 2002; Frederick Douglass Book Prize, 2004); *From Slavery to Freedom* (New York University Press, 1999); and *Tocqueville and England* (Harvard University Press, 1964).

Jon Elster is Robert K. Merton Professor of Social Sciences at Columbia University. His most recent books, all published by Cambridge University Press, are *Closing the Books: Transitional Justice in Historical Perspective* (2004), *Ulysses Unbound* (2000), and *Alchemies of the Mind* (1999). He is working on a comparative study of constitution-making in France and the United States in the eighteenth century.

Robert T. Gannett, Jr., is an independent scholar and director of the Institute for Community Empowerment in Chicago. He is the author of *Tocqueville Unveiled: The Historian and His Sources for "The Old Regime and the Revolution"* (University of Chicago Press, 2003).

Arthur Goldhammer is the translator of more than ninety works from the French, including the Library of America edition of *Democracy in America*, which won the French-American Foundation 2005 translation prize for nonfiction. He is a *Chevalier de l'Ordre des Arts et des Lettres* and an affiliate of the Center for European Studies at Harvard University.

Laurence Guellec is Professor of French Literature at the University of Poitiers (France). She is the author of *Tocqueville et les langages de la démocratie* (Paris, Honoré Champion, 2004) and the editor, with Françoise Mélonio, of *Tocqueville. Lettres choisies, souvenirs* (Gallimard, 2003).

Pierre Manent is the Director of the Centre de Recherches Politiques Raymond Aron. English translations of Manent's most important works include *An Intellectual History of Liberalism* (Princeton University Press, 1996); *Tocqueville and the Nature of Democracy* (Rowman & Littlefield, 1996); *The City of Man* (Princeton University Press, 1998); and *Modern Liberty and Its Discontents* (Rowman & Littlefield, 1998).

Harvey C. Mansfield, Jr., is the William R. Kenan, Jr., Professor of Government at Harvard University. He has written on Edmund Burke and the nature of political parties, on Machiavelli and the invention of indirect government, and extensively on American constitutional government and political science. With Delba Winthrop, he translated Tocqueville's *Democracy in America* (University of Chicago Press, 2001).

Françoise Mélonio is Professor of French Literature at the University of Paris IV – Sorbonne. She is the series editor of two modern critical editions of Tocqueville's works for Gallimard and is the author, most recently, of *Naissance et affirmation d'une culture nationale: la France de 1815 à 1880* (Seuil, 2001). Her works available in English include *Tocqueville and the French* (Virginia University Press, 1998); *The Old Regime and the Revolution*, edited with an introduction by François Furet and Françoise Mélonio (University of Chicago Press, 1998); and *The Old Regime and the Revolution, Volume 2: Notes on the French Revolution and Napoleon*, edited with an introduction by Françoise Mélonio (University of Chicago Press, 2001).

Joshua Mitchell is Professor and Chair of the Department of Government, Georgetown University. He is the author of three books: *Not By Reason Alone: Religion, History and Identity in Early Modern Political Thought* (University of Chicago Press: 1993),

The Fragility of Freedom: Tocqueville on Religion, Democracy and the American Future (University of Chicago Press, 1995), and *Plato's Fable: On the Mortal Condition in Shadowy Times* (Princeton University Press, 2006).

Melvin Richter is Professor Emeritus of Political Science, City University of New York Graduate School and Hunter College. His publications include *The Politics of Conscience: T. H. Green and His Age, The Political Theory of Montesquieu,* and *The History of Political and Social Concepts: A Critical Introduction.* He has edited *Essays in Theory and History; Political Theory and Political Education; The Meaning of Historical Terms and Concepts* (with Hartmut Lehmann); and *Dictatorship in History and Theory: Bonapartism, Caesarism, and Totalitarianism* (with Peter Baehr).

James T. Schleifer is Professor of History and Dean of the Library at the College of New Rochelle. He is the author of *The Making of Tocqueville's "Democracy in America"* (University of North Carolina Press, 1980; second edition, Liberty Fund, 2000), co-editor of the Pléiade edition of *De la démocratie en Amérique* (Gallimard, 1992), and the translator of the forthcoming English version of the Eduardo Nolla critical edition of *Democracy in America* (Liberty Fund, 2006).

Dana Villa is Professor of Political Science at the University of Southern California. He is the author of *Arendt and Heidegger* (Princeton University Press, 1996); *Politics, Philosophy, Terror* (Princeton University Press, 1999); and *Socratic Citizenship* (Princeton University Press, 2001). He is also the editor of *The Cambridge Companion to Hannah Arendt* (Cambridge University Press, 2000).

Cheryl B. Welch is Professor and Chair of the Department of Political Science and International Relations at Simmons College. She is the author of *Liberty and Utility: The French Idéologues and the Transformation of Liberalism* (Columbia University Press, 1984); *Critical Issues in Social Thought* (with M. Milgate, Academic Press, 1989); and *De Tocqueville* (Oxford University Press, 2001).

Delba Winthrop is Lecturer in Extension and Administrator of the Program on Constitutional Government at Harvard University. She has written widely on Tocqueville and, with Harvey Mansfield, translated and wrote the Introduction to Tocqueville's *Democracy in America* (University of Chicago Press, 2001).

Olivier Zunz is Commonwealth Professor of History at the University of Virginia. His publications include *The Changing Face of Inequality* (University of Chicago Press, 1982; French translation, 1983); *Making America Corporate* (University of Chicago Press, 1990; French translation, 1991); *Why the American Century?* (University of Chicago Press, 1998; with translations in French, 2000, Chinese, 2001, Italian, 2002, and Japanese, 2005). Olivier Zunz is currently serving as president of The Tocqueville Society. He is writing a history of American philanthropy.

ACKNOWLEDGMENTS

I am happy to acknowledge the friends and colleagues who have nurtured *The Cambridge Companion to Tocqueville* and sustained me along the way. My first debt is to the Tocqueville scholars published here – their professionalism and responsiveness made the task of assembling the volume a pleasure. Particular thanks for advice about essay assignments and the editorial process are due to Seymour Drescher, Françoise Mélonio, Mel Richter, Jim Schleifer, Dana Villa, and Olivier Zunz.

Ed Parsons was a wonderful editor during the writing stage. I much appreciated his enthusiasm, intelligence, judgment, and graciousness whenever the project hit a snag. And Ronald Cohen's meticulous and thoughtful editorial hand much improved the manuscript and saved me from many errors.

A generous grant from The Florence Gould Foundation made it possible to include several contributions from French scholars – superbly translated by Art Goldhammer – with whom it was a privilege to work.

My own contributions to the volume have been enriched by too many scholars to thank individually. For careful readings, I am particularly indebted to Art Goldhammer (whose penetrating and erudite criticism always arrived by return email), Nancy Rosenblum (whose guidance in distinguishing forests from trees came at a crucial moment), and John Welch (whose counsel on matters from copyright to commas was, as usual, invaluable).

Finally, I am grateful to family, friends, and colleagues for their tolerance of my Tocqueville obsessions. My undergraduate research assistant, Catherine Lague, tracked down obscure references and transposed text with unfailing intelligence and good cheer. Meghan

xiii

Field and Jack Welch provided bibliographical help at key points. Zachary Abuza, Kirk Beattie, and Leanne Doherty Mason were always willing to take up departmental slack. And the support, technical assistance, and warm friendship of Maria Callejas and Jessica Robash made it possible for me to juggle teaching, chairing, writing, and editing.

TEXTS AND ABBREVIATIONS

Œuvres, P	*Œuvres de Tocqueville*, edition Pléiade. Paris: Gallimard, 1991–2004.
TA	Tocqueville Archives.
TA (Beinecke)	Tocqueville Archives for *Democracy in America* at Yale University's Beinecke Library.

MAJOR ENGLISH TRANSLATIONS

AR (trans. Gilbert)	*The Old Regime and the French Revolution.* Translated by Stuart Gilbert. New York: Doubleday, 1955.
AR, 1 (trans. Kahan)	*The Old Regime and the Revolution.* Edited by François Furet and Françoise Mélonio. Translated by Alan S. Kahan. Chicago: University of Chicago Press, 1998.
AR, 2 (trans. Kahan)	*Notes on the French Revolution and Napoleon.* Edited by François Furet and Françoise Mélonio. Translated by Alan S. Kahan. Chicago: University of Chicago Press, 2001.
DAI or *DAII* (trans. Bevan)	*Democracy in America and Two Essays on America.* Translated by Gerald E. Bevan, with an Introduction and Notes by Isaac Kramnick. London: Penguin, 2003.
DAI or *DAII* (trans. Goldhammer)	*Democracy in America.* Translated by Arthur Goldhammer, with a chronology by Olivier Zunz. New York: Library of America, 2004.
DAI or *DAII* (trans. Lawrence)	*Democracy in America.* Edited by Max Lerner and J.-P. Mayer. Translated by George Lawrence. New York: Harper and Row, 1966.

DAI or *DAII* (trans. Mansfield and Winthrop)

Democracy in America. Translated with an introduction by Harvey C. Mansfield, Jr., and Delba Winthrop. Chicago: University of Chicago Press, 2000.

DAI or *DAII* (trans. Reeve-Bowen-Bradley)

Democracy in America. Translated by Henry Reeve, revised by Francis Bowen, and further revised by Phillips Bradley. New York: Knopf, 1945. Introduction by Harold Laski [reprinted, New York: Vintage Books, 1990. Introduction by Daniel J. Boorstin].

S (trans. Lawrence)

Recollections: The French Revolution of 1848. Edited by J.-P. Mayer and A. P. Kerr. Translated by George Lawrence. New York: Anchor Books, 1971.

SELECTED ENGLISH TRANSLATIONS OF OTHER WORKS

Journey to America (trans. Lawrence)

Journey to America. Edited by J.-P. Mayer. Translated by George Lawrence. New Haven: Yale University Press, 1960.

Journey in Ireland (trans. Larkin)

Alexis de Tocqueville's Journey in Ireland. Translated and edited by Emmet Larkin. Washington, DC: Catholic University of America Press, 1990.

Journeys to E and I (trans. Lawrence)

Journeys to England and Ireland. Edited by J.-P. Mayer. Translated by George Lawrence. London: Faber and Faber and New Haven: Yale University Press, 1958.

Memoir on Pauperism (trans. Drescher)

Tocqueville, Alexis de, *Memoir on Pauperism*. Translated by Seymour Drescher. Introduced by Gertrude Himmelfarb. Chicago: Ivan R. Dee, 1997.

Political and Social Condition (trans. J. S. Mill)	"Political and Social Condition of France." *London and Westminster Review.* Translated by John Stuart Mill, no. 3 and no. 25 (April 1836), 137–69.
Selected Letters (trans. Toupin and Boesche)	*Selected Letters on Politics and Society,* Edited by Roger Boesche. Translated by James Toupin and Roger Boesche. Berkeley: University of California Press, 1985.
T on Empire and Slavery (trans. Pitts)	*Writings on Empire and Slavery.* Translated by Jennifer Pitts. Baltimore: The Johns Hopkins University Press, 2001.
T Reader (ed. Zunz and Kahan)	*The Tocqueville Reader: A Life in Letters and Politics.* Edited by Olivier Zunz and Alan S. Kahan. Oxford: Blackwell, 2002.

CHRONOLOGY

1805   Alexis Charles-Henri Clérel de Tocqueville is born in
                    Paris on July 29, the third son of Hervé and Louise-
                    Madeleine de Tocqueville.

1805–13   Tocqueville is tutored by Abbé Christian Lesueur, a
                    conservative priest with Jansenist leaning who had
                    been Hervé de Tocqueville's tutor.

1820   Tocqueville joins his father in Metz and enters the
                    Lycée.

1824–26   Tocqueville studies Roman law, the Napoleonic civil
                    code, civil and criminal procedure, and criminal law,
                    receiving his degree in 1826.

1827   In April, Tocqueville is appointed a *juge auditeur*
                    (apprentice judge) at the tribunal in Versailles.

1828   Tocqueville moves into an apartment in Versailles
                    with Gustave de Beaumont, a lawyer at the tribunal
                    of Versailles. During the year, he meets and falls in
                    love with Mary ("Marie") Mottley, an English
                    woman of middle-class origin.

1829   Tocqueville attends, along with Beaumont, the
                    course on the history of French civilization taught
                    at the Sorbonne by François Guizot, whose lectures
                    he finds "extraordinary." (Guizot was a leader of the

liberal opposition to the Bourbons, as well as one of the most influential historians of the nineteenth century. Along with the political philosopher and famous orator Pierre-Paul Royer-Collard, Guizot was a major figure in the "Doctrinaires," a group of political thinkers who had reconciled the liberal principles of the Revolution of 1789 with the legitimacy of the monarch.)

1830

Tocqueville closely follows the French expedition against Algiers.

Protests against the July ordinances in Paris lead to three days of street fighting ("les trois glorieuses") from July 27 to July 29.

Tocqueville takes the oath of loyalty required of public officials on August 16 and repeats it in October, chilling relations with some members of his pro-Bourbon family.

In October, he and Beaumont petition the minister of the interior to send them to the United States to study the American penitentiary system.

1831–32

On April 2, 1831, they sail from Le Havre on an American ship, and on May 9 they land at Newport, Rhode Island. Tocqueville and Beaumont remain in America for nine months. They travel to New York City, upstate New York, the Great Lakes, Canada, New England, Philadelphia, and Baltimore. By steamboat, they traverse the Ohio and the Mississippi to New Orleans, by chance witnessing the removal of the Choctaw to Arkansas. From New Orleans they travel by stage coach across Alabama, Georgia, South Carolina, and North Carolina, to Norfolk, Virginia, where they again take a boat to Washington, DC. Returning to New York by way of Philadelphia, they embark for Le Havre on February 20.

1833   *Du système pénitentiaire aux États-Unis et de son application en France,* their joint report on prisons written mostly by Beaumont, appears in January. (An American edition, translated and edited by Francis Lieber, is published in Philadelphia later in the year.) In August, Tocqueville travels to England to witness what he describes as "the last performance of a beautiful play" as English society moves away from aristocratic dominance.

In September, Tocqueville returns to Paris to work on his book on America.

1835   Volume One of *De la démocratie en Amérique* is published in Paris on January 23.

Beaumont publishes *Marie ou l'esclavage aux États-Unis, tableau de moeurs américaines,* a novel about the doomed love affair of a French immigrant and a white American woman with a distant mulatto ancestor.

Tocqueville writes *Mémoire sur le paupérisme,* an essay published later in the year by the Academic Society of Cherbourg.

In March, Tocqueville meets Henry Reeve, a young Englishman who agrees, after some hesitation, to translate *De la démocratie en Amérique.* (*Democracy in America* is published in England later in the year; an American edition of the Reeve translation, edited by John Canfield Spencer, is published in 1838.)

Tocqueville and Beaumont travel to London. Tocqueville meets again with Nassau Senior, Lord Radnor, and Henry Reeve; is introduced to the Whig politicians Lord Lansdowne and Lord Brougham; and begins a friendship with John Stuart Mill, who is one year his junior. In late June, he and Beaumont leave London and visit Coventry,

Birmingham, Manchester, and Liverpool, investigating the growth of industrialization and urban poverty, before traveling to Ireland in early July.

On October 26, he marries Marie Mottley. As a commoner and a foreigner, and a woman nine years older than her husband, Marie is never fully accepted by the Tocqueville family, although she has formally abjured Protestantism and fervently embraced Catholicism.

1836   After his mother's death, Tocqueville is given the château de Tocqueville, uninhabited since the Revolution, and also the title of *Comte*, which he will never use. With the château he also receives land that will provide most of his income.

At the request of John Stuart Mill, Tocqueville writes *L'état social et politique de la France avant et après 1789*, his first study of the Old Regime.

1837   Tocqueville publishes two unsigned letters on Algeria in the newspaper *La Presse de Seine-et-Oise*, June 23 and August 22, expressing the hope that French colonists will be able to coexist peacefully with the Arabs in Algeria.

He runs for election to the Chamber of Deputies, but on November 4 loses in the second round of voting.

1838   Tocqueville is elected to the *Académie des sciences morales et politiques* on January 6.

1839   On March 2, Tocqueville takes his seat in the Chamber of Deputies as deputy for Valognes.

He gives his first major speech on foreign affairs on July 2, outlining the diverging interests of France, Russia, and Great Britain in the Middle East.

On July 23, he submits a report to the Chamber on slavery in the French colonies of Martinique,

Guadeloupe, French Guiana, and the Isle of Bourbon
(Réunion), calling for the immediate emancipation of
all slaves, the payment of an indemnity to the slave
owners, and a state-guaranteed wage for the freedmen during a transitional period.

1840   The second volume of *De la démocratie en Amérique* is published by Gosselin on April 20. (A
translation by Reeve appears in London simultaneously, and is published in New York with a preface
by Spencer later in the year.)

1841   Tocqueville travels to Algeria with his brother
Hippolyte and friend Gustave de Beaumont.

1842   In his inaugural speech at the Académie Française,
Tocqueville denounces Napoleonic legend. On July 9,
he is reelected to the Chamber.

1843   In January, Tocqueville publishes in *Le Siècle* six
unsigned letters in which he accuses "unprincipled"
politicians of killing liberty while speaking in its
name. Tocqueville has increasingly come to see
Guizot as the leader of a centralizing, manipulative,
and corrupt ministry and believes former prime
minister Thiers to be equally unscrupulous.

From October to December, Tocqueville publishes
another series of six unsigned articles in *Le Siècle*
calling for slave emancipation in the French
colonies.

During the fall, he works on a study of British rule
in India begun in 1840 (it is never finished).

1844   During a debate in the Chamber over state control of
Catholic secondary education, Tocqueville defends
the independence of Church schools. Tocqueville
joins with a group of friends in buying *Le Commerce*
and establishing it on July 24 as an independent

opposition newspaper. In June 1845, Tocqueville ends his involvement with the failing paper.

1846   During a debate in the Chamber in June, Tocqueville criticizes Bugeaud and the Guizot ministry for failing to effectively promote agrarian colonization in Algeria. He easily wins reelection to the Chamber on August 1. In October, he makes a second trip to Algeria, this time accompanied by his wife Marie.

1847   In the winter session of the Chamber, Tocqueville and a few parliamentary friends fail in their attempt to create a "young left" party of "the really honest men" with a program to end corruption and reduce the burden of taxation on the poor. Tocqueville submits two reports on Algeria to the Chamber in late May criticizing the failure of the government to establish effective political, legal, and administrative institutions in the colony.

1848   In a speech to the Chamber on January 27, Tocqueville warns of growing popular discontent.

After the government prohibits a political banquet, demonstrations begin in Paris on February 22 that quickly turn into a popular revolution. The Second Republic is proclaimed at the Hôtel de Ville on the evening of February 24. On March 5, elections are called for a Constituent Assembly to be chosen by universal male suffrage, and Tocqueville becomes a successful candidate in his department of the Manche. The Constituent Assembly meets on May 4 with moderate republicans in the majority.

Tocqueville, Beaumont, and sixteen other members are elected from May 17 to 19 to serve on a commission charged with drafting a new constitution. In the constitutional commission, Tocqueville cites American examples and proposes creating a bicameral legislature in order to strengthen the power of local elites, but the commission rejects bicameralism, as well as his repeated attempts to lessen its plans for centralized rule.

Tocqueville supports Cavaignac in the presidential campaign, while Thiers backs Louis-Napoleon Bonaparte, whom he describes as "this imbecile we will manipulate." On December 10, Louis-Napoleon Bonaparte is elected with 74 percent of the vote.

1849   On May 13, Tocqueville is elected to the Legislative Assembly.

On June 2, Tocqueville is appointed minister of foreign affairs in a cabinet presided over by Odilon Barrot. Tocqueville's major diplomatic challenge is the restoration to temporal power of Pope Pius IX, who had been forced to flee Rome in 1848 by the republican coalition led by Guiseppe Mazzini. In Europe, Tocqueville seeks to support moderate republican regimes throughout the continent while maintaining friendly relations with the reactionary powers of Prussia, Austria, and Russia.

Tocqueville serves as minister of foreign affairs for only five months. On October 31, Louis-Napoleon Bonaparte dismisses the entire cabinet and replaces them with subservient ministers.

1850   In March, Tocqueville is seriously ill, showing symptoms of tuberculosis.

During the summer in Normandy, he begins writing *Souvenirs*, his memoir of the 1848 revolution (published posthumously in 1893).

In December, the Tocquevilles, seeking a warm climate, rent a house in Sorrento in southern Italy. He continues working on *Souvenirs* and begins conceptualizing a major book on the French Revolution.

1851   In September, he writes the third part of *Souvenirs* in Versailles.

Prohibited by the constitution from seeking a second term, Louis-Napoleon Bonaparte stages a military coup d'état on December 2. Tocqueville is arrested, along with more than 200 protesting members of the Assembly, and is held in jail until December 4.

1852   Tocqueville resigns from the Conseil général of the Manche to avoid having to swear allegiance to the new regime and retires from political life.

On December 2, Louis-Napoleon Bonaparte becomes Napoleon III as the Second Empire is proclaimed.

1853   With his health failing, Tocqueville settles in the Loire Valley, and in nearby Tours he reads the files of the royal administration of the province of Touraine.

1854   Tocqueville decides to devote a full volume to the causes of the Revolution. After learning German, he goes with Marie to Bonn in June to research feudalism in Germany.

1856   Beaumont helps him proofread the first volume of his book on the Old Regime. Seeing a continuity with the American work, Beaumont suggests "Démocratie et liberté en France" to Tocqueville as a possible title. His father, Hervé de Tocqueville dies on June 9.

L'ancien régime et la révolution is published in Paris on June 16 by Michel Lévy and is given an enthusiastic reception. (*The Old Regime and the Revolution*, translated by Henry Reeve, is published simultaneously in London.) The book is understood as a work of liberal opposition to Napoleon III and gives Tocqueville renewed political prominence.

1858   Tocqueville goes to Paris in April planning to do extensive research in the libraries for a second volume on the unfolding of the Revolution and the creation of the Empire. By the middle of May, he falls ill.

1859   John Stuart Mill sends Tocqueville a copy of his *On Liberty*. After a brief remission in February, Tocqueville continues to decline as his tuberculosis worsens. Marie convinces her husband to confess and receive Holy Communion, but it is not known whether he recovers his faith. Tocqueville dies on the evening of April 16.

This chronology is a substantially abridged version, with slight textual changes, of "Chronology" by Olivier Zunz, published in *Democracy in America*, trans. Arthur Goldhammer (New York: Library of America, 2004), pp. 878–906.

THE CAMBRIDGE COMPANION TO
TOCQUEVILLE

Introduction
Tocqueville in the Twenty-First Century

One of the most surprising intellectual turns of the twentieth-century – a phenomenon that shows no signs of abating – was the revival of interest in the writings of Alexis de Tocqueville. In 1900, the French had almost forgotten Tocqueville, and Americans were beginning to find his famous portrait of early nineteenth-century America of dubious relevance to their increasingly industrial immigrant nation. Yet in 2000, the *Journal of Democracy* asked public intellectuals to discuss issues affecting the future of democracy – the end of history, the problem of civil society, European federalism, race and ethnicity, the collapse of communism, war and foreign policy, international inequality, women and the family, even the democratic aesthetics of post-modernism – through Tocqueville's texts. The editors commented, "one may say with little exaggeration: *We are all Tocquevilleans now.*"[1] Or, as Jon Elster has put it, "A generation ago it would have seemed absurd to see Tocqueville as the greatest political thinker of the nineteenth century. Nowadays, there is nothing unusual in this view."[2]

Tocqueville's appeal has stemmed less from his ability to offer a grand theory of society and politics than from his curious role as intellectual *provocateur*, a writer who mysteriously appears to address the reader's own concerns.[3] Indeed, from the mid-twentieth century to the present, Tocqueville has manifested a unique power to bring certain political anxieties into sharper focus: anxieties stemming from efforts to sustain civic cultures that will support the practices of self-government; from attempts to create such cultures in unlikely circumstances; and, finally, from troubling questions about the need for unifying moral beliefs as the basis for democratic viability. Tocqueville aspired to create a democratic language with which to negotiate the nineteenth-century European transition to democracy. Although he failed in that aim, the persona he created has paradoxically succeeded in becoming a powerful voice in subsequent democratic discussions, and not only in Europe.[4]

Contemporary interest in Tocqueville has been accompanied by a surge in both primary and secondary texts, including two modern critical editions of his works.[5] The Œuvres complètes de Tocqueville – begun in 1951 and edited by J. P. Mayer, André Jardin, and Françoise Mélonio – has now reached seventeen volumes, with several books of correspondence to come. The three-volume Pléiade critical edition, also edited by Jardin and Mélonio, was completed in 2004. In addition, there have been many new versions of his major works, most recently an edition of letters with the Recollections that serves a valuable biographical function.[6] New editions of Tocqueville's letters and political writings and speeches have also been appearing in English, and it seems that twenty-first century Americans can't have too many translations of Democracy in America.[7]

The secondary literature on Tocqueville – both casual and scholarly, in French and English (and many other languages) – has also continued apace. But these critical conversations have sometimes been isolated and parochial. In particular, collections of secondary work on Tocqueville in English have generally fallen into camps, either bringing together only scholars from one point of view or discipline, or dealing with only one major text (Democracy in America). One of the goals of this Cambridge Companion to Tocqueville is to cross at least a few of these national, ideological, disciplinary, and textual boundaries. A short volume cannot pretend to comprehensiveness; however, I hope that this Introduction may indicate where this book's contributors fall on the map of recent Tocqueville scholarship. To that end, I briefly gloss the twentieth-century Tocqueville revival, and then address in turn the topics used to organize this volume: Tocqueville as theorist, as writer of classical texts, as explorer of democratic themes, and as interlocutor in two ongoing conversations about democratic identity – American and French/European.

Tocqueville wrote to his friend Eugène Stoffels in 1835, "My work appeals to people of opposite opinions, not because they understand me, but because, by considering only one side of my work, they find arguments favorable to their current whims."[8] For this reason, Tocqueville has become a perennial favorite of politicians, who are not above bungling the quotations or citing apocryphal chapter and verse in their efforts to invoke his benediction. Yet Tocqueville also attracts those – perhaps more today than in the past – who attempt seriously to understand him. Indeed, in the twentieth century, he was claimed by several academic disciplines as a founding father. Today his work figures prominently in political science, sociology, and history; moreover, it has infiltrated the academic ranks of philosophy and literature. A consensus on what exactly constitutes "Tocquevillean" analysis, however, remains elusive.

I. THE REVIVAL OF TOCQUEVILLE

George Wilson Pierson's masterful *Tocqueville in America* (1938) gives us a convenient date to mark the emergence both of the American (or Yale) school of Tocqueville scholarship and to note a quickening of interest in Tocqueville by public intellectuals in the United States. After the war, Tocqueville's analysis of nineteenth-century American politics became a touchstone for theorists such as David Truman and Robert Dahl, who drew on America's practice of democracy – allegedly both exceptional and exemplary – to inform a new theory of democratic pluralism. Related to this reading, which saw in Tocqueville's attention to civil associations and parties a forerunner of interest-group theory, was the Tocqueville who allegedly explained why liberalism was hegemonic in America. Here it is hard to overestimate the lasting resonance of Louis Hartz, who brilliantly recast Tocqueville's thesis that America was exceptional because it lacked a feudal past.[9] The Hartzian thesis that America's peculiar history inoculated it against class warfare has served as both stimulus and irritant to numerous counter-arguments about how to theorize political conflict in America. Indeed, the term "Tocquevillean" routinely appears as a synonym for views that privilege the notion of a liberal consensus as the most suitable framework from which to analyze American politics and its history, occasionally provoking such exasperated outbursts as "Beyond Tocqueville, Please!"[10]

More recently, however, "neo-Tocquevillean" has become a label for those American political scientists who find in the associations of civil society the "social capital" on which liberal democracy allegedly must draw in order to function well. Unlike earlier readers, these neo-Tocquevilleans are less attuned to the directly political functions of associations than to their indirect psychological and moral ones. They draw on the second volume of *Democracy in America*, which warns of the dangers of an isolating pathological individualism, and laud the unintended social consequences of voluntary association. Association combats individualism by dragging democratic individuals out of their private concerns, thus indirectly producing socialized and moralized citizens rather than atomistic consumers. In the battle over the place of associations, "neo-Tocquevillean" sometimes seems to be a shorthand substitute for the claim that civil associations automatically create the necessary social substratum for the effective functioning of political democracy; they are an American treasure that has been squandered.

This lament for a lost associational culture and a golden age of community transcends political divisions; it can emerge among both right-wing social conservatives and participatory democrats. One may attribute the alleged decline of associations, after all, to radically different causes. On the right, the culprit is the loss of individual moral fiber, muscle that was once made strong by tough forms of capitalism or traditional families and churches, but that has now become flabby with the welfare state and self-indulgent popular culture.[11] On the left, the villain is a global capitalism so caustic that it tends to corrode not only inherited social ties but all new attempts to arrest its spread throughout the world.

It sometimes seems, then, that Tocqueville has been embraced more than studied by political scientists, who use small Tocquevillean passages to stake out large theoretical territory. Indeed, in the post-war period, it was not in political science, but rather in sociology or the new field of "American Studies" that Tocqueville was read closely and integrated into university curricula. In the 1950s and 1960s, on both sides of the Atlantic, Tocqueville's works were reconstructed to provide an analysis of society and politics that could serve as a theoretical interlocutor of Durkheim, Weber, and especially Marx. Raymond Aron's *Les étapes de la pensée sociologiques* (1967), translated into English the next year, established Tocqueville as the heir to a particular Montesquieuian sociological tradition, a tradition that focused on political culture and the comparative method. American sociologists began to find in the second *Democracy* a deep critique of the isolating and fragmenting culture of modern America. Among historians and students of American literature, the emergence of the United States as a superpower also encouraged reflection on its national identity, a reflection that always seemed to begin with *Democracy in America*. The Tocqueville read seriously by several generations of students in post-war America, then, was often a political sociologist who offered a perspective on the transition to modernity that contrasted with Marx, or a preternaturally insightful foreigner whose observations of American history and culture provided the orthodoxy with which critical thought must engage.

Tocqueville's revival in France began later and developed differently. In the last third of the twentieth century, a generation of readers – among the most important, Raymond Aron, François Furet, Claude Lefort, Raymond Boudon, and Michel Crozier – rediscovered Tocqueville in the context of reclaiming the French liberal tradition.[12] In the 1970s, for example, Furet used his reading of Tocqueville to contest the dominant historiography of the French Revolution, to urge an abandonment of economic and structural theoretical lenses for cultural and contingent ones. In this way, he also assessed the burden of inherited political cultures on the democratic present, and in particular explored the twin legacies of absolutism and revolution that inhibited France's emergence as a liberal republic. Today, French interest in Tocqueville has broadened to a wide current of historical scholarship contextualizing his work among nineteenth-century historians and liberals.[13] Among political theorists, the twentieth-century receptions and major interpretations of Tocqueville have themselves become a subtle medium for reflecting on contemporary French political philosophy and for exploring the resources of a "republican" language of politics.[14]

The Tocqueville revival, then, has inspired political scientists, instructed sociologists, provided a necessary foil for those who study American history and literature, and produced more than one historical and theoretical epiphany in France. As we move further into the twenty-first century, what does it mean to be a theoretical "Tocquevillean"?

II. THEORY

One cannot begin to grasp Tocqueville's approach to explanation without understanding that his thinking is always and everywhere inflected by a restless comparative movement among what he perceives to be the relevant cases, a movement that creates the generalizations that inform his new "science" and "art." He once confessed, "without comparisons, the mind does not know how to proceed."[15] But comparison is not simply a way of gaining a theoretical purchase on the new logic of democracy that Tocqueville saw unfolding everywhere around him; it also clarifies the possibilities for action. As Seymour Drescher notes, "comparative analysis posits plurality – of pasts and presents." Thus, comparison for Tocqueville also means the recognition and renegotiation of alternatives, "a means of navigation towards a differently imagined future," a series of moral choices as well as a method of empirical clarification.[16] Drescher's essay gives an overview of the comparative dimensions of Tocqueville's thought (his global reach as well as his core preoccupation with Europe). He argues that despite Tocqueville's urge to rise to an ideal-typical level of abstraction, he in fact remained tied to his core cases, and in particular to a complex and shifting conceptualization of Anglo-America as against France-Europe. Drescher, then, does not attempt to find in Tocqueville a sociological model or an all-encompassing theory, but rather extracts theoretical guidance from Tocqueville's practice, from his repeated attempts to look beyond his own society in order to understand it.[17]

In "Tocqueville on 1789," Jon Elster draws a different kind of theoretical inspiration from Tocqueville's practice. Like Drescher, he thinks it a mistake to seek a theoretical consistency "of the whole"; indeed, he has argued elsewhere that in Tocqueville, "the details are of greater interest than the whole, the reasoning is more compelling than the conclusions, and the partial mechanisms more robust than the general theories."[18] Those details, insights, and partial trains of thought, according to Elster, provide a remarkable conceptualization of social psychological causal mechanisms that revolve around desires, beliefs, and actions. In *Political Psychology*, Elster examined the "equilibrium analysis" of *Democracy in America*; in this essay, he analyzes the process of long-term social change as presented in the *Old Regime and the Revolution* and in Tocqueville's notes for a second volume. In both, Elster seeks to isolate particularly fertile causal hypotheses – patterns in which psychological effects interact to produce larger-scale social phenomena. "Tocqueville on 1789," beyond offering new insights into the essential structure of the text, breaks down Tocqueville's explanation of the fragmentation of elites in the old regime into the different causal "mechanisms" surrounding envy and hatred, and also analyzes Tocqueville's own versions of the "Tocqueville paradox" (the insight that reforms may trigger revolutions). Elster thus sees Tocqueville as a theoretical ally: a powerful generalizer who rises above mere narrative, but who nevertheless avoids arid nomological dead ends, achieving, in his best moments, a "superb understanding of social explanation."[19]

Tocqueville, then, continues to inspire those who are attracted to a particular kind of explanation of social phenomena, an explanation that falls somewhere between cultural reconstruction and theoretical generalization, and that illuminates precisely because it works in this "half-light."[20] Perhaps more surprising, however, is the recent inclusion of Tocqueville in the pantheon of political philosophers on both sides of the Atlantic. In the past, rarely placed among the great political philosophers, or even among the canonical theorists who figure in histories of political ideas, Tocqueville is now included on the syllabus for the French *agrégation de philosophie*, and generates an unusual amount of attention among academic political theorists. One might well echo Pierre Manent: "what are we to think of this belated promotion of Tocqueville to the rank of philosopher?"[21]

Harvey Mansfield and Delba Winthrop explore this question by finding yet another kind of theoretical inspiration in Tocquevillean practice. Developing themes articulated in the introduction to their translation of the *Democracy*, they argue that Tocqueville's new political science, "embedded in fact rather than abstracted in a theory," must be inferred from the practice of Americans, and preeminently from their characteristic manner of promoting religion, pursuing self-interest, and practicing democratic *moeurs*.[22]

They position this political science against the old political science of Hobbes, Locke, and Rousseau, which defined itself by a focus on political legitimacy and the techniques of liberal government. Tocqueville, then, is a democratic liberal who unsettles the modern liberal project by ignoring its characteristic apparatus (the state of nature, the social contract, the right of consent, and sovereignty) and substituting an implicitly Aristotelian concern for judging and training souls. And this is the crux of Pierre Manent's elevation of Tocqueville to the role of philosopher: democracy reveals itself as one of the two possible archetypes of the human soul – democracy and aristocracy. These archetypes serve as modern reincarnations of ancient regimes. Indeed, the polarity between democracy and aristocracy is expressed in "the very language in which politics was first articulated when it was brought to light in the political life, and through the political philosophy, of ancient Greece."[23]

For Mansfield and Winthrop, as well as for Manent, Tocqueville's subtle juxtaposition of what one might call the different "life-forms" of aristocracy and democracy presents the reader with implicit lessons about how to rise above both the mediocrity and the dangers of the democratic état social. Manent's is perhaps the darker view of those dangers. On his account, equality of conditions (le fait générateur) fused with the dogma of the sovereignty of the people (le principe générateur) unleashes human willfulness in a destructive cycle that continually threatens to undermine the natural order of human life. But for all three theorists, Tocqueville can be understood to have reintroduced an irresolvable tension (conceptualized as a theoretical gap between greatness and virtue, or between grandeur and justice) that is more ancient than modern.

Theorists who are influenced by Leo Strauss's view of the modern project are not alone in reading Tocqueville in two uncommon contexts – as against the political thought of the ancients and against the modern liberal tradition of natural rights from Hobbes to Rousseau. For example, Sheldon Wolin in Tocqueville Between Two Worlds also situates Tocqueville in the company of theorists that he rather conspicuously avoided. Tocqueville had, after all, "barely read" Plato and Aristotle,[24] he admonished himself not to use inapt examples from the ancient world,[25] and he hardly mentions the modern liberals. These silences seem not to matter. Tocqueville becomes a political philosopher because of his implicit critique of modernity – his view that democracy tends to obliterate pride, or greatness, or, in the case of Wolin, those episodic, rare, and heroic moments when the truly political is possible.

III. TEXTS

Tocqueville has left us four major texts: the two volumes of *Democracy in America*, the posthumously published *Recollections*, and the *Old Regime and the Revolution*. Perhaps the most striking evidence that Tocqueville has become a "great" is that these works are now routinely referred to as literary classics.[26] And one reads a classic not simply for what can be culled to further an intellectual agenda, but with a peculiar kind of respect for a unique textual world that deserves to be understood in its own terms. Thus Tocqueville is not just someone whom we can mine for guidance about our own problems, not just an alternative to Marx, or precursor of Weber, or liberal sage, or denouncer of tyranny; rather, he represents a complex puzzle in his own right. The appearance of concurrent English translations of *Democracy in America* has tended to intensify this focus on language, style, tone, and rhetoric. How did Tocqueville create the distinctive voice that speaks to us from his texts?

Both James Schleifer and Arthur Goldhammer, translators who have spent years living with the text of Tocqueville's *Democracy in America*, remind us of his extreme self-consciousness as a writer, his effort to shape his insights about democracy into a persuasive rhetoric of common sense and reassurance, and his conviction – in Goldhammer's words – that the "classical armature" can be made adequate to rendering new things and persuading a new generation. (The relationship of Tocqueville's style to the French classical moralists is also elegantly dissected in Françoise Mélonio's situation of Tocqueville in the French literary tradition.)

James Schleifer's study of the unpublished notes and archival sources for the two *Democracies* reveals a writer constantly rethinking, rewriting, and attempting to distill new material into concise deductive trains of reasoning or into striking spatial and visual metaphors. He shows us a Tocqueville – we will see the same authorial impulse at work in the *Old Regime* – omitting distracting exegesis and deliberately suppressing his sources in order to establish a direct tie to his readers and better influence their practice. Goldhammer reflects explicitly on this rhetorical attempt both to describe and shape democratic practice by focusing on two allusive Tocquevillean terms: *l'intérêt bien entendu* and *l'instinct*. By textualizing these terms (within *Democracy in America*), contextualizing them (within Tocqueville's literary universe), and exploring their resonances (in French and English), Goldhammer meditates on the "art" of shaping politics and texts. He employs a classical metaphor also frequently revived in the nineteenth century: writers and statesmen as voyagers navigating uncharted and dangerous waters. The legislator and the translator sail by "instinct," and only retrospectively – by a safe arrival in port – know whether their choices are justified.

Laurence Guellec and Robert Gannett take up, among many other matters associated with the composition of his texts, Tocqueville's own failure to arrive safely in port. Tocqueville's rhetorical stance in the *Democracy* failed to persuade. Indeed, undermined by his own awareness that democracy demotes the all-seeing "writer-orator" to the status of just another competitor for the public's ear (an awareness revealed by his irony, his distancing metaphors, and his self-confessed failure to achieve the "divine point of view"), Tocqueville abandoned his initial effort to create a new democratic language. Hence the very different writerly persona of the posthumous *Recollections* (satirical chronicler who mocks the grotesque language of democracy) or of the *Old Regime and the Revolution* (master archivist who unearths shocking historical secrets). At the end of her essay, Guellec raises a question that becomes one of Gannett's "shifting puzzles." What are we to make of Tocqueville's statement in the *Old Regime* that liberty is a sublime taste, even an inexplicable gift of grace, appreciated only by the few?[27] Gannett's scholarly reconstruction of the genesis and composition of the *Old Regime* revisits several historical controversies about the text, but perhaps most importantly suggests that these statements about liberty should be taken neither as retreat nor as lament. Rather they are consistent with a new rhetorical strategy to confront citizens with the nature of their servitude, to shame them with their long acquiescence in despotism, and to jolt them into a new form of prideful self-assertion.

It has often been noted that certain fundamental preoccupations orient Tocqueville's *œuvre*. With a mind that was profound but narrow, he "tirelessly examined just one question over and over again – the relation between freedom and equality in modern societies."[28] One continually meets in Tocqueville's texts various formulations and conceptualizations of liberty, equality, centralization, despotism, individualism, religion, and, of course, democracy itself.[29] This volume can provide only a small sampling of the ways in which contemporary scholars are engaging with these preoccupations. Yet I want to call attention specifically to several new "Tocquevilles" that are beginning to make an appearance in the twenty-first century.

A. Tocqueville and the Debate Over Civil Society

I noted earlier that although Tocqueville lends his name to disputes over social capital and communitarianism in the United States, his own texts are rarely analyzed for direct theoretical insight. But this is beginning to change. And a serious engagement with Tocqueville's texts focusing on the theme of civil society suggests that Tocqueville is strong precisely where neo-Tocquevilleans are thought to be weak – in his appreciation of the interaction between associations, political institutions, and the state. Indeed, as James Schleifer and Dana Villa both suggest, the pendulum is swinging back to the 1835 *Democracy*, with its emphasis on the intrinsically political aspects of civil society and the self-governing nature of federalism.[30]

Dana Villa begins by comparing Tocqueville's notion of an intermediary sphere between individual and state to Hegel's more self-consciously articulated *bürgerlicher Gesellschaft*. Villa concludes that Tocqueville's is the more profound conception because it reveals the manner in which public-political life may colonize and fully inhabit what we now call social life. Villa makes two major points against the current neo-Tocquevillean understanding of civil society in the United States. In his view, these theorists mistake both the nature of Tocqueville's theory of voluntary association and the significance of his distinction between *la société civile* and *le monde politique*. Voluntary association comprises not only spontaneous civil associations, but also the press, political parties, and the permanent associations of town and county government. These are voluntary in the sense that they replace the ascriptive *corps intermédiares* of aristocratic life with bodies created by choice and election. Tocqueville, of course, does distinguish between a sociocultural realm of ideas, feelings, and *moeurs* and the institutions and practices of government, a distinction that suits the moralizing intentions of neo-Tocquevilleans focused on character, community, and volunteerism. This distinction, however, does little theoretical work. Rather, the vital distinction for Tocqueville is between central organizations of power, action, and administration, and local ones. Thus Villa insists that Tocqueville's concept of civil society is more political than "civil."

One might also show that Tocqueville himself would be a critic of naïve neo-Tocquevilleanism by turning to the *Old Regime and the Revolution* instead of to the *Democracy*. Indeed, even a cursory examination of Tocqueville suggests that he fully realized the drawbacks of a certain kind of group life, and the importance of state policy for the "social investment climate." In the *Old Regime*, Tocqueville describes a counter-type to *l'intérêt bien entendu* and a healthy "art and science of association." Eighteenth-century France provides one example of *intérêt mal entendu* and a failed art of association: an active group life within a state infrastructure that both deliberately and inadvertently thwarted political cooperation. Robert Gannett notes that the neo-Tocquevillean Robert Putnam's comparative study of civic traditions would benefit more from considering the sophisticated articulation of political "path dependency" that emerges in Tocqueville's *Old Regime* than from nodding in the direction of the *Democracy*.[31]

Another contemporary twist on this "civil society Tocqueville" applies his study of the preconditions of a healthy democratic civil society to new settings or situations. How might Tocqueville's view of the functions of associations, for example, illuminate the travails of post-colonial African states?[32] Tocqueville's analysis of the preconditions of successful political democracy may also be applied to the chronic problem of the democratic deficit that plagues the project of European unification.[33] Indeed, in *Democracy in America*, Tocqueville often chooses the "evasive strategy" in

Seymour Drescher's words, of contrasting America not with France, but with Europe.[34] This language has struck unexpected chords. As Mélonio reminds us in her "Tocqueville and the French," Tocqueville was dealing not only with French identity but by extension with "continental Europe, scarred by absolutism and struggling to establish liberal democracies."[35]

B. Tocqueville and Despotism

Along with a renewed appreciation of the ways that civil society can foster freedom in democracy is a concern with how to characterize its absence. Tocqueville has often been seen as the Cassandra of democratic despotism, a seer who anticipated the horrors of twentieth-century totalitarianism. Melvin Richter argues that Tocqueville's views of despotism, like many of his other *idées-mères*, were not constant, but rather shifted over the course of his life, and "should serve as one marker for tracing the trajectory of his political, social, and historiographical thought."[36] One of the most illuminating conclusions of Richter's study is the way in which Tocqueville's constant awareness of his audience could misfire. Tocqueville refused to coin a new word (or adopt any of the neologisms available to him) for the new forms of democratic unfreedom that were brought to life so vividly in his texts. Instead he blunted the edge of his own innovative analysis by accepting the platitudinous conflation of tyranny and despotism. Thus Richter's analysis reinforces the view of a writer whose rhetorical choices masked his own subtleties, a writer who failed at times to move his contemporaries but mysteriously reached beyond them to inform later debates.

C. Tocqueville and Religion

Another classic Tocquevillean theme that is undergoing a metamorphosis is the relationship between democracy and religion. Older discussions of Tocqueville and religion in France focused on his possible relationship to the Catholic party, or on whether he himself was a closet son of the Church. Americans, on the other hand, tended to study the functional relationships between religion and democracy in Protestant America. Today we have deeper and more complex readings that place Tocqueville directly in a line of religious and philosophical speculation preoccupied with the uneasy dialectic of the spirit and the flesh. Mansfield and Winthrop, for example, find the particular combination of "self-disgust and self-elevation" in Tocqueville to be a key premise of his political science.[37] Mélonio reminds us that Tocqueville's analysis of religious sentiment is key to his portrait of democracy because democracy is the first regime in which human nature emerges in its "primordial simplicity," and human nature is defined by a sense of incompleteness and a desire for the infinite.[38] Indeed, one recent discussion of Tocqueville's relationship to religion enmeshes him in a particular anthropology of Christian alienation that will eventually fracture into the twentieth-century discussions of Husserl, Arendt, and Merleau-Ponty. Informed by Augustine's two cities, deeply marked by a confrontation with Pascal, Tocqueville thus becomes a guide to the spiritual disequilibrium inherent in modern life.[39]

What can we make of this close attention to the subterranean moral and spiritual world that informs Tocqueville's texts? It betrays, perhaps, a widespread longing for a transcendent dimension of democratic practice now that the unsurpassable horizon of our time is no longer socialist utopianism, but liberal democracy. In any case, the strong French resistance to considering Tocqueville's emphasis on a close link between the spirit of liberty and the spirit of religion seems to be lessening as the struggle between *laicité* and Catholicism recedes, and as the relationship of religion to civil society comes to the fore in French social theory. Certainly, theorists in both Europe and America are exploring new – and more traditional – intersections between religion and politics. Joshua Mitchell has argued that Tocqueville's religious sensibility allowed him to illuminate the fragility of freedom in modern democracy.[40] In his contribution to this volume, Mitchell continues this theme, tracing the ways in which emotional and ontological attachments to religion may compensate for the abstraction of modern society, and hence may be fueled by modernity itself. Mitchell argues that Tocqueville's analysis in *Democracy in America* helps us to see just such a paradoxical connection between religious fundamentalism and equalization of social conditions.

D. New Tocquevilles

Civil society, democratic despotism, and civic religion are relatively familiar themes in Tocqueville scholarship, even if they are emerging in new guises. I now want to mention several new "Tocquevilles" that are stranger and perhaps even counter-intuitive. These new readings are the product of the prodigious increase in Tocqueville's writings that are now available in the complete works, and, increasingly, in English translation.

One unfamiliar Tocqueville is read for insight into the tensions arising from industrialization and economic globalization. The old image of Tocqueville as ignorant of economics and industrialization still makes an occasional appearance in print.[41] This theme was most persuasively articulated by Raymond Aron fifty years ago, and it is obviously true that *Democracy in America* focuses more on egalitarian political culture than on the contradictions of capitalism. Yet new readings, drawing on an appreciation of Tocqueville's active role in French politics and writings on social reform, directly refute the view that he was uninformed and unconcerned about the "material bases" of life.[42] Relying on Tocqueville's involvement with the school of Catholic social economy, his attempts to develop policies to defuse the social question and to develop a program for what he called a "new left" in the 1840s, these readings emphasize Tocqueville's concern with managing economic transformation and his attempt to steer a third way between state and market. Indeed, James Schleifer's reflections on working manuscripts and notes for the *Democracy* confirm that Tocqueville had a "stronger and more sophisticated grounding in economics and economic matters than many critics have charged."[43]

A second unfamiliar Tocqueville is the one who analyzes the ways in which egalitarian democracy coexists with difference, and may intensify or reinscribe it. Several new readings of Tocqueville, for example, are particularly sensitive to the ways in which he uses gendered imagery – and not only in the chapters on women – or in which he struggles with his own ambivalence over the European colonial project.[44] My own essay focuses on Tocqueville's writings on slavery and empire. I argue that his famous chapter on the dynamics among Anglo-Americans, aboriginal peoples, and newly freed slave populations in the United States and his writings on

slavery and empire from the 1830s and 1840s can be read as a
coherent whole. The same combination of ironical judgment about
the tendency of European civilization to break through moral limits
and unwavering commitment to European expansionism marks all
of these writings. His ambivalence, struggles for clarity about
democracy's contrary tendencies, and uneasy compromises in some
ways mirror our own and can inform the democratic dilemmas of a
post-colonial world.

V. TWO TRADITIONS

While Tocqueville's writings have an important reach beyond the
United States and France, it is in these two countries that he has
entered most deeply into debates over democratic national identities and the nature of modern liberty. Juxtaposing the essays by
Françoise Mélonio and Olivier Zunz reveals the ways in which
texts take on different "physiognomies" – to use a Tocquevillean
word – in different milieus. Mélonio, expert guide to the reception
of Tocqueville in France, focuses here on his roots in French culture. Taking up themes articulated by other contributors, she shows
his deep embeddedness in the French political tradition and in a
particular post-revolutionary moment. She also reads him in the
lineage of the French moralists, emphasizing that the structure of
his writing and ideas cannot be fully appreciated apart from the
particular cadences of prophetic moralism.

With the immediacy of vivid reconstruction, Olivier Zunz
reveals what happens when this text emigrates to nineteenth-century America. The full story of Tocqueville's reception in the
United States has not yet been told, but Zunz's "Tocqueville and
the Americans: *Democracy in America* as read in Nineteenth-
Century America" for the first time carefully lays out its initial
chapter. Tocqueville, as he feared, was nowhere understood to have
said what he meant; his text was hijacked not only by his own
ambiguities (which did not travel well), but also by Americans' preconceptions about their democracy, post-colonial anxieties, desires
for approval, and refusal to be judged. Yet Zunz's narrative also
reveals how traumatic events can completely alter the reception and
perception of a writer. The American Civil War, in this account,

created a new generation of readers suddenly capable of entering into a deep dialogue with Tocqueville.

In retrospect, it is clear that this post-Civil War conversation was only the beginning of an ongoing series of "turns to Tocqueville," moments in which Americans first unravel and then re-stitch the intellectual fabric of their common life. Tocqueville's ability to stimulate such new beginnings – in the United States, Europe, and beyond – is perhaps his most lasting legacy and the reason that he remains an indispensable companion, even in the twenty-first century.

NOTES

1   *Journal of Democracy* 11:1 (2000), 9.
2   *Political Psychology* (Cambridge: Cambridge University Press, 1993), 101.
3   James Schleifer notes that every major American editor has remarked that "Tocqueville seems to be speaking to his own time, whether 1838/ 40, 1862, 1898, 1945, 1966, or 1981" in "Tocqueville's Reputation in America," Andrew J. Cosentino, ed., *A Passion for Liberty: Alexis de Tocqueville on Democracy and Revolution* (Washington, DC: Library of Congress, 1989) 19. An inspection of subsequent introductions to editions of *Democracy in America* supports this claim.
4   In this volume, see especially the essays by Goldhammer, Guellec, Mélonio, Richter, and Schleifer for discussions of Tocqueville's attempts to fashion a persuasive rhetoric from the common language. Tocqueville's contemporary appeal can be gauged by the many major academic conferences that marked the bicentennial of his birth. A partial list of countries that hosted one or more such conferences in 2005 includes France, Japan, the United States, Canada, Poland, and Belgium.
5   There is also a nineteenth-century edition of the collected works edited by Gustave de Beaumont: *Œuvres complètes d'Alexis de Tocqueville*, 9 vols. (Paris: 1864–66).
6   Françoise Mélonio and Laurence Guellec, *Tocqueville, lettres choisies, souvenirs* (Paris: Gallimard, 2003), cited here as *Lettres, S.*
7   In addition to older translations of Tocqueville's writings on social reform, voyages to England and Ireland, and letters, Olivier Zunz and Alan Kahan published for the first time (in 2002) a reader that contains selections from Tocqueville's entire *œuvre*, cited here as *T Reader* (ed. Zunz and Kahan). In 2001, Jennifer Pitts published an English edition of

the most important writings on slavery and empire, cited here as *T on Empire and Slavery* (trans. Pitts). This *Companion* is fortunate to have as contributors four scholars who have recently translated or are translating *Democracy in America*: Harvey Mansfield and Delba Winthrop brought out a new translation in 2001 published by the University of Chicago Press; the Library of America published Arthur Goldhammer's translation in 2004 (the only translated work ever to appear in this series of classic American writers); and the Liberty Fund will bring out a translation of Eduardo Nolla's critical edition by James Schleifer (with Tocqueville's extensive notes and alternate passages) in 2006. There is also a recent translation of *Democracy in America* by Ernest Bevan in a Penguin edition (2003); moreover, the Reeve/Bowen/ Bradley and Lawrence translations are still in print. *L'ancien regime et la revolution* and Tocqueville's notes for an unpublished second volume have been translated by Alan Kahan, with introduction and critical notes by François Furet and Françoise Mélonio, in a two-volume edition published by the University of Chicago Press, cited here as *AR*, 1 and *AR*, 2 (trans. Kahan). The Gilbert translation of the *Old Regime* is also still in print.

8 Tocqueville to Eugène Stoffels, February 21, 1835, *Lettres, S*, 315.

9 Louis Hartz, *The Liberal Tradition in America: An Interpretation of American Political Thought Since the Revolution* (New York: Harcourt Brace, 1955).

10 Jacqueline Stevens, "Beyond Tocqueville, Please!" *American Political Science Review*, 89:4 (1995), 987–990.

11 The use of Tocqueville's critique of individualism as a cultural critique of modern egalitarianism has its analogue in France as well. See, for example the selections by Gilles Lipovetsky, Anne Godignon, and Jean-Louis Thiriet, in Mark Lilla, ed., *New French Thought: Political Philosophy* (Princeton: Princeton University Press, 1994), 209–231.

12 Mélonio, p. 357, note 24. [Subsequent citations by author and page, without further attribution, refer to the essays published in this *Companion*.] For Tocqueville's reception in France from the nineteenth century to the present, the intricacies of which cannot be traced here, see Mélonio, *Tocqueville et les français*, translated into English as *Tocqueville and the French*, trans. Beth G. Raps (Charlottesville, VA: University Press of Virginia, 1998).

13 The bicentennial of Tocqueville's birth occasioned many new works of Tocqueville scholarship in France, including a new biography by the editor of Tocqueville's familial correspondence that gives a fuller sense of the private man. see Jean-Louis Benoît, *Tocqueville: Un destin*

paradoxal (Paris: Bayard, 2005). For other works published in the bicentennial year, see notes 14, 19, and 26.

14 See, for example, Serge Audier, *Tocqueville retrouvé: genèse et enjeux du renouveau tocquevillien français* (Paris: Vrin-EHESS, 2004).

15 Tocqueville to Ernest de Chabrol, October 7, 1831, *Selected Letters* (trans. Toupin and Boesche), 59.

16 Drescher, p. 41.

17 Drescher, p. 42.

18 *Political Psychology*, 101.

19 Elster, p. 64. A more general case for the relevance of Tocqueville's sociological "method" can be found in Raymond Boudon, *Tocqueville aujourd'hui* (Paris: Jacob, 2005).

20 In a letter to Pierre Freslon, September 20, 1856, Tocqueville noted that he wished to work in "that half-light (*demi-clarté*) that allows one to glimpse the country and to ask the inhabitants to point out the way." *Lettres, S,* 1213.

21 Manent, p. 108.

22 Mansfield & Winthrop, p. 85.

23 Manent, p. 114.

24 Manent, p. 115.

25 Schleifer, p. 125.

26 The second *Democracy* (1840), for example, is now a part of the program for the *agrégation de lettres* in France. For Tocqueville's literary stature, see *Tocqueville et la littérature*, ed. José-Luis Diaz and Françoise Mélonio (Paris: PUPS, 2005).

27 *AR, Oeuvres*, P 3, 195.

28 Françoise Mélonio, *Tocqueville and the French*, 2.

29 James Schleifer, *The Making of Democracy in America*, 2nd edition (Indianapolis: Liberty Fund, 2000), 161–162.

30 On this renewed appreciation of the role of federalism in Tocqueville's thought, and hence of the 1835 *Democracy*, see Barbara Allen, *Tocqueville, Covenant, and the Democratic Revolution: Harmonizing Earth with Heaven* (Lanham, MD: Lexington Books, 2005).

31 Gannett, p. 214, note 51.

32 For example, the interdisciplinary Workshop on Political Theory and Policy Analysis at Indiana University, Bloomington, under the leadership of Elinor and Vincent Ostrem, has long had an explicitly "Tocquevillean" inspiration. The Workshop is planning a book applying Tocqueville's theory of civil society to non-European settings: *Tocquevillean Analytics: A Comparative Perspective*.

33 See, for example, Larry Siedentop's *Democracy in Europe* (New York: Columbia University Press, 2000), 1–24, which explicitly tries to apply

the preconditions for American federalism explored by Tocqueville –
the habit of local self-government, a shared language, the seminal role
of lawyers, and shared mores – to assess the chances of Europe's
success in pushing its inherited political culture in a more democratic
direction.

34 Drescher, p. 32.
35 Mélonio, p. 345.
36 Richter, p. 269.
37 Mansfield and Winthrop, p. 86.
38 Mélonio, p. 349.
39 See the penetrating analysis in Agnès Antoine, *L'impensé de la
    démocratie: Tocqueville, la citoyenneté, et la religion* (Paris: Fayard,
    2003). For another recent work that treats Tocqueville's agnostic
    spirituality and particular version of Christian humanism as keys to
    his life's work, see Jean-Louis Benoît, *Tocqueville Moraliste* (Paris:
    Champion, 2004).
40 *The Fragility of Freedom: Tocqueville on Religion, Democracy and the
    American Future* (Chicago: University of Chicago Press, 1995).
41 See, for example, Garry Wills, "Did Tocqueville 'Get' America?" *The
    New York Review of Books*, April 29, 2004.
42 See a new edition of Tocqueville's writings: *Textes économiques:
    anthologie critique*, ed. Jean-Louis Benoît and Éric Keslassy (Paris:
    Pocket, 2005). See also Éric Keslassy, *Le libéralisme de Tocqueville à
    l'épreuve du paupérisme* (Paris: L'Harmattan, 2000) and Michael
    Drolet, *Tocqueville, Democracy and Social Reform* (London: Palgrave,
    2003).
43 Schleifer, p. 132.
44 In retrospect, Delba Winthrop's article focusing on women as symbolic
    markers of Tocqueville's larger democratic theory looks prescient. See
    "'Tocqueville's American Woman and 'the True Conception of
    Democratic Progress.'" *Political Theory* 14:2 (1986), 239–61. In
    contrast to Straussian readings, we now have at least one sustained
    feminist reading of *Democracy in America* using a psychoanalytic lens
    to interpret Tocqueville's use of familial and gendered imagery. See
    Laura Janara, *Democracy Growing Up: Authority, Autonomy, and
    Passion in Tocqueville's Democracy in America* (Albany NY: State
    University of New York, 2002). See also the essays in *Feminist
    Interpretations of Tocqueville*, ed. Jill Locke (University Park, PA:
    Penn State Press, forthcoming 2007).

1 Tocqueville's Comparative Perspectives

"It was necessary to glance briefly beyond France in order to make sense of what follows; for I dare say that whoever has studied and seen only France, will never understand anything about the French Revolution."[1] These words, appearing in 1856 in Tocqueville's last published work, were indicative of his perspective about every subject to which he turned his attention. A generation earlier, his attendance at François Guizot's influential course of lectures on the history of civilization was preceded by a long meditation on the lessons of English history.[2] These reflections were formulated in his very first letter to Gustave de Beaumont, who was to be Tocqueville's lifelong friend and traveling companion in America and England.

The quotation from the Old Regime speaks not only of studying but of seeing what one wished to understand, of viewing from without what one wishes to understand within. Tocqueville believed deeply in the importance of personal, even first, impressions. Again and again, the first volume of the *Democracy* (1835) would frame an observation in personal terms. One had to "go to America" to appreciate the extraordinary and pervasive sensations of political and economic activity, of personal mobility and religious belief that pervaded American life.[3]

Impressions were also registered as general comparisons: "On passing from a free country into another which is not free, one is struck by a very extraordinary sight. In the former all is activity and movement, in the latter all seems calm and immobile." On his first day in Algeria, in 1841, Tocqueville wrote: "The architecture...depicts the social and political condition of the Muslim and oriental populations: polygamy; the sequestration of women; the

21

absence of any public life; a tyrannical and suspicious government that forces one to conceal one's existence constrains all sentiments within the circle of the family."[4]

Tocqueville's appetite for personal observations far exceeded his life's itinerary. During the American journey, he would have liked to have visited the free colored colony of Wilberforce in Canada. He regretted not having spent more time in the United States South.[5] In the 1840s, he began an intensive study of India in preparation for a serious study of that country. He got no further than a first draft of reflections before abandoning the project. As he later wrote to an English friend, one would have to visit India in person in order to properly complete such an ambitious project.[6]

I. GLOBAL COMPARISONS

Nevertheless, Tocqueville's comparative perspective ranged far beyond places that he actually visited or intensively studied. At one point or another, his interest extended across most of the globe: in Europe, from Russia to Ireland; in the Pacific, from Australia to New Zealand; in Asia, from China to the Ottoman empire; in North Africa, from Egypt to Algeria; in the Western hemisphere, from Canada to South America. At many points in his writings and notes, he made historical references to pre-modern polities and civilizations. Given his intense curiosity about the interplay between politics and *moeurs*, it is hardly surprising that Tocqueville devoted considerable energy to studying the sacred texts of the Muslim and Hindu religions.

In most cases, his references to individual societies were brief and casual. French Canada made cameo appearances in the *Democracy* and the *Old Regime* as a relatively stagnant society, trapped in old French *moeurs* and a centralized state, and unable to capitalize on the full potential of its situation in the New World. It was compared unfavorably to the more dynamic and decentralized Anglo-American colonies to its South. Mexico was also a foil for Tocqueville's analysis of the stable democracy of Anglo-America. Entrapped between anarchy and military despotism, backward in civilization, corrupt in its *moeurs*, Mexico also served as an example of the difficulty of adapting the complex Anglo-American political system without its nexus of *moeurs*.[7]

Other societies made equally brief appearances in Tocqueville's published writings or working drafts. In the *Democracy*, Egypt is invoked as an extreme case of despotic egalitarian centralization within a nation of "hommes très ignorants et très égaux," of "very equal and very ignorant men," located at the level of "incomplete civilization." China is assigned a similar role as "the most perfect emblem of the kind of social well-being that a highly centralized administration can offer to people who submit to it." Its civilized people had sunk into almost barbaric stagnation. Of all these relatively peripheral societies, Russia made the most dramatic entrance in Tocqueville's writings. It bursts onto the final page of the *Democracy* of 1835 as the embodiment of the principle of servitude, providentially designed to hold the destiny of half of the world in its hands.[8]

Most of the inhabitants of these societies inhabited a world of their own, with prospects that deviated widely from those of Europeans. Tocqueville's rare overviews of the globe evoked an implicit distinction between peoples of European descent and others. In opening his discussion of the three races in the *Démocratie* of 1835 he wrote: "Among these diverse men inhabiting the United States, the first to attract attention, the first in enlightenment, power and happiness, is the white man, the European man par excellence; below him appear the negro and the Indian."[9] The future, too, belonged to Americans of European descent. Why this inequality, he asked himself, in a draft of his manuscript for a book predicated on the providential equalization of humanity – "Why this unequal sharing of this world's goods"? His response was only: "Who can say?" Tocqueville sustained this vision at the end of the second *Democracy* in 1840. As he once again extended his imagination to embrace the globe, it was "to the limits of the vast area occupied by the European race." The prophet of democracy looked no further. Casually, rather than analytically, Tocqueville traced civilization's boundary of power, knowledge, and well-being. Beyond that lay the half-civilized, the barbarian and the savage.[10]

If Tocqueville foresaw the inevitable end of institutionalized servility within Europe's domination, then, he also foresaw the expansion of imperial domination of colonized peoples. Europeans generally viewed Britain's conquest of India as an extraordinary and inexplicable event. Tocqueville considered it to be the paradigmatic example of the asymmetrical relationship between the European and non-European worlds. One need only compare his observations on communal New England in 1831 with his observations on communal India ten years later. New England's local government was treated as the miraculous seed of America's decentralized egalitarian liberty. The Indian commune was also the "social soil" of that nation, each village a complete and autonomous society. It offered its members everything necessary for human existence and civilized life. In contrast to New England, however, India's communal laws, education, and mores combined to keep society rigidly hierarchical, static, and stable. Secular and religious authority, and village membership itself, were all defined by heredity. Birth ascribed rights and duties to every individual in these tiny aristocratic republics. India's decentralization, more complete than that of England itself, facilitated submission both to external domination and internal hierarchy.[11]

For Tocqueville, the fact that a country was easily vanquished was, in itself, a signifier of backwardness and defectiveness. His *Old Régime* of 1856 casually refers to China's "imbecile and barbarous government," which a handful of Europeans could overcome at will. In that book, the French Physiocrats' admiration for Chinese administration is clinching evidence of the extent to which the authoritarian Physiocrats were infatuated with the principle of despotism.[12]

In this respect, power was a marker of both cultural and political robustness. The British conquest of India was what made it most worthy of sustained analysis. Tocqueville considered the very durability of British domination as indicative of one of the world's great revolutions. India's contribution to Britain's strategic position and world power, not its very questionable contribution to British wealth, justified British domination. Tocqueville adopted a similar rationale for France's retention of Algeria: "In the world's eyes abandonment would clearly announce our decadence." Here Tocqueville foreshadowed a major rationale for European imperial expansion for generations to come. If Tocqueville's *Democracy* appears to announce the end of the era of dependent individuals, its author clearly accepted the principle of indefinitely dependent peoples.[13]

II. CORE COMPARISONS

Despite Tocqueville's sorties into global perspectives, his political and literary output as a whole shows that the core of his comparative interest lay in a much narrower compass. As indicated in the opening quotation of this essay, Tocqueville's comparative perspective was usually invoked in reference to his own nation. The central mission of Tocqueville's life and work was to understand and influence the future of France. For this project, the most promising models lay within the English-speaking world. His journeys to America and the *Democracy* itself were only early indicators of a lifelong orientation. Tocqueville subsequently relied upon American and English examples to address many French public issues: welfare policy, foreign policy, slave emancipation, and colonial expansion.

Anglo-America maintained its central position in Tocqueville's perspective because it clearly embodied two major themes of his world-view. From the Introduction to the *Democracy* (1835) to the Preface to the *Old Regime* (1856), Tocqueville succinctly summed up his philosophy of history. Humanity was inescapably moving along a temporal axis from inequality towards equality, from aristocracy towards democracy. It was a trajectory "that one can hope to moderate and channel, but not to overcome."[14] This "historical axis" was superimposed upon an axis of political choice. As men approached equality of social condition, they had to locate themselves between despotism and liberty. In adumbrating the implications of these two themes, the political liberty of the Anglo-American world was crucial to Tocqueville. As he thought his way through three decades of political turmoil, Tocqueville continually reconfigured Anglo-America in relation to France and continental Europe.

His first critical choice, at the outset of his career, was that the United States, not England, constituted the society against which France should measure itself and draw its principal lessons for achieving lasting liberty. He reasoned that England had retained its freedom in an aristocratic social and political framework. Even the English Revolution was made primarily for *freedom*. Its French counterpart was made chiefly for *equality*. Subsequently, England remained profoundly aristocratic and monarchic. France was already more fundamentally democratic.[15]

Throughout his writings, Tocqueville understood that to compare was to choose, within as well as between societies. Between
1831 and 1835, Tocqueville was quite selective in what he regarded
as the highest standard of American political democracy. He
repeatedly noted that the further westward one moved from the
essentially "New England" core of his subject, the weaker and more
disorderly became the participatory politics that Tocqueville hoped
to see transferred to France. Popular sovereignty and disorder
became increasingly stronger at the periphery of American
democracy. Even when he turned to analyzing civil society in the
Democracy of 1840, Tocqueville's notes indicate that "the New
England American" still constituted the essential and particularly
desirable democratic exemplar.[16]

Tocqueville encountered a still more challenging anomaly to
democracy at the Mason-Dixon line. Had he not decided, at the last
moment, to include a final chapter on the "three races" in America,
the South would certainly have been nearly as peripheral to the
Democracy of 1835 as it is to the sequel of 1840. It is frequently
observed that Tocqueville began this final chapter of the 1835 text
by emphasizing the irrelevance of America's multiracial problems
to the future of French and European democracy. Less noted is the
fact that by this same criterion, Southern whites were assigned the
same marginal status as non-whites. As it turned out, the Western
world's most striking representatives of both aristocracy and
democracy were to be found in America.[17]

Tocqueville never expressed himself with greater vehemence
against aristocracy *in principle* than in his drafts for this final
chapter. In the *Democracy*, Southern white slaveholders are designated as an aristocratic entity. The South's leaders are privileged,
leisured, traditional, landed, and almost feudal. They are endowed
with the appropriately aristocratic *moeurs* and codes of honor
generically outlined in the second *Democracy*. Particularly striking
are passages in the 1835 manuscript, deleted before publication: "It
is affirmed that Americans, in establishing the universal vote
and the dogma of its sovereignty have demonstrated the advantages
of equality to the world. For my part, I think that they have chiefly
offered such proof by establishing servitude; and I find that they
demonstrate the advantages of equality less by *democracy* than
by *slavery*..." and, "America assuredly proves the goodness of

equality by liberty and by slavery, but more certainly by the latter than by the [former]."[18]

The *Democracy* of 1835 also confidently asserts slavery's economic inadequacy as well as its moral turpitude. It is portrayed as an institution in retreat. In 1840, Tocqueville still remained so averse to admitting that slavery might be economically efficient that the *Democracy* denies Southerners any entrepreneurial role in the astonishing expansion of Southern sugar and cotton during the 1830s. Southern agricultural dynamism is exclusively attributed to migrant Northerners, bringing with them their "industrial passions." By 1840, of course, Tocqueville realized that slavery was embedded in the growth sector of the American economy. This perspective is ironically acknowledged, only privately, to an American correspondent.[19] This revision of Tocqueville's assessment of slavery's economic robustness never made its way into the second *Democracy*. Nevertheless, as we shall see, it probably played an important part in Tocqueville's reconsideration of the respective roles of England and America as exemplars of liberty two decades later.

Tocqueville's perspective on England underwent far more significant changes. In the *Democracy* of 1835, England represents aristocracy, and is particularly useful in accounting for remnants, good and bad, of some "aristocratic" phenomena in the United States. Even where English and American institutions seemed both analogous and desirable, Tocqueville assiduously emphasized the difference between the two sides of the Anglo-American Atlantic. While taking note of the importance of association and decentralization in both societies, the *Democracy* of 1835 carefully distinguishes between the egalitarian basis of the American variant and the aristocratic basis of the English. Occasionally, the convergence of Anglo-American opinion is put to good use. The testimony of both American anti-democrats and English anti-aristocrats in favor of decentralization is deployed as a clinching argument in the *Democracy* of 1835.[20]

Beginning with the publication of that volume, Tocqueville's interest in England became more systematic and continuous. He began to devote more time and energy to the study of British official reports than to those of any other foreign nation. His second journey to England, in 1835, turned Tocqueville's attention to Britain's rapid commercial and industrial growth and to its positive and negative implications for liberty. In seeking to incorporate those commercial and industrial elements into his original "aristocratic" model, Tocqueville reconfigured England's historical situation as a transitory condition between true aristocracy of birth and democracy – an "aristocracy of wealth." The second *Democracy* focuses on the tensions in such an aristocracy. A silent status war reigns between all English citizens as a consequence of the ambiguity inherent in such an unstable social formation. In his notes, Tocqueville also played with ideas that might explain the conundrum of an aristocracy ruling modernity's economic vanguard.[21]

Tocqueville's investigations during his second English journey of 1835 led him to reevaluate democracy in England. The implementation of the New Poor Law of 1834 reinforced his suspicion that democratization was linked to an egalitarian bias in favor of administrative centralization.[22] Equally important, Tocqueville and Beaumont discovered the presence of strong "democratic" layers in English society, both old and new. They increasingly analogized segments of English and American civil society. The United States and Britain no longer occupied discrete positions on an aristocratic/democratic axis: "If I take a general overview of English society, I see that the aristocracy indeed rules the provinces, but if I look more deeply into the administration of parishes, there at least I discover the whole society governing itself [self government]. I see that all emanates from it [variant: from the people] and comes back to it. I see officials who, freely elected by the whole of the citizenry, concern themselves with the poor, inspect the roads, direct church affairs, and almost autonomously manage communal property. I acknowledge that the authority thus created is very limited but it is essentially democratic. Extend the circle of its attributions and you would quickly believe yourself to be transported to one of the townships of Massachusetts [New England].... Therefore, nothing that is nowadays created by the English is an entirely new formation. The English are not creating democracy; they are expanding the democratic spirit and customs within England."[23]

Tocqueville now perceived a full-blown social layer of American democracy in English civil society. The Anglo-American analogy struck him with particular force during his visit to industrial Birmingham in 1835. Although England's "democratic" middle class is not explicitly identified, the preparatory notes for the second *Democracy* demonstrate its enduring significance. In a long passage, Tocqueville cited that class as exemplifying democracy's potential for a combination of material well-being and religious belief: "I will not use the [example of the] Americans to prove it [my point]; their origins set them apart. But I will cite, above all, that of the English. The middle classes of England form an immense democracy in which everyone is unceasingly busy improving his condition, and where all seem to be consumed with the love of wealth. However, the English middle classes cling faithfully to their religious beliefs and demonstrate in a thousand ways that these beliefs are powerful and sincere [manuscript variant: true]. Nevertheless, England for all of its traditions and memories, is not relegated to some corner of the universe. Unbelief is no stranger to its neighborhood. The English themselves have spawned several famous unbelievers. Yet up to the present moment, the middle classes of England have remained firmly religious and it is these sincere Christians who have produced the industrial marvels that astonish the world."[24] In the Anglo-American orbit, it was the English middle classes that supplied the United States with "its principal and, so to speak, its *only* elements." Hence, "America composes, as it were, a part of the English middle classes."[25]

What was the most significant implication of this reconfiguration of English society during the nine-year gestation of the *Democracy*? The first *Democracy* begins with America at birth. When the first English migrants arrive in the New World, the prolific germs of free institutions and popular sovereignty are already deeply implanted in them. Their colonies, as well those of other Europeans, all contain at least the germ of complete democracies. For Anglo-Americans, equality and liberty are coeval.

At its end, in 1840, the *Democracy* makes a strikingly different point. The first Anglo-Americans still arrive with their heritage of free institutions and *moeurs*. But they spend considerable time in the New World before becoming equal. Therefore, "with Americans... it is liberty that is old; equality is comparatively new." In Tocqueville's estimation, liberty and equality were never coeval. On the European continent, equality was an "old fact" when liberty was still new. Because America and England were similar in proceeding from liberty towards equality, the threat of despotism was always correspondingly less for them than for continental Europeans. Among the latter, and their white colonists, equality was introduced primarily by centralizing monarchs before their first aspirations to liberty. Revolutions might exacerbate or hasten egalitarian centralization, but European history as a whole demonstrated that revolution is incidentally, rather than necessarily, linked to the threat of democratic despotism. The vulnerability of any egalitarian society to despotism ("the science of despotism") could be best understood by comparing Anglo-America, on the one hand, to continental Europe on the other.[26]

The same perspective affected Tocqueville's evaluation of the relationship between the British people and its rulers. English democracy did not operate only at the local level. The nation's most vigorous and most durable national popular movement offered decisive evidence of the ability of democratic peoples to focus upon great political achievements and to persist in them over generations. Colonial slave emancipation was probably more consistent with the full range of Tocquevillian political values than any other major reform to which he committed himself during his twelve years in French national legislatures. For Tocqueville, Britain's nonrevolutionary road to expanding freedom constituted an almost ideal model of democracy in action. The British had led 800,000 human beings, their fellow subjects, from social death to civil equality. The transformation occurred on single day and without loss of a single life.[27]

Moreover, this democratic reform was "the work of the nation and not of its rulers." Nothing as exemplary of associative democracy was ever described so glowingly anywhere in Tocqueville's writings. British abolitionism was identified as a mass movement for mass liberation. It was the product of idealistic passion, not the result of calculated interest. The people prevailed over an aristocratic government that fought to delay the final outcome as long as it could. For fifteen years before 1807, the political elite postponed the abolition of the British slave trade. For another twenty-five years, it resisted the abolition of colonial slavery, "always in vain; always the popular torrent prevailed and swept it along." In identifying "two Englands" in the French Chamber of Deputies, Tocqueville could nationalistically demand that "democratic" France abandon its servile "acquiescence" in aristocratic England's foreign policy, while urging his countrymen to match democratic England's emancipation policy. The "freest and most democratic nation on the continent [i.e. France] could not do otherwise."[28]

III. AN ELUSIVE COMPARISON

In all of Tocqueville's comparisons, the most important component remained France itself. The political condition of his country determined both the subject he chose to examine and the terms of comparison. Whatever role he might assign to providence in viewing American, British or Russian expansion into distant parts of the world, the "greatest theater of human affairs" [was] not in Sidney or even (yet) Washington, it is still in our Old Europe." In the first Democracy (1835), the principal targets of comparison were France and the United States, with England playing a large secondary role. In the Old Régime (1856), England and Germany were the main counter-examples to France. In the Democracy of 1840, however, Tocqueville's comparative approach is less obvious. In 1835, Tocqueville had a dual purpose in publishing an extended analysis of democracy the United States. America's political example might facilitate France's escape from the malignant cycle of revolution and despotism. The Democracy calls on its French readers to become a free and equal political association of citizens. Tocqueville's secondary aim in 1835 was to portray America as a nation in which the process of equalization was reaching "its natural limits" socially, culturally, and religiously. The United States was to be the empirical benchmark for assessing the generic impact of "equality of conditions" and of "democracy itself" on civil society – its habits, its ideas, and its moeurs. In short, Tocqueville wished to use America to imagine the future of the West.[29]

In the second Democracy, America ceases to be the privileged, or indeed even the primary, empirical source for fathoming democracy's destiny. By 1840, Tocqueville had shifted his focus from "America" to the "Democratic Type."[30] He even intended to entitle the 1840 study, "The Influence of Equality on Human Ideas and Sentiments." For various reasons, he went back, at the last minute, to Democracy in America. The original title more correctly reflects the book's objective. It was meant to offer a vision of the whole egalitarian future. For this reason, it has sometimes been argued that the "national-typical" categories of the *Démocratie* of 1835 were unsuitable, indeed illogical, sources for deriving a "pure" democratic "type": If America was exceptional, if England was a mix of aristocracy and democracy, if France was revolutionary, comparison had to yield to synthesis or an ideal-typology.[31]

Careful scrutiny of Tocqueville's preparatory reflections and the final text, however, shows that Tocqueville obscured, but never abandoned, his comparative frame of reference. His crucial methodological step was to shift America from the category of best model of the future to that of best exception to the rule. The second *Democracy* quietly abandons one major premise of the first. The Introduction of 1835 designates the United States as the optimal point of departure for thinking about the future. In 1840, the marginalization of America constituted an analytical shift. Tocqueville himself did not realize its full significance until he reread his own half-finished manuscript in 1838, and committed a hundred pages of it to the fire.

Moving America from exemplar to exception did not therefore necessitate making it melt into a generic model. On the contrary, one can still read many chapters of the 1840 volumes as transparent distillations of Tocqueville's America. Indeed, his notes for the sequel carefully document his ongoing efforts to furnish himself with empirical examples of American ideas and culture. It is the *non*-American element that gives the second *Démocratie* its distinctive tone and analytical thrust. In some chapters, only the titles or passing phrases refer to the United States. In even more chapters, America literally disappears. In André Jardin's precise calculation, the discussion of things American occupies only a fifth of the first three parts of the sequel. America's share falls to a mere two percent when Tocqueville revisits political society "Deuteronomy" of *Democracy*.[32]

Did Tocqueville cut himself loose from the comparative/empirical approach at any point in his *Democracy* of 1840? A careful look at his drafts suggests the opposite. Tocqueville's allusiveness regarding the "European" component of his comparison was already evident in the first *Democracy*. Its brief closing discussion is entitled, "Importance of the Foregoing in Relation to Europe." The author's father, Hervé de Tocqueville, was a close reader of the draft manuscript. He detected its evasive strategy: "the author speaks about all of Europe and nevertheless draws all of his arguments only from the present condition of France," a social condition that did not resemble those of several other great European nations, nor would for many years to come. "All his descriptions," concluded Hervé, "paint what is happening in France and not elsewhere. All belong to France and are applied to Europe as a whole."[33]

Tocqueville's reasons for speaking generically about Europe were grounded in his personal and tactical ambitions. They need not deter us here. The significant point is that he adopted exactly the same strategy in writing the highly charged closing chapters of the second *Democracy*. The book refers overwhelmingly to "European" or "democratic" societies. In the final fourteen chapters of the 1840 work (revolutions, war, military and administrative organization and, above all, the growth of governmental power), contemporary France is referred to as infrequently as the United States.

Nevertheless, as Hervé de Tocqueville remarked of the 1835 draft, the "European" chapters of 1840 are principally about France. Tocqueville's manuscripts are replete with evidence that France formed the silent, but very persistent empirical basis of his "pure," "generic" or "ideal typical" model of democracy. The preparatory notes are a running commentary on French articles, events, and contemporary political figures, positing quite explicit comparisons with America and England. As Tocqueville forcefully insisted to his English translator just before publication, he was writing principally for France and from a French point of view.

In writing his chapter on the accumulation of sovereign power in European nations, Tocqueville reminded himself: "State the facts without explaining them. They are apparent to readers because they are French facts." In another note, he observed that he had to delve more deeply into the mechanisms of centralization in a detailed way for France in particular, "because there is I think the chief source of danger for the future."[34]

In his final manuscript draft for the *Democracy*, Tocqueville avowed his belief in France's exemplary position in modernity. In a closing note to the final chapter, "General View of the Subject," he wrote: "I cast my eyes on my country and I see a universal transformation. I extend my view, I carry it forward ever closer to the extreme limits of the vast area occupied by the European race; I am struck everywhere by an analogous sight." In 1840, democracy in *America* is thus transmuted into democracy in the *world* via democracy in *France*. In this panoramic vista, there remains "only one aristocracy that still knows how to defend itself, that of England. All the rest are but general staffs without armies."[35]

If France gradually displaced America as the principal source of democratic "facts," is the *Democracy*'s perspective still a comparative one? As Tocqueville moved through his final peroration, he paused to contrast his new, generically packaged, French-oriented version of democracy with the American example. In 1840, the United States was still offered to French readers as the antidote to the European trajectory of democratization. In a marginal annotation to his final comparison, Tocqueville wrote: "I am very happy to have hit on this idea because I think it just and the only way of getting America to appear in my last chapters which *really only deal with France*."[36] If France now furnished the preponderant examples of democratization, America remained the preferred alternative.

Some scholars have interpreted the *Democracy* of 1840 as a bleaker more pessimistic vision of American democracy. The second *Democracy* actually offers readers far fewer direct criticisms of American institutions and *moeurs* than did the first. This observation has frequently escaped both admiring and critical commentators.[37] Such assessors usually fail to note the ironic fate of Tocqueville's most notorious reservation about American political life. In 1835, Tocqueville identified the tyranny of the majority as the principal threat to political freedom in the United States. Five years later, the phrase "Tyranny of the Majority" simply disappears. Just two references to the democratic majority emphasize its *passive* intellectual and moral dimensions. The *Democracy* of 1840 is concerned with the moral weight of the majority to inhibit both intellectual and political novelty, not to the direct political abuse of majoritarian power.[38]

The complete abandonment of "tyranny," as applicable to the behavior of either the rulers or ruled, stands in dramatic contrast to Tocqueville's invocation of American democracy as the antidote to a more sinister threat to democratic freedom. *Individualisme* is the most novel concept introduced into the *Democracy* of 1840. *Individualisme* refers to democracy's central thrust toward civic apathy, withdrawal and self-imposed powerlessness. It is the opposite of self-government. In 1835, the individual in America is envisioned as learning from birth that he must depend upon himself to overcome life's challenges. He or she relies minimally upon social power. The individual human will is strengthened only by the free combination of collective power, both in political and civil life. In 1835, even American isolation is a heroic choice, illustrated in Tocqueville's moving portrait of a pioneer family in the wilderness.[39]

There are anticipations of *individualisme* in the first *Democracy*, but isolation and apathy are characteristic only of the demoralized and vanishing aristocratic element in the United States. Deprived of access to public power and deference, America's old elites retreat to private life and tactfully conceal both their wealth and their opinions. In 1835, the French analogue to the retreating American elite is the nobility, among whom Tocqueville counted many friends and relatives. They too had forsaken public life in the wake of the Revolution of 1830.

A second group of unpolitical French citizens briefly appears in the *Democracy* of 1835. It has no counterpart in the United States. A footnote refers to the role of the French bureaucracy, spreading an "invincible apathy" among the inhabitants of French communes and reducing political life to a vegetative existence. The footnote in the first *Democracy* takes center stage in the second. Here we encounter an isolationism so pervasive that the very souls of men lose touch with each other. The old spectre of a tyranny of aggressive collective majorities is displaced by a *morcellement* of opinion and the degradation of the public sphere: "Don't you see that opinions are dividing more quickly than patrimonies, that each one encloses himself tightly within his own spirit like the farmer in his field? That sentiments become more individualized every day and that men will soon be more separated by their beliefs than they ever were by inequality of condition"?[40]

Individualisme is now a voluntary abdication of citizenship, the loss of a will to power and to participation. For maximum impact, Tocqueville's two chapters on *individualisme*, written late in the composition of the second *Democracy*, were relocated to the beginning of the section on "The Influence of Democracy on the Feelings of Americans." The argument is dramatically repeated in the final chapter of the book.[41] Of equal importance is the fact that the word "America" never appears in the chapter on *individualisme*, and is followed by the *Democracy*'s most sustained series of chapters on the United States. These chapters also offer the most uninterrupted positive commentary on America in 1840. Tocqueville consciously chose to make America literally shine as the antidote to *individualisme*: "Americans have fought the individualism to which equality gave birth, and they have conquered it." Individuality in the United States is the counter-example to *individualisme*.[42]

IV. COMPARATIVE PASTS

By the time Tocqueville wrote the *Old Regime*, his political ambitions no longer placed any constraints upon his comparative bent. Louis Napoleon's coup d'état of 1851 thrust him outside the political arena. The same event underlined France's continued entrapment within the cycle of revolution and despotism. Tocqueville now turned his full attention to the long-term causes of this bitter outcome to his hopes for political liberty, with no end in sight. For comparative purposes, he chose three European societies that shared a "medieval constitution." England and Germany became his benchmarks for comparison with old regime France. The Anglo-American world again offered him the foremost examples of free orderly societies before and after 1789.

In more than one respect, liberty's possibilities had sharply diminished in the 1850s. France was no longer an endangered free polity. It was a failed one. The European Continent was in the grip of counter-revolutionary authoritarianism. Across the Atlantic, in the United States, the American empire of slavery had not shrunk by a single state since Tocqueville's journey. On the contrary, slavery had not only expanded, but now threatened to expand indefinitely. Southern dominance of the presidency of the American federation, combined with a clear pro-slavery bias in the conduct of foreign relations, supported widespread speculation that the United States was not just a slaveholding but a slaveholders' republic.[43]

At least as important as slavery's dynamism was the growing threat that its expansion posed to the survival of the Federal Union. To find American models of liberty in the 1850s, Tocqueville had to shift his gaze downward. He could still point to America's republican state and local institutions as worthy of emulation, especially in their adherence to principles of constitutional liberty and the rule of law, so recently flouted in France. In the *Old Regime*, the decentralized New England township of the *Démocratie* re-emerges untarnished. It remains a model of successful local political freedom in comparison with French centralization.[44] Tocqueville, however could hardly help not sharing the anxiety of other Europeans. The fragmentation of the United States might occasion a further devaluation of liberalism and of self-government, compounding the demoralization of European liberals in the wake of the failed revolutions of 1848.

In the *Old Regime*, the standard-bearer of freedom is therefore one closer to home – Tocqueville's *seconde patrie intellectuelle*. In the 1850s, Britain was the world's most advanced economy, its most stable polity, and its most global empire. In a book about the long-term origins of France's political failures, its author had no qualms about linking England's present prosperity and power to its past freedom. *Old Regime* references to England's contemporary success abound: its advanced and entrepreneurial farmers, its small police force, its aristocracy's opulence, its security, its institutions, and, above all, its *moeurs* of freedom: "Nothing is more superficial than to attribute the greatness and power of a people to the mechanism of its laws alone; for, in this matter, it is less the perfection of the instrument than the strength of the motors that determines the result. Look at England: how many of its laws today seem more complicated, more diverse, more irregular than ours! Is there, however, a single country in Europe where the public wealth is greater, individual property more extensive, more secure, and more varied, the society richer or more solid? This does not come from the bounty of any particular laws, but from the spirit which animates English legislation as a whole. The flaws of certain organs make nothing impossible, because their vitality is powerful."[45] For good measure, Tocqueville added three solid pages of notes on English Law to this paean to liberty. Not by accident, the *Old Regime* then immediately switches to the perverse impact of prosperity, in the absence of freedom, on pre-Revolutionary France. Without liberty, wealth actually exacerbates hatred of the nation's privileged orders and its ancient laws. Ultimately, prosperity destabilizes despotism.

Again and again, the *Old Regime* returns to the same perspective. On one side of the Channel, political liberty averts disorder and maximizes prosperity. On the other shore, absolute monarchy drains the medieval constitutions of their libertarian component. In collusion with the privileged orders, the ruler alienates the educated classes from each other and all of them from the peasantry.

Even *individualisme* retrospectively colonizes the *Old Regime*. The *corporate individualisme* of the privileged is just another mechanism of alienation. The vacuum created by the absence of a public sphere is filled by a literary spirit undeflected by public debate and countervailing interests. When the nation finally gathers together after two centuries of isolation in 1789, these alienated components of France combine to destroy the old monarchy. After shredding the fabric of its old institutions, revolutionary despotism tears apart the fragile new political institutions as well.

In the *Old Regime*, England is France's counter-history. It is offered as an alternative mode of transition from Europe's ancient constitution to modernity. Notably absent from this account are any of the *Democracy*'s earlier references to the "silent warfare" created by the amorphousness of England's status boundaries, or the instability of a transitional "aristocracy of wealth," with its stability of an aristocracy of "birth." The *Old Regime* literally inverts the contrast. Now, the very ambiguity of social status in England mitigates the social and political tensions inherent in all hierarchical class relations. Ambiguity becomes one of the major strengths of England's successful transition to modernity. Its rulers have avoided the generic aristocratic tendency to become a "caste" because of the continuous political interaction inherent in its parliamentary and municipal systems. When an English peer does not need the public, he is "naturally the proudest, the most exclusive, and often the harshest of all nobles. It is political freedom which has softened and bent his iron."[46] Liberty trumps alienation and revolution.

In the *Old Regime*, two medieval aristocracies, quite similar in the fourteenth century, follow divergent historical trajectories. The result is that "England has an aristocracy, France had a nobility."[47] The different tenses in Tocqueville's terse description resonate.

France's ruling class *had* ossified into a caste. It was complicit with France's rulers in exacerbating the worst crime of the old monarchy – the division of classes. The *Old Regime's* portrayal of the French nobility reflects its author's abiding disappointment with the whole French elite, past and present. Exactly twenty years before, Tocqueville benignly portrayed French pre-Revolutionary elites as having played a role analogous to that of England's aristocracy. The French nobility was credited with fostering a vibrant libertarian current in the eighteenth century. If medieval liberty had disappeared from French institutions, liberty sustained itself as persistently as ever in French *moeurs*.[48]

In the *Old Regime*, this vision of parallel Anglo-French histories of liberty vanishes. In 1856, Tocqueville insists on emphasizing the narrowness of elite resistance to monarchical power. Far from being oppressed, the privileged groups were often "too free." They too easily gained exemptions from royal power to the detriment of the people. Their greater bargaining power produced yet deeper resentment. The result was a terrible preparation for a modern world based upon civil equality: "So wrong is it to confound independence with liberty. There is nothing less independent than a free citizen."[49]

The divergence of Anglo-French history in the *Old Regime* is matched by the convergence of Anglo-American history. If references to America almost vanish from the *Old Regime*, this is probably not due to any lack of "relevance" to the subject.[50] As the United States moved closer to the brink of disunion in the 1850s, America was increasingly ill-suited to be the "success story" of liberty. Yet something else seems to have been at stake in Tocqueville's avoidance of Revolutionary America. After all, the *Old Regime* does note, if only in passing, that the American Revolution had a profounder effect upon the French than the rest of Europe. Perhaps, but it is extraordinarily curious that Tocqueville avoided writing a single word on the significance of the American Revolution for at least one other European nation. England, after all, was more deeply involved in that Revolution – militarily, materially and ideologically – than was France. However successfully England ultimately navigated the shoals of the "Age of Revolution," its political system initially failed to avert, and then to overcome, the Anglo-American world's most violent division in three centuries of expansion. The American Revolution may have gotten short shrift in the *Old Regime* because it ran counter to Anglo-America's assigned role: liberty trumping alienation and revolution.[51]

Wherever America briefly appears in the *Old Regime*, it is as England's partner in a seamless Anglo-American heritage. Transatlantic conflict and transatlantic slavery are both kept discreetly offstage. The modern New England township is the twin of the modern English parish. Both are descendants of the self-governing medieval towns and villages, the "petites republiques démocratiques" that acted as a counterpoint to Europe's aristocratic medieval constitution. Tocqueville's working notes indicate the author's stark Anglo-American contrast with France at every level: *"How one finds disfigured traits of the English Parish and the American Township in the Parish of the Old Regime."*[52]

Local government remains the locus of "self-government." The *Democracy*'s contrast becomes retrospective in the *Old Regime*: the family resemblance of medieval European local governments; their thriving descendants in Atlantic Anglo-America; their ossified remnants in pre-Revolutionary France. At the local level in America, "everything *is* alive." In France, everything was dead. The debris of French local government offers the clue to its vanished vitality. Recall, again, Tocqueville's aristocratic parallel: "England *has* an aristocracy. France *had* a nobility."

The comparison with Anglo-America occurs a third time in the *Old Regime's* juxtaposition of centralized colonial French Canada with decentralized colonial British America. Ontogeny repeats phylogeny. Colonies exaggerate metropoles. Even when all of the progeny are socially egalitarian, the English colonies display the *republican* element that is the base of English *moeurs* and the English constitution. At the lowest institutional unit of human action, *individualisme* is conquered again, In England, individuals do much; in America, "individuals uniting together do everything." By contrast, in old French Canada, there was not even the shadow of municipal government. Its inhabitants were even more submissive to state power in the absence of old-world upper classes.[53]

Traditions persist through time and despite egalitarian revolutions. The English decentralize in America; the French centralize in

Algeria. In 1856, perhaps evoking the Revolution of 1848, Tocqueville contrasted revolutionaries' contempt for the feelings of "the majority" with the respect shown by the English and the Americans for their fellow citizens. England and America are conjoined in an eminently democratic sentiment of respect for the majority: "Among the latter, reason is proud and self-confident while ours [i.e. French revolutionaries] only invented new forms of servitude."[54] Here, too, North America's disconcerting "peculiar institution" is passed over in silence. Even in the wake of Napoleon III's tutelary, plebiscitary empire, Tocqueville remained committed to majoritarian legitimacy. Political rationality in Anglo-America is also contrasted starkly with bureaucratic/revolutionary rationality on the continent.

One must not allow Tocqueville's silences to obscure the central message of the *Old Regime*. Tocqueville sought to break out of a world in which he was living his own worst nightmare. His nation was bereft of political freedom. All too many of his fellow citizens were indifferent to its absence. Anglo-America released him from the weight of political silence in his internal exile. As long as he believed that America or England could affect the movement of his own country towards liberty, he was neither politically divorced from his own age nor from the future. The unexpected success of the *Old Regime* in 1856 in France and his extraordinary triumphal journey to England in 1857 raised his hopes as well as his spirits. During the final months of his life, he rejoiced in the fact that the English political scene was still "the greatest spectacle in the world, though not all of it is great."[55]

V. CONCLUSION

For Tocqueville, comparison lay at the heart of clear thought and informed action. It represented a means of creating a new science for a new age of politics. It enabled him to confront the enormous weight of the past and the political tragedy of his nation. Comparative analysis posits plurality – of pasts and presents. Comparison meant the recognition and renegotiation of alternative political systems, alternative cultural systems, and alternative historical patterns.[56] For someone who so keenly believed that his society had been entrapped in, and seduced by, certain patterns of ideas and action, comparison offered Tocqueville a means of navigation towards a differently imagined future.

Despite his own prophetic style, Tocqueville knew that one cannot truly foresee the future, "that enlightened and upright judge who always, alas! arrives too late!"[57] His political mission was more modest: the articulation, the preservation and, if necessary, the rebirth of liberty in France. Each moment, each situation demanded its own comparative perspective. Locating himself on the cusp of a transition from aristocracy to democracy, he sought to engage his countrymen in looking outward in order to identify a realistic image of the possibilities and constraints of democratic freedom. His fundamental assumption – that people must look beyond themselves to understand themselves – has never seemed more relevant.

NOTES

1   *AR, OC* 2:1, 94. For an analysis of Tocqueville's general approach to comparative political analysis with special reference to methodological antecedents, see Melvin Richter, "Comparative Political Analysis in Montesquieu and Tocqueville," *Comparative Politics*, 1 (1960): 129–160. See also Alan Macfarlane, *The Riddle of the Modern World: of Liberty, Wealth and Equality* (London: Palgrave, 2000), 153–247.

2   Tocqueville to Gustave de Beaumont, 5 October 1828, *OC*8:1, 49–71.

3   See, inter alia, *DAI* (Nolla), 229.

4   *DAI* (Nolla), 252; "Notes du Voyage en Algérie de 1841," *OC* 5:2, 191–192.

5   See, inter alia, *DAI* (Nolla), 275 note d. and 297 note v.

6   *DAI* (Nolla), 275 note d, and 297 note v; "L'Inde" *OC* 3:1, and Tocqueville to Lord Hatherton, 27 November 1857, *OC* 6:3, 281.

7   *DAI* (Nolla), 127, 131–132.

8   *DAII* (Nolla), 249 and note o; 47 note a; *DAI* (Nolla), 313–314. On Tocqueville's expansive use of national units as categories of comparative analysis, see also Françoise Mélonio, "Nations et Nationalismes," *The Tocqueville Review*, 18:1 (1997): 61–73; Enrique Krauze, "La culture de la démocratie en Amérique Latine: Variations sur un thème de Tocqueville," *ibid.*, 21:1 (2000): 175–187; and Lawrence Saez, "Tocqueville's Fragmented Encounter with India," ibid., 21:2 (2000): 157–170.

9   *DAI* (Nolla), 241 and note c.

10 *DAI* (Nolla), 246 note c, and *DAII* (Nolla) 279 note c. Regarding the uprising in India in 1857, see Tocqueville to Lady Thereza Lewis, 18 October 1857, *OC* 6:3, 275.

11 "L'Inde," *OC* 3:1, 443, 450 ff., 466, 508. For Tocqueville's serious investigation of communes in various countries of Europe, see Robert T. Gannett, Jr., "Bowling Ninepins in Tocqueville's Township," *American Political Science Review*, 97 (2003): 1–16.

12 *AR, OC* 2:1, 213; also *AR*, 1 (trans. Kahan), 213. For a similar perspective on Russian despotism in relation to the peasantry, see "Constitution de la classe agricole en Russie," *OC* 16, 561–567 (October 1853). See also Tocqueville to Gustave de Beaumont, 3 November 1853, *OC* 8:3, 164. For Beaumont's comparison of American democratic self-government, individual initiative, decentralization with the leveling equality of Russian life, with its communal patterns of agriculture and its autocratic state, see Beaumont, "La Russie et les États Unis sous le rapport économique," *Revue des deux mondes*, ser. 2, 5 (1854): 1163–1183. For Tocqueville's comment on the article, see Tocqueville to Gustave de Beaumont, 9 April 1854, *OC* 8:3, 204.

13 "L'Inde," *OC* 3:1, 213, 444, 478. For scholarly analyses of Tocqueville's perspective on French expansion and colonization, see, *inter alia*, Melvin Richter, "Tocqueville on Algeria," *Review of Politics*, 25 (July 1963): 362–399; Jennifer Pitts, "Empire and Democracy: Tocqueville and the Algerian Question," *Journal of Political Philosophy*, 8:3 (2000): 295–318; as well as the Introduction to her edition of Tocqueville's *Writings on Empire and Slavery* (Baltimore: The Johns Hopkins University Press, 2001), ix–xxxviii; Michael Hereth, *Alexis de Tocqueville: Threats to Freedom and Democracy*, trans. George Bogardus (Durham, NC: Duke University Press, 1986), 145–165; Cheryl B. Welch, "Colonial Violence and the Rhetoric of Evasion: Tocqueville on Algeria," *Political Theory*, 31:2 (2003), 235–264. Their general assessment is that the relation of European colonization to Tocqueville's thought constitutes a conundrum or paradox. See also, Seymour Drescher, *Dilemmas of Democracy: Tocqueville and Modernization* (Pittsburgh: University of Pittsburgh Press: 1968), 191–195.

14 *AR, OC* 2:1, 73. For recent general assessments of Tocqueville's political thought, see, inter alia, Cheryl Welch, *De Tocqueville* (New York: Oxford University Press, 2001); Sheldon Wolin, *Tocqueville Between Two Worlds: The Making of Political and Theoretical Life* (Princeton: Princeton University Press, 2001); and Pierre Manent, *Tocqueville and the Nature of Democracy*, trans. John Waggoner (Lanham, MD: Rowan and Littlefield, 1996).

15 On Tocqueville's decision to travel to the United States, see André Jardin, *Tocqueville: A Biography*, trans. Lydia Davis with Robert

Hemenway (New York: Farrar Straus Giroux, 1988), ch. 6. For comparisons between England and France in terms of democratization, see "Quelques notes sur la révolution de 1688 et 1830," *OC* 16, 560; and *AR OC* 2:2, 334–335, and *AR*, 2 (trans. Kahan), 286–287, "Similarities and Differences of the Revolutions of 1640 and 1789"; and *DAI* (Nolla), 37: "The salient point of the social condition of the Anglo-Americans is to be essentially democratic."

16   *DAII* (Nolla), 152 note d.

17   *DAI* (Nolla), 228 and 246 note a.

18   *DAI* (Nolla), 268 and *DAII Oeuvres*, P: 404 note a.

19   *DAII* (Nolla), 138; "Discours improvisé...à l'Académie des Sciences Morales et Politiques de l'Institut" [20 April 1839], *OC* 16, 165–167; Tocqueville to Jared Sparks, 13 October 1840, *OC* 7, 83.

20   "Voyage en Angleterre de 1833," *OC* 5:2, 29–43; *DAI* (Nolla), 183 and notes j and k. In ibid., 196, Tocqueville denied any significance or relevance to claims that the democratic elements in English (or any aristocratic) society could have been of real significance in the past. See also, ibid., 36–37. But he was equally certain that "some nations come to democracy as the English will do; others come through absolute power, as we have done." Quoted in Jean-Claude Lamberti, *Tocqueville and the Two Democracies*, trans. A. Goldhammer (Cambridge, MA: Harvard University Press, 1989), 112.

21   See *DAII* (Nolla), 126 note c; 138 note f; 140 note c; 149 and note c. See also "Voyage en Angleterre et en Irelande de 1835," *OC* 5:2, 63–64, 84, 89–92; and "État social et politique de la France avant et depuis 1789," *OC* 2:1, 50–51. For the impact of Tocqueville's English and Irish journeys and readings on his political, economic, and social thought, see Seymour Drescher, *Tocqueville and England* (Cambridge, MA: Harvard University Press, 1964), ch. 4–7; *Tocqueville and Beaumont on Social Reform*, ed. and trans. Seymour Drescher (New York: Harper and Row, 1968), Parts I and III; Michael Drolet, *Tocqueville, Democracy and Social Reform* (London: Palgrave, 2003), esp. 149–160; and Eric Keslassy, *Le libéralisme de Tocqueville à l'épreuve du pauperisme* (Paris: L'Harmattan, 2000), 117–188.

22   "Voyage en Angleterre...de 1835," *OC* 5:2, 49, 68; Mémoires "Sur le paupérisme" (1835 and 1837), *OC* 16, 117–157; also in *T and B on Social Reform* (trans. Drescher), 1–27; *Alexis de Tocqueville's Memoir on Paupérism* (Chicago: Ivan R. Dee, 1997); and Drescher, *Tocqueville and England*, ch. 5.

23   *DAII* (Nolla), 166 note e. See also ibid., 184 and 246. Tocqueville was dismissive about the quality of democratic elements in England during his first journey of 1833. He treated an election meeting in London

(15 August 1833) as one of "these saturnalia of English liberty," leaving him with feelings more akin to disgust than fear (*OC* 5:2, 14).

24 *DAII* (Nolla), 131 note h; and, above all, 246: The English who came to found a democratic society in the wilderness of the New World, were all accustomed, in the mother country, to take part in public affairs...Among Americans it is therefore liberty which is old; equality is comparatively new."

25 Ibid., 44 note f.

26 See *DAI* (Nolla), 24–27, and 37–38. In writing the first *Democracy*, Tocqueville was quite emphatic. In a manuscript note to the chapter on the "Point of Departure," he wrote: "*Point de départ*. In my perspective the most important [cause] of all.... Equality. Democracy imported in germ." Compare with *DAII* (Nolla), 94–95, and 245–246. In 1840, the distinctiveness of America and Britain is reserved primarily for discussions of language and oratory in the *Democracy* of 1840. See ibid., 67–72; 89.

27 "L'emancipation des esclaves" (1843), *OC* 3:1, 91 ff. See also *T and B on Social Reform* (trans. Drescher), 138, 150–153.

28 Tocqueville to Henry Reeve, 26 March 1853, *OC* 6:1, 143; *OC* 3:1, 81, 91–93; *T and B on Social Reform*, 140.

29 *DAI* (Nolla), 14, 16.

30 For the title, see Tocqueville to John Stuart Mill, 14 November 1839. For discussions of Tocqueville's shifting focus and the decision to change the title, see Seymour Drescher, "Tocqueville's Two *Démocraties*," *Journal of the History of Ideas*, 25:2 (1964): 201–216; and "More than America: Comparison and Synthesis in *Democracy in America*," in *Reconsidering Tocqueville's Democracy in America*, A. S. Eisenstadt, ed. (New Brunswick: Rutgers, 1988), 77–93; Jean-Claude Lamberti, *Tocqueville and the Two Democracies*, trans. Arthur Goldhammer (Cambridge, MA: Harvard University Press, 1989); *DAI* (Nolla), "Introduction," liii (note); James T. Schleifer, "Epilogue: How Many Democracies," in *The Making of Tocqueville's "Democracy in America*," 2nd ed. (Indianapolis: Liberty Fund, 2000), 354–368; Robert Gannett, "Bowling Ninepins," 16–18; and Robert Gannett, *Tocqueville Unveiled: The Historian and His Sources for The Old Regime and the Revolution* (Chicago: University of Chicago Press, 2003), 5–6. For the probable motives in Tocqueville's decision to switch back to *Democracy in America*, see Françoise Mélonio, *Tocqueville and the French*, trans. Beth G. Raps (Charlottesville, VA: University Press of Virginia, 1998), 30.

31 Mélonio, *Tocqueville and the French*, 57. For a similar emphasis on Tocqueville's motivation as a methodological search for an "ideal

typology" in the second *Democracy*, see, inter alia, Richter, "Comparative Political Analysis," 155–158. Schleifer's *Making* emphasizes Tocqueville's diminishing attention to America, an increasing shift to Europe and to what was generically or theoretically democratic. See Schleifer, *Making*, 222, 235. The most elaborate argument in favor of the typological hypothesis is in Lamberti, *Tocqueville and the Two Democracies*, passim. Although some of Tocqueville's chapters are congruent with a typological approach, this still leaves Tocqueville's explicitly "American" chapters anomalous and unaccounted for in the *Democracy* of 1840. Equally important, there are very few of Tocqueville's (non-American) designations of "democratic" phenomena or characteristics that cannot be accounted for by direct reference to French (and, to a lesser extent) European examples. In assessing the simultaneously austere style and the rhetorical aim of the second *Democracy*, one must consider Tocqueville's goals. They were intended to garner "both attention from his readers and eventual glory for himself." ... So he cloaked his text in "mystery while forging a useful shield to conceal his artistic exaggerations." (Gannett, *Tocqueville Unveiled*, 151.)

32 Jardin, *Tocqueville*, 251. Jardin notes that in the first *Democracy*, the natural parallel was between democratic America and aristocratic England. In the second, the important comparison, often implicit, was between the two democracies, the United States and France (ibid., 252). One should also not overlook the fact that Tocqueville's notes show him referring more frequently to England in the second *Democracy* than in the first. For Tocqueville's burning of some of his early draft chapters, see "Tocqueville to Beaumont," 5 December 1838, *OC* 8:1, 328.

33 *DAI* (Nolla), 241 note t.

34 *DAII* (Nolla), 257 note s and 255 note o.

35 Ibid., 279 and note c; also 268 note j.

36 Ibid., 248 note k. (my emphasis).

37 For some recent examples, see Garry Wills, "Did Tocqueville 'Get' America?" *New York Review of Books* (April 29, 2004): 52–56; and Harvey C. Mansfield and Delba Winthrop, "Editors' Introduction" to *Democracy in America* (Chicago: University of Chicago Press, 2000), xvii.

38 See, *inter alia*, Schleifer, *Making*; and *DAII* (Nolla), 22–25; 234 and *DAI* (Nolla), 146. The one reference to the "omnipotence of the majority" at the beginning of the *Democracy* of 1840 is explicitly linked to the United States. The same page, dealing with democratic societies in

general, refers to "the infallibility of the masses." Toward the end of the book, "tyranny" is explicitly rejected as a concept relevant to the democratic future. Toward the end of the *Democracy* (part 4, chapter 2), "omnipotence" itself is embedded in a discussion of French, not American, society. The conceptual migration is complete. For a balanced and extended analysis of the concept in Tocqueville's *Democracy*, see James Schleifer, *The Making of Tocqueville's Democracy in America*, 2nd ed. (Indianapolis: Liberty Fund, 2000), ch. 14, 15.

39 The longest note in the *Democracy* of 1840 is a portrait of the heroic solitude of an American pioneer family, ibid., 282–284.

40 *DAI* (Nolla), 75 note 51; *DAII* (Nolla), 275 note t.

41 ibid., 96, 267 and note, 278 note b.

42 ibid., 101 and note k, 122, and 204 note j.

43 See Don E. Fehrenbacher, *The Slaveholding Republic: An Account of the United States Government's Relations to Slavery* (New York: Oxford University Press, 2001).

44 "Rapport sur un ouvrage de M. Theodore Sedgwick," July 1858, *OC* 16, 245.

45 *AR*, I (trans. Kahan), 221; *AR*, I *OC* 2:1, 222.

46 Compare *DAII*, 150 note e, and *AR*, I (trans. Kahan), 268. Compare the *Old Regimes* reiteration of England's unqualified contentment, past and present, with the portrait presented in a note of the *Democracy* of 1840. "Look at England through the whole course of the eighteenth century. Never did a nation bathe itself in more incense; never was a people happier with itself; all was well with its constitution, every glaring defect immune criticism. Today a host of Englishmen seem bent on demonstrating that the very same constitution was defective in a thousand ways. Who was right, last century's English or those of our own day?" *DAII* (Nolla), 284.

47 Ibid., 368.

48 "État social et politique de la France avant et depuis 1789" (1836), *OC* 2:1, 60–64. This essay was originally published as "Political and Social Condition of France: First Article," trans. John Stuart Mill, *London and Westminster Review* 3/25 (April 1836): 137–69.

49 *AR OC* 2:1, 302.

50 For this argument, see Françoise Mélonio and François Furet, Introduction to *AR, I* (trans. Kahan), 30.

51 See, *inter alia*, Stephan Conway, *The British Isles and the War of American Independence* (New York: Oxford University Press, 2000). The *Democracy* of 1840 dismisses the impact of British parliamentary orators. During the American Revolution, the voices from "the great

theater of English freedom" had little resonance beyond Great Britain, compared with those of the colonial assemblies of America. *DAII* (Nolla), 89. When setting out to investigate the impact of the French Revolution, however, "Tocqueville read in their original English the complete corpus of Burke's speeches, public letters, and private correspondence on the French Revolution" (Gannett, *Tocqueville Unveiled*, 61). Their impact on Europeans was considerable. Burke's influence on the making of the *Old Regime* is carefully analyzed by Gannett.

52 *AR, OC* 2:1, 115, *AR, I* (trans. Kahan), 125, 345–346.

53 *AR, OC* 2:1, 286–287; *AR,* 1 (trans. Kahan), 280–281.

54 *AR, OC* 2:1, 306; *AR, I* (trans. Kahan), 300.

55 Tocqueville to George Cornewall Lewis, 5 September 1858, *OC* 6:3, 303.

56 For the protean potential of Tocquevillian comparative perspectives beyond his own core zone see, *inter alia*, Carlos A. Forment, *Democracy in Latin America* (Chicago: University of Chicago Press, 2003); Fritz Stern, "The New Democracies in Crisis in Interwar Europe," in *Democracy's Victory and Crisis: Nobel Symposium no. 93*, Axel Hadenius ed. (New York: Cambridge University Press, 1997): 15–22. Robert D. Putnam, *Bowling Alone: The Collapse and Revival of American Community* (New York: Simon and Schuster, 2002), expands Tocqueville's comparative range to a far broader range of national units than his predecessor.

57 *S, OC* 12, 89.

2 Tocqueville on 1789

Preconditions, Precipitants, and Triggers

I. INTRODUCTION

In his discussion of the causes of the English Revolution, Lawrence Stone distinguishes among preconditions (1529–1629), precipitants (1629–39), and triggers (1640–42). The preconditions "made some form of redistribution of political power almost inevitable [...], but whether these changes would come about by peaceful evolution, political upheaval, or force of arms was altogether uncertain." Later, the "precipitants of the 1630s turned the prospects of a political breakdown from a possibility into a probability," whereas the trigger was provided by "a sequence of short-term, even fortuitous events which turned the probability into a certainty."[1] The dates are of course somewhat arbitrary, but indicate points of inflexion in the likelihood that observers, whether writing at the time or with the benefit of hindsight, might assign to a revolutionary outcome.

One can try to make a similar distinction with regard to Tocqueville's writings on the French Revolution.[2] The preconditions, discussed in Book II of the *Ancien Régime* (AR), were established over the period from 1439 to 1750. The precipitants, which are the topic of Book III, developed from 1750 to 1787. The triggering events, which are discussed in the notes for Books I and II of the planned second volume, occurred from 1787 to 1789. Although roughly adequate, this periodization is not quite true to his analysis, which points to a further inflexion point around 1770. In Ch.III.i of AR he points to 1750 ("vers le milieu du siècle") as a watershed, marked by the appearance and intellectual hegemony of a certain kind of abstract philosophical radicalism. At that time, however, the mood was reformist rather than revolutionary.[3] In fact,

49

an enlightened monarch on the throne might have averted the Revolution.[4] Twenty years later, the mood had changed.[5] Tocqueville cites, as one example, popular reaction to the abolition of the *parlements* in 1771, and adds that from that point onwards, a radical evolution was inevitable.[6]

The rhetoric of inevitability is, as always, hard to decipher. There are two possible counterfactuals we might envisage, and in fact Tocqueville seems to rely on both. In a weak counterfactual, the Revolution was inevitable if neither Louis XV and Louis XVI, *such as they were*, could have done anything to prevent it. In a strong counterfactual, it was inevitable if it would have occurred even *had they been different from what they were*. Concerning Louis XV, Tocqueville asserts that although the latter might have initiated a peaceful reform around 1750 and averted the Revolution, it was not in his character to do so.[7] Thus the Revolution was weakly inevitable by 1750. When Tocqueville asserts that it was only by 1771 that a radical revolution had become inevitable, he must therefore have the strong sense in mind. Yet when he also asserts that Louis XVI could have taken a number of preemptive decisions that would have steered the course of events in a less radical direction,[8] he must rely on the weak counterfactual, since none of these far-sighted choices could have been made by the notoriously indecisive Louis XVI. Given his character, the Revolution was a certainty.

A further problem of interpretation arises from Tocqueville's explanatory style. As in the somewhat analogous case of Marx, Tocqueville oscillates between intentional and functional explanation (see Section III), between structural explanation and event-based explanation (see Section V), and between explanation and irony (see Section VI). Compared with Marx, he is, to be sure, much more firmly committed to intentional, event-based explanation, as shown by his analysis of what has come to be known as the "Tocqueville effect" (see Section IV).

I shall proceed as follows. In the brief historiographical Section II, I indicate some of the ideas that Tocqueville may have taken from his predecessors, or that they may all have taken from a common source. In Section III, I consider Tocqueville's view of the pre-conditions of the Revolution: the absolute monarchy as it existed around 1750. Section IV focuses on the precipitants that made a revolution increasingly likely in the years up to 1787. In Section V,

I discuss some of the events that triggered the violent turn of the Revolution. Section VI offers a brief conclusion.

II. MME DE STAËL AND JOSEPH DROZ

Tocqueville's pithy analyses of the Revolution and the events leading up to it had several predecessors. He was probably familiar with Mme de Staël's *Considérations* and certainly with the *Histoire du règne de Louis XVI* by Joseph Droz, by whom he "set great store."[9] Both works excel in the politico-psychological mode of analysis that we now associate with Tocqueville. Reading them, one can glean an impression of what was relatively commonplace and, by implication, what was novel in Tocqueville's analyses. The following offers some instances in which his ideas had already been stated by these two writers. A few other examples are cited in the notes.

1. A central idea in Book II of the AR is that the French nobility had broken the two implicit contracts that justified its privileges in the public eye: to do military service in exchange for tax exemptions[10] and to provide public goods to the peasantry in exchange for feudal dues.[11] Mme de Staël was fully aware of the first breach of contract[12] as well as of the second.[13]

2. Another key theme of Book II is the pervasive combination of envy and resentment from below and contempt from above in the relations within[14] and between[15] the different orders of the old regime. Droz is very eloquent on this topic, as when he refers to "a cascade of contempt"[16] in the old regime or to the illusion of the nobles at Versailles that they could subdue the third estate by displaying their contempt.[17]

3. In Book II, Tocqueville argued that in its policy towards criticism, the monarchy contributed doubly to its own downfall by allowing free discussion of dangerous if abstract ideas while forbidding constructive criticism of the acts of the administration.[18] The former policy, in his view, was something like a safety-valve or consolation prize.[19] Droz, while noting the same paradox, offered a simpler explanation

of the toleration of radical ideas, appealing to the frivolity of the officials rather than to their Machiavellianism.[20]

4. In a striking comment in Book II, Tocqueville notes that while usually taking an aloof stance towards officials, the nobles behaved deferentially towards them when they came soliciting.[21] Again, Droz makes a very similar observation.[22]

5. Although in Book III Tocqueville recognized that the parlements were useful in some respects, he also asserted that they had more power to prevent good than to prevent evil.[23] In Droz's (equivalent) language, they had more power to do evil than to do good.[24]

6. A central idea in Book III (and in the notes for the second volume) is that under Louis XV and Louis XVI, the administration constantly failed to see that *half-measures* would work contrary to their intended purpose, an idea that Tocqueville applied to concessive[25] as well as to repressive[26] policies. Mme de Staël refers to the ineffectiveness of the repressive half-measures taken on the day of the oath of the Jeu de Paume.[27] Droz refers both to concessions[28] and to repressive measures[29] that were counterproductive because they did not go far enough in their respective directions.

7. Another important idea in Book III is the inconsistent attitude of the privileged classes towards the people, an amalgam of sympathy and contempt.[30] Droz makes the same point and, like Tocqueville (but referring to a different behavior), spells out how the attitude also led to inconsistent practice.[31]

8. In the notes for the second volume, Tocqueville makes the strong claim that one cannot at one and the same time be courageous against despotism and against anarchy.[32] Having successfully resisted the king, the *constituante* could not also stand up against the people of Paris. Again, we find Droz making the same observation.[33]

I have no direct evidence that would allow me to tell whether these instances reflect a direct influence of de Staël and Droz on Tocqueville, or whether the three writers simply expressed ideas that were in common circulation at the time. It seems to me that the similarities documented in (3) and (8) are so striking and specific that a direct influence rather than a common cause is plausible. The main point, however, is that even when we find his observations very striking, we should be careful about making claims about Tocqueville's originality. He *was* extremely original and innovative, so that even if we take away some of his claims to fame, there are plenty of them left. And if Tocqueville did borrow some ideas from his predecessors, it would be absurd to condemn him for not citing them. Here, as elsewhere, Tocqueville wrote with the pride of an aristocrat and a historian, hiding his traces and demolishing his scaffolding.

III. *ON NE S'APPUIE QUE SUR CE QUI RÉSISTE*

These words ("You can lean only on what offers resistance"), spoken to Napoleon by the poet François Andrieux, can be used to summarize a major strand in Tocqueville's argument in Book II of the AR.[34] In a nutshell, he claimed that the successive French kings were so successful in reducing the nobility to a state of political impotence that when Louis XVI needed their help to resist the Revolution, they had nothing to offer. Only in the west of France, where the nobles had resisted the summons of the king to come to the court, did they come to his assistance.[35] In fact, the administration had undermined *all* intermediary bodies, so that even in an ordinary crisis it could not enlist the assistance of anybody.[36]

An important reason for the feebleness of the nobles was their isolation from the bourgeoisie that followed from their own tax exemption.[37] Because they were not subject to the same taxes, the two classes had few common interests and few occasions to take concerted action.[38] Moreover, the tax exemption was a visible symbol of privilege that fueled the resentment of the bourgeoisie. As part of the "cascade of privilege," to paraphrase Droz, the bourgeoisie was almost as isolated from the people as the nobility was from the bourgeois.[39] Although Tocqueville does not use the phrase "divide et impera," it is very clear from his analyses that this was the strategy he imputed to the kings.[40] Yet as we know from Simmel,[41] the fact that party C may benefit from a fallout between parties A and B is not by itself proof of intentional "divide et impera." There is always the possibility of an accidental third-party benefit, "tertius gaudens." Does Tocqueville offer any proof in favor of the more intentional or Machiavellian thesis?

Tocqueville's interest in triadic structures, such as king-nobility-people, goes back to his early days. In a letter to Beaumont from 1828, he offers a more conventional idea of the relations among the three, asserting that the French kings first allied themselves with the people ("les communes") to destroy the nobility and then were in turn destroyed by the people in 1789.[42] The discussion in the AR is subtler and, up to a point, convincing. Tax exemption for the nobles seems in fact to have combined material interest with the symbolic value of *distinction*. "The privileged insisted, and had largely obtained, that when taxed at all, they would be listed in rolls distinct from those for commoners. [...] For the nobles, the wish to avoid having their names contaminated by residing on the same piece of paper with those of commoners was joined with the benefit of obfuscating their relatively low rates of assessment."[43] Following Tocqueville, one might argue that the tax exemption had *mainly* symbolic value, since the tax paid by a tenant cut into the rents commanded by the lord.[44] Whether through its material or symbolic effects or both, the exemption might plausibly generate "the suicidal consequences of elite fragmentation."[45] The question remains, however: did Tocqueville show that the fragmentation was deliberately brought about by the kings rather than being an unintended by-product of actions undertaken for other purposes?

In addition to his analysis of the *effects* of tax exemption for the nobles, Tocqueville offers an account of the *origins* of the exemption – namely, that the nobility "cowardly" accepted tax exemption as a bribe to let the king impose new taxes without calling the Estates-General.[46] Before I pursue this point, let me signal the extraordinary causal importance that Tocqueville attached to the desire of the kings to avoid having to convoke the Estates-General. The venality of offices is also ascribed to this desire,[47] as is the political importance of the *parlements*.[48] In each case, Tocqueville also invoked the king's need to hide for the French the nature and the extent of their real oppression. There is more than a hint of functionalism in this argument, as there was in his claim, discussed earlier, that the administration allowed criticism of religion as a "consolation" and (I shall now argue) in his claim that the tax exemption was a strategy of "divide et impera."

In functional explanation, one cites the beneficial consequences (for someone or something) of a behavioral pattern in order to *explain* that pattern, neither showing that the pattern was created with the *intention* of providing those benefits nor pointing to a *feedback loop* whereby the consequences might sustain their causes.[49] When not supported in either of these two ways, the alleged explanation is spurious, since it does not exclude the possibility that the benefits could have arisen in some accidental way. A typical example is the explanation of conflict behavior in terms of third-party benefits without excluding the notice that the latter might belong to the category of "tertius gaudens." Strictly speaking, Tocqueville does not offer a functional explanation of the tax exemption, since he does impute a divide-and-conquer intention to the kings. Yet, since he provides no evidence for this intention, it is hard not to conclude that he just inferred the *ex ante* intention to benefit from the factual *ex post* benefits, combining "post hoc ergo propter hoc" with "cui bono?"

Going back to the granting of the exemption that was "cowardly" accepted by the nobles, we see that Tocqueville here offers a perfectly reputable intentional account that in no way relies on "divide et impera": the king offered the immunity as a bribe so that he would not have to call the Estates-General. As an additional explanatory factor, Tocqueville notes that when Charles VII first established the *taille* on a national basis, it would have been dangerous to impose it on the nobles,[50] especially as it was likely to be used against them.[51] Again, this is a reputable intentional explanation, but it does not support the story according to which the kings granted tax exemptions to the nobles in order to undermine their political power. In fact, to complicate matters, Tocqueville at one point asserts that the exemptions were a "consolation" for that loss,[52] thus reversing the causal chain.

The exemption of the nobles from military service occurred at the same time as the establishment of the *taille* from which they were also exempt.[53] In one perspective, the creation by Charles VII in 1439 of a national tax and of a national army financed by that tax was the beginning of modern France. Tocqueville emphasizes, however, the disastrous consequences of exempting the nobility from the obligation to pay taxes and from the responsibility to make up the king's army. As we have seen, the exemption from the *taille* prevented any form of joint action with the bourgeoisie. The exemption from military service was another poisoned gift.[54] Without the obligation of public service, the nobility lost its energy and became a mere ornament. Individually, they might appear greater, but collectively they lost out.[55]

Here, we should take public service to include the provision of public goods to the local peasantry – notably, law, order and famine relief – as well as raising troops for the king's service. Just as the royal militia replaced the nobles in the latter function, the royal *intendant* and his *subdélégué* replaced the *seigneur* in the former. And just as the tax exemption fueled the envy of the bourgeois for the nobles, so did the withdrawal of the nobles from local administration fuel the hatred the peasantry felt for them.[56]

These two emotions, *envy* and *hatred*, form the core of Tocqueville's social psychology in the AR.[57] Although his vocabulary is somewhat inconsistent,[58] I believe that the main thrust of his argument is the following. If we distinguish between emotions of comparison and emotions of interaction,[59] envy falls in the former category and hatred in the latter. Because, as we have seen, nobles and bourgeois had few occasions to interact, the latter tended to envy the former rather than to hate them. By contrast, the constant and intense interaction between the peasant and the seigneur[60] tended to produce hatred rather than envy. In both cases, the emotions arose from the lack of any obligations on the part of the nobles that might justify the tax exemptions and feudal dues from which they benefited.[61]

Given these powerful emotions, no wonder that the peasants burned their castles and that the Third Estate destroyed their privileges. In this respect, France was unique among the major European countries. The German bourgeoisie may have felt envy towards the nobility because of unequal access to noble possessions, high office or the court,[62] but not on grounds of unequal tax burdens. In fact, Tocqueville cites one of his German interlocutors to the effect that when the German nobles ceased to do military service, they became subject to a new tax.[63] (Elsewhere he remarks that a similar surcharge would have been appropriate in France.[64]) Because of the participation of the German nobility in local administration, the conditions for hatred were not present.[65] In England, there were no breeding grounds for envy, since tax exemptions were enjoyed by the poor rather than by the rich,[66] nor for hatred.[67]

There is one gap in this otherwise admirably tight argument: why, how, and when did the *intendant* (or his *subdélégué*) take the place of the seigneur in local administration? Virtually all references to the *intendant* in the AR are to his functions in the eighteenth century, and there is no mention of the creation of the office in the sixteenth century. It seems plausible, however, that Tocqueville connected the undermining of seigniorial power with the abolition of the *taille seigneuriale*[68] and of private armies[69] decreed in the 1439 ordinance. We are led, therefore, to ask if Tocqueville did not needlessly complicate his explanation of the decline of the nobility. From Charles VII onwards, the French kings were constantly trying to reduce the power of the nobles, constrained at each step by the power they still retained. Although in this process the kings certainly played the nobles off against each other, the idea that they offered them tax exemptions in order to play them off against the bourgeoisie is far-fetched and undocumented. More plausibly, as Tocqueville himself asserts, the kings made the nobles exempt from the tax because they were not strong enough to impose it on them. Later, this exemption may well have redounded to the kings' benefits, but if so, the mechanism was that of "tertius gaudens," not "divide et impera."

In England, the nobility continued to serve as a check on royal power. Although it did not have that role in France, other institutions served, however imperfectly, the same end. The Estates-General ceased early to be an effective counterweight, but the two institutions that (according to Tocqueville) were introduced so as the kings would not have to convoke them took up their function. In his analysis, the venality of office[70] and the parlements[71] illustrated what is nowadays called the *principle of the second-best* – namely, that "it is not true that a situation in which more, but not all, of the optimum conditions are fulfilled is necessarily, or is even likely to be, superior to a situation in which fewer are fulfilled."[72] Applied to the present case, and assuming that the arbitrary royal administration, the parlements and the venality of office were all sub-optimal institutions, the principle asserts that given the first of these, the presence of the second and the third could well make things better rather than worse. Although Tocqueville made this assessment as an observer, the participants in the system might also subscribe to it, at least in part. The venality of office never enjoyed much support beyond that of its beneficiaries,[73] but the parlements were increasingly seen as a bulwark against despotism,[74] whence their brief but crucial role in the prelude to the Revolution.

IV. THE "TOCQUEVILLE PARADOX"

In the social sciences, the "Tocqueville paradox" refers to the idea that subjective discontent (and hence the likelihood of revolution) and objective grounds for discontent may be inversely related to each other.[75] In the AR, Tocqueville offers two synchronic versions and one diachronic version of the paradox. At the beginning of Book II, he asks why the Revolution occurred in France rather than in Germany, given that feudal burdens were lighter in France.[76] The resolution of the paradox, as we saw, is that in Germany the nobles still performed the administrative functions that justified their appropriation of feudal benefits. In the absence of peasant hatred, bourgeois envy could not by itself trigger a revolution.

In Book III, Ch. iv, Tocqueville notes that another synchronic version of the paradox could be observed within France itself.[77] The areas in Île-de-France where the Revolution would break out enjoyed greater personal freedom and lower taxes than the western lands that would be the bastion of the counterrevolution.[78] Tocqueville's resolution of this version of the paradox is ambiguous. On the one hand, as we have seen, he can cite the fact that in the west of France (as in Germany), the nobles were still involved in local administration. On the other hand, he appeals somewhat confusingly to a diachronic version of the paradox. He states, first, that the better their conditions, the more the French found them intolerable.[79] Although the statement by itself allows for a diachronic as well as a synchronic reading, the discussion leading up to it *unambiguously* favors the latter. He then, however, goes on to restate the paradox in one of the most famous statements in the whole work, to the effect that revolutions often occur as one goes from the worse to the better rather than the other way around.[80] Although the context makes it clear *without any doubt whatsoever* that this is a diachronic statement, it is presented, misleadingly, as equivalent to the synchronic one that immediately preceded it.

There is no reason to accuse Tocqueville of being disingenuous, but he was obviously subject to a rare slip of the mind.

Let us focus, then, on the diachronic paradox, and first approach it as part of the larger question of how governments respond to an actual or predictable crisis. Broadly speaking, we may distinguish four responses: preemption, concession, moderate repression and severe repression. Wisdom dictates preemption – meeting popular demands before they are formulated, or granting more than is demanded. Both Louis XV[81] and Louis XVI[82] were sorely lacking in this quality of mind. Severe repression, for its part, requires a decisiveness that was also absent. Although Tocqueville does not mention the well-known aversion of Louis XVI for spilling the blood of his subjects, he does cite the more general tendency of the eighteenth-century monarchy to be *fortiter in modo, suaviter in re*.[83] The administration was left, therefore, with the alternatives of concession and moderate repression. As we saw, "half-measures" (Droz), "half-constraints" (Tocqueville), "shadow freedoms" (Tocqueville), and "small reforms" (Droz) often work against their purpose. In particular, the tendency of concessions to inflame rather than to appease the population offers one explanation of the diachronic paradox. For each demand that is granted, more will spring up until the capacity of the system to absorb them is broken.

Why does one concession generate the demand for more? Generally speaking, it could be because it induces a change in the *beliefs* of the citizens, in their *preferences*, or in both. On the one hand, the granting of a demand may provide new information about the resolve of the administration, and support the belief that further demands will also be met with a positive response. In Ch.III.iv, Tocqueville does not appeal to this mechanism, although he cites it elsewhere to argue why the recall of the *parlement* of Paris in September 1788 was a point of no return for the monarchy.[84] On the other hand, reforms that satisfy a given desire may at the same time cause dormant desires to appear on the horizon. This was Tocqueville's answer.[85] The key idea, already stated in the Introduction to *Democracy in America*,[86] is that people do not resent the evils that appear to them as an inevitable part of the natural or social order. Once one such evil has been removed, however, similar evils will appear as removable and therefore as intolerable. A cognitive change (the evil is not inevitable) triggers a motivational change (it is intolerable). Although this argument would seem to apply to preemption as well as to concessions, we may note that preemptive measures do not signal lack of resolve. To make Tocqueville consistent with himself, we may speculate that the self-defeating consequences of concessive measures were due to a combination of signaling effects and induced preference change.

In this argument, improvement causes discontent. In another argument, improvement and discontent are traced back to a common cause – namely, increased economic activity. Because the expanding fortunes of the individuals were so closely linked to the finances of the state,[87] the utter disorder of the public sector generated frustration in the increasing number of individuals that had to deal with it.[88] Tocqueville's analysis of the relation between the individual investor or entrepreneur and the state has some similarity with his discussion of the relation between the peasant and his lord. The hatred of the peasant towards the lord and the irritation of the capitalist with the bureaucracy are generated by their constant *interaction* with these authorities rather than by the objective burden the latter impose on them.

The two last paragraphs have dealt with two of the three grievances Tocqueville cites as subject to the diachronic paradox: *liberty* and *money*.[89] The abolition of abuses creates more suffering, not less; increased prosperity generates more discontent, not less. Applying the logic of the paradox to the third grievance, *equality*, we would expect him to assert that as society advances towards equality, the greater is the discontent caused by inequality. There are two ways to understand this idea. First, there is the view that Tocqueville developed in *Democracy in America*, according to which increased equality in one dimension causes inequality *in that dimension* to appear as more and more intolerable.[90] Second, there is the idea of *status inconsistency*, according to which increased equality in one dimension causes inequality *in other dimensions* to appear as more and more intolerable. For instance, if status barriers to occupational choice remain constant or even become more rigid while economic conditions are becoming more equal, rich commoners will feel increasingly frustrated. There is a hint of this idea in a draft of Ch.II.9,[91] although Tocqueville does not tell us under which conditions the tension will lead to individual efforts (for examples, for rich commoners to seek ennoblement) and when it will trigger collective action (for examples, to demands for the abolishment of nobility).

Ch.V of Book III does not address the "Tocqueville paradox" as usually understood, but another paradoxical effect of the initiatives of the old regime. Earlier, I mentioned Tocqueville's claim that a wise preemptive policy in 1750 might have prevented the Revolution. In Ch.III.5, he refers to various disinterested measures to alleviate the misery of the people – measures *not* undertaken under the pressure of demands – from the years immediately before the Revolution.[92] However wise the measures themselves may have been, the wisdom of the way they were proposed was highly questionable. The privileged classes publicly stated their own responsibility for the plight of the peasantry, as if their intention were to create disturbances rather than to prevent them.[93] Adding insult to (the perception of) injury, they also used contemptuous language when referring to the individuals they intended to help,[94] as if the latter were unable to understand what they were saying. Thus the precipitants of the Revolution included proactive no less than reactive attempts to improve the situation of the population.

V. TRIGGERS OF THE REVOLUTION

Whether Tocqueville really pulled off the trick announced in the title of the final chapter of AR – "Comment la Révolution est sortie d'elle-même de ce qui précède" – is debatable. Maybe an argument could be made that, given the preconditions and precipitants outlined in Books II and III, it would take so little to trigger the Revolution that, by the laws of probability, it was morally certain to occur. Tocqueville did not, however, want to limit himself to a structuralist explanation. In the second volume, he intended to go beyond the argument that the revolution *had to* happen, in one way or another, to spell out the way in which it *did* happen. In the notes for Books I and II of the second volume of the AR, Tocqueville covers events from the first *assemblée des notables* in 1787 to the end of 1789, with brief remarks on the summer of 1790. The tantalizing fragments offer elements of an explanation, but no "idée-mère."

A. Assemblée des Notables and Parlements

The role of these bodies in the run-up to the Revolution was mainly to expose the frailty of the administration. Even when the government proposed measures that were in the interest of the country, the people supported those who refused to ratify them. The notables in the first assembly were applauded when they opposed Calonne's proposal to abolish the corvée, tax exemption for the nobles, and internal tariffs.[95] When in 1787 the king granted a very democratic organization of the provincial assembly in the Dauphiné, the regional parlement that refused to endorse it was glorified rather than vilified by the people.[96] Tocqueville drew the conclusion that in politics, the approval or disapproval of a proposer causes approval of disapproval of his proposals rather than the other way around.[97]

B. Events in the Dauphiné

Among the triggers of the revolution, Tocqueville emphasized the enormous importance of events in the Dauphiné. As just noted, until it was squashed by the parlement, the proposed assembly of 1787 had an unusually democratic form. A year later, the immensely influential assembly in Vizille achieved an unprecedented unity of action among the three orders,[98] made possible in part by the fact that the tax system used in the province did not involve personal exemptions from the taille.[99] An effect (or a sign) of their unity was the adoption of the system of "cross-voting"[100] in electing deputies to the Estates-General. In this system, deputies for a given order were chosen jointly by members of all three orders, just as once the Estates were in place, the Third Estate demanded that the credentials of deputies from a given order be verified jointly by the three orders. Tocqueville asserts that the Estates-General might have found it easier to agree if this electoral system had been universally adopted.[101] As the estates elsewhere were more deeply divided, this was a remote contingency.

C. Division of the Privileged Orders

One reason the Revolution succeeded was indeed that the privileged classes did not begin to cooperate until it was too late. The *cahiers de doléance* already displayed the "suicidal elite fragmentation" to which I referred earlier.[102] During what Tocqueville refers to as "the era of class struggle," the fragmentation became "vertiginous"[103] and of a different character. Whereas previously the conflicts within and between the privileged orders had benefited the government, they now became so virulent as to bring it down.[104] Tocqueville is somewhat inconsistent, however, in his treatment of the tension between the upper and lower clergy. He asserts that Necker's report to the king of December 27, 1788, was intended to create a split between the bishops and the parish priests, but adds that in the light of their later reunion, the decision did not matter.[105] Elsewhere he recognizes, however, the important role of the lower clergy in the struggle over the verification of credentials,[106] well before the reunion forged by the abolition of the tithe, the confiscation of the church goods and the civil constitution of the clergy.

D. The Half-Measures of Louis XVI

The tendency of the royal administration to resort to concessive and repressive half-measures, discussed earlier, persisted throughout this period. In his comments on the report of December 27, 1788, Tocqueville asserts that its most disastrous provision was the one granting the Third Estate as many deputies as the other two orders combined, while leaving it undecided whether votes would be taken by head or by order. In his view, the king would have been better off either insisting on the old forms (vote by order) or imposing a new system (vote by head). The compromise he offered was more risky than either extreme.[107] Once it turned out that this half-reform set in process a motion that ended with the Third Estate's declaring itself the National Assembly and the deputies taking the oath of the Jeu de Paume, Louis XVI tried to impose his own program in the *séance royale* of June 23. Before[108] as well as after[109] that session, he tried to intimidate the deputies by various petty methods, which again worked against their purpose.

E. The Role of the Bourgeoisie

On the basis of the correspondence of the deputies from Anjou to their constituency, Tocqueville asserts that well before the meeting of the Estates-General, the bourgeoisie had formed a plan of action that anticipated the events that eventually took place.[110] This statement is clearly intended to refute the commonly held view that the six-week interval between the meeting of the Estates-General and their self-transformation into the National Assembly was crucial for that metamorphosis to occur. Apart from the fact that Tocqueville's very general claim can hardly be supported by this single source, it does not fit with his observation that as late as March 1789, Mounier took seriously the "mad illusion" that even with double representation and vote by head, the Third Estate would easily be dominated by the privileged classes.[111] Had it not been for the six weeks of isolated deliberation that allowed the Third Estate to consolidate itself, the old habits of deference might have prevailed.

VI. CONCLUSION

The AR is Tocqueville's greatest achievement. *Democracy in America*, while full of striking insights of lasting value, is badly structured and often incoherent. Brilliant, exuberant and messy, it is very much a young man's first book. By contrast, his study of the French Revolution is the work of a mature and highly disciplined mind. The use of telling details to illuminate general ideas is striking, as is Tocqueville's performance as a *character reader* of the old regime. Being closer to it in time, Joseph Droz had perhaps an even better intuitive understanding of how it operated, but he did not have Tocqueville's powerful generalizing mind.

The main flaw in Tocqueville's analysis is that it is sometimes *too* systematic. Oscillating between intentional and functional explanation, he strives to find *meaning* in what were more plausibly accidental or incidental outcomes of political struggles. The most important example of this tendency is the analysis of how the king benefited by granting tax exemptions to the nobility, but it is also at work in his statements about various institutions being created as "consolations" to this or that group or to "hide" the reality of oppression from the oppressed. Tocqueville had an acute sense of irony, and a superb understanding of social explanation, but he stumbled when he confused the two genres.

NOTES

The passages cited in the notes have been translated by Arthur Gold-hammer for this chapter. References to the *Ancien régime et la révolution* have been translated from the 1866 edition published in *OC*, B. Page references without attribution are to that edition; for convenience, corresponding pages to the *Œuvres*, P are also given. Page references to the notes for the projected volume two of the *Ancien régime* are to the materials published in *Œuvres*, P 3:319–1286.

1   *Causes of the English Revolution* 1529–1642 (London: Routledge, 1986), 127, 135.
2   For Tocqueville's brief comments on the relation between the revolution of 1640 and that of 1789, see *Œuvres*, P 3:343.
3   "By about 1750, the nation as a whole showed itself not more exigent in regard to political liberty than the economists themselves. It had lost the taste for and even the idea of such liberty by losing the use. It wanted reforms more than it wanted rights" (243; *Œuvres*, P 3:192).
4   "[If] at that time the throne had been occupied by a prince of the magnitude and temperament of the great Frederick, I have no doubt that he would have achieved any number of the greatest changes that the Revolution brought about in society and government, not only without losing his crown but with a considerable augmentation of his power" (ibid.).
5   "Twenty years later, things were no longer the same: the image of political liberty had presented itself to the French and came to seem more attractive to them with each passing day" (ibid.).
6   "I believe that from that moment on, this radical revolution, which would ultimately reduce what was best and what was worst in the old regime to an identical state of ruin, became inevitable" (*AR*, 245; *Œuvres*, P 3:193).
7   "We are assured that one of Louis XV's cleverest ministers, M. de Machault, anticipated this idea and pointed it out to his master. No one undertakes such a venture on the advice of another, however. One is apt to succeed in an enterprise of this kind only if capable of conceiving it" (*AR*, 243; *Œuvres*, P 3:192).
8   Tocqueville lists at least five such decisions. First, announcing the deficit to the first assemblée des notables before being requested to do so. Tocqueville lists this as one of the main errors of Louis XVI: "In convoking an assembly to ask for advice on finances, he did not anticipate all the demands for information it might make and believed that it would help him to eliminate a deficit the extent of which he did not wish to reveal" (*Œuvres*, P 3:1135). Second, "doubling [the

representation of] the Third Estate and allowing the three orders to vote in common" in the convocation to the Estates-General. In that case, "the leading classes would have adapted in advance to an inevitable fate. Feeling the pressure of the monarchy on themselves as well as that of the Third Estate, they would have grasped their helplessness from the start. Rather than fight madly to preserve everything, they would have fought so as not to lose everything" (ibid., 497). Third, universalizing the mode of election to the Estates-General used in the Dauphiné, where "the deputies to the Estates-General were elected by the assembly, so that each nobleman had bourgeois among his electors and each bourgeois, noblemen, and each of the three deputations, while remaining distinct, thus became in a sense homogeneous. Represented in this way, the three orders might have been able, if not to meld into a single assembly, then at least to maneuver in the resulting assembly without clashing too violently" (ibid., 497–498). Fourth, adopting the principle of a unicameral assembly and universal eligibility from the beginning. "If, from the beginning, the intention had been to form just one assembly to which anyone could have been elected, there is reason to believe that many noble and ecclesiastical landowners would have been elected in the countryside, which would have yielded a far less dangerous assembly" (ibid., 561). Fifth, proposing in the opening session of the Estates-General the reform program announced seven weeks later. "If that had been done two months earlier, it is certain that affairs would have proceeded in this direction for some time, and the Revolution, which I believe to have been inevitable, would have come about in a somewhat different way, and without the fiery impetuosity impressed upon it by the class struggle" (ibid., 570). The two references to what was "inevitable" suggest that whereas profound changes were inevitable, the violence of the Revolution was not.

9 André Jardin, *Tocqueville* (New York: Farrar, Straus & Giroux, 1984), 484.
10 "[Nobles had been] relieved of the very onerous obligation to make war at their own expense, yet their immunity from taxation had been maintained and in fact expanded considerably. In other words, they retained the indemnity while shedding the burden" (*AR*, 118; *Œuvres*, P 3:119).
11 "[I]f the French peasant had still been subject to the administration of his lord, feudal dues would have seemed far less unbearable to him" (*AR*, 45; *Œuvres*, 3:78).
12 "If the French nobility had remained purely military, people might have tolerated its advantages much longer out of admiration and

gratitude." Germaine de Staël, *Considérations sur la Révolution française* (Paris: Tallandier, 2000), 145.

13 "The nobles of France were neither magistrates by dint of peerage, as in England, nor suzerain lords, as in Germany" (ibid.).

14 "These miserable prerogatives [tax exemptions for members of the Third Estate] filled those deprived of them with envy and those who possessed them with the most selfish pride" (*AR*, 138; *Œuvres*, P 3:131). In his notes on Germany, Tocqueville asked himself, "Did there exist between nobles of different origins the feelings of contempt and envy that one observed in France?" (*Œuvres* P 3:321).

15 "The system of ennoblements, far from diminishing the commoner's hatred of the nobleman, rather increased it without bound. It embittered that hatred with all the envy that the new noble inspired in his former equals" (*AR*, 133–134; *Œuvres*, P 3:128).

16 "There was [...] something like a cascade of contempt that passed down from rank to rank and did not stop at the Third Estate. The judge of a small tribunal had for the merchant the same contempt that the merchant had for the artisan." Joseph Droz, *Histoire du règne de Louis XIV pendant les années où l'on pouvait prévenir ou diriger la Révolution française* (Paris: Renouard, 1860), 1:81.

17 "To wound the amour-propre of the Third Estate and to vanquish the Third Estate were ideas that coincided in the frivolous minds of courtiers" (ibid. 2:129).

18 "[The government] rather readily tolerated attacks on the fundamental principles on which society then rested, and even discussion of God himself, provided that one refrained from comment on the most insignificant of its agents" (*AR*, 95; *Œuvres*, P 3:106).

19 "The French must always be allowed the sweetness of a little license to console them for their servitude" (ibid.).

20 "It was far more difficult to circulate judicious comment on certain administrative acts than to publish criminal texts. The former offended people in power, whom the latter amused" (Droz, 1:63).

21 "Noblemen themselves were sometimes great favor-seekers. ... In general, nobles never addressed intendants as anything but Monsieur, but I have noticed that in these circumstances they always addressed them as Monseigneur, just as the bourgeois did" (*AR*, 104; *Œuvres*, P 3:112).

22 "A very sharp demarcation line separated the nobility of the sword from the nobility of the robe, whose origins were not as ancient. The former spoke proudly of the blood they had shed for the state and had but little consideration for the honorable though peaceful functions of the magistracy. Yet when it was necessary to beg the indulgence of the

judges, no one hesitated to show signs of deference, no matter what title he wore" (Droz, 1:79).

23 "[T]he parlements, which alone bore the responsibility of standing in for political bodies, could not prevent the harm the government did and often prevented the good it wished to do" (*AR*, 238; *Œuvres*, P 3:189).

24 "[T]he parlement was powerful when it came to doing ill, for its resistance often aroused storms, and at the same time impotent when it came to doing good, for the *lits de justice* and exile triumphed over the most just of its efforts" (Droz, 1:109).

25 "[A]t the beginning of a revolution, these enterprises [granting no real liberties but only their shadow] always fail and merely inflame the people without satisfying them" (*AR*, 213; *Œuvres*, P 3:175).

26 "The half-measure of constraint imposed on the enemies of the Church at that time did not diminish their power but rather increased it. [...] Authors were persecuted just enough to make them complain but not enough to make them tremble. They were hobbled in a way that provoked resistance without incurring the heavy yoke that might subdue it" (*AR*, 224–225; *Œuvres*, P 3:181–182). See also *Œuvres*, P 3:483, where the struggle of the government against the parlements is characterized as "employing violence to the point of irritation but never pushing it to the point of fear." See also Section V for more examples.

27 "The danger was obvious enough to give them the air of courage, yet not real enough for timid men to surrender to it" (Staël, 148).

28 "Breteuil ... made a great deal of noise about some minor reforms, the effect of which was not so much to quiet demands as to encourage them" (Droz, 1:315).

29 When Louis XVI tried to suppress Necker's work on the administration of finances that appeared in 1784, the government "took half-measures that did not prevent readers from satisfying their curiosity and merely proved to them that what pleased them displeased the government" (Droz, 1:369). The measures taken on August 4, 1789, "were intended to calm the people but only aroused them more" (ibid., 2:312).

30 "[The people] had already become the object of their sympathy [i.e., of the sympathy of the assemblies of nobles] but without having ceased to be the object of their disdain" (*AR*, 271; *Œuvres*, P 3:209).

31 "Instead of preventing groups from forming early on [...], the gatherings were allowed to increase in size [...] and things proceeded from excess to excess until fears of pillage arose. Then the troops received the order to fire, to the great surprise of the multitude, which had so often heard it repeated that arms would never be used against it. This strange way of maintaining order resulted from a mix, very

common at the time, of contempt for the people, which made it impossible to believe that its agitation was grounds for fear, with so-called philanthropy, which opposed the application of a firm hand" (Droz, 2:71).

32 "Every assembly is obedient to the thought surrounding its creation. The Constituent Assembly of '89 was dispatched to fight aristocracy and despotism, and it was quite vigorous in opposing those enemies but [not] in opposing anarchy, which it was not prepared to combat. [...] It is rare for a man, and almost impossible for an assembly, to have the ability to alternately make violent efforts in two opposite directions. The energy that launched it violently in one direction impeded its progress in the other" (Œuvres, P 3:610; see also ibid., 604). He also claims, very dubiously, that the Constituent Assembly of 1848 had been "elected especially to combat anarchy," presumably to explain why it did not resist the rise to power of Louis Napoleon. He asserted, however, that his maternal great-grandfather Malesherbes had defended Louis XVI against the people *and* the people against Louis XVI. See Françoise Mélonio, *Tocqueville et les Français* (Paris: Aubier, 1993), 9. Elsewhere he takes a moralizing attitude: qualifying the failure of the assembly in July 1789 to adopt Lally-Tolendal's resolution condemning popular violence as "the Constituent Assembly's greatest blunder, or one might say, its great crime," he adds that "from that day forward, it was destined to obey and not to command; the people of Paris became the sovereign. Power had passed briefly to the Assembly only to end with the people. [...] If [per impossibile!] it had sensed its power and influence, it would have stood up to both the monarchy and the people and retained leadership of the Revolution in its own hands" (Œuvres, P 3:576).

33 "Many men are half-brave: some are brave against despotism, others against anarchy. Very few are capable of attacking both scourges with equal dedication" (Droz, 2:271). Yet he also notes that "Lally-Tolendal attacked anarchy as he had fought against despotism" (ibid., 269). He might equally have cited Clermont-Tonnerre: "You did not wish to obey armed despotism; will you obey popular turmoil?" *Réimpression de l'ancien Moniteur* (Paris: 1840ff), 1:400.

34 In fact he makes a quite explicit (if grammatically somewhat opaque) statement to that effect in the notes for the second volume: "In the time of Henri IV, these princes, great lords, bishops, and wealthy bourgeois ... could ... limit the movement to which they gave rise and support the monarchy even when they might have resisted it. Under Louis XVI, these same classes [...] could still stir up the people, [but] they were

incapable of leading it" (Œuvres, P 3:467–468, amended in the light of marginal note (c) cited in ibid., 1134).

35 "The letter of an intendant responding on this subject has survived. He complains that the nobles of his province are pleased to remain with their peasants rather than discharging their duties at Court. Now mark this well: the province described in these terms was Anjou, later known as the Vendée. The nobles who we are told refused to do their duty to the king were the only ones in France to take up arms to defend the monarchy" (AR, 182; Œuvres, P 3:155–156).

36 "[I]n time of scarcity [...] the central government took fright at its isolation and weakness. It would have liked to revive for the occasion the individual influences and political associations it had destroyed. It called on them for help, but no one answered the call, and the government was regularly astonished to find dead those whom its own actions deprived of life" (AR, 194–195; Œuvres, P 3:163–164).

37 "Of all the ways of introducing distinctions among men and discriminating between classes, inequality of taxation is the most pernicious and the most apt to add isolation to inequality and make both in a sense incurable" (AR, 132; Œuvres, P 3:127).

38 "[O]nce the two classes cease to be equally subject to taxation, there is virtually no further reason for them ever to deliberate together, no further occasion to experience common needs and feelings. Keeping them apart is no longer a concern: they have in a sense been deprived of the opportunity and desire to act together" (ibid.). See also Œuvres, P 3:410.

39 "[W]hat one sees above all in all the actions of this bourgeoisie is the fear of seeing itself confused with the people and the passionate desire to escape from the people's control by any available means" (AR, 139; Œuvres, P 3:131).

40 "Nearly all the unfortunate defects, errors, and prejudices I have just described in fact owe either their origin or their duration to the skill of most of our kings at dividing men in order to govern them more absolutely" (AR, 200; Œuvres, P 3:167). In the notes for the second volume, we read that "kings were able to create this unchecked power only by dividing the classes and isolating each of them amid its own peculiar prejudices, jealousies, and hatreds so as never to have to deal with more than one at a time" (Œuvres, P 3:485). In his notes on England, he writes that in France "those who worked most effectively to prevent landowners from becoming in this way members of a single body and forming an aristocracy rather than a caste were the kings who, for reasons of financial expediency dating back to the thirteenth

century, conceived the idea of levying a special tax on commoners who owned fiefs" (ibid., 342).

41 *Soziologie* (Berlin: Duncker and Humblot, 1908), 82–94.

42 The king "called the commons to his aid, joined forces with them, led them by the hand, enlisted their assistance to destroy feudalism, and was finally devoured when he found himself face-to-face with them in 1789" (*Letters, S,* 122).

43 J. Markoff, *The Abolition of Feudalism* (University Park, PA: Pennsylvania State University Press, 1996), 171. See also Droz, 1:40: "The authorities verified the commoner's income and taxed it strictly, whereas they contented themselves with the noble's declaration, which was almost always too low and sometimes scandalously false."

44 "Inequality, though great, was admittedly still more apparent than real, for the noble was affected by the tax on his farmer from which he was himself exempt. In this realm, however, the inequality that one can see causes more pain than the inequality that one feels" (*AR,* 131; *Œuvres,* P 3:126). Conversely, he agreed with Sieyès that abolition of the tithe would only benefit the lords: following the night of August 4, 1789, "Sieyès gave a speech in which I see nothing to criticize, in which he showed that abolishing the tithe instead of simply declaring it redeemable was quite clearly to make a gift to the great landowners" (*Œuvres,* P 3:596).

45 G. Shapiro and J. Markoff, *Revolutionary Demands* (Stanford: Stanford University Press, 1998), 284.

46 "I dare to affirm that on the day the nation, tired of the interminable disorders that had attended the captivity of King Jean and the dementia of Charles VI, allowed kings to levy a general tax without its consent, and when the nobility was cowardly enough to allow the Third Estate to be taxed provided that it remained exempt itself – on that day the seed was sown of practically all the vices and abuses that ravaged the Ancien Régime for the remainder of its existence" (*AR,* 147–148; *Œuvres,* P 3:136).

47 "These institutions [the venality of offices] were established precisely in opposition to them [the estates]. They were born of the desire not to convoke them and of the need to hide from the French a tax that one did not dare show them in its true guise" (*AR,* 157; *Œuvres,* P 3:142).

48 "This same desire to escape the tutelage of the estates led to the attribution to the parlements of most of their political prerogatives. This entangled the judicial power in government in a manner that was highly prejudicial to the orderly conduct of affairs. There was a need to appear to provide guarantees to replace those that had been eliminated, because the French, who put up rather patiently with absolute power as

long as it was not oppressive, never liked the sight of it, and it was always wise to raise some apparent barriers in front of it, barriers which, though they could never stop it, at least hid it a little" (ibid.).

49 J. Elster, *Explaining Technical Change* (Cambridge: Cambridge University Press, 1983), chap. 2.

50 "When the king undertook for the first time to levy taxes on his own authority, he understood that he would have to begin by choosing one that appeared not to fall directly on the nobles, because at the time they constituted a class that was a rival and danger to the monarchy and would never have tolerated an innovation so prejudicial to themselves. He therefore chose a tax from which they were exempt; he selected the taille" (*AR*, 149; *Œuvres*, P 3:137).

51 In his notes for the second volume, Tocqueville first quotes Turgot: "Under Charles VII one began to mount a permanent paid militia, and it was in this period that the taille was established on a permanent basis" and then adds that "since the purpose of the paid troops was to subdue the nobles or at least to circumvent them, it was quite natural that, in order to pave the way for the transition, they were not themselves asked to provide the money to be used against them" (*Œuvres*, P 3:413).

52 See the text cited in note 66.

53 In addition to the text quoted in note 46, one may cite the statement that "the original purpose of the taille was of course to enable the king to buy soldiers who would dispense nobles and their vassals of the need to perform military service" (*AR*, 189–190; *Œuvres*, P 3:160–161). From the account in G. Picot, *Histoire des États Généraux*. 5 vols. (New York: Burt Franklin, 1963 [1888]), 1:321–31, it seems that the point of Charles VII's ordinance of 1439 was not so much to exempt the nobles from military service as to prohibit them from raising private armies.

54 "The French nobility remained obstinately apart from the other classes. Noblemen ultimately allowed themselves to be exempted from most of the public duties they had once discharged. They imagined that they could maintain their grandeur without performing these duties, and at first this appeared to be the case. Soon, however, an invisible internal malady seemed to have attached itself to their status, which gradually diminished, though no one lifted a finger to make this happen. They grew poorer as their immunities increased" (*AR*, 199; *Œuvres*, P 3:166).

55 "What seems peculiar to France, moreover, is the fact that even as the noble order was thus losing its political powers, the nobleman individually acquired any number of privileges that he had never possessed and expanded privileges he already held. One might say that

the limbs gained at the expense of the body. The nobility enjoyed the right to command less and less, but nobles more and more claimed the exclusive prerogative of being the master's principal servants" (AR, 130; Œuvres, P 3:125–126).

56 "Why, then, did the same feudal dues inspire in the hearts of the French people a hatred so powerful that it outlived its object and thus seemed inextinguishable? The cause of this phenomenon was in part that the French peasant had become a landowner and in part that he had entirely escaped the government of his lord" (AR, 44; Œuvres, P 3:78); see also the text cited in note 11.

57 The distinction is clearly made by Droz, 1:85: "The onerous privileges of the leading orders rankled the Third Estate, but the sentiment it experienced was not so much hatred as envy."

58 He refers, for instance, to "the wealth of hatred and envy that accumulated" in the heart of the peasant (AR, 46; Œuvres, P 3:79) and to the "envious hatred" of the legislation of the old regime (Œuvres, P 3:392). See also the texts cited in note 15 and note 93.

59 J. Elster, Alchemies of the Mind (Cambridge: Cambridge University Press, 1999), chap. 3.

60 "Whatever he does, [the peasant] always finds these inconvenient neighbors in his way, spoiling his pleasure, impeding his work, eating his produce, and when he has done with them, others, dressed in black, appear to take from him the better part of his harvest" (AR, 46; Œuvres, P 3:79).

61 Concerning envy: "If one notes that the nobility, having lost its former political rights and having ceased, more than anywhere else in Europe, to administer and guide the population, nevertheless not only preserved but greatly increased its pecuniary immunities and the advantages enjoyed by its members individually [...], it will come as no surprise that its privileges seemed so inexplicable and hateful to the French, and that the sight of it so inflamed democratic envy in their hearts that it burns there still" (AR, 301; Œuvres, P 3:225). Concerning hatred: "Feudalism remained the greatest of all our civil institutions while ceasing to be a political institution. Thus diminished, it aroused far more hatred than ever" (ibid.).

62 "[T]he bourgeois could not in general purchase equestrian properties or obtain the highest posts in the civil service. Nor were they hoffähig, which is to say, they could not appear at court. [...] As in France, this inferiority was all the more hurtful because this class grew more enlightened and influential with each passing day. [...] Irritation with the privileges of the nobility, which would contribute so much to the

Revolution in our country, explains why the Revolution was initially received with approval in Germany" (AR, 339–340; Œuvres, P 3:249).

63   "[O]nce they ceased to wage war at their own expense, a tax [...] was levied on them [...] for the specific purpose of replacing military service" (Œuvres, P 3:322).

64   "Today, the privilege of the tax, which was based on the fact that only nobles were obliged to serve, is combined with the privilege the nobles enjoy of not serving if they so wish, for nobles and even their valets are not subject to the laws governing the militia. Thus grounds for relief from the charge no longer exist, though a surcharge would be justified" (ibid., 414).

65   "In the very parts of Germany where princes were most successful [...] in freeing themselves from noble oversight in general affairs of state, they allowed the nobles in large part to continue as administrators of the countryside" (AR, 41; Œuvres, P 3:76).

66   "In the eighteenth century in England, it was the poor man who enjoyed the tax privilege. In France, it was the rich man. There, the aristocracy took the heaviest public responsibilities on itself so that it would be allowed to govern; here, it retained the tax exemption to the end to console itself for having lost the government" (AR, 146–147; Œuvres, P 3:135).

67   "England was administered as well as governed by the principal landowners" (AR, 37; Œuvres, P 3:75–76).

68   Briefly and indirectly mentioned in AR, 149; Œuvres, P 3:137.

69   Even more indirectly mentioned in the text cited in note 51.

70   "The government, in its desire to turn everything into money, had first put most public offices up for sale and thus deprived itself of the faculty to grant and revoke them at will. One of its passions had thus greatly interfered with the success of the other: its greed had worked counter to its ambition. In order to act, it was therefore continually reduced to using instruments it had not fashioned itself and could not break. Hence it often saw its most absolute wishes enfeebled in execution. This bizarre and faulty constitution of public functions took the place of any kind of political guarantee against the omnipotence of the central government. It was a strange and ill-constructed sort of dike that divided the government's power and blunted its impact" (AR, 162; Œuvres, P 3:144).

71   "The irregular intervention of the courts in government, which often disrupted the proper administration of affairs, thus served at times to safeguard liberty: it was a great ill that limited a still greater one" (AR, 172; Œuvres, P 3:150).

72 R. G. Lipsey and K. Lancaster, "The General Theory of Second Best,"
    Review of Economic Studies 24, 11–12.

73 "It was this same need of money, coupled with the desire not to request
    it of the estates, that led to the inception of the venality of office, and
    little by little this turned into something so strange that nothing like it
    had ever been seen. Thanks to this institution, born of a certain
    conception of state finances, the vanity of the Third Estate was held
    spellbound for three centuries and directed solely to the acquisition of
    public offices" (*AR*, 155; *Œuvres*, P 3:140–141).

74 "When the parlements were destroyed in 1771, the same public that
    had so often been obliged to suffer from their prejudices was profoundly
    moved by the sight of their downfall. With them the last barrier still
    capable of containing royal arbitrariness seemed to have fallen" (*AR*,
    244; *Œuvres*, P 3:193).

75 See R. Boudon, "The Logic of Relative Frustration," in J. Elster, ed.,
    Rational Choice (Oxford: Blackwell, 1986).

76 "[T]he Revolution, the essential purpose of which was to abolish every
    last vestige of medieval institutions, did not break out in countries
    where, because those institutions were better preserved, their confining
    and rigorous nature was most manifest, but rather where it was least so;
    thus their yoke seemed most intolerable where in reality it was lightest"
    (*AR*, 33; *Œuvres*, P 3:71). The following paragraphs make it clear that he
    is comparing France and Germany.

77 "[T]he parts of France that were to become the principal center of that
    revolution were precisely those where progress was most evident" (*AR*,
    257; *Œuvres*, P 3:201).

78 "If one studies what remains of the archives of the former généralité of
    the Île-de-France, one can easily convince oneself that it was in the
    regions around Paris that the old regime reformed itself soonest and
    most profoundly. [...] Nowhere, by contrast, did the old regime
    maintain itself better than along the Loire, toward its mouth, in the
    marshes of Poitou and moors of Brittany. It was precisely there that civil
    war flared up and spread and that the most durable and violent resistance
    to the Revolution occurred" (*AR*, 257–258; *Œuvres*, P 3:201–202).

79 "[O]ne might say that the better the situation of the French became,
    the more unbearable they found it" (ibid.).

80 "[I]t is not always going from bad to worse that leads to revolution.
    What happens most often is that a people that puts up with the most
    oppressive laws without complaint, as if they did not feel them, rejects
    them violently when the pressure is alleviated. The regime that a
    revolution destroys is almost always better than the one that
    immediately preceded it, and experience teaches that the most

dangerous time for a bad government is usually when it begins to reform" (*AR*, 259; *Œuvres*, P 3:202).

81 See the text cited in note 7.

82 "Decree of January 21, 1776, concerning the destruction of rabbits. [...] The preamble and body of this edict came from Louis XVI himself, who showed it to M. Turgot with the comment, 'Do you suppose I do no work of my own?' Poor and excellent king, who, on the eve of so great a Revolution, approached reform by way of rabbits, precisely seventeen years to the day before mounting the scaffold" (*Œuvres*, P 3:407).

83 "[I]n this eighteenth-century monarchy, although the forms were terrifying, the penalty was almost always moderate. One preferred to frighten rather than harm, or, rather, one was arbitrary and violent out of habit and indifference and mild by temperament" (*AR*, 283; *Œuvres*, P 3:215). Although the comment refers to criminal justice, it also applies to the preference for moderate over severe repression.

84 "The king [...] recalled Parlement and rescinded the stamp law and the territorial tax. [...] If the king wished to remain the king of the old monarchy, this was precisely what he should not have done. From that moment on, all sorts of concessions were indispensable" (*Œuvres*, P 3:1141–1142).

85 "The evil that one endures patiently because it appears inevitable seems unbearable the moment its elimination becomes conceivable. Then, any abuse that is ended seems only to call attention to those that remain and to make their sting more painful: the ill has diminished, to be sure, but sensitivity to it has increased" (*AR*, 259; *Œuvres*, P 3:202).

86 "The people, never having imagined a social condition other than their own and never expecting to become the equals of their leaders [...] loved their superiors when they were clement and just and submitted to their rigors without hardship or ignominy as if bowing to inevitable woes imposed by the hand of God" [*DAI* (trans. Goldhammer), 8–9].

87 "The number of people who did business with [the government], who were interested in its loans, lived on its stipends, and speculated on its contracts, had prodigiously increased. Never had the fortunes of the state and private fortunes been so intertwined" (*AR*, 261–262; *Œuvres*, P 3:204).

88 "Thus in 1789 the state owed nearly 600 million to creditors, nearly all of whom were debtors themselves and who, as a financier said at the time, found in their grievances against the government partners in all whom the government's inexact methods associated with their plight. Note, moreover, that as the number of malcontents of this sort increased, their vexation grew" (ibid.).

89 "Men had developed to the point where they had a clearer sense of what they lacked and suffered more from it, even though the sum total of their suffering was much smaller than before. Their sensitivity had grown far faster than their relief. This was true of the want of liberty and equality as well as the want of money" (*Œuvres*, P 3:1073).

90 "When all conditions are unequal, no inequality is great enough to be offensive, whereas the slightest dissimilarity seems shocking in the midst of general uniformity. The more complete the uniformity, the more unbearable the sight of inequality" [*DAII* (trans. Goldhammer), 795].

91 "It is a commonplace to say that inequality of rights, while no greater as the Revolution approached, seemed more unbearable because the real equality of conditions was great. I add that inequality of rights was in certain respects much greater and of a far more shocking nature than at any previous time" (*Œuvres*, P 3:1110). The last remarks probably refer to the rigid rules for access to officer status introduced in 1781.

92 "One must recognize that in France the upper classes of society began to worry about the fate of the poor before the poor made themselves feared. [. ...] This became especially evident in the ten years prior to '89" (*AR*, 269–270; *Œuvres*, P 3:208).

93 "This was to inflame each and every individual by rehearsing his woes, identifying those responsible, revealing their small number in such a way as to embolden the victim, and piercing his heart to the quick to set it ablaze with greed, envy, and hatred" (*AR*, 273; *Œuvres*, P 3:210).

94 "What is most peculiar, moreover, is that to these striking assertions of interest in the people they added from time to time public expressions of contempt. [...] The provincial assembly of Haute Guyenne, in warmly pleading the cause of certain peasants, referred to them as ignorant and crude creatures, troublesome people, rough and untamed characters. Turgot, who did so much for the people, was scarcely different in his language" (*AR*, 271; *Œuvres*, P 3:209; see also *ibid.*, 377).

95 "All these measures were consistent with the spirit of the time. All were opposed or delayed by notables. Yet it was the government that was unpopular and the notables who had public opinion in their favor" (*Œuvres*, P 3:469).

96 "*Despite this huge concession, the king and ministers who made it were wildly unpopular, while the Parlement, which opposed it, enjoyed the fanatical support of the people.* No less noteworthy is the fact that the minister who made [...] this huge concession, which could not fail in short order to make the Third Estate the absolute master of affairs, was execrated by the people, while the Parlement,

which opposed enforcing a law that was so democratic for the time, received the people's fanatical ovation" (ibid., 507; italics in original). Droz had already made the same observation: "How did [parlement] win popularity through actions that harmed popular interests?" (Droz, 2:10).

97 "[I]n politics it is always wrong to judge the impression that a measure will produce by its intrinsic value, whether for good or for ill. Its influence depends primarily on the circumstances in which it is put forward and above all on the person with whom it originates. That is why politics cannot be a science or even an art. In politics, one finds no fixed rules, not even the rule that in order to please people, one must do what they consider useful. When circumstances conspire to make a government popular, one willingly suffers ill at its hands. When it is unpopular, even its good deeds are painful" (Œuvres, P 3:1136).

98 "The assembly of Vizille was in a sense a material and visible sign to all that this new union had taken place and showed what effects it might have. Thus an event that took place in a remote corner of a tiny province in the Alps proved decisive for all of France, and a minor incident suddenly became the main event. It brought to the attention of all what had been visible to only a few, showed everyone where power lay, and thus decided the victory in an instant" (ibid., 485). The last sentence, not in the Pléiade edition, is taken from AR, OC 2:2, 78.

99 "In Dauphiné, the taille was real and not personal. Hence nobles were not as much at war with the Third Estate over this issue as they were in many other places and did not have to concede equality on as many points." (This comment, not in the Pléiade edition, is taken from AR, OC 2:2, 74, note 1).

100 J. Elster, "Cross-voting," Journal of Political Philosophy (forthcoming).

101 "If the vote in common had to be adopted, it is unfortunate that what was done in Dauphiné was not done everywhere, because there the deputies of all three orders were chosen by all three orders, and this might have favored an accord" (Œuvres, P 3:531). See also the text on 497–498 cited in note 8. Elsewhere he notes that in Qu'est-ce que le tiers état? Sieyès "rejected the idea of having the orders elected by everyone. This idea, which was applied in the Dauphiné and which might be regarded as an acceptable bargain that would inevitably lead quickly to an amalgamation of the entire nation in one common mass, was deliberately rejected by Sieyès" (ibid., 541; italics in original).

102 After citing complaints by the clergy over the trespassing of the lords on the property of their tenants, Tocqueville adds that "several other cahiers [of the clergy were written] in the same spirit and with the same bitterness of peasants become curés. Later on we will see the

clergy come in for similarly strong abuse from the nobility. The two orders had yet to learn to make common cause" (ibid., 424).

103 "When I come to the era of class warfare, show clearly how dizzying the disintegration was. It was not just the bourgeoisie that made war on the nobility but the lesser nobility that attacked the greater, the lower clergy the higher [...] until the Revolution simplified the division and established harmony among the various occupants of the same social compartment" (ibid., 1147).

104 "Nothing serves more to [...] fuel despotism [than] the hatred [and] jealousy of the various classes. But with the proviso [that] this hatred and envy are nothing more than a bitter and tranquil emotion, just enough to prevent people from helping one another but not enough to spur them to fight. There is no government that will not collapse once violent clashes between the classes have begun" (ibid., 497).

105 "[T]his text also shows clearly that the electoral law promulgated in the wake of this report was deliberately designed to make curés the principal representatives of the clergy and to set off a disruptive internal battle between the bishops and their flock [sic]. This had no great consequences because the attacks on the clergy in general soon tightened this body's internal bonds" (ibid., 546).

106 "Arrival of three curés from Poitou seeking authentication of their credentials. Speaking for the group, one said, 'We come, preceded by the torch of reason and guided by love of the public good, to take our places alongside our fellow citizens.' (Obviously these curés were more of their age than of their church.) Greeted with applause. This was the stone falling from the vault above" (ibid., 567).

107 "Finally, *supreme* blunder, the question of voting by head, rightly identified as the principal issue, debated in a way favorable to the Third Estate and so as to arouse its hopes and passions and yet not decided, in other words, the worst of all imaginable ways of proceeding. If the king had clearly ruled out voting by head in advance, it would have been more difficult for the commons to demand it. If, in advance, the king had ordered voting by head, it would have been difficult for the privileged to hope that the torrent could be turned back. The Revolution would have been accomplished, but with a greater likelihood of a smooth transition and a tranquil spirit. But to raise hopes of voting by head and yet not authorize it was to spur the Third Estate to attack and allow the privileged to resist. In other words, it was suddenly to turn reform into violent revolution" (ibid., 546; italics in original).

108 "Same attitude of power mixed with incomplete violence and disdain" (ibid., 569).

109 "The assembly, irritated and aroused rather than demoralized by this mild pressure from the government, increasingly adopted the attitude of being in charge" (ibid., 570).

110 *The Tennis Court Oath in everyone's mind and anticipated six weeks before it took place.* As early as May 9, the deputies of Anjou informed their principals that for a few days they would use 'all means of conciliation capable of uniting the privileged orders with the Third, and after these means have been exhausted, we will constitute ourselves as a National Assembly.' Thus it was not the heat of battle that drove the representatives beyond the point they wished to go. They intended beforehand to reach that point, and everybody [sic] was aware of it" (ibid., 563); see also ibid., 481 (italics in original).

111 "We find Mounier devoting a chapter to combating the fears of those who believed that even with the doubling of the Third and voting by head, the nobility and clergy would still dominate the assembly. How can we be surprised that the nobles were wildly deluded as to their importance and strength, given that their adversaries also were?" (ibid., 550; my italics). This seems inconsistent, however, with the statement that in the debate on the proposal to convert the Estates-General into the National Assembly, "when some called for a vote, 60 or 80 opponents vehemently insisted that it be postponed for two days. During that session, the gallery was already inserting itself into the debate in a violent manner. Those who called for postponement were shouted down as traitors. [...] Thus, even within the isolated Third Estate, there was a minority, which though not very numerous was nevertheless quite determined, and this would have allowed the two orders, even with common voting, to hold the balance of power or at least slow the pace and cushion the consequences" (ibid., 567–568).

3 Tocqueville's New Political Science

"A new political science is needed for a world altogether new."

(*DAI* Intro., 7)[1]

Here is a striking statement, given a paragraph to itself, from the Introduction to Tocqueville's *Democracy in America*. Although it could hardly be more prominent, as an implied promise it is disappointing because Tocqueville never delivers the new political science. More cautiously, one could say that he never directly tells his readers what that political science is, what is wrong with the existing political science, and why political science is needed. Nonetheless, there is good reason to think that the new political science is in that book, and elsewhere in Tocqueville's writings, and that he left it implicit and scattered rather than explain it systematically, also for good reason.

To begin with the question why political science is needed, one might compare Tocqueville with two benchmarks, Aristotle and *The Federalist*.[2] Aristotle is pre-modern; *The Federalist* is modern and American. In all three, political science is needed not only to describe politics but also to have a good effect on it. Contrary to the value-free "empirical" political science of our time, the task of their political science is to bring reform in the act of describing. For Aristotle, political science is a practical science. Though the political scientist is an outside observer rather than a participant, by virtue of his knowledge he comes to be a participant, but a better one on a higher level than ordinary practitioners. Aristotle presents the political scientist (or philosopher) as the judge of claims of justice made by the ordinary practitioners who assert against other claims that their party alone espouses justice (1282b14–1283a42).[3] He also presents the political scientist with less elevation above politics, as a kind of gymnastic trainer who improves the fitness of ordinary people as well as the best athletes (1288b10–20). In the first treatise written on politics, Aristotle was seeking to establish the right of the political scientist to intervene with helpful advice.

The Federalist, however, takes this right for granted. In recommending the new republican constitution for America, it rests its principal argument on the difference between ancient and modern republics that has been established by modern political science. Against the traditional authority originating in Aristotle (and repeated in Montesquieu) that republics must be small, the American constitution sets up a large republic with new institutions designed by political science to keep the people from forming or operating the "majority factions" that throughout history had so bedeviled small republics. To make the experiment, The Federalist puts full faith in the discoveries of "modern" political science as against the republican tradition (9, 40–41).[4] Although political science will not automatically produce success, and so statesmanship is needed too, the role of political science is positive and decisive. Without political science, republicanism would fail in America as it had elsewhere.

Tocqueville takes neither of these views entire but mixes them. Like The Federalist (1, 1), he regards America as the most modern regime, the arena in which the happiness and liberty of mankind are at stake in a new experiment. Yet, while he praises the making of the American Constitution, he does not share the wholehearted enthusiasm of its makers. In effect he abandons the distinction in Federalist 10 between democracy (exemplified by ancient republics) and republic (with modern safeguards) to say that in America, the power of the people overcomes the republican restraints of representative government owed to modern political science (DAI 2.1, 165). He regards the ancient republics, based on slavery, as a kind of aristocracy – and thus irrelevant to democracy, which is modern (DAII 1.15, 450–51). This conclusion was very different from Aristotle's, but it did not prevent Tocqueville from adopting the dual role of judge and trainer – now as two ways of instructing democracy – that Aristotle assigns to the political scientist.[5] Near the end of the Introduction to *Democracy in America* (11–12), he describes six parties and judges them all to be wrong, not so much in deed as in thought; they exhibit "intellectual miseries." The six boil down to two – the party of religion and that of freedom – and Tocqueville's political science will undertake to reconcile them.[6]

Tocqueville the trainer recognizes certain good effects of modern political science, and the other three occasions in the *Democracy* when he speaks of "political science" refer to its daily role in the practical thinking of Americans. Americans down "to the last ranks of society" (*DAI* 1.8, 156) readily understand the difficulties of living under so artificial a system as federalism ("a great discovery in the political science of our day" (*DAI* 1.8, 147), and they also appreciate "an axiom of political science" (*DAI* 2.3, 176) that a free press will regulate itself if the number of newspapers is multiplied rather than reduced. In general, however, Tocqueville takes note of the beneficial practices of Americans as they govern themselves, praises and encourages them, and makes suggestions for improvement. While judging from a distance, seeing "not differently, but further than the parties" (*DAI* Intro., 15), he does not content himself with remote observations, however impressive, but also notices activities close to him and offers recommendations.

Like Aristotle, Tocqueville considers that the political scientist must be occupied with the character of human souls, and yet he values souls as a liberal would, in contrast to Aristotle. Just after announcing the need for a new political science, he remarks that souls in his time are "degraded" (*DAI* Intro., 8). Aristocracy, he says, was based on the mutual illusions of nobles and serfs, but these illusions were held to be legitimate. In modern democracy, however, the use of power and obedience to it are held to be illegitimate, and it is illegitimate power that degrades souls. Yet legitimacy, not a concern for Aristotle, had been the central self-assumed task of modern political science since Hobbes prior to Tocqueville. It seems that the "new political science" before Tocqueville's has failed in its main object. It has produced not consensus but "intellectual miseries," issuing in the confusion of parties that he laments. It had had little to say about souls, for it assumed that any provision in politics for the improvement of souls gave an opportunity to priests, who wanted in diverse ways to intervene in politics to save souls. Modern political science had attempted to bypass the state of souls in order to starve societies roiling in religious dispute of material for conflict; it would look for "legitimacy" rather than any sort of political health that included the health of souls. Tocqueville does not say that the object of democratic politics can be the health or perfection of soul.[7] He is a liberal willing to accept the justice of democracy rather than counsel perfection. But he also denies that modern theories can attain legitimacy. A new political science is needed because the modern political science preceding Tocqueville's did not succeed in its principal aim of resolving conflict by means of legitimacy without degrading souls. The modern theorists believed they could have legitimacy without concern for souls; Tocqueville disagrees.

LIBERALISM IN PRACTICE

Why is it necessary for a new political science to be concerned with the soul, like the old political science of Aristotle and unlike the existing political science that had once also claimed to be new? Tocqueville does not discuss the existing, modern political science that circumvents the soul. Notably, he does not discuss the political theory of Hobbes, Locke, and Rousseau that is characterized by formal principles such as the state of nature, the social contract, the sovereign, and the right of consent. Although he dwells on the American Constitution in *Democracy in America*, he does not even mention the Declaration of Independence on whose Lockean principles the Constitution is based. Instead of devoting himself to the formulation and derivation of principles, he immerses himself in the practice of liberty by Americans, praising, criticizing, but above all describing with marvelous verve and insight so that his book is equally concerned with democracy and America. He prefers liberalism in practice to liberalism in theory because liberalism in practice is liberalism with soul.

The degree of soul necessary to liberalism, according to Tocqueville, is not perfection but pride.[8] A free individual must have the pride to think himself capable and worthy of governing himself; he must have at least a modicum of ambition. Pride is the spur to action required for the practice of liberty, and it works through ambition, petty and grand. Pride may be held a vice, but Tocqueville says "I would willingly trade several of our small virtues for this vice" (*DAII* 3.19, 604). The trouble with liberal theory is that it is too hostile to pride. It posits self-preservation as the strongest human desire, while occasionally calling for a proud defense of liberty (as with Locke) or advising surrender of liberty for the sake of security (as with Hobbes). The penchant for security is all too consistent with democracy because democracies tend to judge things by the standard of the common needs of humanity rather than the particular goals that arouse individual pride (*DAII* 3.18, 589–90, 598–99).

In *Democracy in America*, Tocqueville describes two harmful kinds of democratic theorists who disregard human pride – the pantheists and the democratic historians.[9] The pantheists show the universe to be a unity that dissolves individual differences, and the democratic historians understand history to be determined by general causes rather than particular individuals (*DAII* 1.7; *DAII* 1.20). In the practice of democracy, however, democratic citizens show their pride. Tocqueville remarks in the chapter on parliamentary eloquence following the one on democratic historians (*DAII* 1.21) that a democratic representative, as opposed to an aristocratic one, feels the need in his bombastic rhetoric to show how important he and his constituents are. Thus the spirit of the democratic representative contradicts the insignificance attributed to individuals by the democratic historian (from which, of course, the historian exempts himself). The democratic representative believes that he is important, hence that humanity is important. Tocqueville does not start from a theory about human nature but draws, or allows readers to draw, the theoretical implication from the practice described. This is the method of his new political science.

To see how Tocqueville theorizes by implication from practice, let us look at what he says about religion, self-interest, rights, and mores. In his account of religion as practiced in America, he implies a due degree of reliance on pride, neither too much nor too little; from American devotion to self-interest, a self that is more soul than material enjoyment; from the exercise of rights in America, the necessity of forms in democracy; from American mores, the inadequacy of liberal theories of sovereignty that give primacy to law over custom. In America, Tocqueville says he sought "an image of democracy itself." (*DAI* Intro., 13) The image is there to be seen, but in his political science it is embedded in fact rather than abstracted in a theory. Democracy for him is *in* America, and America is not merely an example of democracy outside his political science. The "intellectual miseries" Tocqueville saw in Europe are not to be disputed in dialogue as bad arguments but rather to be refuted with his description and analysis of democratic politics in America.

PRIDE AND MODERATION IN RELIGION

Religion in Tocqueville's presentation is mainly about the immortality of the soul and secondarily about God's providence. It is not about knowledge of God except as it follows from the nature of the human soul.[10] To explain the immortality of the soul, Tocqueville begins from his observation of Americans, and notes that, contrary to the expectation of eighteenth-century philosophers and to the opinion of Europeans influenced by them, Americans, as they advance in freedom and enlightenment, continue in their zeal for religion. He finds the reason for this in the complete separation of church and state by which clergy are excluded from politics. By staying out of politics, the clergy stay above partisan hatreds and religion actually increases its influence on society – and therefore on politics (*DAI* 2.9, 282–83).

What is the soul's immortality? Tocqueville says: "Alone among all the beings, man shows a natural disgust for existence and an immense desire to exist: he scorns life and fears nothingness" (*DAI* 2.9, 283–84). But this is pride. In fact, it resembles what Plato calls *thumos*, the willingness to risk one's life in order to protect it, the combination of self-disgust and self-elevation.[11] Tocqueville endorses the pride of religion because it stands in the way of the impious maxim that "everything is permitted in the interest of society" (*DAI* 2.9, 280). To have this effect, religion must distinguish humans from the rest of nature and God from His Creation; we must reject the pantheism, so powerful an idea in democratic ages, that confuses these necessary distinctions and subjects every notable thing, especially the human individual, to nature and thereby to society (*DAII* 2.7). Pantheism is the postulate arising from the modern idea of rational control, associated with democracy, of controlling human aberrations, great and small, "in the interest of society." The idea of subjecting prideful human individuals to a new, rational society intoxicates men (and especially theorists), whereas religion makes them moderate. "Religion prevents them from conceiving everything and forbids them to dare everything" (*DAI* 2.9, 280).

Moderation does not arise from every religion, but it might be taught even by a false religion as long as it does not attempt "to stop the free ascent of the human mind" (*DAII* 1.5, 418). In a striking passage, Tocqueville indicates that religion is on the one hand an authority and on the other a science. Men have need of authoritative ideas about God, the soul, and their duties because doubt on these fundamentals would deliver them to chance, and thus to disorder and impotence. Philosophers may study these things – Tocqueville does not mention theologians – but the best they can discover is "a few contradictory notions" that are much above the average capacity of men, who in any case have no leisure for such study. He suggests that philosophers would consent to the formulation, but not the imposition, of religion that would provide secure answers "intelligible to the crowd" and serve as a "salutary yoke on the intellect" (*DAII* 1.5, 418). These unnamed philosophers of whom he approves – or should we say Tocqueville himself? – do not find dogmatic beliefs of the right kind to be incompatible with the free ascent of the mind. The right kind of religion is the Christianity of the Gospels, and the wrong kind is the religion of Mohammed. Mohammed's doctrine included political maxims, which involve the church with the state, and scientific theories that interfere with freedom of the mind. The Gospels do neither; they achieve a universality that is above politics and apart from science. But they can be understood as among the sciences, or part of political science, because their daily use in providing authority against doubt is indispensable – even though they must be shielded from "the habitual action of individual reason" (*DAII* 1.5, 418).

Tocqueville says that man can never have both political and religious independence: "[I]f he has no faith, he must serve; and if he is free, he must believe" (*DAII* 1.5, 418–19). What is so bad about doubt? Doubt in the realm of the intellect frightens men with uncertainty as to fundamental questions they cannot suppress about their place in the universe and how they should live. Instead of being braced by the challenge of meaningless flux, they seek a way out in self-concern (or what Tocqueville called individual-ism)[12] and in love of material enjoyments (*DAII* 1.5, 419).[13] In their weakness, "they give themselves a master" and lose their freedom (*DAII* 1.5, 418).

As Tocqueville praises Socrates for his spiritualism, shown especially in his arguments for the immortality of the soul, so he denounces the modern materialist philosophers who encourage the "very dangerous instincts" that can come with the great goods of equality (*DAII* 1.5, 419; *DAII* 2.15, 519–20).[14] Excessive love of material enjoyments is a vice endemic in democracy on its own, and it needs to be counteracted, not promoted. But why should materialism in philosophy promote materialism in a democratic way of life? Rightly understood, Tocqueville remarks, materialism should make men modest about themselves as capable of nothing high or grand, but he finds modern materialists particularly offen-sive for the manner in which they flaunt their dispiriting conclu-sions. Having established that men are only brutes, "they show themselves as proud as if they had demonstrated men were gods" (*DAII* 2.15, 519). Their pride (which goes against their philosophy) is explained by the fact that they do not really mean to sow doubt either in their readers or in society at large. Descartes, the leading example, doubted everything in order to overthrow traditional authority and to replace it with a rational method that resisted doubt. But Tocqueville does not argue with him or with other philosophers better known for espousing materialism. He attacks the idea of rational control over society by which modern materi-alists carry their doctrines into practice, transforming doubt into dogma and liberty of the individual into tyranny by society.

Rational control is best explained in Tocqueville's later work, *The Old Regime*, but his hostility to it underlies the whole of *Democracy in America*.[15] We believe it is the alternative to the new political science that he proposes, the enemy he has in view.[16] He terms it "democratic despotism" (as well as "administrative" or "mild despotism") even though it originates long before in the faint beginnings of democracy that he discerns in the eleventh century. Democratic despotism is mild because in opposing traditional ways, it appears rational and well-intended. To be rational, it concentrates all intelligence and power in one central sovereign power so as to issue uniform, yet detailed rules that apply to all equally. These benevolent rules are intended to improve the people, not exploit them. As the people are made more healthy and secure, they are taught how to live more rationally.

But popular enlightenment comes at the cost of freedom. Democracy does not require a democratic form of government, or self-government; as happened in France, a democratic social state can thrive under a monarch who adopts the policy of allying with the people against the nobles and replaces feudal authorities with a simpler, more uniform order based on "equality of conditions."[17] This result was so far from happenstance, however, that it reveals the dangerous instinct of democracy to destroy self-government. When all are similar or equal, no one stands above the crowd as an authority and a guide. Looking around, all citizens find no other guide than themselves, than public opinion. Being subjected to public opinion, citizens are, so to speak, under their equals, thus led without any sense of being commanded. But public opinion, like the vast impersonal forces portrayed by the democratic historians, seems too big for one citizen to control, and it is easy and seems reasonable to hand over the governing of society to one centralized, enlightened state. An "immense tutelary power" over democratic citizens, Tocqueville says sarcastically, takes away "the trouble of thinking and the pain of living" (DAII 4.6, 663).

In practice, the political science of rational control does not work. Tocqueville shows that the French monarchy tried to bring rational progress to the people in all things – for example, by teaching farmers how to farm better. In doing so, it raised higher expectations than it could meet. It made the people impatient with detailed regulation and contemptuous of lax enforcement. While the monarchy eliminated all intermediary institutions and habituated the people to depend on nothing but itself, it won no gratitude and little support. The only enthusiasm to be found for rational progress was in the French literary intellectuals who were determined to eliminate risk and rationalize life. Consumed with ambition themselves, they failed to recognize or prize it in others. Their rationalism had no room for irrational pride in free self-government. Rather like social scientists today, they focused on security rather than action, preferred centralization to local initiative, and simplified problems as well as solutions.

In Tocqueville's view, religion in democracy is "the most precious inheritance from aristocratic centuries" and must be treasured (DAII 2.15, 519). Its central dogma, the immortality of the soul, is necessary to the greatness of man, and politicians "should act every day as if they themselves believed it" (DAII 2.15, 521). Tocqueville almost says that not humility but pride is the practical essence of Christianity, at least in America. Religion in America is superior to materialism, its great modern rival, above all in its treatment of pride. The materialist theorists have their own pride, but it stands in blatant contradiction with their opinion that man is no more than matter, and materialist theory keeps democratic citizens from displaying their pride by teaching them that they must submit to the impersonal forces that have replaced God in materialist theory.

Religion both elevates humans through the immortality of their souls and restrains them, because of that immortality, from "limitless independence" (DAII 1.5, 418). Limitless independence places all its hopes in the state. This perversion of freedom regards nothing as sacred, pretends it can play God, fails to deliver, earns ridicule and contempt, enervates those it claims to benefit, and smothers real freedom in its suffocating embrace. Religion holds man subject to God so that man cannot claim to know or do everything and thus would not attempt the project of rational control. Yet religion also engages human pride in the very task of providing its own moderation. Although man cannot be God, he can be immortal, and for this he needs and deserves to be proud enough to be free.

Religion is the first premise of Tocqueville's new political science, but in a way peculiar to him.[18] Rather than supporting monarchy or any other non-democratic authority (to say nothing of calling for a theocracy), Tocqueville's religion endorses the separation of church and state; and more, it grounds the proud freedom that makes self-government possible. It opposes the rationalist, materialist political science of the modern state that attempted to replace religion; it is an anti-materialist religion, an anti-anti religion. The religion Tocqueville mentions is in the Christian Gospels, for that is what he saw at work in godly Americans. But it does not seem that his religion, or the religion of his political science, has to be Christian.[19] Its function, which is not quite the

Gospel message, is to protect freedom by allowing the right amount of pride.

While religion protects pride, it supports politics even more. If religion is his first premise, the activity it grounds is politics. In times of faith, Tocqueville says, religion permits its devotees to acquire a "taste for the future" (DAII 2.17, 524) and to develop long-term undertakings worthy of human pride. In times of doubt, people lose confidence in the future and scramble for quick satisfactions in the present – a condition made worse in the "tumult of democracy" (DAII 2.17, 523). To recover the future, moralists and politicians "must strive above all to banish chance ...from the political world" (DAII 2.17, 524). They can do this if they prevent "the sudden and unmerited elevation" of persons who have gained popular favor without the effort of advancing science or rendering a service (DAII 2.17, 524). The American dream (as we think it today) of work rewarded with success must not be confounded by examples of unmerited luck. Tocqueville advocates the re-creation of religion where its influence has disappeared, but in the spirit of American enterprise rather than that of patience and piety. The notion of the immortal soul lengthens the reach of the mortal soul, enabling it to resist temporary desires and to accomplish long-term projects. By this means, the providence of God is redirected in American mores from the prodigal son of the Bible to the dutiful, deserving son of the American dream.

For Tocqueville, it is not as if religion were the expression of an anxious human desire to know what will happen, what one's fortune will be – as was said by some modern philosophers. The latter were then able to equate religion with the desire of science to extend human power, only misapplied by the vulgar to God. But Tocqueville wants religion to extend human power much more in politics than in science, and to do it through human pride and not for the sake of self-preservation. Thus we turn now from religion in Tocqueville to the politics that his notion of religion endorses.

The self-preservation that is the basis of liberal political science in John Locke is hardly found in Tocqueville. Instead, we find self-interest, which might be termed self-preservation in social practice, for gain rather than survival, as opposed to the theoretical state of nature. But Tocqueville does not conceive self-interest in the fashion of Adam Smith as calculation merely for one's individual advantage. Self-interest for him comes in his famous formulation, "self-interest well understood," and is, like religion, an American practice from which he draws principles of political science. What must be *well understood* about self-interest? Like religion again, self-interest comes in a doctrine "preached in America"; it is not spontaneous or unconsidered (*DAII* 2.8, 503). Natural self-love is enhanced by the notion that one ought to care only about oneself, and it is supported by the notion that everyone has equal reason to do this. The result is a strong tendency toward material well-being, a goal that is both individual and within reach of all. But this "honest materialism" (*DAII* 2.11, 509), promising an easy and comfortable, if mediocre, way of life, produces citizens who are subject to restive discontent. Their material well-being has to confront the fact of their mortality, and they see that in limited time they cannot enjoy everything, but do not know what to choose and thus enjoy nothing. Moreover, the getting of wealth may lead to the creation of an industrial aristocracy and thus prove incompatible with democratic equality.

SELF-INTEREST AND ASSOCIATION

The doctrine of self-interest well understood combats the individualism that harms democracy, says Tocqueville, but he indicates that it may also aggravate individualism. It brings individuals to cooperate with one another rather than to take advantage of others, but in addressing their needs and accommodating their weaknesses, it confirms their love of material well-being (*DAII* 2.8, 502). It teaches them to make small sacrifices of their interest to secure greater gains, and hence to be satisfied with mediocrity. Democrats are also genuinely compassionate, but that feeling is easy for them because their dogmatic belief in equality prompts them to see others as similar to themselves. Their compassion is a tacit bargain that the support they give now will be available to them later if needed (*DAII* 3.4, 545). Justice too is in the "well understood" supplement to self-interest, and is also based on a facile equality (*DAII* 3.18, 589–90).[20] Neither compassion nor justice has much strength except when united with self-interest. Democracy presupposes strong individuals who take pride in running their own lives, but democratic life tends to produce weak, soft, timid individuals who cannot see how they can manage, and are strongly tempted to give up their pride and have recourse to the "immense being" of tutelary government to run their lives for them (*DAII* 4.3, 644).

Yet Tocqueville nourishes hope in what he calls the "art" or the "science" of association, as practiced in America, that democracy need not wither because of the weakness of democratic individuals. His political science is designed to avoid despair as much as false confidence, for these evils are allied when the despair of individual weakness breeds false confidence in centralized government. The art of association is part of self-interest well understood, and so is not hostile to the calculation of interest. It is not based on compassion, piety, or generosity. But it is hostile to the kind of calculation that accepts the viewpoint of the isolated individual as natural, as if each of us were entitled to return in our minds to the state of nature while calculating. For Tocqueville, the desire to associate is not a mere consequence of one's interest but also a part of one's nature, though in one's nature it comes second to one's interest. Hence one calculates as a member of a community, not as an alien might. "In the United States...the inhabitant applies himself to each of the interests of his country as to his very own" (*DAI* 1.5, 90). He feels himself glorified in his country's glory; his interest is not cold and indifferent but rises to patriotic passion.

Tocqueville does not begin from an abstract theory of associations but analyzes the associations in which America excels. In those associations he sees a shared idea or sentiment in the members that they want to impart to the community, to publicize. America being a democracy, its associations are voluntary rather than inherited; that is why America needs an art or science to guide the use of associations. Though the members have an interest in furthering the goal of the association, they also take pride in it and satisfy their ambition by serving it. As members, they subordinate but do not surrender their wills to its ends and to its officers; they achieve strength and independence together in association (as "team players"), not separately. This the members do out of habit rather than expedient calculation, and they are sustained by a general, favorable opinion and successful practice of association among their fellow-citizens.

Besides these shared characteristics, associations are divided into civil and political by Tocqueville, but not in such a way as to make "civil society" altogether distinct from politics.[21] For example, a civil association like the temperance movement can have a political goal as well as a moral or civil one. Tocqueville even cites the creation of temperance societies as examples both of *civil* associations (*DAII* 2.5, 489, 492) and of the prodigious *political* activity of Americans (*DAI* 2.6, 232). Civil associations, he says, get people into the habit of associating, but political ones show them why they associate (*DAII* 2.7, 496–97). These are hardly distinct qualities, for civil associations, one might say, become more political as they reflect more on the implications of their goals. The political character of all associations can be seen in Tocqueville's recommendation of democratic partisanship and in his urgent insistence on the need for maintaining forms and formalities in a democracy.

Associations formed to promote a sentiment or an opinion often find themselves in opposition to existing habits and beliefs and are thus compelled to become partisan, or they may simply begin with partisan passion. Associations in this way temper the tyranny of the majority because they expose the majority as merely temporary and as open to persuasion or revision. In any case, to act freely is rarely a non-partisan experience. Theories of self-interest by individual calculation aim to reduce partisanship by showing that anyone would act in predictable fashion when following his self-interest. One should not get angry with someone who is merely doing what you would do in his situation. But the idea of self-interest well understood has room for voluntary choice, therefore for pride in a good choice, and therefore for partisanship on behalf of that choice. Partisan feeling is neither individual interest nor an altruistic sacrifice of individual interest but in between the realism of the former and the idealism of the latter. To exercise your freedom you have to become exercised, and that will almost always make you a partisan. Partisanship needs to be schooled, however, and political associations such as parties are "great schools, free of charge, where all citizens come to learn the general theory of associations" (*DAII* 2.7, 497).

According to Tocqueville, self-interest ill understood is always open to renegotiation and permits only temporary coalitions, but self-interest well understood lasts longer; the coalitions are formal institutions. Every association has a formal structure with officers and rules enabling it to last over time, as Americans know from experience.[22] But the most formal institutions are those of government, and government is among the democratic associations of America. Tocqueville is against big government, but he is not against all government. He believes not in the maximum of freedom from interference or restraint but in freedom that sustains pride and dignity through opportunity for satisfied ambition. He prizes forms and formalities in the first instance for being barriers to the shifting caprices of popular will – for example, the long terms in the American constitution for the President, Senate, and Supreme Court. But he prizes them even more for keeping citizens active and satisfying their desire not merely for participation in our sense of self-expression but for actual accomplishments.

The formal structure of American government is particularly friendly to political association. Its federal character combines a highly artful central government (a "work of art" [*DAI* 1.8, 157]) with natural and spontaneous local government (*DAI* 1.5, 57). What Tocqueville calls "governmental centralization" permits the political direction of common interests and rewards the ambition of the most outstanding citizens (if elected!), but "administrative decentralization" permits initiative or at least freedom of action by local and state governments while opening many offices to ordinary citizens. In America, a plethora of elections keeps citizens active and prevents the rule of a centralized bureaucracy. It is true that many office-holders are mediocre and vulgar, but Tocqueville is willing to suffer their inefficiency for the sake of their activity. America prospers, he says, not because the elected magistrate makes it prosper, but "because the magistrate is elective" (*DAII* 2.4, 488). At the end of *Democracy in America*, Tocqueville reiterates "the utility of forms" in democracy for countering its naturally impulsive temperament and bringing order and patience to its actions (*DAII* 4.7, 669). A respect for forms prevents, or inhibits, immediate pleasure or the satisfaction of desire. In Europe, freedom and order are understood to be in conflict; in America, they are together.

Tocqueville's famous discussion of the New England township is a prominent feature of his political science of associations. The township is so much by nature that it seems to "form by itself." Yet a free township is a "rare and fragile thing" that grows slowly once the laws permit it to exist. A government would not have the "spirit of freedom" without a free township (*DAI* 1.5, 57–58). Tocqueville uses the township, again by contrast with the state of nature of theoretical liberalism, to explain how authority in a democracy becomes legitimate. In a democracy, each individual is supposed to be as enlightened, as virtuous, and as strong as any other, so why should he obey society? He obeys society not because he is inferior to anyone but because he knows that society is useful to him, and that obedience is necessary to society. The reasoning resembles that of Thomas Hobbes, but it is drawn from social experience rather than individual imagination, mixes rights and duties rather than distinguishing them, establishes the authority of "selectmen" rather than a sovereign representative, and results in patriotic strength and independence among the citizens rather than fear and subjection. Here is freedom from the ground up, making weak individuals strong by advancing beyond individual interest to the exercise of pride and ambition when put to work among one's neighbors.

The critical discussion of associations in *Democracy in America* occurs in the section devoted to democratic sentiments (*DAII* 2). There Tocqueville develops the American practice of association into an art, even a science or "general theory" (*DAII* 2.7, 497). The science presupposes the art (rather than the reverse), and the art is discovered in practice.[23] The art, one may suggest, has to do with the use of forms so as to reconcile the equality of conditions in democracy with the inequalities necessary to common action and to transform weak individuals in a mass and confronted by vast forces into strong and capable citizens. The science, if we may speculate, might be a picture of God and nature that satisfies "the true friends of freedom and human greatness," like Tocqueville (*DAII* 4.7, 670). He has high praise for the American constitution, but he begins from the township. To be capable, free men require association, and to be great, they must govern themselves. Tocqueville can be said to have desired to restore politics, and therewith greatness, to the political science of liberalism.

RIGHTS AND MORES

Tocqueville's treatment of rights and mores reveal more of the soulfulness of his new political science. Like other liberals, he accepts the idea that rights are central to politics. Unlike other liberals, who mostly define rights as against virtue, he asserts that rights are intermingled with virtue. Rights are virtue introduced into politics, for it is by rights that men, especially in democracy, define what is license and tyranny. In a democracy with respect for rights, a citizen can obey without being submissive and command without being arrogant, and as a society practices such respect through time and troubles, it gradually learns "the art of being free" (*DAI* 2.6, 227–29). A people cannot be free simply by declaration of a theorist that "man is born free" but must develop its virtue by standing up for its rights. In discussing rights, Tocqueville does not mention theorists but instead says that in America the idea of individual rights was "taken from the English aristocracy" (*DAII* 4.4, 648). In democratic times, a people must constantly be on its guard to prevent the sacrifice of rights, even of the most obscure citizen, to the power of society (*DAII* 4.7, 670). At stake in the protection of rights is not so much the security as the greatness of a people. Tocqueville implies that human greatness is rooted in the importance of the individual, however obscure. Every individual has a soul that makes him an individual and in which he takes pride. Not every individual is great, of course, but human greatness begins from the individuality that appears in every individual. Insofar as democratic respect for the rights of all requires respect for individuality, it implies appreciation of greatness. Tocqueville's reasoning puts democracy in a position where, with equal rights, it could level its citizens and yet lift them.

Mores as well as rights are featured in Tocqueville's political science. As determined as he is to recommend the formality of rights, so he insists on the importance of mores, which show how rights are exercised. Mores or "habits of the heart" (informal) are contrasted with laws (formal), yet mores develop gradually out of laws so that they do not appear to be legislated.[24] Mores combine human legislation, which is by choice, with what is by nature and cannot be legislated – the law and the resistances to law (*DAI* 2.9, 274–75, 295–96). In American democracy, mores are both an informal expression of popular sovereignty and an informal check on it. Religion is one example of mores, as we have seen, and another is the place of women. Men and women seem to have been made unequal by nature; then how does American democracy come to terms with this awkward fact? In the part of *Democracy in America* devoted to mores, Tocqueville finds that American women freely choose to submit to the "bonds of matrimony" and stay in the home, where, with functions separate from those of men, they achieve a democratic equality (*DAII* 2.10, 566). It is not the only democratic equality, for, to Tocqueville's dismay, some in Europe try to make women not only equal but alike. Tocqueville recommends the American way, in which women "show themselves to be men in mind and heart" though not in station (*DAII* 3.12, 574). These prideful qualities of soul save women from inferiority and democracy from infidelity to itself.

TOCQUEVILLE'S INNOVATIONS

So far we have discussed elements of previous liberalism that Tocqueville adopted and made over: religious toleration, self-interest, rights, legal sovereignty. But there are also three substantial innovations in his political science that need mention – the social state, the notion of one's similars or those like oneself (*semblables*), and the use of predictions.

The social state (*état social*), a concept Tocqueville was the first to develop, is said to be both product and cause.[25] It is a product of both fact and laws that then becomes the "first cause" of most of the laws, customs, and ideas that regulate nations (*DAI* 1.3, 45). As such, it replaces, almost reverses, Aristotle's notion of the regime (*politeia*) that makes government the cause of society (*Pol.*, 1276a40–b12). It might be better to say that Tocqueville replaces Aristotle's view (which is not free of complication) with deliberate confusion, for he speaks of democratic and aristocratic social states, naming them by their government as if they could not be social without one. In any case, for him America has a "point of departure" – the Puritans – rather than a deliberate founding. A founding is imposed, but a social state causes the society without ruling over it. That is why an aristocracy, which is the rule of a part imposing itself on the whole, is less of a social state than is a democracy.

Because a democratic social state can sustain both liberty and tyranny, government is the crux, not merely a consequence. In the second volume of *Democracy in America*, Tocqueville came to see that a passive, mild despotism was the greatest danger in democracy, not an active majority tyranny, as he had said in the first volume, and mild despotism is more invited by the people than imposed on them. The social state wields its power through public opinion, through private opinion made public, a process in which the distinction between private and public is blurred and mere consensus among private individuals settles into the more confining influence of public opinion. The sovereignty of the people is exercised through public opinion, not by a definite sovereign, and that is because it comes out of the social state rather than a state of nature, whose function in previous liberal theory is to prepare the selection of an explicit, legally identifiable sovereign. Yet in Tocqueville's view, the democratic social state comes increasingly to resemble the state of nature;[26] it turns democratic citizens into private individuals by robbing them of their sense of being able to act effectively. His general theory of associations, designed to remedy this harmful individualism, appears then as a replacement for the liberal social contract that is meant to remove individuals from the state of nature. Associations, which make possible democratic liberty, already exist in the American version of the democratic social state, not mere potentialities of human nature.

Individuals in the democratic social state are those like oneself (*semblables*).[27] In that state, all regard themselves as equal; whether or not they are equal in fact, they see one another as equal. Human equality does not have to be proved, nor is it subject to disproof; it is practiced spontaneously and taken for granted in every encounter. There is no problem of the self encountering the other to whom it must become reconciled, as in Hegel's theory, since no one is considered truly different in the first place. There is no distinction between the few and the many as is characteristic of Aristotelian political science, in which the many constitute a multitude opposed to the few who claim to be better. While Aristotle thought that democracy represented the triumph of the many over the few, for Tocqueville the claim of the few is simply not made or heard. There is no mixed regime in America because there is no fundamental distinction between democracy and oligarchy that would be necessary to mix. Tocqueville declares that the mixed regime is a chimera (*DAI* 2.7, 240), and the moral force of the democratic majority is unopposed. Aristocracy and democracy are successive eras in history, not constant possibilities for human beings to choose between or to mix, as Aristotle argued.

The few, for Tocqueville, cannot speak in their own name to deny that the majority is like them. The few of greater intellect are the likely victims of majority tyranny, and he denounces the "moral empire" of the majority based on the false idea that "there is more enlightenment and wisdom in many men united than in one alone" (*DAI* 2.7, 236). On behalf of these few Tocqueville declares that "there is no freedom of mind in America," that in a democracy, tyranny "leaves the body and goes straight for the soul" (*DAI* 2.7, 245, 244). Freedom, for Tocqueville as we have seen, is in the realm of the soul, which is the realm of pride. Although one might think that the intellectual few desire understanding rather than satisfaction of pride, Tocqueville puts understanding and pride together. The danger to freedom of mind, he says, attacks "the pride of man in its last asylum" (*DAI* 2.7, 236). The few rich also have to defer to the majority especially if they wish to be elected to office, and they are subject to envy because they are regarded as similar and not naturally superior to the poor.

Underneath the insistently asserted similarity of democratic citizens in America are a number of features Tocqueville calls aristocratic in origin, though now democratized in appearance and function. His official theme that democracy and aristocracy are contraries rises to a climax at the end of *Democracy in America* when he declares that they are "as it were, two distinct humanities" (*DAII* 4.8, 675). Throughout, he makes excellent use of the contrast between them, from which we learn much more about democracy than from our democratic theory today, which knows no other regime. Although he denies the possibility of a mixed regime, a number of democratic mores and institutions are said to be aristocratic in one way or another: Christian religion, as we have seen, is an aristocratic inheritance; rights must be applied with a "political spirit that suggests to each citizen some of the interests that make nobles in aristocracies act" (*DAII* 3.26, 634); America's taste for local self-government, its jury system, its free press, its idea of individual rights are all said to have been brought from aristocratic

England (*DAII* 4.4, 646, 648); democratic associations are comparable to "aristocratic persons" (*DAII* 4.7, 667–8); lawyers constitute
an American aristocracy (*DAII* 2.8, 257); and the Constitution itself
was the work of the Federalists, a party inspired by "aristocratic
passions" (*DAI* 2.2, 170). Tocqueville does not add up these hidden
aristocratic elements in American democracy, perhaps because the
sum would seem considerable. He does say that in America, freedom is old, democracy comparatively new (*DAII* 4.4, 646). So much,
from this modern liberal, for the new freedom promised by modern
political science.

Tocqueville's political science, in its concern with facts, repeatedly makes predictions of trends and tendencies. It does not seek to
determine exactly what will happen in the fashion of some political
science today, but it does say what one can expect to happen, unless
someone intervenes or something interferes. His most famous
prediction occurs at the end of the first volume of *Democracy in
America*, when he says that America and Russia represent the
democratic future, freedom or servitude. Here the prediction is a
choice set for us by "a secret design of Providence" (*DAI* 2.10, 396).
Behind this choice is Tocqueville's overall prediction for the future,
the democratic revolution that produces an ever-increasing equality
of conditions. This he calls a "providential fact" (*DAI* Intro., 6).
What does he mean by providential fact?

We may begin with Tocqueville's use of "fact." Today, political
science speaks of fact (or data) but not of "nature," while in
Aristotle one finds nature but not fact. Tocqueville uses both
terms.[28] He does not trace aristocracy and democracy to different
aspects of human nature, each of which may in principle be chosen,
like Aristotle. Democracy is the fact that all must adjust to now,
and the task of political science is not to offer advice as to a choice
between regimes but rather to show how to choose democratic
liberty over democratic tyranny. The democracy common to these
choices is a social state, not a regime. Tocqueville agrees with
Aristotle that political science deals with choice, not merely with
fact, but he introduces fact to narrow the choice and to specify that
it be made with reference to fact.

The fact of democracy is both "generative," in generating other,
particular facts, and "providential." He does not explain "providential," but from his description in the Introduction to *Democracy*

in America of a long train of events, all going in the direction of democracy, we can infer what he means. A providential fact is a trend of contingencies too consistent not to have been planned, yet not within the planning capacity of human beings, not even a full generation of them. Such a fact would be in some sense sacred, not to be gainsaid, and irreversible. Clearly Tocqueville wanted the reactionaries of his day to consider democracy irreversible. But providence can also serve to restrain the radical liberalism of rational control that he opposed. Providence does not preside over a philosophy of history with rational stages that determine the course of events; there is something mysterious about it that prevents human beings from knowing how it operates even if they can sense its direction. Tocqueville says that God rules providence, but God's mind being unknown to us, we do not see all that God sees, which is human beings with all their similarities and differences (*DAII* 1.3, 411). We see human beings as alike, which is democracy, or as separate and distinct, which is aristocracy – each being a partial view. Tocqueville tries to do better; he enters into the "point of view of God" (*DAII* 4.8, 675) so as to see human beings in both aspects. But he does not know God's plan (*DAI* Intro., 12); though he speaks of providence, he does not claim to discern what must happen. His notion of providence preserves human choice, which means that it preserves politics.[29] The providential fact of democracy guides us by advising not to challenge democracy itself, but frees us to choose liberty over tyranny. If we knew too much, we would not be free; if we knew too little, we would not be able to choose. The providential fact leaves us between the extremes of determinism and arbitrariness (which amount to the same).

Tocqueville makes it clear that democracy needs religion as its instrument, but his political science goes further because it depends on religion. Political science today takes for granted the whole of nature when it claims to be universal; the political scientist can see everything he needs to see without being an American or a Christian. But for Tocqueville, the political scientist cannot be so readily impartial in this way. The object of political science is politics as divided into democracy and aristocracy, but this generality is wrapped in the particular fact that providence has made our age a democratic revolution. The politics we need to know is democratic, and to repeat, democracy is *in* America – so that the study of democracy is the study of American politics. And what is the "first cause" of America? Surely it is the American Revolution and the American Constitution, but these are enshrouded and enshrined in the point of departure, a particular beginning from the Puritans. And where does democracy come from? Tocqueville is not ashamed to say: "[I]t was necessary that Jesus Christ come to earth to make it understood that all members of the human species are naturally alike and equal" (*DAII* 1.3, 413). The upshot for political scientists is to pay attention to particular facts, not only to general truths, and this lesson is aristocratic in character rather than democratic. Impartiality for the political scientist has to be attained by both immersing oneself in our democratic age and also by rising above it. It cannot be assumed as a mere consequence of being a theorist, for democracy and theory are in close, illicit alliance.

NOTES

1   Page references to *Democracy in America* in the text are to *DA* (trans. Mansfield and Winthrop).
2   For the context of Tocqueville's political science, see Cheryl Welch, *De Tocqueville* (New York: Oxford University Press, 2001), esp. 13–42; Larry Siedentop, *Tocqueville* (Oxford: Oxford University Press, 1994), 20–40; Pierre Manent, *An Intellectual History of Liberalism*, trans. Rebecca Balinski (Princeton: Princeton University Press, 1994).
3   Aristotle, *The Politics*, trans. Carnes Lord (Chicago: University of Chicago Press, 1984).
4   Alexander Hamilton, James Madison, and John Jay, *The Federalist Papers* (New York: NAL Penguin, 1999).
5   Raymond Aron (*Main Currents in Sociological Thought* [New Brunswick, NJ: Transaction Publishers, 1998]) says that Tocqueville remains within the tradition of classical political philosophers "who would not have conceived of analyzing regimes without judging them at the same time," 261–62. Aron also considers Tocqueville's links to Montesquieu, connecting both in turn to Aristotle.
6   Among the parties, the only one about whom Tocqueville has nothing kind to say are those "who in the name of progress, [strive] to make man into matter." For Tocqueville's critique of materialist doctrines, see Ralph Hancock, "The Uses and Hazards of Christianity," in *Interpreting Tocqueville's Democracy in America*, ed. Ken Masugi (Savage, MD: Rowman and Littlefield, 1991) 355–61.

7 For Tocqueville in contrast to Aristotle, the end of politics appears to
   be "independence and dignity" (*DAII* 4.7, 666) or "freedom and human
   greatness" (*DAII* 4.7, 670), not the highest and most authoritative good
   (*Pol.*, 1252a1–6). For Tocqueville, the political association is distinguished from other associations by its greatness (*DAII* 2.7, 496–97), not
   by the comprehensiveness of its end (Aristotle, *Nicomachean Ethics*,
   trans., Martin Ostwald [Upper Saddle River, NJ: Prentice Hall, 1962] I
   1094a19–b11, 1097b22–28, 1098a8–18). Greatness, in Tocqueville's
   mind, is not simply identical with virtue. He remarked of Napoleon
   that he was "as great as a man could be without virtue" (Discours de
   M. de Tocqueville, prononcé dans la séance publique du 21 avril 1843,
   en venant prendre séance à la place de M. le Comte de Cessac, *OC*
   16:263). Hancock, in his analysis of *DAII* 2.15, says that Tocqueville
   wants to show the legislator how to encourage "the fullest activity of
   the best human faculties" ("The Uses and Hazards of Christianity,"
   355). This comes close to Aristotle's position (*NE* I 1098a15–18), but
   when a legislator in a democracy takes special care for man's "most
   sublime faculties," it is because democracy on its own tends toward
   materialism. The ruling principle will not be the perfection of the soul.
8 For an analysis of soul and pride in Tocqueville's political science, see
   Peter Augustine Lawler, *The Restless Mind: Alexis de Tocqueville on
   the Origin and Perpetuation of Human Liberty* (Lanham, MD:
   Rowman and Littlefield, 1993).
9 Tocqueville is also highly critical of the racialist theory of his friend
   Arthur Gobineau, which he declares to be "very probably wrong and very
   certainly pernicious." He understands it to be "a kind of fatalism" and "a
   cousin of pure materialism." Tocqueville to Gobineau, November 17,
   1853, *Selected Letters* (trans. Toupin and Boesche), 297–301.
10 The chief purpose and benefit of any religion is to furnish fixed, general
   ideas about "God and human nature" (*DAII* 1.5, 416–17). Of the nature
   of man and even of himself, a human being always has only partial
   knowledge (*DAII* 1.17, 462). God, in contrast, perceives at once each
   human being and the race as a whole (*DAII* 1.3, 411; 4.8, 674). While
   Tocqueville strives to accept God's presumed judgment that what
   matters most is the greatest well-being of all and thus that democracy's
   equality is just and therefore great, he never claims to have achieved
   God's knowledge (*DAII* 4.8, 674–75). As Sanford Kessler observes in
   *Tocqueville's Civil Religion: American Christianity and the Prospects
   for Freedom* (Albany: State University of New York, 1994), 44, in order
   to grasp Tocqueville's understanding of religion's political benefits, one
   does well to begin with his discussion of poetry and its root in man's
   partially obscured view of the soul.

11 Plato, *The Republic*, trans. Allan Bloom (New York: Basic Books, 1968), bks. 3–4, esp. 439a–41c.

12 The term "individualism," a new word when Tocqueville wrote, was not coined by him, but defined and developed by him. See James T. Schleifer, *The Making of Tocqueville's "Democracy in America"* (Chapel Hill: University of North Carolina Press, 1980), 251–59.

13 For an argument that Tocqueville points to the conclusion that mature democratic citizens must confront the challenge of meaningless flux, see Laura Janara, *Democracy Growing Up: Authority, Autonomy and Passion in Tocqueville's Democracy in America* (Albany: State University of New York Press, 2002), 70.

14 For Tocqueville's place in the philosophic tradition and his opposition to it, see Lawler, *The Restless Mind*.

15 James Ceaser argues that Tocqueville intended to oppose not just rationalism, but the traditionalism of the followers of Edmund Burke, who had too little regard for reason and science. James W. Caeser, *Liberal Democracy and Political Science* (Baltimore: Johns Hopkins University Press, 1990), ch. 7. His intention was to "rescue the original core of rationalism from its later distortions" (166).

16 For Tocqueville's critique of the earlier "political scientists," see *AR*, 2 (trans. Kahan), 2:1, 3:1.

17 Harvey C. Mansfield, Jr., and Delba Winthrop, *Liberalism and Big Government: Tocqueville's Analysis,* (London: Institute of United States Studies, University of London, 1999), 6.

18 Tocqueville refers to himself as "a man ... convinced that man's true grandeur lies only in the harmony of the liberal sentiment and religious sentiment, both working simultaneously to stimulate and to restrain souls, and ... one whose sole political passion for thirty years has been to bring this harmony about" (Tocqueville to Corcelle, September 17, 1853, *Selected Letters* (trans. Toupin and Boesche), 294–95.

19 In 1843, Tocqueville commissioned his protégé Gobineau to research the distinctiveness of modern morality, and this led to an extended correspondence (*OC* 9:45–69). Tocqueville proposed that the sharp break in morality occurred between the ancients and the Christians; modern morality had for the most part "only developed, extended the consequences of the morality of Christianity without changing its principles" (Tocqueville to Gobineau, September 5, 1843, *Selected Letters* (trans. Toupin and Boesche), 46). The new principles that Gobineau finds in modern morality Tocqueville either attributes to a weakening of religious faith (Tocqueville to Gobineau, October 2, 1843, 58) or understands to be "only new consequences that the state of our civilization, our political laws and our social state have us draw

from the old principles of Christianity" (Tocqueville to Gobineau, October 22, 1843, 68).

20 Tocqueville says that justice is one of two standards of moral evaluation. It arises from the "permanent and universal needs" of the human race (*DAII* 3.18, 589). An example of such a need or interest is that men not kill one another (590). The second standard, always peculiar to a people or a class, emerges from its special needs (589), helps sustain courage among those who fall under it (593), and thus enables the group to maintain its dominion. Relying on the first standard alone would be appropriate in a world in which humans no longer distinguished themselves from one another by "any characteristic feature" (599).

21 Tocqueville always uses the term "civil society" alongside "government" or "the political world," never suggesting that the one can subsist without the other. Indeed, he connects them: "[The] agitation, constantly reborn, that the government of democracy has introduced into the political world, passes afterwards into civil society" (*DAI* 2.6, 233). See also *DAII* 2.1, 479 and *DAII* 3.8, 562.

22 "From school onward," Tocqueville notes (*DAI* 2.4, 180).

23 In a speech delivered to an academy in 1852, Tocqueville distinguishes between the art of government and political science. He warns his fellow academicians that they are a "learned society and not a political body." They should be devoted to "pure theory and abstract science" as opposed to the political science of the French Revolution, which was made "precisely by the men of those times who never took the least part in public affairs." Political science should respect the art of government either by drawing rules from it, like Tocqueville himself, or by not laying down rules for it, like the literary theorists of the Revolution. See the "Discours prononcé à la séance publique annuelle de l'Académie des Sciences Morales et Politiques du 3 Avril 1852 par M. de Tocqueville, Président de l'Académie," *OC* 16:229–42.

24 "Thus as long as township freedom has not entered into mores, it is easy to destroy it, and it can enter into mores only after having subsisted for a long time in the laws" (*DAI* 1.5, 57).

25 The term *état social* had been used by others, most notably Guizot, whose lectures Tocqueville had attended and whose works he had read as a young man. As to the difference in their use of the term, see Manent, *An Intellectual History of Liberalism*, 103–04.

26 See Pierre Manent, *Tocqueville and the Nature of Democracy*, trans. John Waggoner (Lanham, MD: Rowman & Littlefield, 1996), 26–28.

27 *Semblable* is a "general notion" that is readily recognized only in democratic centuries. The term is italicized – rare for Tocqueville – as this point is made (*DAII, Œuvres*, P 2, 613).

28 Tocqueville uses the term "fact" eleven times in his thirteen-page introduction to *Democracy* alone; the term "nature," in the sense of a natural order, occurs twice there.

29 Hadari argues that Tocqueville's apparent lack of intellectual rigor was a price he willingly paid to preserve free will in the face of the deterministic causal explanations to which the social sciences tend. Saguiv A. Hadari, *Theory in Practice: Tocqueville's New Science of Politics* (Stanford, CA.: Stanford University Press, 1989), esp. 46–50. Sheldon Wolin in *Tocqueville Between Two Worlds* (Princeton: Princeton University Press, 2001), 184–86, has Tocqueville prophesizing a universal condition of revolutionary egalitarianism in order to invest a form of scientific determinism with moral authority while presenting his new political science as "an epical form of theoretical action that both submits to God's decrees and selectively combats some of them" by containing the providentially decreed democracy. See also Aron (*Main Currents*, 293), for the importance of unpredictability, hence action in Tocqueville's thought.

4   Tocqueville, Political Philosopher

Translated by Arthur Goldhammer

Since 2002, texts by Tocqueville have been included in the syllabus for the French *Agrégation de Philosophie*. What are we to think of this belated promotion of Tocqueville to the rank of philosopher? Did the sages who draft the syllabi give in to the winds of fashion? Or did their selection finally reveal the true nature of the "Norman aristocrat?" I shall try to answer this question.

I. A TOTALLY NEW WORLD

We see Alexis de Tocqueville first of all as a citizen, a politician, and statesman confronting a temporal discontinuity. The old order has been swept away; the new order is not firmly established. If instability and disorder are prevalent in institutions, it is because they already affect men's souls: "The laws of moral analogy have ... been abolished."[1] If one is to become capable of acting in and on the new society, one must first know it. But what does it mean "to know the new society?" A "new political science" of unparalleled prestige already existed, that of Montesquieu. Benjamin Constant held fast to Montesquieu's conclusion that the "modern difference" was the difference introduced by the development of commerce and the institution of regular political representation. In a style all his own, François Guizot ratified and extended the science of "representative government."

Tocqueville was more acutely aware than the two other great liberals that times had changed. The novelty of the new age was wider and deeper than imagined by those who contemplated the historical procession with satisfaction as it finally reached the stage of "commerce" and "concern for the public good" (*publicité*).

The conclusions of liberal political science and the techniques of liberal government (separation of powers, religious neutrality of the state, representation, freedom of commerce, and so on) were not equal to the novel difficulties and unprecedented problems that modern humanity faced for the first time. Something *totally* new had appeared: "A world that is totally new demands a new political science."[2]

These novel difficulties and unprecedented problems concerned not so much the government per se as the element in which the government operated, in which it was immersed – namely, the new society, the society that Tocqueville called *democratic*.

II. LIBERALISM AND SOCIOLOGY

Tocqueville was the last-born of the great French liberal political thinkers and commentators on public affairs of the early nineteenth century, two of whom I have just mentioned. Because he situates the most important and interesting aspect of the modern condition in "society," we must also locate his position in another, quite different series: the sociologists. This is what Raymond Aron did in his now-classic work, *Les étapes de la pensée sociologique*, in which he considers Tocqueville in relation to Auguste Comte, Karl Marx, and Max Weber.

Tocqueville thus belonged to at least two series or "traditions": on the one hand, the series of liberal statesmen and political commentators, and, on the other hand, the series of sociologists. This union of liberal politics and sociology in the person of Tocqueville – this "personal union" – is proof, or at any rate empirical evidence, that the two are not incompatible, in contrast to what one might infer from the overwhelming tendency of the sociological discipline itself, which is primarily concerned with revealing social "necessity." In any event, the two series inter-sected before Tocqueville in the work of Montesquieu and would intersect again after him in the work of Weber. Indeed, if sociology tends to create estrangement from liberalism, the liberal politician is a sociologist of necessity, since the fundamental liberal outlook or disposition is not to attempt to rule society arbitrarily in the name of some pre-existing idea of the True, the Good, or the Just but, on the contrary, to "let it be," to allow it to develop freely in keeping with its own interests, to respect its laws, and to take the fullest possible account of public opinion without seeking to force or manipulate it. Liberal politics tries to distinguish between state and society or even to separate the two rigorously: knowledge of society – hence sociology – is the condition as well as the consequence of liberal politics.

Nevertheless, despite the brilliance of the works of Montesquieu, Tocqueville, and Weber, the overwhelming tendency of sociology itself can fairly be called anti-liberal. The reason for this is not simply the epistemological requirement to identify causal "necessities." Or, rather, this epistemological reason derives from a deeper political one. In saying that it is right and good to "leave society free," to allow it to develop in its own way, the liberal political thinker grants "society" a value, an authority greater than that granted to free government itself. Society "is more" than the political body in which the free political choices made by citizens culminate. The sociologist systematizes and, if I may put it this way, "professionalizes" this judgment, which is incorporated into the structure of the liberal regime itself. In considering society in itself – that is, insofar as it is distinct from the political body – he naturally and necessarily sees it as the primary *cause* of the phenomena of contemporary life. He therefore tends to regard the political body as a "superstructure" without substance or meaning of its own, as an *effect* of the social cause, of the cause that is society. Enveloped in this way by social causes, political liberty loses much of its luster. That is why sociologists are often inclined to be contemptuous of liberalism. It will suffice to mention Comte and Marx. (I say that sociologists tend to be "contemptuous" of liberalism or of liberal institutions: they are not essentially or straightforwardly anti-liberal like the "reactionary" writers who sought to restore the superior legitimacy of political command. For both Marx and Comte, though in different ways, liberal institutions and procedures are in a sense mere transitory appearances, feeble and misleading effects of the social movement that will soon absorb them, whereupon society as newly defined will henceforth reign alone as causes and effects at last become adequate to one another.)

In short, liberal politics tends to imply a devaluation of the political, which sociology tends to extend and radicalize until liberal politics is destroyed.

III. A POLITICAL SOCIOLOGY

Sociologists who share a similar contempt for liberalism may hold very different ideas about society and what makes it run. For Marx, modern society is by definition *capitalist* society, based on private ownership of the means of production, whereas for Comte, it is *industrial* society, based on the application of science to the exploitation of nature. Both definitions emphasize economic, social, and intellectual factors, not political ones. Hence we can ask how Tocqueville proceeds, given that he has the rare though not unique distinction of being both a liberal in politics and a sociologist – a liberal sociologist.

Like his colleagues, Tocqueville posits society, or what he calls "the social state," as a cause. Society is the Cause. But how does he go about giving a more precise definition of modern society? He defines it as *democratic*. The originality of this definition is immediately apparent: the essential attribute of modern society belongs to the political order, or at any rate stems from the language of politics. Tocqueville is an unusual sociologist because in conceiving "democracy" as a "social state," he defines the social in political terms.

Tocqueville's terminology has puzzled some commentators on his work. Yet it is this distinctive, "non-rigorous" use of terminology that takes us to the heart of Tocqueville's thought. His sociology is incomparably "more political" than that of Marx or Comte: the political terms it contains retain a meaning, though not necessarily their usual meaning. Social causality does not encompass – or at any rate does not subsume – the political, as it does in Marx and Comte. For Tocqueville, in fact, the same social "base" – "democracy" – can correspond to two antithetical political regimes, one democratic in the ordinary sense of the word, the other "despotic," but involving a novel form of despotism. In any case, this well-known proposition confirms that the political plays a much larger role in Tocqueville's work than in that of most – and perhaps *all* – other sociologists. He is the most political sociologist. For further proof, consider the fact that when it comes to treating the ills of modern society, his primary recommendation is to employ political remedies rather than economic, social, scientific, or "cultural" ones – political remedies that constitute his political liberalism in the proper sense of the term.

IV. DEFINING EQUALITY OF CONDITIONS

What is the democratic "social state?" Answer: "equality of conditions." What is equality of conditions? At the very beginning of *Democracy in America*, Tocqueville calls equality of conditions a "fact" that has had a "prodigious influence" on the development of societies, and indeed he designates it as the "original fact," but he does not give a more precise definition of exactly what it is. It is not clear that he ever provides such a definition in the remainder of the work. On the other hand, the whole book will serve as an explanation, a development, a deployment of this "factual" or "causal" thesis. In a way, Tocqueville explains what democracy does or produces without achieving a clear definition of what it is – indeed, without worrying a great deal about the need for such a definition. With wonderful breadth and subtlety, he shows us how "democracy" transforms every aspect of human life, even the most personal and intimate. In this sense, his major work is a systematic study of social causality. Here, in fact, Tocqueville can be seen as "more sociological" than, say, Marx, who, though he asserts in a general way that the "superstructure" of human life depends on the "infrastructure" defined by the relations of production, has little precise, much less convincing, to say about the "details" that constitute the texture of that life, which Tocqueville so vividly captures.

To be sure, Tocqueville already says a great deal when he characterizes equality of conditions as a "fact," indeed "the original fact" (*le fait générateur*). In the constant change of all things human in Europe, one thing does not change: democracy as "democratic revolution," as equalization of conditions, which is "the oldest, most continuous, most permanent fact known to history."[3] The unchanging fact is change of a certain type. What is permanent is the way in which things change and the direction in which they move. The original fact, it seems, is not so much equality of conditions as equalization of conditions, constant movement toward ever-greater equality of conditions. If so, what might the destination of that movement be, knowledge of which would alone enable us to define equality of conditions?

Some will say that the reason Tocqueville offers no further explanation is that the normally constituted reader needs none. Everybody knows what equality of conditions is because everybody knows its opposite – namely, inequality of conditions – when some people, "nobles," monopolize land, titles, and prerogatives. The French Revolution had recently been waged against what became the Old Regime, against "feudalism," in order to abolish "privilege." All this gave meaning to equality of conditions.

Was this really so, and, if so, is it sufficient? We do of course possess empirical knowledge of the Old Regime and inequality of conditions. But do we achieve a clear definition by defining equality of conditions as the negation of inequality of conditions? Is this definition sufficient? Can one really *define* something as the negation of something else, a "fact" by the negation of another "fact?" Furthermore, although the Old Regime was overturned and equality of conditions was in principle established, progress toward greater equality of conditions continued as if the Revolution had not yet achieved anything, as if this "fact" had yet to become a fact at all. Toward what destination or final state are we moving? Indeed, in the United States, where there was no Old Regime and which was founded *on the basis* of equality of conditions, a steady movement toward greater, more complete equality could be observed. It was in the American West that "democracy [was] pushed to its ultimate limit."[4] Tocqueville explains:

In these states, in a sense improvised by fortune, people lived on land to which they had come only a short while before. They barely knew one another, and none knew the history of his nearest neighbor. In this part of the American continent, the population therefore escaped the influence not only of great names and great wealth but also of that natural aristocracy which derives from enlightenment and virtue.[5]

We were expecting a definition of the destination of equality, of its "ultimate limit," that would at last provide us with a criterion for equality of conditions, and what do we find? A description not of a society but of a scattered collection of people, a sort of dis-society. Is this dispersed collection of dissociated individuals what is meant by equality of conditions?

V. DEMOCRACY AND ARISTOCRACY

In any case, it appears that the driving force in democratic change is rejection and flight from "aristocracy," not only in Europe, which had lived for a long time under an Old Regime, but even in the United States, which was born in equality. Tocqueville's interpretation of European history and of contemporary social change was based on the polarity between equality and inequality of conditions, or between "democracy" and "aristocracy." Thus the language of Tocquevillean sociology is the very language in which politics was first articulated when it was brought to light in the political life, and through the political philosophy, of ancient Greece.

Yet Tocqueville uses the terms "democracy" and "aristocracy" to denote realities apparently quite different from those designated as such by Plato and Aristotle. For Aristotle, "aristocracy" and "democracy" were the two fundamental political regimes of the city, "aristocracy" referring to government by the "few" or "the best," while democracy referred to government by the "many," the majority of free men. The difference between Tocqueville and the Greek philosophers is apparent from the fact that Tocqueville includes the democratic regimes of the Greek cities, including most notably Athens, under the heading "aristocracy." His grounds for this classification are clear: the citizens of democratic Athens, though a relatively large number in the Greek context, amounted to only a "few" of the citizens of Attica. But what is the value of a classification or typology that puts Pericles' Athens in the same category as France under Philip Augustus or Louis XIV? Is it possible to imagine more different polities? Are we not obliged to conclude that Tocqueville's terminology betrays a certain rough-and-ready improvisation, not to say a certain incompetence?

In fact, if we look at Tocqueville's use of these terms a little more closely, we see that "aristocracy" and "democracy" denote what we would today call two broad "anthropological types," two different types of human being: aristocratic man and democratic man. The former sets himself lofty goals; his soul orients itself toward what is "great"; he is moved by the idea of "grandeur" and "superiority." The latter turns his back on grandeur and rejects the very idea of superiority; he aspires to equality because his basic emotion is the "feeling of human similarity." Now it appears that calling Athenian democracy "aristocratic" was not so bizarre after all. Not for the obvious arithmetic reason that the Athenian *demos* still comprised only a "few" men, but because it insisted on participating in the aristocratic city and shared the "agonistic" inclinations and ideal of "honor" characteristic of the "few" in the strict sense, the *eupatrides*.[6]

Furthermore, Tocqueville's analysis establishes a close relationship between dispositions of the soul and forms of communal life, including the two overarching forms "aristocracy" and "democracy," which led him to rediscover the most fundamental intuition of Plato and Aristotle, which he repeats freely (because he had barely read them) but faithfully – namely, that there exists a close correspondence between the order of the city and the order of the soul.[7] Because he develops all aspects of this correspondence with marvelous finesse, Tocqueville, liberal politician and sociologist, is a full-fledged if unintentional member of the school of political philosophy founded in Athenian democracy.

VI. JUSTICE AND GRANDEUR

To be sure, numerous and important differences separate Plato and Aristotle on the one hand from Tocqueville on the other. I shall mention two of these. First, Tocqueville's classification is "looser," so to speak: he sees only two broad "types," whereas Plato and Aristotle distinguish as many as six different political regimes. As subtle as his analysis is, his classification is more summary than that of the Greek philosophers. Second, the Greek classification is not only descriptive but also evaluative, ranging the various regime types on a scale from best to worst. Greek philosophers looked at political life in terms of the "best regime," hence the best human life. They did not shrink from making what we would nowadays call value judgments. By contrast, Tocqueville seems to have aimed for "value-neutrality." At the very end of his great work, when he offers a "general view of the subject" that sums up the results of his long and scrupulous comparison of aristocracy and democracy, he writes: "These are like *two distinct humanities*, each of which has its peculiar advantages and drawbacks, its inherent goods and evils. Hence we must be careful not to judge nascent societies by ideas drawn from societies that are no more. To do so would be unjust, for these societies are so extraordinarily different as to be *incomparable.*"[8]

This conclusion could not be clearer, yet it leaves us in doubt. This is because Tocqueville is not a modern "post-Weberian" sociologist or anthropologist for whom mankind is essentially "plastic," taking on as many forms as there are "cultures" (of which the number is endless), and who carefully refrains from making judgments not only as between cultures but also within a given culture. The post-Weberian's only purpose is to explain the internal coherence of each form. Tocqueville in effect presents mankind as taking on only two anthropological forms, and he usually uses the language of value judgment without the slightest hesitation – and nowadays some would say without the slightest precaution. In fact, a few paragraphs before the "value-neutral" passage I cited, he says: "I chose to speak out publicly about the dangers that equality poses to human independence because I firmly believe that those perils are the most formidable that the future holds, as well as the least anticipated."[9] In several places, Tocqueville speaks of the perils to which democracy subjects "human grandeur." More generally, his comments are pitched throughout in the contrasting and complementary keys of praise and blame, and he proposes a very explicit "scale of values" as a guide to human action. How can we reconcile a political and moral analysis so sure of its judgments with a general conclusion so uncertain and "skeptical?" Can we say that Tocqueville the politician and moralist was as sure of himself – as sure of what was good for his contemporaries – as Tocqueville the philosopher was hesitant about what was good for man in general? That Tocqueville knew the malady and the remedy but hesitated to define health?

These questions are currently resolved as follows: Tocqueville was a political man of old noble stock who made a resolute choice for democracy in his head while his heart remained filled with aristocratic "nostalgia." Thus we have a man inwardly divided and a thought ultimately uncertain of itself. This sort of portrait is of course plausible and pleasantly dramatic. It can even claim justification in certain of Tocqueville's own statements.

But it does not yield the answer we are after. In the first place, it neglects the fact that while Tocqueville was indeed a Norman aristocrat by birth, he was by nature and vocation a politician and statesman, and this nature and vocation insisted for their full development on the political liberty that is intimately intertwined with modern democracy. Tocqueville's most persistent and salient ambition was intimately associated with the new possibilities opened up by modern democracy. Furthermore, to assert that Tocqueville's intellectual judgment in favor of democracy could be offset by his "nostalgia" for aristocracy is seriously to underestimate him as a thinker. An author capable of succumbing to such a weakness would not be worthy of interest as a guide to understanding modern democracy and acting within it.

How, then, are we to understand Tocqueville's professed neutrality between aristocracy and democracy, two "distinct and incomparable humanities?" *In his own mind*, I believe, there was a tension that I would define as follows:

- On the one hand, the perspective of *justice*. From this point of view, the modern, democratic conception of liberty – liberty as equal rights – is undoubtedly the just one. The ancient, aristocratic conception of liberty as privilege has to be given up. This judgment "of the head" was also a judgment "of the heart": Tocqueville, the "Norman aristocrat," shared the primary emotion of democracy when he spoke of men as "obviously similar."
- On the other hand, the perspective of *grandeur*, or *independence*, which he also calls *liberty* – but this is a liberty different from "equal liberty." Here the concern is no longer primarily with relations among men but with the quality of each man's soul, of his "tone," of his "stature" or "grandeur." For Tocqueville, as for Aristotle, the perspective of "magnanimity" does not coincide with that of "justice", and sometimes comes into contradiction with it. For Tocqueville, man insofar as he is "capable of grandeur" is particularly imperiled in modern democracy.

VII. THE TWO DEMOCRATIZATIONS

Tocqueville's ambivalence toward democratic equality stems not from his biography but from his thought, and more precisely from his understanding of equality. In order to grasp this point, it will be worthwhile to make a brief detour by way of Greece.

Athens, like Europe, underwent a process of "democratization" of which the primary cause was military necessity. When the city needed its poorest citizens, when "the sailor rabble" ensured its victory at Salamis, Athens opened its regime to the "extreme of the populace."[10] The many insisted on *political* participation in a city previously constituted by the few. The poor man and the rich man remained what they had been, but now the rich man was obliged to obey the poor man when the latter was magistrate. The "resemblance" between the rich man and the poor man consisted in the fact that both took turns as "commander" and "commanded." What equality existed between them was a *direct* product of the political order and a part of that order.

The "equality of conditions" characteristic of modern democracy is something quite different. It does not originate with more extensive participation in civic life, in increased "politicization." On the contrary, it stems from a long process of "de-politicization" of which the monarchy was the instrument: "In France, kings proved themselves to be the most active and constant of levelers."[11] What is distinctive about modern democracy in Europe, and particularly in France, is the *prior* institution of a "plan of equality" by means of the sovereign state. In the French Revolution, political and civic demands came from members of society whose crucial collective experience was that of a non-political equality that was at once recent, imperfect, and threatened. French democracy was a political demand, and therefore a demand of liberty, issuing from a humanity whose primordial passion was, in Tocqueville's phrase, the "passion for equality."

Of course, all this had important consequences for Tocqueville's political sociology. Democratic society was indeed the "original fact," the cause, of the democratic life that Tocqueville describes, but that cause was in turn caused by a political institution to which a representation was attached. The political institution was the sovereign, leveling state, the state that produced the "plan of equality"; the representation was the idea of equality as human resemblance, with the passion that accompanied it. Thus the "original fact" was in turn engendered by the political institution – a "de-politicizing" political institution.

VIII. THE SOVEREIGNTY OF THE PEOPLE AND PHILOSOPHY

The political character of modern democracy comes to the fore explicitly and formally when Tocqueville posits the "dogma of popular sovereignty" as first cause:

In the United States, the dogma of popular sovereignty is not an isolated doctrine unrelated to either habits or the whole range of dominant ideas. On the contrary, one can think of it as the last link in a chain of opinions that rings the whole Anglo-American world. Providence equipped each individual, whoever he might be, with the degree of reason necessary to guide his conduct in matters of exclusive interest to himself alone. This is the great maxim on which civil and political society in the United States is based: fathers apply it to their children, masters to their servants, towns to the people they administer, provinces to towns, states to provinces, the Union to the states. Extended to the whole nation, it becomes the dogma of popular sovereignty. Thus, in the United States, the generative principle of the republic is the same principle that governs most human actions.[12]

Whereas equality of conditions was defined as the "original fact" (*fait générateur*) at the beginning of volume one of *Democracy*, at the end of the volume it is the dogma of popular sovereignty that is declared to be the "generative principle" (*principe générateur*). Social causality appears as both "fact" and "condition," whereas political causality appears as "principle" and "dogma." This second causality is obviously richer and more significant in human terms since it serves to regulate most human actions from within and is inextricably associated with a "dogma" – in this instance, an opinion about the human world that possesses incontestable authority.

Aristotle described the life of the city as centered on the competing demands of the few and the many to participate in government. In this sense, the Greek city, unlike the modern city, was "undogmatic." It asked itself, Who governs? Modern democracy is based on a "dogma," since only one demand is recognized as legitimate: the many, now in the guise of "all citizens," govern, while the demands of the few are rejected as illegitimate.[13]

Tocqueville extends the inquiry initiated by Greek philosophy in conditions made less favorable to philosophy by the institutionalization of the dogma that quashes the dispute between the few and the many with the authority of "all" or the "generality." By instituting the confrontation between "aristocracy" and "democracy" in his work and declaring that the debate between these two forms of humanity – between justice and grandeur – cannot be resolved, he reopens the question that our dogmatic passion declared to have been settled in advance. How can we deny the name "philosopher" to the liberal sociologist who leads us out of the social cave?

NOTES

1   *DAI Œuvres*, P: 12–13; *DAI* (trans. Goldhammer), 12.
2   *DAI, Œuvres*, P: 8; *DAI* (trans. Goldhammer), 7.
3   *DAI, Œuvres*, P: 3; *DAI* (trans. Goldhammer), 3.
4   *DAI, Œuvres* P: 56; *DAI* (trans. Goldhammer), 58.
5   Ibid.
6   See Christian Meier, *La naissance du politique* (Paris: Gallimard, 1995), 56–70.
7   See *Republic*, 544d–45a.
8   *DAII, Œuvres*, P: 852; *DAII* (trans. Goldhammer), 833; italics added.
9   *DAII, Œuvres*, P: 849; *DAII* (trans. Goldhammer), 830.
10   See Aristotle, *Politics*, 1277b3, 1296a1, 1304a22–24.
11   *DAI, Œuvres*, P: 5; *DAI* (trans. Goldhammer), 4.
12   *DAI, Œuvres*, P: 462; *DAI* (trans. Goldhammer), 458.
13   Marx had a striking formulation of this point: "Man declares by political means that private property is abolished as soon as the property qualification for the right to elect or be elected is abolished, as has occurred in many states of North America." Karl Marx, *La question juive* (Paris: Aubier Montaigne, 1971), 71.

5 Tocqueville's *Democracy in America* Reconsidered

I. INTRODUCTION

This chapter focuses on *Democracy in America,* certainly the most famous – and probably the most important – of the works of Alexis de Tocqueville. It is an effort on my part to re-examine and to rethink the making of Tocqueville's classic book, based upon my work over the past five years as translator of the forthcoming English language version of Eduardo Nolla's critical edition of the *Democracy.*[1] In 1990, this invaluable contribution to Tocqueville studies was published first in a Spanish translation and then in the original French.[2] The Nolla work was the first, and remains by far the fullest, critical edition of Tocqueville's *Democracy.*[3] It presents a very broad and extensive selection of early outlines, drafts, manuscript variants, marginalia, unpublished fragments, and other materials relating to the writing of Tocqueville's book. These working papers are largely drawn from the Yale Tocqueville Manuscripts Collection, which is housed at the Beinecke Library at Yale University and contains, among other treasures, Tocqueville's original working manuscript for the *Democracy* and large quantities of his drafts. Included in the apparatus of the Nolla critical edition are editorial notes, a selection of important appendices, excerpts from and/or cross-references to Tocqueville's travel notebooks, his correspondence, and his printed sources, as well as significant excerpts from the critical commentary of family and friends, written in response to their readings of Tocqueville's manuscript. In short, the Nolla edition allows the interested reader to follow along, from 1832 to 1840, as Tocqueville's ideas developed and as the *Democracy* took shape; it recreates much of Tocqueville's long process of thinking (and rethinking), writing (and rewriting). With the appearance of the English translation of the Nolla edition, all of these materials will, for the first time, become available in print to scholars and others interested in Tocqueville who work primarily in English.

My task as translator has required a close and careful rereading of Tocqueville's masterpiece and manuscripts, and it has therefore engaged me in an ongoing reconsideration of Tocqueville's work. The process of translation has also led me to a re-examination of *The Making of Tocqueville's "Democracy in America"* – my own earlier attempt to tell the story of how Tocqueville's ideas and book developed.[4]

II. TOCQUEVILLE'S METHODOLOGY AND SOURCES

Translation provides an invaluable opportunity to study and to appreciate a text in new ways. It demands special attention to, and awareness of, an author's vocabulary, use of language, stylistic traits, turns of phrases, and other writing characteristics, all of which in turn reveal his patterns of expression and ways of thinking. So the task of translating the *Democracy* means a re-evaluation of Tocqueville's methodology.

Several major recurring characteristics of the way Tocqueville's mind worked are inescapable for a translator. Perhaps most strikingly, Tocqueville thought very deductively, even syllogistically. In the *Democracy* and in his working papers, he frequently presented deductive sets of ideas, expressed in chains of paragraphs or sentences (or even in chains of phrases within a single, long sentence). We often read segments of the *Democracy* that are essentially syllogisms: Since ... , and since ... , thus ... . Moreover ... , so ... , consequently ... . Characteristically, Tocqueville often attempted to carry the reader along by the sheer force of logic, without any (or very little) reliance on fact or example. The tight logical sequence of his ideas is particularly evident in the many early outlines of segments and chapters of the *Democracy*, especially of the 1840 portion, which appear in the critical edition.

Tocqueville also commonly wrote in parallel structures, in matched phrases, sentences, or paragraphs. This feature reflects another important intellectual trait. He tended to think in pairs, and especially in contrasting pairs, or pairs in tension. This attention to contrasting pairs is, of course, related to one of Tocqueville's favorite techniques: comparison and contrast. Probably the most famous examples are his repeated discussions of the differences between the aristocratic and the democratic social states, and the running comparison between America and France, between a healthy, well-regulated democracy and a disjointed and unstable one. But there are many other examples in the pages of the *Democracy*, including his contrasting descriptions of the American North and South and of the right and left banks of the Ohio River. And the closely related concept of pairs in tension, of opposites (or near opposites) in balance, often defines what Tocqueville understood as an harmonious society. Notably, for example, he praised the way in which American society had blended the spirit of liberty and the spirit of religion, a pair that in France was at war rather than being in balance. His inclination to think in pairs and his belief that harmony meant pairs in equilibrium also explain his repeated assertion that, for a healthy society, the social and political worlds must be matched. In the United States, the social and political realms were equally democratic, so the republic was stable. In France, the two realms were out of joint – a democratic social state co-existed with a political state that was, at best, only emerging as democratic. The resulting mismatch, made worse by revolution and the revolutionary spirit, produced a society marked by bitter discord and destructive passions.

If he was not relying on the power of syllogism, Tocqueville often resorted to the device of images or word pictures to clarify his ideas and to persuade his reader. This use of the portrait was part of his larger effort to put his ideas in the clearest, simplest terms.

[The] principal quality of style is to paint objects and to make them perceptible to the imagination. ... Without having myself a style that satisfies me in any way, I have however studied a great deal and meditated for a long time about the style of others .... . There is in the great French writers, whatever the period from which you take them, a certain characteristic turn of thought, a certain way of seizing the attention of readers that belongs to each of them. ... But there is a quality common to all writers; it serves in a way as the basis of their style; it is on this foundation that they each then place their own colors. This quality is quite simply good sense. ... So what is good sense applied to style? That would take a very long time to define. It is the care to present ideas in the simplest and easiest order to grasp. It is the attention given to presenting at the same time to the reader only one simple and clear point of view ... It is the care to use words in their true sense, and as much as possible in their most limited and most certain sense, in a way that the reader always positively knows what object or what image you want to present to him. ... What I call good sense applied to style is to introduce into the illustrations only things comparable to the matter you want to show ... [The] illustration is the most powerful means to put into relief the matter that you want to make known .... .[5]

A translator repeatedly encounters certain images favored by Tocqueville: the circle or sphere, which defines limits; beams or rays of light converging; and roads coming together at some central point. (Note that all of these are essentially geometric illustrations.) Other favorites included rising floodwaters or raging rivers, and a host of set pieces relating to light and sight. Tocqueville often used images of shadows, of the fading of light, of seeing, of eyes, of light and darkness.[6]

Related to this technique of the telling snapshot is Tocqueville's device of deducing a broad picture from a small, specific detail or fact:

There are a thousand means indeed to judge the social state and political laws of a people once you have well understood what the various consequences are that flow naturally from these two different things. The most trivial observations of a traveler can lead you to truth on this point as well as the searching remarks of philosophers. Everything goes together in the constitution of moral man as well as in his physical nature, and just as Cuvier, by seeing a single organ, was able to reconstruct the whole body of the entire animal, someone who would know one of the opinions or habits of a people would often be able, I think, to conceive a fairly complete picture of the people itself. ... So if you see each man dress himself more or less as he pleases, speak or keep quiet as he desires, accept or reject generally received formulations, subject himself to the rule of fashion or escape from it with impunity, if each man escapes in some way from common practice and easily gets himself exempted, do not laugh; the moment has come to think and to act. These things are trivial, but the cause that produces them is serious. You have before your eyes the slightest symptoms of a great illness. Be sure that when each man believes himself entitled to decide alone the form of an item of clothing or the proprieties of language, he does not hesitate to judge all things by himself, and when the small social conventions are so badly observed, count on the fact that an important revolution has taken place in the great social conventions.[7]

His tendency to seize upon an image and to use a single detail to grasp the larger society also helped to lead him to models as a favored rhetorical and logical device. Throughout the *Democracy*, he posed three fundamental social states: aristocratic, democratic, and transitional. And for each one, he presented a model: England, the United States, and France, respectively. These models were not one dimensional, however. France served as a model for at least three major concepts: the transitional state; a nation that has undergone a revolution and is marked by the revolutionary spirit; and (as I indicated earlier) a country afflicted by mismatched social and political realms. And England shifted somewhat between the 1835 and 1840 volumes, from being primarily the model of a traditional, landed aristocracy to being, as well, the model of an aristocracy of wealth, an open aristocracy.

The Nolla edition also shows Tocqueville rejecting certain standard models. The working papers, as well as the published text, reveal his great discomfort with the traditional inclination of most social and political thinkers to draw lessons about democracy from the ancient and Renaissance republics. At times, he seemed to follow the usual path and occasionally cited the republics of antiquity or of Renaissance Italy to illustrate various ideas. But usually, especially in his drafts, Tocqueville reminded himself that the modern democratic world was entirely unprecedented. The earlier republics, therefore, had little to teach his contemporaries:

I do not know when people will tire of comparing the democracy of our time with what bore the same name in antiquity. The differences between these two things reveal themselves at every turn. For me, I do not need to think about slavery or other reasons that lead me to regard the Greeks as very aristocratic nations despite some democratic institutions that are found in their midst. ... It is enough for me to contemplate the statues that these peoples have left. I cannot believe that the man who made the Belvedere Apollo emerge from marble worked in a democracy.[8]

In another draft he declared: "I would very much like people to stop citing to us, in relation to everything, the example of the democratic republics of Greece and Italy." And in a marginal note, he suggested to himself that he "Show how what was called democracy in antiquity and in the Middle Ages had no real analogy with what we see in our times."[9] So if Tocqueville made lavish use of certain models, there were other conventional ones that he almost always rejected.

Several other characteristics of Tocqueville's way of thinking should also be mentioned. He had an almost playful fondness for reverse proofs as a way of turning logic on end and persuading by surprise. He asserted, for example, that the American republic proved the benefits of equality better by the horrors of slavery than by the advantages of liberty.[10]

More significantly, in his drafts, as well as in the published text, Tocqueville presented some of the reasons for his intellectual choices. He explained that, although he was aware of other dimensions of a particular issue, he sometimes decided very consciously to focus on the dimension he most wanted to address and to set the other dimensions aside. In the Foreword of the 1840 *Democracy*, he wrote:

I must immediately warn the reader against an error that would be very prejudicial to me. Seeing me attribute so many diverse effects to equality, he could conclude that I consider equality as the unique cause of all that happens today. This would assume a very narrow view on my part. There is, in our time, a host of opinions, sentiments, instincts that owe their birth to facts foreign or even contrary to equality. ... I recognize the existence of all these different causes and their power, but talking about them is not my subject. I did not undertake to show the reason for all our inclinations and all our ideas; I only wanted to show to what extent equality had modified both.[11]

And in one of his drafts, he explained:

After doing a book that pointed out the influence exercised by equality of conditions on ideas, customs and mores, another one would have to be done that showed the influence exercised by ideas, customs and mores on equality of conditions. For these two things have a reciprocal action on each other. ... If I examined separately the first of these influences, without concerning myself with the second, it is not that I did not know and appreciate the extent and the power of the latter. But I believed that in a subject so difficult and so complicated, it was already a lot to study separately one of the parts, to put the parts separately in relief, leaving to more skillful hands the task of exposing the entire tableau to view all at once.[12]

This kind of decision marked the *Democracy* in important ways, including the way Tocqueville addressed economic matters, as we will see. It reaffirms the judgment of many Tocqueville scholars that some of the silences (or near silences) of the *Democracy* do not betray blind spots or lack of awareness, but rather Tocqueville's choices about what he preferred to address, what was closest to his heart and to his most personal moral and philosophical beliefs, and what he decided to leave to others.

The working papers and other materials included in the Nolla critical edition demonstrate other interesting features of Tocqueville's methods of thinking and writing. In the drafts, we find several highly excited and unrestrained passages (often related to the French Revolution). They reveal Tocqueville in a less balanced, less moderate pose. But he almost always put these passages aside for fear of offending readers or showing himself too partisan. Almost all of these intensely passionate fragments were deleted from the text and remain only in the drafts and unpublished fragments.[13]

The manuscript materials also disclose more of his personal moral, religious, and philosophical convictions, and in some cases, show specific connections between those deeper beliefs and particular topics under consideration in the text of the *Democracy*. So sometimes the variants offer a more profound and intimate counterpoint to the theme at hand; they link Tocqueville's published ideas to the broader network of his beliefs.[14]

The Nolla edition also documents Tocqueville's repeated and sometimes unfinished efforts to define key terms, including such words as aristocratic persons, despotism, democratic despotism, revolutionary spirit, great revolution, and, most significantly, democracy itself. His papers provide many examples of working definitions and show him grappling, throughout the long process of writing the *Democracy*, with the challenge of teasing out all of the subtle meanings of concepts central to his thought. This ongoing effort to define terms again reflected his propensity for constantly turning and re-turning ideas.

Still another methodological feature was particularly important in the making of the *Democracy*. A close rereading of all of the materials of the Nolla critical edition exposes Tocqueville's intense self-awareness as a writer. The working papers, especially the original working manuscript, are full of the author's queries to himself about his ideas and his style. His own most unrelenting critic, Tocqueville was highly judgmental about his own work.

Marginalia and other comments show him:

- — reconsidering his ideas; reflecting on how they are interconnected; weighing which ideas were more important and which ones should precede the others for maximum clarity and persuasion;
- — wondering whether he is repeating an idea or indulging in an unnecessary digression;
- — outlining and reviewing the sequence of his ideas and chapters;
- — analyzing his own drafts; summarizing his key points; pointing out to himself the weaknesses of a particular version; reminding himself about what he is really trying to say; considering how best to structure and to support his argument;
- — consulting family and friends; reacting to their comments; and sometimes incorporating their suggestions and even their phrases;
- — deciding which chapters and fragments to include; and explaining to himself why or why not;
- — determining whether he needed to support a given idea with an example, a fact or an image;
- — examining and refining his style, for word variation, sentence balance, clarity of expression, definition of terms, impartiality; trying always to move toward a more elegant, more literary, and more moderate language and presentation; and
- — reminding himself about his intended audience; considering who his readers would be, what they would want, what they would accept or reject, what they would understand; wondering whether he risked boring, losing,

or puzzling his readers; questioning whether he needed to moderate his language or his viewpoint in order not to offend the political or national sensibilities of segments of his audience (French or American).

In addition to demonstrating Tocqueville's methodology, the materials presented in the critical edition also expand the known list of Tocqueville's sources. As a result, the Appendix, "Works Used by Tocqueville," which Eduardo Nolla presents at the end of the work, includes new titles that appear only in Tocqueville's notes, drafts, and other working papers, as well as more familiar sources cited in the published text of the *Democracy*.[15] These additional sources are diverse, and some are obviously more important than others. Some merely gave Tocqueville facts or illustrations to support already existing ideas; others provided the germs of new insights or deepened the internal conversation going on in Tocqueville's mind.

The critical observations of Tocqueville's family and friends, made in response to their readings of the manuscript, as well as marginalia and other fragments that reflect additional conversations with Gustave de Beaumont, Louis de Kergorlay, or other people close to Tocqueville add to our understanding of the important role these individuals played in the making of Tocqueville's book. Louis de Kergorlay, for example, often suggested significant ideas to Tocqueville about moral and religious questions and about more specific matters such as the nature of democratic armies.[16]

Tocqueville's working papers demonstrate, in particular, the important influence of contemporary French political and economic developments, especially during the five years when he was writing the second part of the *Democracy*, from 1835 to 1840. The drafts and other unpublished fragments include various references to conversations with Adolphe Thiers, with friends and supporters of Thiers, and with other named or unnamed political figures. And the working materials also contain numerous excerpts from newspaper accounts of current political issues, particularly from the *Journal des Débats* and from the *Revue des Deux Mondes*. These excerpts often concern the development of industry and transportation in France during the mid- and late-1830s, and the debate over the proper role of government in those undertakings. In these matters especially, rereading these manuscripts made me appreciate much more than ever before the way in which the *Democracy* reflected the issues and debates of Tocqueville's contemporary France.[17]

III. SOME THEMES OF THE *DEMOCRACY*

The close rereading and intensely focused attention demanded by the task of translation also lead to new insights about some of the principal themes and fundamental characteristics of the *Democracy*. My reconsideration of Tocqueville's work brought me back, for example, to the old issue of "How Many Democracies?"[18] Are the two halves of the *Democracy* – the first published in 1835, the second in 1840 – essentially different books? From a translator's perspective, the dissimilarities between the two segments of Tocqueville's book are certainly striking. The 1840 portion presents word use and a considerable amount of vocabulary not encountered in the 1835 half. Even sentence structures are somewhat different in the two parts. Most significantly, the high incidence of abstract words in the 1840 *Democracy* reflects the much more abstract character of the second portion.

But I continue to believe that parts one and two remain two segments of the same work. The working papers demonstrate that during the approximately eight years when Tocqueville was writing the *Democracy*, he was wrestling with essentially the same fundamental issues. Of course, ranks of importance, levels of emphasis shifted; some new concepts and terms emerged; and certain issues or ideas either disappeared or blossomed rather late in the creative process. But by and large, the same questions, problems, and dilemmas were the focus of Tocqueville's attention as he wrote and thought. Numerous outlines and early sketches written for the 1835 *Democracy* and many sentences or brief discussions in the 1835 text itself contain seeds of concepts and chapters that would become important in 1840. Even more strikingly, the solutions to democratic dilemmas that Tocqueville offered in the 1835 and 1840 portions of his work are identical. The drafts and other unpublished materials presented in the critical edition offer no evidence to support the traditional arguments for a radical disjuncture between 1835 and 1840: for a basic shift in the relationship either between democracy and centralization or between democracy and revolution.

My work as translator did suggest a different question, however. Is it time for readers of the *Democracy* to reconsider which of the two parts, 1835 or 1840, is the greater? In the nineteenth century, the usual judgment was that 1835 was the better and more impressive portion. In the twentieth century, common wisdom chose 1840, the second half, as more profound and less dated. Perhaps in the twenty-first century, readers should return to the earlier appreciation of 1835 as the superior effort. The argument would rest on the weakness of 1840 as the far more speculative and abstract portion, which means that it is less grounded, more dubious, and sometimes strangely obscure. Certain chapters in the second half seem, in particular, to overreach and to fall into doubtful speculation. In some ways, 1840 is also less strikingly original than 1835 (in part because 1840 grows so organically out of intellectual seeds laid down in 1835). And, certainly, the extraordinarily close reading required for translation exposes the repetitive and sometimes long-winded nature of some of the arguments of the 1840 *Democracy*. I am not asserting that the second half is not a great work of political and social philosophy, only that a case can once again be made for agreeing with serious and informed readers of the nineteenth century and considering the first half, the 1835 *Democracy*, as the more impressive of the two portions.

Close engagement with the Nolla critical edition also strongly demonstrates the presence of America in Tocqueville's book and the key role of the American journey in suggesting new ideas to Tocqueville and in shaping his thought. Repeatedly throughout the *Democracy*, he remarked how he had been struck by some unexpected feature of American society. The list of such "striking" occasions serves as an extended demonstration of how much the American journey taught him.[19] The argument made by some scholars that Tocqueville reached the New World in 1831 with the main elements of his thinking and of his book already in place simply does not withstand these admissions by Tocqueville that in America he was witnessing new things and learning new lessons about the nature of democratic society, about the advantages and dangers of democracy, and about the possible ways to enhance the first and to avoid the second. In all of this, the United States provided essential new elements to his understanding.

The text and the working papers of the *Democracy*, including his travel notes, present a rich, full description of the American republic: physical/environmental, historical, social, political, religious, psychological, cultural, even economic. Some of the elements of his portrayal do not appear in the published text, but they are in the travel notebooks, drafts, discarded fragments, and other working materials. To read them all is to realize the breadth of Tocqueville's portrait. He did not get everything or get everything right, but here again, what is left out of the published *Democracy* is almost always absent not because of ignorance or lack of interest, but because of conscious choices made by Tocqueville.

For example, one of the central features of the America described by Tocqueville was a sense of motion. He was astonished by the pace of change – the move westward, the conquest of the wilderness, the rise of cities, the economic transformation occurring before his eyes, the American assumption or expectation of change, the pace at which Americans went about "doing" whatever they were engaged in at the moment, the speed of American business activity, the headlong rush of Americans toward their own future. Tocqueville was a good historian; he knew a great deal about the American past. He was an astute observer of the American present. And he had a remarkable vision of the future of the American empire. Tocqueville's portrait of the American republic is inescapable in the pages of the *Democracy*.

The sense of movement, which Tocqueville observed in the United States, became one of the essential elements of his understanding and definition of democracy. A democratic society was a society in motion, a society open to change, to the new, to the future.[20] And such a society had profound implications for the American character, for American mores, and for the American psychology. The text and working papers of the *Democracy* are full of descriptions of the American character, and not all of them are complimentary.

My reconsideration of the *Democracy* also persuaded me once again that Tocqueville had a much stronger and more sophisticated grounding in economics and economic matters than many critics have charged. Again, the working papers add significant fragments to discussions that appear in the published text. In his drafts, he asserted notably that what was happening in industry was "the great fact of our time," second only to the march of equality, and that the rise of the industrial aristocracy was "an immense question."[21] But the *Democracy* itself does, after all, contain several chapters on the development of manufacturing, on economic change, on the rise of new industrial classes, especially the manufacturing aristocracy and the industrial working class, on the economy of scale, on the specialization or division of labor, on the impact of democracy on wages, rents, and leases. Even more broadly, Tocqueville saw the way in which democracy favored commerce and industry and how it commercialized many (if not most) areas of society, including changing literature into a business and transforming citizens into consumers. His descriptions of the brutalization of the working class and his condemnation of unchecked capitalism as practiced by the industrial aristocracy are powerful pieces of economic (and moral) analysis.

Moreover, America clearly helped to shape Tocqueville's understanding of economic transformation and of how that transformation could be managed in a way to safeguard liberty and avoid the danger of excessive centralization. Tocqueville noticed that in the United States, major economic undertakings were often shared enterprises. There the government was not becoming the principal industrialist. He recognized the importance in America of the industrial association or corporation; as an economic tool, it freed business or industrial enterprises from the fate and mortality of individual investors, permitted a kind of legal immunity from personal responsibility, and fostered change in remarkable ways. But more broadly, he saw that the preferred American method for accomplishing "internal improvements" was to blend private, state, and federal support. The American system avoided both the risk that most (or all) major economic developments would be in private hands (the danger of the industrial aristocracy) and the threat that most (or all) major undertakings would be done by the government (the French model of the late 1830s, which Tocqueville opposed as leading to administrative centralization and bureaucratic despotism). The Americans, Tocqueville realized, had discovered a mixed system that balanced public and private involvement, public and private responsibility. Their blended approach allowed the Americans to accomplish wonders.[22]

Here, once again, the published *Democracy* was shaped not so much by blindness as by choice. Tocqueville could not write about all of the major features of modern society that he recognized. So he decided to write a "philosophico-political" work[23] and to concentrate on analyzing "democracy." He knew that industrialization was the other great force at work in the modern world, but he chose to leave the full elaboration of that theme to others.

The task of translation also led me to re-examine Tocqueville's attitude toward centralization. In some of his working papers, he asserted that administrative centralization, within certain limits, is a necessary fact in modern societies. The prosperity of a nation, he argued, requires the execution of great national enterprises; such large and costly works were essential to the public good and, in turn, required a centralized State. He also called on the State actively to support, and even to fund, academic and scientific societies; such support would assure continuing research in the theoretical sciences and in other fields not attractive to the immediate, often short-sighted interests of democratic society. The Americans, he noted, were so decentralized administratively and so afraid of centralization that they did not know some of the advantages of centralization. In one draft fragment, with the title "Unity, centralization" and dated March 7, 1838, he wrote:

However animated you are against unity and the governmental unity that is called centralization, you cannot nonetheless deny that unity and centralization are the most powerful means to do quickly, energetically, and in a given place, very great things. That reveals one of the reasons why in democratic centuries centralization and unity are loved so much.

And in another draft, he declared:

Contained within certain limits, centralization is a necessary fact, and I add that it is a fact about which we must be glad. A strong and intelligent central power is one of the first political necessities in centuries of equality. Acknowledge it boldly.[24]

Of course, he also warned that the State, the administration, must not act alone. As we have seen, he praised the American mixed model. And for France, he argued that if the administration became deeply involved in great industrial enterprises, it had to be checked by the legislature and by the courts. If the State acted alone, liberty was in danger.[25] The real question, according to Tocqueville, is not whether or not the State should participate, but where and how to draw the limits of State participation. No involvement endangered national prosperity and progress. Too much involvement threatened liberty and risked bureaucratic despotism.[26]

A close rereading of the materials contained in the Nolla critical edition also clarifies Tocqueville's stance toward democracy. In the working papers, he declared himself "a partisan of democracy" and asserted that "my tendencies are always democratic."[27] Much of the *Democracy* serves as a long exercise in reassurance. In his book, Tocqueville was trying to reassure those disturbed by the advent of democracy, especially his fellow citizens. He said repeatedly, as he treated successive topics in his work, that democracy does not destroy, but instead transforms; it bestows another character, gives things a new twist. Democracy will not necessarily undermine culture and lead to a new Dark Ages, but democratic civilization will certainly be different. In democratic societies, the desire for art, literature, and science will remain, but will be channeled in new ways; democracy will in fact multiply the number of those pursuing the arts and sciences and may lead to a cultural flowering – but of a different sort. Democracy does not eradicate honor; it brings out a new kind of honor. Democracy will not destroy the family, but family relationships will be modified profoundly. Democracy does not necessarily lead to anarchy; a democratic society can be orderly and law-abiding (witness the American republic). But democratic society will be turbulent and in constant motion. Democracy will not necessarily be at war with religion; in a democracy, the spirit of liberty and the spirit of religion can blend in new ways (again witness the United States).

Repeatedly, in the face of the most common accusations made against democracy, especially by his own countrymen, Tocqueville presented his defense. In one sense, his book, particularly the 1840 portion, is a catalogue of the common charges made against democracy and his point-by-point refutation.

IV. CONCLUSION

So, in many ways, the wealth of working materials presented in the Nolla critical edition fosters a reconsideration and a new appreciation of Tocqueville's methodology, sources, and themes. In such a short chapter, there is no room to reproduce examples to illustrate each of the characteristic ways in which Tocqueville thought and wrote, or to show each of the new twists in the substance of Tocqueville's ideas. Instead, I urge those interested in Tocqueville to read the entire critical edition for themselves; they will make their own discoveries.

NOTES

1 The English translation of the Nolla critical edition will be published in 2006 by the Liberty Fund, Indianapolis; all translations presented here are my own, prepared for the forthcoming Liberty Fund edition.

2 *La democracia en América.* Edited and translated by Eduardo Nolla. 2 vols. (Madrid: Aguilar, 1990). And *De la démocratie en Amérique*, ed. Eduardo Nolla. 2 vols. (Paris: Librairie Philosophique J. Vrin, 1990). Hereafter cited as *DA* (Nolla).

3 The other critical edition of the *Democracy*, directed by André Jardin, edited by Jean-Claude Lamberti and James T. Schleifer, was published in 1992 as a single volume in the Pléiade series of Tocqueville's works (*Œuvres de Tocqueville, édition Pléiade. Paris: Gallimard*, 1992). The volume includes important selections from Tocqueville's working papers, but is much more limited in scale than the Nolla edition. The text has been translated into English, but not the critical apparatus.

4 James T. Schleifer, *The Making of Tocqueville's "Democracy in America."* (Chapel Hill: The University of North Carolina Press, 1980). A second, revised edition was published by the Liberty Fund, 2000.

5 *DAII* (Nolla), 63–64, note r; emphasis in the original. The note is largely an excerpt from a letter by Tocqueville to Charles Stoffels, dated July 31, 1834.

6 See, for example, *DAI* (Nolla), 245, note o; *DAII* (Nolla), 281, note j.

7 *DAII* (Nolla), 182–183, note c; emphasis in the original. These comments are from Tocqueville's autograph drafts for the 1840 *Democracy.*

8 *DAII* (Nolla), 56, note k. See especially *DAI* (Nolla), 235, text. Also: *DAI* (Nolla), 302, note d; *DAII* (Nolla), 65, text and notes a and b; 122–123, text and notes e and g; and 187, text.

9 *DAII* (Nolla), 215, notes n and p.

10 See *DAI* (Nolla), Second Part, ch. X, the chapter on the three races.

11 *DAII* (Nolla), Foreword, 7–8.

12 *DAII* (Nolla), 144, note a.

13 See as examples: *DAI* (Nolla), 7, note r; 14, note o; 300–301, note z.

14 See, for example: *DAII* (Nolla), 131, notes h and k.

15 *DAII* (Nolla), Appendix VII, 325–334.

16 See, for example: *DAII* (Nolla), 221–222, note d. There are several other important examples scattered throughout vols. I and II.

17 See as examples: *DAII* (Nolla), 224, note j; 246–247, note d; 254, note k; 255, notes m and n; 258–259, note y; 260–261, notes b and d.

18 Concerning this debate, see especially Seymour Drescher, "Tocqueville's Two Démocraties," *Journal of the History of Ideas* 25 (April–June 1964), 201–216; Jean-Claude Lamberti, *Tocqueville et les deux démocraties* (Paris: PUF, 1983); and François Furet, "Naissance d'un paradigme: Tocqueville et le voyage en Amérique (1825–1831)," *Annales* 39:2 (March–April 1984), 225–239. And consult my earlier article, "How Many Democracies?" found on pp. 193–205 of *Liberty, Equality, Democracy*, ed. Eduardo Nolla (New York: New York University Press, 1992). (This article is also included in Schleifer, *Making*, second edition, Epilogue, 354–368.)

19 See my essay "Tocqueville's Journey Revisited: What Was Striking and New in America." *The Tocqueville Review/La Revue Tocqueville* 18 no. 2 (2006), which addresses the question of the influence of the American journey on Tocqueville's thinking, especially the "striking" lessons that he absorbed in the United States.

20 See, for example: *DAI* (Nolla), 303, 307–308, text; and *DAII* (Nolla), 42–43, note b; 46, note h; 210, note b; 212, note f; and 210–212, 214, text.

21 On this subject, see especially *DAII* (Nolla), 260, note a; and 261. Also: *DAII* (Nolla), 139, note j; 162, text and notes a and b; 163, note g; and 140–142, text and accompanying notes; 257–261, text and accompanying notes. And consult: Seymour Drescher, *Tocqueville and England* (Cambridge, MA: Harvard University Press, 1964); Drescher, ed. and trans. *Tocqueville and Beaumont on Social Reform* (New York: Harper & Row 1968); Drescher, trans. *Alexis de Tocqueville: Memoir on Pauperism* (Chicago: Ivan R. Dee, 1997); and Michael Drolet, *Tocqueville, Democracy and Social Reform* (London: Palgrave, 2003).

22 See *DAII* (Nolla), 106–107, text and notes, especially 106, note s; 249, note p; 257–260, text and notes. Also see *DAI* (Nolla), 266, note 36.

23 Schleifer, *Making*, second edition, 110.

24 *DAII* (Nolla), 243, note c and 268, note p; both are from Tocqueville's drafts. Also see on the American fear of consolidation: *DAI* (Nolla), 293–294, 279, note o; 280, note q; on necessary governmental support for academies and research: *DAII* (Nolla), 47, note a; 90, note h; and on centralization and the appropriate role of government: *DAII* (Nolla), 57, note c; 106–107, text and note s; 139, note j; and 245–249, text and notes a, b, f, g, k, m, and p.

25 See *DAII* (Nolla), 254, note k; 255, note o; 256, notes p and 4; 258–259, notes 5 and y.

26 *DAII* (Nolla), 258–259, note y.

27 *DAII* (Nolla), 186, note m.

6   Translating Tocqueville
The Constraints of Classicism

I. THE CLASSIC

Nearly everyone will grant that Tocqueville's *Democracy in America* deserves to be called a "classic."[1] Does the work's classic status constrain its translator? Should it? And if so, how? These are the questions I want to address.

Tocqueville wrote as the self-conscious heir of a long intellectual tradition of writing about politics. Though never a systematic student of the ancient classics, he is known to have consulted Plato, Aristotle, and Plutarch during the period in which he wrote *Democracy in America*. He also read "classic" writers of the post-classical tradition such as Aquinas, Machiavelli, Montaigne, Bacon, Descartes, Pascal, Montesquieu, and Rousseau.[2] His early education owed a great deal to his tutor, the Abbé Lesueur. Lesueur, who had also been his father's tutor, was a man who belonged more to the eighteenth century than to the nineteenth, and who wrote an elegant French in the manner of that earlier time. When the young Tocqueville won a prize in rhetoric at the Metz lycée, he credited the preparation received from his tutor. The good Abbé, moreover, was an ecclesiastic with Jansenist leanings, who probably imparted the values of that austerely cerebral sect to his pupil, and we know that Pascal, the most sparkling of Jansenist writers, remained an important influence on Tocqueville's thinking.[3] Thus, from his earliest upbringing, Tocqueville had his attention turned from his own time to that earlier period to which the French refer as *l'âge classique*: classic because its authors were the first, in the opinion of many, to fashion from the French language an instrument supple enough to convey ideas and images with the vigor and subtlety of

139

Latin and Greek, and classic, too, in the sense of classicizing, harking back to ancient models as exemplars of the best that had been thought and known.

Unlike his uncle Chateaubriand, the proto-Romantic *prosateur* par excellence, Tocqueville felt no need to forge a new style in order to render new things. If he followed his older relative into the American wilderness, it was not to register the palpitations of his soul before the grandeur and immensity of the new world, even if he does, in the odd passage, take on an almost Chateaubriandesque tone of lugubrious delectation:

As in forests under man's dominion, death here worked its ceaseless ravages, but no one took it upon himself to remove the debris it left behind. Dead wood therefore piled up faster than it could decay to make way for new growth. Yet even in the midst of all this debris, the work of reproduction continued without letup. Climbing vines and other plants crept among fallen trees and worked their way into decaying remains; they lifted and broke the shriveled bark that still clung to the dead wood, thereby clearing the way for young shoots. Thus death in a way served life. Each looked the other in the face, seemingly keen to mingle and confound their works.[4]

But Tocqueville was far too conscious of Pascal's strictures against what a recent editor has dubbed "ego-history" to have followed his uncle down the road to Romanticism. While he admired Montaigne, whom he quotes once in *Democracy in America*, he of course knew what Pascal thought of the Bordeaux magistrate's "sot projet ... de se peindre." Even in this brief Romanticizing prose poem, we feel the continued presence of the classical armature. Note the balance and equipoise of the periods. One doesn't have to count syllables to sense how the sentence that begins with "Climbing vines" rises to its pinnacle in "decaying remains," only to race down the back slope where "young shoots" are poking up through the soil. A quick seven-word haymaker follows hard upon this undulating and almost Proustian left hook, a short, sharp sentence built around the antithesis between death and life, which stuns you with the observation that death serves rather than curtails its double. (In French, there are twelve words; I flatter myself that the greater concision of the English would have pleased

Tocqueville and made up for the slight slippage from *aider*, "to serve".[5]) Thus even this Romantic thrust is mere drapery over the firmly planted pillars of the classical temple that Tocqueville is constructing sentence by sentence.

II. TRANSLATING THE CLASSIC

With respect to stature, substance, and style, Tocqueville's work can thus fairly be called a classic. How does this special status affect the translator's handling of the text? A classic bears a special relation to other texts as well as a special relation to the language in which it is written. There is a passage in which Tocqueville speaks of the ease with which the leading men in aristocratic societies can recognize one another. They stand above the rest, he says, and easily spot each other from one hilltop fortress to the next, as it were. Classics, too, are like this, and Tocqueville clearly recognized certain prominent predecessors as peers with whom he wished to enter into conversation. His is not the way of the modern scholar, however. He does not adorn his text with frequent footnotes to indicate where he has borrowed or with whom he agrees or disagrees. He does not dissect the arguments of others in detail as proof that he has understood and weighed them, not merely dismissed them blindly or out of hand. He wants to influence his contemporaries, and, knowing that many of them will be impatient of any hint of pedantry, he does not wish to burden his prose with exegesis. Often he merely alludes. To the wise, a word is enough to indicate what he is up to, an ironic reference sufficient to indicate what he thinks. He will speak, for instance, of "philosophers and historians" who assert that distance from the equator determines the mores of women, and one knows that behind the "materialist doctrines" he thus stigmatizes in passing, he is indicating his distaste for Helvétius, d'Holbach, and Diderot and his disagreement with a tendency in the thinking of Montesquieu, for whom he elsewhere professes respect.[6] A certain delicacy is required in dealing with such a text lest subtle references – hints contained in a lexical wisp or syntactic murmur – be obscured.

There is a contemporary school of textual interpretation that takes this intertextual subtlety a good deal further. Leo Strauss was its founder. Strauss believed that the classics pose a special kind of interpretive problem. The very fact that they are so widely studied can obscure or falsify their deliberately cryptic messages. Incessant commentary softens the most shocking insights of fundamental works. The temptation to make classic texts "relevant" to contemporary problems dilutes the vigor of their original language and buries their hidden secrets even deeper. For Strauss, lulling commentary on the great works diverts attention from what he calls permanent problems: "Many of our contemporaries are of the opinion that there are no permanent problems and hence no permanent alternatives."[7] The proper way to read the classics, he suggests, is in relation to one another, for at bottom they are engaged in a durable contest, a fundamentally agonistic confrontation between alternative values.

Since these fundamental texts are written in different languages, translation poses a special problem for exponents of Straussian interpretation. The permanent problems were first posed in Greek and Latin, then translated into modern tongues. One thus gains insight into the clash of agonistic values by paying close attention to the way in which modern antagonists inflect certain terms of classical discourse. Reading Machiavelli against Aristotle teaches us more about our own modernity, say Straussians, than contemplating, as Tocqueville does in one of his rare dilations upon a topical theme of actual American politics, Andrew Jackson's opposition to the creation of a national bank. And to be sure, Tocqueville is not so much diverted by the circumstantial detail such an event provides as he is grateful for the opportunity to expound classical topoi such as the susceptibility of democracy to demagogy and the conversion of military prowess into popular appeal. Since what the great philosophers say is often veiled, Straussians contend, because it is dangerous or offensive to established ways of thinking, it is important that the translator refrain from disturbing signs that may be the keys to recovering these encrypted meanings. Similarly, contradictions must not be glossed over, nor should inconsistencies be "harmonized," lest clues to what was unassimilable or contested or overlooked in the appropriation of ancient texts be brushed aside.[8]

If I devote attention to these Straussian dogmas, to which I do not subscribe, it is in part because Straussian scholars have done important work on Tocqueville.[9] It is also because a recent translation of *Democracy in America*, by Professors Harvey Mansfield and Delba Winthrop, explicitly places itself in the Straussian tradition. Before Mansfield and Winthrop, however, other translators had labored to make the text a classic in the United States even as it lapsed in France from popularity into neglect.[10] Tocqueville himself read and commented on the first translation of his work, by Henry Reeve. He had this to say: "Without wishing to do so and by following the instinct of your opinions, you have quite vividly colored what was contrary to Democracy and almost erased what could do harm to Aristocracy."[11] Note well Tocqueville's use of the word "instinct." We'll encounter it again. In any case, defective or not, Reeve's translation, revised first by Francis Bowen and again by Phillips Bradley, has remained in print. I have not studied the original version to see if it merited Tocqueville's disapproval, which seems to credit translation with more damage than it can do if it is at all faithful. Perhaps Tocqueville was merely startled by a reasonably accurate transcription of his own voice, as we often are when we listen to a recording. In any case, we know that Tocqueville's work has become a classic of the English language, and surely it owes that status in part to the quality of the joint effort of Reeve, Bowen, and Bradley, whose inexpensive Modern Library edition, which I have studied, filled the need for a text that made a case for democracy in America in the early years of the Cold War, when Tocqueville's all too famous prediction that the world would one day be divided between America and Russia seemed to be coming true. Then, in the 1960s, George Lawrence published a new translation, which, though it owed a great deal to its predecessor, nevertheless spoke with a distinctly more contemporary voice. Perhaps it was the clarity of that voice, or perhaps it was the changed climate of the Sixties, but commentators seemed to become more aware of certain of Tocqueville's doubts about the democracy to which he had attempted to reconcile himself and his fellow Frenchmen: his concern with corrosive individualism, mediocre conformity, the tyranny of the majority, and similar themes now commanded attention.

In any case, the Mansfield-Winthrop translation appeared shortly after I began work on my own version of the text, taking its place after the well-established Reeve-Bowen-Bradley and Lawrence versions.[12]

If Tocqueville's book was widely studied and admired in American schools, the credit was due largely to Reeve, Bradley, Bowen, and Lawrence. Whatever deficiencies their translations possessed, they were not so debilitating as to rob the text of its claim to be a work "of the highest rank or importance, approved as a model" – a classic, in short. Whatever precedents my predecessors had established, therefore, had to be weighed carefully – not necessarily accepted merely because they were established, but not necessarily rejected solely for the sake of difference or novelty either. In addition, I was now reminded by Mansfield and Winthrop of the possibility that the text might be read in ways that made special demands on the translator, whom they admonished to show "reverence."[13]

Genuflection is one thing, however; translation is another. Take a case in point: one finds in Tocqueville the important concept of "l'intérêt bien entendu." This concept matters a great deal to the author of *Democracy*, because, while he stands in religious awe before the inexorable power of equality to shape human history, what he "loves" is not equality but liberty, and liberty, as we shall see, is precisely the freedom of each person to pursue his own interest as he conceives it. Yet Tocqueville is appalled by the materialist assumption that interest is simply a given, a behavioral manifestation of biological imperatives. The value and ultimately the viability of a society that takes liberty as its first principle depend on the education of interest. How interest is shaped, whether by laws, mores, or history, is thus of primary importance to Tocqueville and in a sense the key to both his appreciation of and his worries about democracy.

III. *L'INTÉRÊT BIEN ENTENDU*

Translating "l'intérêt bien entendu" is therefore a matter worth a moment's reflection. Reeve translated this phrase as "self-interest rightly understood," while Lawrence preferred "properly understood." I myself, in translating, some years ago, *Tocqueville's Two Democracies* by the late Jean-Claude Lamberti, adopted Lawrence's usage. Schleifer glosses the phrase as "enlightened self-interest."[14] But Mansfield and Winthrop, professing a general preference for literalism, for "staying as close as possible to the original," prefer "self-interest well understood."

Now, much discussion of translation revolves around quibbles of this sort, which can be tedious and unilluminating. How, precisely, is one to adjudicate between "interest well understood" or "properly understood" or "rightly understood" or "enlightened"? It's a question of "ear," some will say, but of course the argument is perfectly circular: if "self-interest properly understood" sounds right to you, it may be that your ear, like mine, has already been shaped by prior experience.

Or maybe my ear is just off. There are scholars who say that El Greco painted the human figure as he did because he suffered from severe astigmatism; perhaps it is possible to suffer from an astigmatism of the ear and consequently to prefer faltering rhythms and odd dissonances to compositions favoring regularity, predictability, and conformity to strict rules. What if rhythm and diction change depending on where the writer's attention is focused? What if allusive association with precursor texts attaches to a word used in one context a somewhat different inflection from the same word used in a different context? Shouldn't the translator be alert to these subtle variations? Might not literalism and consistency prove to be misguided?

The argument from literalism seems to me no more persuasive than the argument from instinct. Must "bien" be translated as "well" rather than "properly" simply because it may be translated that way in some contexts? Can one really say that "well understood" is "closer to the original" than "properly understood?" After all, there are many contexts in which it would not be at all natural to translate *bien* as well. What about *c'est bien bon, c'est bien simple,* or *c'est bien bizarre*? What about the formulaic *bien entendu,* which of course means "of course"? Or the closing of a letter, *bien à vous.* Or, to confine attention to *bien* as adverbial modifier of a past participle, *il est bien venu que ..., il est bien entendu que ...*? Or the formula *c'est bien trouvé*? The semantic range of the French morpheme *bien* only partially overlaps the semantic range of the English morpheme well: consider *le bien et le mal, le bien national,* or *est-ce bien le train pour Paris*? The student who receives *une mention bien* may regret that she didn't receive a *très bien, mais quand bien même elle s'est acquittée tant bien que mal, et bien qu'elle ne soit pas trop brillante.* Consider, too, the difference between *je veux* and *je veux bien, je t'aime* and *je t'aime bien*. In none of the foregoing instances can *bien* be translated as "well," hence the defense of such a translation as "literal" seems more a premise than a proof. To complete the proof, one would presumably have to say why *l'intérêt bien entendu* has more in common with *bien fait* or *bien joué* than with *bien venu* or *bien trouvé*.

And that is not all: I haven't yet touched on all that is left out (or smuggled in) when we translate *intérêt* by its simple English cognate interest, for in French one says *il y a intérêt à faire quelque chose* without hinting at a utilitarian doctrine of motivation. As Jon Elster pertinently remarks, La Rochefoucauld denies that the word *intérêt* always refers to "a material interest" (*un intérêt de bien*); more often – in *l'âge classique*, at any rate – it refers to "an interest of honor or of glory."[15] In any event, the footsteps of Adam Smith and Jeremy Bentham dog the Anglo-Saxon writer on political theory far more than they do the French writer, who is likely to think of Helvétius and the rather different philosophical tradition conjured up by his name. For if Helvétius and not Bentham was, as Isaiah Berlin persuasively argues, the true father of utilitarianism, he was also the true heir of materialist mechanism, and it was as such that Tocqueville combated his legacy even as he reached a compact of understanding with Bentham's heir John Stuart Mill.[16] What Tocqueville meant by *l'intérêt bien entendu* is therefore something that must emerge from his text as a whole, and this fact tends to diminish the importance of the merely local choices that one makes in translating this or that word.

So where does this rapid survey leave us? Is there simply no rational basis for choosing? Here is a modest proposal. Let us toy with the hypothesis that "properly understood" is preferable to "well understood" because the latter formulation suggests that there is an unambiguous notion of interest that the actor is well-advised to grasp well, or thoroughly, whereas the former suggests that interest is really a rather slippery concept, that what we take to be in our interest depends crucially on how we view the world and in particular on where we take time's horizon to be situated, and therefore it behooves us to understand our interest not merely well but properly – that is, to choose among the many possible definitions of interest the one that is truly the self's, or that is the true self's.[17] As for "rightly," one might see this as a compromise solution, more ambiguous as to the nature of interest. Is "properly" then a legitimate translation or an illegitimate substitution of the translator's understanding or unconscious preference or opinion for the author's? Does yet another option suggest itself? Or is there perhaps no significant difference at all among the alternatives? Am I imagining the nuance?

To pursue this point a little farther, let me make a Straussian move to clarify the grounds for my objection to the Straussian contention that in the absence of complete knowledge of a text, it is better to translate as literally as possible – whatever "literally" might mean, and I think I have shown already that there is a certain incoherence to the notion. My Straussian move is to cite a writer whom Tocqueville never mentions in *Democracy in America* but is known to have studied closely – Edmund Burke – and to strengthen my belief that I am correctly reading what he does say by contrasting it with what he doesn't say, but Burke does.[18] Let me mention first that Mansfield and Winthrop state in a footnote that "the actual phrase 'self-interest well understood' was apparently first used by Etienne de Condillac in 1798."[19] Of course, what they mean to say is, "the actual phrase 'intérêt bien entendu.'" Attributing responsibility for their translation to a French author is a slip, as is the date 1798, since the *Traité des animaux*, which they cite as the source, was actually published in 1755 (Condillac died in 1780). In any case, we find the following passage in Burke's *Reflections on the Revolution in France*, published in 1790:

These enthusiasts do not scruple to avow their opinion, that a state can subsist without any religion better than with one and that they are able to supply the place of any good which may be in it, by a project of their own – namely, by a sort of education they have imagined, founded in a knowledge of the physical wants of men; progressively carried to an enlightened self-interest, which, when well understood, they tell us, will identify with an interest more enlarged and public.[20]

It is striking to find in Burke the phrase "enlightened self-interest" coupled with the phrase "well understood." Does this rule out "properly understood?" On the contrary, I believe it makes my case. To be sure, Burke's expression here is not sparklingly pellucid. It is not altogether clear who is meant to understand self-interest well, the enthusiastic educators or the men they educate. Is the argument of the "invisible hand" sort – that men so educated work blindly to satisfy themselves but can nevertheless be seen, by those who understand well, to contribute to the "enlarged and public" interest? Or is it that men can be educated to understand that certain kinds of apparent self-sacrifice in fact redound to one's own benefit, hence that it makes sense for self-interested reasons to consider, or, more cynically, to calculate, how one might "do well by doing good?" It is not clear, either, whether Burke's phrase "progressively carried" means that the doctrine of interest is enlarged beyond "physical wants" or confined within the sphere of the material.

Tocqueville in any case appears to share the concern that motivates the reformers whom Burke disparages, for he says that in revolutionary times it is essential "to make the case that the interests of individuals and of the nation are inextricably intertwined, because disinterested love of country has vanished forever."[21] But he also says that while "it is to be expected ... that individual interest will become more than ever the principal if not the sole motive of human action, ... it remains to be seen how each person will interpret his individual interest,"[22] leaving to the individual a freedom to interpret the lessons he is taught that Burke seems to deny to the manipulated pupils of his cunningly coercive educators. And far from seeing self-interest as merely an enlargement of the sphere of physical wants and a substitute for religion, Tocqueville believes that in America it has become an essential prop of religion: "Hence I see no clear reason why the doctrine of self-interest properly understood should turn men away from religious beliefs. On the contrary, I can make out ways in which it might draw them toward religion."

That Tocqueville is perfectly conversant with Burke's "enthusiasts" (not from having read Burke but from his knowledge of the would-be reformers whom Burke disparages) is clear from the following passage, in which he calls them, collectively, "moralists":

But as ... people began to concentrate on themselves, moralists became alarmed by the idea of sacrifice and no longer dared hold it up for the human mind to contemplate. They were accordingly reduced to asking whether citizens might not find it to their individual advantage to work for the good of all, and whenever they happened upon one of the points where the particular interest intersects and converges with the general interest, they were quick to call attention to it. Little by little, such observations proliferated. What was once just an isolated remark became a general doctrine, and ultimately it came to seem as if man, in serving his fellow man, served himself.[23]

But Tocqueville, as I shall show in a moment when I turn to a discussion of the word instinct, sees this development in a more generous spirit than Burke. He emphasizes the variety of ways in which interest can be not only understood but acquired. For him, self-interest is not always material and is not determined in advance by man's biological nature. Nor is it a direct consequence of his position in society: it is not true that the rich or the poor or the few or the many have certain unalterably opposed interests simply because they are rich or poor or more or less numerous. Their interests can be "enlarged" and made more "public" by granting them rights, by involving them in politics:

It is not within the power of the law to revive dying beliefs, but it is within the power of the law to instill in people an interest in the fate of their country. It is within the power of the law to awaken and guide the vague patriotic instinct that dwells permanently in the heart of man and, by linking that instinct to everyday thoughts, passions, and habits, to turn it into a conscious and durable emotion. Let it not be said that it is too late to try: nations do not grow old in the same way as men. Each new generation born among them is fresh material for the lawmaker to mold.[24]

Tocqueville, in other words, sees interests as plastic and their shaping as an art, indeed the political art par excellence: the "new political art," if you will, which must be conjoined to his "new political science" if the latter is to have any useful effect. And Tocqueville wanted more than anything to have useful effect; his theory was intended to be a tool, for as he put it in his Introduction, "science [is] a means of government and intelligence a social force." Clearly he had made his own what Stephen Holmes calls a "pivotal, but largely neglected, liberal idea" first formulated by Locke: "Law, in its true Notion, is not so much the Limitation as the direction of a free and intelligent agent to his proper Interest, and prescribes no further than is for the general Good of those under the Law."[25] And here, mirabile dictu, we have an English-language precedent for coupling the adjective "proper" to the idea of "interest" in a thoroughly enlarged and anti-materialist, hence plausibly Tocquevillean, sense.

So that is my case for believing that "self-interest properly understood" is a better translation than "self-interest well understood." I hope to have made it clear that the choice is not simply one of lexical fidelity. Of course we tend to talk about the lexical rather than other aspects of that overall impression precisely because we can talk about them: it's easy to point to a word and to a dictionary definition and say, "See, that's what it means." In doing so, we take toward prose an attitude rather like that which Dr. Johnson took toward matter when he kicked the rock and said, "I refute Berkeley thus." But Johnson, though a lexicographer, was no literalist: he described his dictionary as "the dreams of a poet doomed at last to wake a lexicographer," and is remembered as much for his extracurricular and poetically licentious glosses on the meaning of words such as "patriotism" as for his efforts to regiment the unruliness of Shakespeare's tongue. Even formal prose like Tocqueville's is rather more ragtag than regimented. The potential alternative uses of "bien" and the conceivable implications of each permissible choice of a translation hover as silent as ghosts around the actual embodiment not only of the author's palpable intent but of possibilities latent in his language that deserve to be preserved for the reader without access to the original. These ghosts influence the translation, as do other unarticulated elements such as the rhythm of the text's sentences, the balance of its periods, the grace or gruffness of its tone, the hint that the author was smiling when he stabbed at his paper with particular vigor in bringing to a full stop a particularly well-turned phrase. In the translator's ear, these mute voices run like a counterpoint to the text's main line, influencing his song even if he would be hard pressed to say precisely how. If he doesn't hear those voices, he isn't likely to achieve the proper overall effect.

Does my argument carry absolute conviction? Surely not. Call it a hunch. Or, to use a Tocquevillean word, an instinct. But an instinct based on a long experience of turning French into English. Not that this argument, trumped up after the fact, reflects the actual thought process of the translator at work. I'm afraid that he is often swayed by the instincts not of his "opinions," for which Tocqueville reproached Reeve, but of his intellect and aesthetic – that is, by the promptings not of his nature but of his second nature, as Pascal styled culture. I had read Holmes' book after translating Lamberti and before undertaking *Democracy in America* but did not in fact remember Locke's use of the phrase "proper interest" until I refreshed my memory in writing this chapter. My argument, such as it is, is not a proper argument so much as a description of the inner landscape that forms the background to the translator's judgment. Why, at this or that juncture, one prompting of his nature should outweigh another is a bit of a mystery, but surely no less mysterious than the defense of one possible translation on the grounds that it is "closer" than some other to the original. Closer by what measure? The belief that literal translation can get us closer to the text than an honest, if inevitably partial, effort to grapple with its meaning strikes me as a kind of scientistic fallacy, in that it seeks to atomize the complexity of language the better to dominate it. It is odd to find such a view of language associated with the name of Strauss, who denounced what he called "the 'scientific' approach to society" as an "abstraction from the moral distinctions by which we take our bearings as citizens and as men. The indispensable condition of 'scientific' analysis is then moral obtuseness."[26] Literal translation, when it defies the instincts of the translator's ear for his own as well as the foreign tongue, seems to me to suffer from a comparable aural obtuseness. But perhaps I have said enough on this point and should leave it at that.

Does it matter if I'm wrong in this choice? Probably not much, or at least I hope not. Unless one happens to be a scholar for whom some argument hinges crucially on this or that word choice, it's usually a mistake to make a fetish out of the lexical dimension of a text. Translation, though practiced as an art of small choices, of relatively delicate, almost imperceptible individual touches and brush strokes, is also, like any art, subordinate to a larger order, to a principle of the whole. In order to achieve that whole, the copyist must be allowed a certain freedom to blend this detail with that. Slavish imitation, being mechanical, saps the work's soul. A translation, like a painting, must make an overall impression if the reader is to care enough to follow its internal gradations and impastos, its subtle or startling effects, its sfumati and pentimenti.

IV. INSTINCT

So instinct is essential in translation, but the instinct I've been talking about is not the brutish kind; it's a rather sophisticated sort of instinct, a cultivated spontaneity. I've tried, moreover, to contrast the instinctive approach to translating to the overly rational one, which would impose either a rule – translate literally – or a method: translate as though your text were in conversation with the classics and concerned ultimately if not exclusively with the "permanent problems." Now these are matters about which Tocqueville had things to say. "Instinct" is a word that occurs frequently in his work. The right relation of rationality to instinct is a matter that concerns him deeply, as we shall see in a moment. And he explicitly warns against believing that classical thought is the best guide to the present: "A world that is totally new demands a new political science."

The old political science that Tocqueville deemed no longer adequate was presumably both the Enlightenment's and Aristotle's, more or less, and Tocqueville certainly knew of Aristotle's dictum that there is no science but of the general. If he aimed at science, he aimed at the general, but generalities were also the occasion of his deepest misgivings. In his very interesting chapter on language, he says:

Generic and abstract terms are the basis of all language. Hence I am not claiming that such words are found only in democratic languages. All I am saying is that men in ages of equality tend to increase the number of words of this type in particular; they tend to take them always in isolation, in their most abstract sense, and to use them incessantly, even when the occasion does not require it.[27]

Thus the virtuous use of language requires striking a just mean in the employment of general terms, hence in the application of science. Tocqueville's wariness of the theoretical and preference for the practical are well known. Pragmatism is one quality for which he praises Americans, the lack of it one vice for which he chastises revolutionaries in France. In aristocratic societies, language can be more concrete than abstract or theoretical, moreover, because it "inevitably partakes of the general ambience of repose. Few new words are created, because few new things come to pass. If anyone did anything new, moreover, he would try to describe it using familiar words whose meaning had been fixed by tradition." By contrast, "the perpetual fluidity that is so prominent a feature of democracy is forever reshaping the face of language as well as of business (*DAII* 1.16, 548)."

If the real is so fluid that language cannot fix it in words, cannot literally transcribe things as they are, then science must be supplemented by art. This was of course true for the old Aristotelian political science as well, but Tocqueville's doubts about the guidance that reason can offer man were unknown to Aristotle. They are informed by a Pascalian pessimism as to man's nature. "Le cœur a ses raisons, que la raison ne connaît pas," Pascal wrote – "the heart has its reasons, which reason knows not." For Pascal, who believed that the divide between head and heart was an abyss, the asceticism of Port Royal was the only possible life. But Tocqueville chose an active life in politics. Clearly he held out hope – did he take it from Rousseau? – that the head might yet heed the heart and the heart be instructed by the head.

For Tocqueville as for Pascal, excessive faith in reason was associated with a name: Descartes. "Cartesianism," Tocqueville tells us, is the "common philosophical method" of the Americans, even though they "do not read Descartes, because their social state discourages speculative studies."[28] He gives several reasons why this should come as no surprise. Equality of conditions is corrosive of authority:

As for the possibility of one intelligence influencing another, it is necessarily quite limited in a country whose citizens, having become more or less identical, can observe each other at close range. Seeing that no one possesses any incontestable mark of greatness or superiority, each person is forced back on the most obvious and accessible source of truth, his own reason. What is destroyed as a result is not only confidence in any particular individual but also the readiness to believe anyone solely on the basis of his word. Each person therefore retreats within the limits of the self and from that vantage ventures to judge the world.

Not only is intellectual authority thus destroyed; so, too, is the authority of classes, of a seemingly natural and settled order of things.[29] Intergenerational authority is also undermined, for "in the constant state of flux that prevails in a democratic society, the bond that ties generation to generation is loosened or broken. People easily lose track of the ideas of their ancestors or cease to care about them."

The upshot of these several blows to authority is that "in most activities of the mind the American relies solely on the unaided effort of his own individual reason." Democratic societies are thus led naturally to adopt a philosophy that Descartes derived from inspection of his own cogito. The consequence of this, for Tocqueville, is an ominous democratic hubris: "Equality of conditions fosters a ... very high and often quite exaggerated idea of human reason."[30]

This is a perfectly Pascalian thought. It owes nothing to skepticism. The skeptic doubts the power of reason to know anything. Tocqueville, like Pascal, had nothing but the highest respect for reason; witness his frequent remarks on the indispensability of *les lumières*, of enlightenment, as a sine qua non of democracy. "All our dignity consists in thought," he could have said with the Jansenist philosopher. Yet if thought constitutes man's nobility, man is still as nothing before the unfathomable depths of the universe: "A vapor, a drop of water, is enough to kill him," said Pascal. "Man is but a reed, the weakest in nature. But he is a thinking reed."

For Pascal, it was the immensity and variability of the universe and of the individual soul that inspired humility and warned against undue confidence in the powers of reason.

I spent much of my life believing that some kind of justice existed, and in that I was not mistaken, for justice does exist, insofar as God has willed that it be revealed to us. But I did not take it that way, and there I was mistaken, for I believed that our justice was essentially just and that I possessed the means to know and to judge it. Yet I found myself so often wanting right judgment that in the end I became wary of myself and then of others. I have seen changes in all countries and all men, and I understood that our nature was one of constant change.

For Tocqueville, the providential increase in the equality of conditions signaled the kind of justice that God intended but did nothing to bolster man's feeble reason in the face of the immensity of the unknowable, including what was unknowable or at the very least unavowable within himself. Indeed, the passage to a democratic social state entailed debilities in the faculties of reason not contemplated by Pascal. Man now found himself alone, isolated, helpless, and weak vis-à-vis not just the multitudinous universe but also the multitudes of his fellow men. With the transfer of intellectual authority to the mass, opinion gains a power it had not previously possessed (*DAII* 1.2). The end of studious idleness as a result of the universal injunction to work means that the few who have a taste for higher studies may lack the opportunity for it, while those who acquire the opportunity may have lost the taste. The restless mobility of the democratic social state forsakes fixed ideas for the bewildering swirl of amorphous opinion, which Tocqueville compares in a fine metaphor to "intellectual dust, blown about by every wind and unable to coalesce into any fixed shape."[31]

What, then, was the point of a new political science, if ideas commanded so little authority, if their imprecision led to error rather than insight, and if reason in the best of cases was dwarfed by immense and dimly understood forces and combated within the bosom of man himself by the power of the passions? Let me say in advance where I am headed: the new political science, I believe, was intended to direct the new political art, whose purpose was to shape man's instincts, for when the light of reason fails and circumstances are unprecedented, instinct is all that man possesses to set himself on the right course.

Several passages from Pascal bear on this point. Let me enumerate them first, then gloss them in an effort to suggest how Tocqueville transformed Pascal's thoughts. Pascal tells us that "two things instruct man by way of his entire nature: instinct and experience. Instinct seems to be aspiration to the good, memory of our primitive perfection; experience is knowledge of our misery and our fall." There is, Pascal says, "intestine warfare in man between reason and the passions;" as a result of this war, those "who wanted peace divided into two sects. Some sought to renounce the passions and become gods; others sought to renounce reason and become brute beasts." "But they were unable to do so. Reason persists always, accusing the baseness and injustice of the passions and disturbing the repose of those who yield to them; and the passions live on in those who would renounce them."

Now, how did Tocqueville read this account of a tragic and inexpugnable doubleness in the soul of man? First, he did not believe that men could purge themselves of their passions and become gods. His contemporary Hegel held that history had carried out such a purification by setting man's reason over against man himself in the form of the bureaucratic state, a human construct that nevertheless presented itself as the embodiment of suprahuman rationality. Marx assigned a similar role to a different actor, the working class, whose interests he assumed to be identical with the interests of man as species. Tocqueville's realism on this point set his thinking on a radically different course that established him for posterity as the principal theoretical adversary of the Hegelian-Marxist understanding, a circumstance that undoubtedly played a part in securing his present classic status. Hence we must pay particular attention, when reading Tocqueville, to words that open up a middle ground between causal forces and human actions. Man, for Tocqueville as for Pascal, is a moral actor, free to raise to consciousness the forces that impinge on him and to choose his course in relation to his understanding of his situation; yet if he is free in principle to achieve a proper understanding of his interest, he often fails to do so in practice. This failure defines his fallen state.

Second, Tocqueville agreed with Pascal about the instructive value of instinct and experience. Pay particular attention to the former word, instinct. It occurs in no fewer than forty nine of the eighty three chapters of *Democracy in America*. Tocqueville uses it in its etymological sense, meaning "instigation, impulse, or prompting." There was originally no connotation of innateness, and in fact Tocqueville speaks in some places of instincts as things that can be acquired or that depend on society for their nurturing, so clearly he does not assume that instincts are inborn and immutable.[32] This original meaning was still current in Tocqueville's French. He shared it in fact with those "materialist philosophers" whose hostility to religion made them his enemies. Pierre Naville, a student of the writings of the Baron d'Holbach, remarks that "d'Holbach emphasizes above all the acquired character of what is called instinct (physical or moral)."[33] Furthermore, he is keen to show that "moral instincts – what we would call penchants, dispositions, attitudes, behaviors – are no more 'innate' than physical instincts."[34]

Now, I've compiled a long list of passages in which Tocqueville uses the word "instinct". I won't enumerate them all. Instead I'll summarize the varied and even contradictory ways in which

Tocqueville uses the word. Several themes stand out. They are not consistent with one another, and in certain places Tocqueville will emphasize one connotation of the term and suppress others.

First, he sometimes sets instinct in opposition to reason, just as Pascal does. Reason is light; it sees. Instinct is blind. Reason reflects upon itself and is cold or calculating, instinct warm and passionate and immediate. Thus the purpose of *Democracy in America* is to "substitute ... understanding of true interests for blind instinct."[35] "Egoism is born of blind instinct."[36] Yet Tocqueville can also say that "what was calculation becomes instinct."[37] This last quote suggests a narrowing or bridging of the gap between instinct and reason such as we find already in d'Holbach, who wrote that "to have instinct (*avoir de l'instinct*) means simply to judge promptly and without need of lengthy argument."[38]

Second, instinct, as for the materialists, is associated with an array of other unreflective motivations such as taste, thirst, passion, character, tendency, predilection, proclivity. All are forms of what Aristotle would call disposition, consequences of the way a thing is constituted, of the nature or arrangement of its parts. "The majority ... often has the tastes and instincts of a despot."[39] Students of the law acquire "a taste for forms and a sort of instinctive love of regular sequence in ideas."[40] "A taste for the tangible and the real ... as well as contempt for traditions and forms" are "general instincts" of individuals living in conditions of equality.[41]

Third, when it comes to indicating the strength of instincts relative to other motives for action such as reason, interest, or opinion, Tocqueville speaks in two distinctly different registers. Sometimes an instinct is a weak form of desire, an attenuated passion. These are the passages in which he associates instinct with taste and its cousins. At other times, however, instinct is an all but irresistible force, a drive not unlike the drives or instincts in Freud or concupiscence in Aristotle. Tocqueville doesn't speak of subconscious drives but he does attach great importance to "secret instincts."[42] "All bodies ... harbor a secret instinct that impels them toward independence."[43] Nothing is "more contrary to nature and to the secret instincts of the human heart" than the subjection of a people to a noble caste.[44]

Fourth, instinct is a force that reason or spirit or cunning may choose either to resist or to enlist. "Religion, by respecting all democratic instincts not hostile to it and by enlisting some of them in its own behalf, successfully struggles against the spirit of individual independence, which is for it the most dangerous."[45] "Suppose that a man ... resists instinct at every turn and coldly calculates all the actions of his life."[46] There can be "constant tension" between "the instincts to which equality gives rise and the means it provides for their satisfaction," and this tension "torments and tires the soul."[47]

Fifth, man is part brute, part angel, and in the contest between the two, the instincts are ambivalent: "The instinct and taste of the human race support this doctrine" of spiritualism and "often save it from men themselves,"[48] yet men also "lapse easily into that state of complete and brutish indifference to the future that is only too consistent with certain instincts of the human species."[49]

Finally, we must consider the temporal nature of instincts. Are they durable dispositions, properties of a thing's nature, intrinsic qualities, as Tocqueville's language sometimes suggests? Or are they, as he implies elsewhere, like certain passions: products of circumstance, transitory, inconstant? "Democratic instincts were awakened."[50] "Parties are an evil inherent in free governments, but their character and instincts are not always the same."[51] "The periodical press seems to me to have instincts and passions of its own, independent of the circumstances in which it operates."[52] "When opinions are in doubt, people end up relying on instinct and material interest to guide them."[53] But it is difficult to judge the "permanent instincts of democracy."[54] As often as not, instinct occupies a middle position: it is like love, at once circumstantial and durable. Indeed, "instinctive love" of one's country "stems primarily from the immediate, disinterested, indefinable sentiment that ties a man's heart to the place where he was born." It is a "habit" and "attached to memories." As such it links up with another key term in Tocqueville, mores, whose definition he says he takes from the Ancients: "I apply [the term] not only to mores in the strict sense, what one might call habits of the heart, but also to the various notions that men possess, to the diverse opinions that are current among them, and to the whole range of ideas that shape habits of the mind." Instincts, then, are in this guise like mores in the strict sense, "habits of the heart," quasi-durable and unreflective dispositions to act in certain ways, yet subject to modification by a range of notions, opinions, and ideas, which together determine "habits of the mind."[55]

To sum up, the word instinct conjures up for Tocqueville the Pascalian ambiguity, uncertainty, and doubleness of man's situation. Reason by itself is too feeble an instrument to guide him in life's storms. He must use reason wherever he can, but, knowing in advance that it may fail him in crucial moments, he must live his life and constitute his society in such a way as to cultivate those instincts most likely to save him when reason fails.

V. INSTINCT AND ART

The new political art is needed precisely in order to accomplish this, to prepare both hearts and minds for those tests that reason cannot altogether foresee. How is this to be done? Tocqueville's answers are characteristically nuanced and frustratingly scattered throughout his text. He envisions for society times of stability and times of instability. Instinct is likely to be tenacious, opinions and ideas more volatile but by the same token more supple and adaptable. Hence one might be well advised to place confidence in instincts during times of stability and in ideas in times of flux. But flux can be so rapid as to cloud the mind and discourage the heart. In such dark times, neither instinct nor reason can be counted on, but the legislator instructed in the new political science may seek to order the parts of a polity in such a way that its instincts in the face of unforeseen circumstance offer it the best chance of survival. Here I must allow myself to quote Tocqueville at greater length:

In the life of a nation ... there may come a time when ancient customs are transformed, mores decay, faiths are shaken, memories lose their prestige, but enlightenment has yet to complete its work and political rights remain insecure or limited. At such times the only light in which men can see their country is a feeble and dubious one. Patriotic feeling no longer attaches to the soil, which to the people who live on it has become mere inanimate earth; or to ancestral customs, which they have learned to see as confining; or to religion, of which they are skeptical; or to the laws, which they do not make; or to the lawmaker, whom they fear and despise. Hence they cannot see their country anywhere, in either its proper guise or any other, and they withdraw into narrow, unenlightened selfishness. They have escaped prejudice but not yet embraced the empire of reason. Lacking both the instinctive patriotism of monarchy and the considered patriotism of a republic, they find themselves stuck somewhere between the two, surrounded by confusion and misery.[56]

Deprived of the guidance of both instinct and enlightenment, man is rudderless. In such a predicament, a conservative might be expected to appeal to traditional values, to invoke the need for order, to rely on prescriptive authority. Tocqueville's proposal may therefore surprise those who think of him as a conservative:

What to do in such a situation? Retreat. But nations no more revert to the sentiments of their youth than do men to the innocent desires of childhood. Though they may long to feel such feelings again, nothing can revive them. So there is no choice but to proceed forthrightly and with all deliberate speed to make the case that the interests of individuals and of the nation are inextricably intertwined, because disinterested love of country has vanished forever.

Far be it from me to suggest that in order to achieve this end, full political rights must immediately be granted to all men. Nevertheless, the most powerful way of persuading men that they have a stake in their country's fate, and perhaps the only way still available to us, is to see to it that they participate in its government. The civic spirit today seems to me intimately intertwined with the exercise of political rights, and I think that from now on the number of citizens in Europe will rise and fall in proportion to the extension of such rights.[57]

If instinct fails in a crisis that unfolds more rapidly than reason can grasp it, disaster follows. It is therefore prudent for political science to nurture healthy instincts in the citizenry before crisis strikes. To accomplish this, interest must be properly understood, by which I mean, and I think Tocqueville meant, that the way in which interests arise out of instincts, and hence the link between the core of the self and its rational expressions, is central to the art of politics. Tocqueville wants no part of Burke's contempt for reform, even if he shares Burke's scorn for those reformers who think they can lead the herd by feeding its appetites. He believes that men can be educated not by a direct application of reason – not by abstract argument or manipulative calculation – but by participation in a polity contrived by reason to nurture true instincts. Once confronted with the practical problems of government, men will see, concretely, that "they have a stake in their country's fate." Their instincts will be modified accordingly – instincts in the sense of tastes. In the language of neoclassical economics – the intellectual heir of that materialist utilitarianism that Tocqueville greeted initially not with Burkean sarcasm but with the irony of the moralists of *l'âge classique* – their schedule of preferences will change, and hence their interests. So interest, an abstract that which in Tocqueville's lexicon starts out on the side of calculation and Cartesian reason, is drawn by the art of politics to the side of virtue, to the idea of a conscious and deliberate fashioning of the self. It is not simply that the sphere of private interest is "enlarged" to encompass the public interest. At the same time, the public spirit is compressed and concentrated in the individual mind. The soul of democratic man undergoes modification through his participation in government. Just as, in the democratic family, "habit and need" foster "intimacy" between father and sons that "makes the father's authority less absolute"[58] but develops a new and vital family instinct unknown in aristocratic society, so too can the legislator craft laws intended to develop new instincts in the citizens of a democracy.

Let me return now to translation. The transition may seem abrupt, but there is, I believe, a connection between the art of politics and the art of translation. Tocqueville wrote that "the legislator is like a navigator on the high seas. He can steer the vessel on which he sails, but he cannot alter its construction, raise the wind, or stop the ocean from swelling beneath his feet."[59] The translator finds himself in a similar predicament. Whatever his preparation for his task may be, he cannot bring to the text precisely the same presuppositions as the author. He cannot alter the construction of the work, but he can study its most minute details. He can prepare himself as well by exploring many other texts before facing the challenge. In confronting a classic, he will also need to take account of the winds of conflicting interpretation that blow from every quarter of the compass. But in the moment, with the blank page before him and all his prior reading and translating stretched out behind him like a wake on the surface of the sea, and all the swirling maelstrom of commentary set to one side, he has only his instinct to rely on. He is, if I may presume to make a rather grandiose comparison, like the statesman in a moment of crisis. Argument, explication, criticism, comparison – the tools of reason – all these are occupations for dry land. Instinct is not much of a defense for his spur-of-the-moment decisions unless he arrives safely in port. And that, ultimately, is not in his power to decide, any more than it is in the power of the legislator to divine what fate holds in store for the people whose instincts he has tried to shape, to make ready for every contingency.

So I have written at some length only to tell you that in the end I translated one phrase, "self-interest properly understood," exactly as one of my predecessors did, and that despite the complex web of meanings and allusions that Tocqueville wove around the word instinct, I felt I had no choice but to translate it by its misleading English cognate. Here you see what is so humbling about the work of the translator. He has to wear his learning so lightly that he is likely to appear naked, and in the end he must rely on his own instincts to do the right thing and on the instincts of his readers to divine when he has done so. Translation is thus an act of faith, or at any rate the simulation of faith. For unless one has faith that in translating it is possible to do better than literal transcription, one won't do better. Recall Tocqueville's own words, which echo the wager of Pascal:

What I am about to say will do me no good in the eyes of politicians. I believe that the only effective way for governments to honor the dogma of the immortality of the soul is to act every day as though they believed in it themselves. And I believe that it is only by conforming scrupulously to religious morality in great affairs that they can boast of teaching citizens to know it, love it, and respect it in small ones.[60]

Similarly, what I am about to say will do me no good in the eyes of my critics, but if the translator truly wishes to honor the notion that the work before him is a classic, that it has the power to instruct, to inspire, to command respect, he must translate as though he believed it. He must not, while professing humility, imperiously strip the work of the mystique from which it derives its immortality. If, as Pascal says, "instinct seems to be aspiration to the good," the denial of instinct is wrong, the insistence on method a trap, and the repudiation of freedom a betrayal that would leave mastery exclusively to the masters of a method sanctioned only by themselves. Classicism properly understood isn't a constraint; it's a liberation.

NOTES

1 A somewhat different version of this chapter appeared in *The Tocqueville Review/La Revue Tocqueville* 24 (1): 2004. I would like to thank David Bell, Daniel Gordon, Patrice Higonnet, Stanley Hoffmann, Sophia Rosenfeld, Steven Vincent, Cheryl Welch, and Olivier Zunz for helpful comments on earlier versions.

2 James Schleifer, *The Making of Tocqueville's "Democracy in America"* (Chapel Hill, NC: University of North Carolina Press, 1980), 26.

3 André Jardin, *Alexis de Tocqueville* (Paris: Hachette, 1984), 44.

4 *DAI* 1.1 (trans. Goldhammer), 25. All subsequent citations to *Democracy in America* without attribution are to my translation.

5 The French is: "Ainsi la mort venait en quelque sorte y aider à la vie." Bradley has: "Thus decay gave its assistance to life." Lawrence: "Thus death in some way helped life forward." Mansfield and Winthrop: "Thus death came in a way to the aid of life."

6 *DAII* 3.11, *Œuvres*, P 718.

7 Leo Strauss, *Thoughts on Machiavelli* (Chicago: The University of Chicago Press, 1958), 14.

8 See, in the Mansfield-Winthrop translation of *Democracy in America*, "A Note on the Translation," xci–xciii, and especially Harvey C. Mansfield and Delba Winthrop, "Translating Tocqueville's *Democracy in America*," *The Tocqueville Review* 21 (1) 2000: 155. Cf. my "Remarks on the Mansfield-Winthrop Translation," *French Politics, Culture & Society* 21 (1) 2003:110 (available on-line at http://www.people.fas. harvard.edu/~agoldham/articles/Mansfield.htm), and Harvey C. Mansfield and Delba Winthrop, "Reply to Our Critics," ibid., 139.

9 Cheryl Welch, *De Tocqueville* (Oxford: Oxford University Press, 2001), 245: "Some of the most penetrating American scholarship ... on Tocqueville's thought has been produced by political theorists who identify with Strauss's approach to the study of political philosophy."

10 Françoise Mélonio, *Tocqueville et les Français* (Paris: Aubier, 1993).

11 Letter from Tocqueville to Henry Reeve, October 15, 1839; *OC* 6.1, 48.

12 There is also a third new translation by Gerald E. Bevan, published by Penguin, which I have not yet examined in any detail.

13 Mansfield and Winthrop, xci: "A book as great as Tocqueville's should inspire a certain reverence in translators."

14 J. Schleifer, *Making*, 237.

15 Jon Elster, *Alchemies of the Mind: Rationality and the Emotions* (Cambridge, England: Cambridge University Press, 1999), 91.

16 Isaiah Berlin, *Freedom and Its Betrayal: Six Enemies of Human Liberty* (Princeton: Princeton University Press, 2002), 20: "Bentham was a complete disciple of Helvétius, and although the word 'utilitarianism' is normally associated with him, I think it is fair to say that there is little – among the cardinal ideas, at least – in Bentham which does not stem directly from Helvétius."

17 Interesting comments on the topics discussed in the rest of this essay can be found, with somewhat different emphases, in the influential work of Albert Hirschman, *The Passions and the Interests* (Princeton: Princeton University Press, 1977), and Stephen Holmes, *Passions and Constraints: On the Theory of Liberal Democracy* (Chicago: The University of Chicago Press, 1995), 42–68.

18 Robert Gannett, *Tocqueville Unveiled* (Chicago: The University of Chicago Press, 2003), 60–77, argues persuasively that Tocqueville did not read Burke carefully until the early 1850s. My argument here does not depend on his having read Burke but only on his instinctive opposition to the position that Burke imputes to reformers in order to reject it.

19 Mansfield-Winthrop translation, 501 n.

20 Edmund Burke, *Reflections on the Revolution in France*, par. 271.

21 *DAI* 2.6, 270.

22 *DAII* 2.8, 613.

23 *DAII* 2.8, 610.

24 *DAI* 1.5, 106.

25 S. Holmes, *Passions and Constraints*, 66.

26 Strauss, *Thought on Machiavelli*, 11.

27 *DAII* 1.16, 553.

28 *DAII* 1.1, 483.

29 Also: "Nor can the inhabitants of such a society derive their beliefs from the opinions of the class to which they belong, because in a sense there are no longer classes, and those that do still exist are so variable in their composition that the body can never exert any real power over its members."

30 *DAII* 1.2, 490.

31 *DAII* 1.1, 487.

32 The suggestion of innateness probably grew out of the use of the word as a verb. The *OED*, for example, cites this sentence from 1549: "The good simple people of the olde golden worlde ... lived onely as Nature taught and instincted them." Hence it was the idea that nature prompts people to act in certain ways that gave rise to the notion of

instinct as an innate prompting, an instigation by nature. The original sense vanished from English some time after 1730, the date of the last example given in this sense by the *OED*.

33 Pierre Naville, *D'Holbach et la philosophie scientifique au XVIIIe siècle* (Paris: Gallimard, 1967), 285.

34 Ibid., 289.

35 *DAI*, Introduction, 7.

36 *DAII* 2.2, 585.

37 *DAII* 2.4, 594. Other examples: The American revolution stemmed from "a mature, reflective preference for liberty and not a vague, indefinite instinct for independence" (*DAI* 1.5). "Instinctive love" of country is an "unreflective passion" that can be contrasted with "another, more rational form of patriotism" (*DAI* 2.6).

38 Ibid., 289, quoting d'Holbach, *Système de la nature*, vol. 2, 38.

39 *DAI* 2.8, 301.

40 *DAI* 2.8, 303.

41 *DAII* 1.10, 522. Other examples: Man exhibits "both a natural disgust for existence and an overwhelming desire to exist. ... These divergent instincts constantly compel his soul to contemplate the other world" (*DAI* 2.9). Men in aristocratic societies "feel an instinctive distaste" for general ideas (*DAII* 1.3).

42 Other examples: "The patriotic instinct" is "a powerful force in the heart of man" (I 1.8). Instinctive love of country "inspires great but transitory efforts rather than persistent ones" (I 2.6). "As long as a religion draws its strength from sentiments, instincts, and pas-sions ... it can resist the work of time" (*DAI* 2.9). "What keeps large numbers of citizens subject to the same government is much less the rational determination to remain united than the instinctive and in some sense involuntary accord that results from similarity of feeling and likeness of opinion" (*DAI* 2.10). The President is "encouraged in his vendetta ... by his sense that the majority with its secret instincts supports him" (*DAI* 2.10). Jackson obeys the "half-divulged instincts" of the majority, "anticipating its desires before it knows what they are" (*DAI* 2.10).

43 *DAI* 2.10, 445.

44 *DAI* 2.10, 461.

45 *DAII* 1.5, 509.

46 *DAII* 2.9, 615.

47 *DAII* 2.13, 627.

48 *DAII* 2.15, 636.

49 *DAII* 2.17, 639.

50 *DAI* 1.3, 53.

166   ARTHUR GOLDHAMMER

51 *DAI* 2.2, 198.
52 *DAI* 2.3, 208.
53 *DAI* 2.3, 214.
54 *DAI* 2.5, 224.
55 *DAI* 2.9, 331.
56 *DAI* 2.6, 270.
57 Ibid.
58 *DAII* 3.8, 688.
59 *DAI* 1.8, 185.
60 *DAII* 2.15, 637.

7 The Writer Engagé
Tocqueville and Political Rhetoric

Translated by Arthur Goldhammer

"The overwhelming fact of our time – the advent of democracy – changes the conditions of the revelation of ideas." So said Victor de Laprade, a poet, critic, and admirer of Lamartine whose name has passed into oblivion.[1] Nevertheless, his 1843 formulation precisely captures the question that Tocqueville faced in *Democracy in America*, and which he answered in a style different from that of both the great "romantic magi" and "the school of disenchantment," to use Paul Bénichou's categories. His style differed as well from that of his colleagues in liberalism: Guizot, Cousin, and, from an earlier time, the liberals of Coppet, even though he aspired as they did to a role as enlightened guide of public opinion. With the July Revolution – after which the waggish Jules Janin[2] described a scene in which Lamartine had "retired from the world of poetics" to become a deputy; Carrel, "the finest pupil of Tacitus," had moved into journalism after renouncing history; and Guizot and Villemain wielded power as ministers – the liberal illusion of a harmonious union of "literature" (or "science") with political institutions and a revolutionized society faced a crisis brought on by the test of power. *Democracy in America* echoed these doubts: indeed, the treatise pondered the implosion in France of the liberal philosophy that called itself, in the words of Victor Cousin, a philosophy of "the true, the beautiful, and the good" and that had been elaborated with unwavering concern for the benefits it might yield for society.

Nevertheless, Tocqueville, to whom the events of 1830 had made concrete the meaning of historical change and the urgent need for thinking about democracy,[3] did not give up on intellectual liberalism's earlier aspirations. *Democracy in America* was an attempt to renew the conceptual framework without abandoning the original impetus, especially that of forging a style capable of combining thought and action, of imparting knowledge while simultaneously shaping the world. Yet the work also shows that Tocqueville was tempted to escape into philosophy, to flee the constraints imposed by democratic public space and by rhetoric, the art of persuasion. For Tocqueville constantly faced a terrible paradox: in order to conceptualize democracy, one must leave the city, yet only in the city is action permitted. His *Recollections* of the revolution of 1848 and the Second Republic, written when France was on the brink of collapsing into yet another authoritarian regime, literally enacted his retreat into the antirhetoric of an autobiographical text. Written for himself and destined to be published only posthumously, these memoirs expressed Tocqueville's (temporary) removal from the scene of political action, his refusal to ascribe to the event a meaning intelligible to all, and the tragic failure of his public language.

I. LIBERAL RHETORICS

Liberalism in early nineteenth-century France certainly cannot be reduced to a unified body of doctrine: Lucien Jaume has demonstrated this in exemplary fashion in his book on "the elided individual,"[4] in which he distinguishes three schools: the individualist liberalism of Benjamin Constant, the state liberalism of François Guizot, and the liberal Catholicism of Lamennais, Montalembert, and Lacordaire. Nevertheless, there was a liberal style of thought, and Tocqueville (who is difficult to categorize in terms of this classification) shared in it. Indeed, it is easy to associate the Tocqueville of *Democracy in America* with the ambitions of intellectual liberalism as Rémusat still defined them in 1847 in the preface to *Passé et présent*:

Simultaneously to explain a great historical event and legitimate the results, reveal and found institutions, set the tone of a real epoch and a real society, and yet maintain, in the realm of the true, the beautiful, and the abstract, that detachment from everything that is merely useful and evanescent, that disinterested loftiness, which is characteristic of science and art itself.[5]

Beyond this agenda, one must add the link that the liberals wanted to establish between political thought and political action. Tocqueville also declined to divorce the scholar from the politician. That is why *Democracy in America* must be read as an argumentative text that is as much concerned with consolidating the contemporary political understanding of democracy, the key to the present and the future, as with rallying an expanded public in support of liberal democracy and laying the groundwork for the institutional reforms needed to allow France to make the transition to democracy without untoward incident – in other words, without another revolution. Thus Tocqueville's "political science" was invested with the same civic function that Madame de Staël assigned to "literature" in the broadest sense: "Everything that ultimately touches on the exercise of thought in writing."[6] This was a useful science, and the very one that Guizot identified with history at the end of the first lecture of his course on "The History of Civilization in France":

For us, what is at stake is something quite different from knowledge. - ... Science is beautiful, no doubt, and in itself worthy of man's labors, but it is a thousand times more beautiful when it becomes a potent force (*une puissance*) and engenders virtue. That, Gentlemen, is what we need to make it: we need to discover the truth and give it outward reality, in external facts, for the benefit of society.[7]

Tocqueville, in the role he attributed to "science" and "literature" in post-revolutionary society, was indisputably the heir of the Coppet liberals and the *doctrinaires* of the Restoration, and, like them, he aspired to act concretely on representative institutions, such as those that the liberal revolution of 1789 gave to France. Though perhaps a man of letters and surely a writer and thinker, Tocqueville nevertheless aspired to political action, the mature form of his commitment. While immersed for eight years in the writing of his great work, he simultaneously sought election as a deputy in the Chamber, a position he finally achieved in 1839. Whatever disappointments he may have met with in the political swamps of the July Monarchy, it should never be forgotten that in his eyes the duty to serve always outweighed the rewards of intellectual work and the gratifications of authorship. In 1837 he wrote to Louis de Kergorlay: "Do not suppose, my dear friend, that I suffer from any reckless enthusiasm for the intellectual life. I have always placed action above everything else."[8]

Tocqueville was wary of a "republic of professors" in the form already imagined by the Idéologues at the end of the Revolution. "The institution of reason," or the grand project of educating the people by shaping an enlightened public opinion through the Ecoles Normales, was not enough to form citizens in the way Tocqueville imagined. The contemporary example of Guizot as a reformer of elementary education also demonstrated the limits of the educational system, from the standpoint not of knowledge but of liberty. Nor was Tocqueville in the same camp as Michelet and Quinet, republicans who from their chairs at the Collège de France would promote a definition of democracy very different from his liberal, Catholic, and Americanist one. For Tocqueville, the citizen's apprenticeship took place not in the classroom but in the "free schools" offered by local government and jury service – that is, in the habit of practical and frequent participation in "democratic institutions." It was through this metaphor, then, that he appropriated Enlightenment ambitions for political pedagogy and adhered to the ideal of practical reason in the hope of educating the new sovereign. In this respect, *Democracy in America*, rightly belongs in the category of "democratic" discourse associated with the "political *Aufklärung*," in which the relation between elite and people, orator and audience, writer and readers is "of the pedagogical type."[9] Hence the often monitory figure of the author in the treatise and the very insistent presence of the "reader" or addressee who is repeatedly invoked and exhorted with much solicitude to follow the arguments, though the more subtle of them will largely escape the majority in any case. In the sometimes tiresome repetitions of *Democracy in America* we see all the modesty of a teacher eager to make himself understood and all the determination of a rhetorician for whom, by his own admission, the value of his book will be measured by its power to convince, and to convince broadly.

"The realm of the true, the beautiful, and the abstract." In the program that Tocqueville set for himself in 1835, "to teach and impart morality to democracy," the constitution of political knowledge and its transmission to the public go hand in hand, for Tocqueville as for Rémusat and Mme de Staël, with the establishment of a morality as the indispensable premise of the new science of government. "Let us therefore, to begin with, establish morality as a fixed point."[10] For liberals, standing firm on aesthetics (the realm of "the beautiful") also meant refusing to reduce knowledge to either the calculus of social probabilities (with which the Idéologues had sought to impede revolutionary madness) or art and literature (which they saw as inexact representations, couched in metaphor and symbol). The strictness of style, in Tocqueville as in Rémusat, is at times merely a polite concession to the taste of the time. In this rhetoric, where, as in all rhetoric, the point is to "marshal men by marshaling words,"[11] the ornaments are chosen as a function of their capacity to persuade, and images for the most part are used as needed to further the argument. Yet Tocqueville was not so naïve as to believe in the literal, and in that respect his preoccupations were "literary." He knew that language was problematic, and he devoted to this subject an entire chapter of the second book of *Democracy*, in which we find him exploring the "democratic" tendency to generalize the use of abstract words.

What degree of abstraction to adopt? Where exactly to situate oneself in the "realm of the abstract"? This question, which Tocqueville is forced to face as he tries to reshape traditional concepts, is intimately intertwined with any intellectual venture. Yet it takes on a particular coloration when a body of knowledge is conceived as an educational curriculum, when it seeks to impose a shape on reality and give meaning to the collective destiny, or as Tocqueville, whose imagination found it easier to depict the negative than the positive, put it, "to indicate if possible ... how it is possible to escape tyranny and bastardization by becoming democratic."[12]

Under a variety of names, the problem of abstraction obsessed the minds of thinkers during and after the Revolution, when "abuse of language" – and first and foremost of the word "equality" – was common, according to analysts as diverse as Volney, Laharpe, Sébastien Mercier, and Mme de Staël. Liberals did not renounce reason on the grounds that it sometimes went awry, as we see from the fact that Constant devoted a chapter of *Des réactions politiques*

(1797) to defending and demonstrating its principles. They were nevertheless wary of all abstract metaphysics, especially when it touched on the science of government, because philosophical radicalism and revolutionary extremism joined to advocate wiping the slate clean. That is why the liberals' recognition of their debt to the Enlightenment philosophy that inspired 1789 was always accompanied by cautions as to the socio-historical conditions under which the thought of the *philosophes* was elaborated: "Actions and texts must be judged according to their date," wrote Mme de Staël.[13] She pardoned Rousseau for his theoretical audacity on the grounds that he was a stranger to real politics, but she censured statesmen for having taken the spirit of *The Social Contract* literally. Even as she was importing German idealism into France, she continued, in writing *Considérations*, to believe that "in fiction one is right to be original, but when real institutions are involved, one is only too glad if they enjoy the warrant of experience."[14] Tocqueville echoes these sentiments in a chapter of the second book of *Democracy* devoted to the French passion for "general ideas in political matters." After briefly establishing the genealogy of this passion – the "imaginary democracy" in which an entire century indulged, as he would later put it in *The Old Regime and the Revolution* – he recommended "experience" instead:

On any subject about which it is particularly dangerous for democratic peoples to embrace general ideas blindly and over-enthusiastically, the best corrective is to make sure that they deal with that subject in a practical manner on a daily basis. Then they will have no choice but to delve into the details, and the details will reveal the weak points in the theory.[15]

II. THE IMPENDING SEPARATION OF PRACTICES

The holy alliance between thought and action in the man and the work; the confidence, however qualified, in the virtues of explanatory pedagogy; morality as the "fixed point"; rigor of style and faith in ideas – Tocquevillean rhetoric involves all these things. What one saw after 1830, however, was, for a conservative like Nisard, a flight of all "serious" talent into politics; for Sainte-Beuve it was a "wholesale shift of forces."[16] For others, these literary realignments portended a breath of fresh air for romanticism, while the frantic jockeying for position among writers who had formerly contributed to the newspaper *Le Globe* came as a revelation of the bourgeoisie's will to power. This crisis of intellectual liberalism after 1830 formed the backdrop against which Tocqueville wrote, at a time when "this conjunction, or, rather, this coalescence of the political, the literary, and the philosophical" that had characterized the liberal position since the Empire was coming undone.[17] On the one hand, Tocqueville rejected "Parnassian" liberalism.[18] He refused to fall back haughtily on pure philosophy, thereby rejecting the advice of Royer-Collard, who stood as a living embodiment of the bad conscience of July Monarchy liberalism. On the other hand, he was no more willing to accommodate to the liberalism of compromise represented by Guizot, Rémusat, and Cousin – the old avant-garde, who now claimed to have stopped history in its tracks. It was this uncomfortable – and marginal – position that gave rise to the analysis in *Democracy in America*, which anticipates and explores as a problem the impending separation of three distinct types of practice: literature, scientific discourse, and political eloquence.

As Françoise Douay-Soublin has ably demonstrated in her work on nineteenth-century rhetoric, under the July Monarchy, and indeed for some time after 1848, the word "literature" still signified "the entire range of oral and written utterances possessing some importance for our collective destiny, whether political or cultural."[19] Nevertheless, the relation of Tocqueville "the writer" to literature is problematic, or, rather, paradoxical, when he characterizes his mission as a "holy occupation" in terms quite close, in effect, to a "lay vocation,"[20] while at the same time envisioning the desacralization of the writer by democratic society. There is nothing very original in his attacks on the absence of style in journalists, the proliferation of "salesmen of ideas," the "industrial" future of literature, or the oddities of the Romantics, and to anyone familiar with the philippics of the time against "facile literature" and "literary democracy," the strictures in *Democracy in America* will seem rather mild.[21] By contrast, his analyses of political eloquence and the language of democracy are more innovative, and from them it emerges that, for Tocqueville, the writer can no longer be the republic's designated orator or even an authority with the power to lay down the law in matters of language and style. Literature had not disappeared from democratic society, and Tocqueville, countering the pessimists, argued that the Americans "will have one in the end." Against the Staëlian ideal of the great man as commentator on public affairs, and against the Romantic image of the leader of men or spokesman for the people, he offered the modest person of the democratic representative chosen by the suffrage of a majority of people just like himself – far indeed from brilliant or sublime. He also showed how democracy inevitably relegates literature to the rank of one form of language *among others*, the extreme opposite of the magisterial ambitions that literature conceived for itself in France when it "sacralized" the figure of the writer-orator.

In so doing, Tocqueville dethroned himself, of course, and introduced suspicion at the heart of his enterprise, which also explains the distance maintained throughout the treatise by irony, which had become the refuge of elite souls – distance from a society that seemed indifferent to the values of culture without actually denying them. The mix of styles that Tocqueville noted in American language – a mix of what Kenneth Cmiel calls "middling styles"[22] quite characteristic of new ways of speaking, which were attacked in America itself by the cultivated English elite – proved to his satisfaction that democracy is serenely indifferent to taste. And what was "taste" for Mme de Staël if not the virtue that preserved a person from the "vulgarity" and violence of the people as well as the faculty of articulating the beautiful and the good in the language of the orator, the writer, and the statesman? The absence of style and confusion of genres in egalitarian societies made it difficult for liberals to conceptualize the combination of aesthetics and morality other than as "classics," for they refused to admit that a new art, and therefore a different morality, could originate in a mix of high and low.

In *Democracy in America*, Tocqueville nevertheless came close to renouncing, in theory at any rate, the stylistic proprieties that democracy violated ("Harmony and homogeneity are only secondary beauties of language. These qualities are largely matters of convention, and if necessary one can do without then").[23] But his obvious incomprehension of Romanticism betrays his resistance to other mixtures, of elite and people, of aristocracy and mob: to convince oneself of this, one has only to reread the accounts of the writer's encounters with insurgents in his *Recollections* of 1848. In any case, there is a great risk of seeing the exaltation of morality degraded into a defense of good manners, a danger that Tocqueville barely avoids thanks to his Pascalian vision of the human. Yet he fails to paint morality in colors other than those of utility when he transposes Montesquieu's republican virtue into the American morality of "self-interest properly understood": "In the United States, people rarely say that virtue is beautiful. They maintain that it is useful, and give proof of this daily."[24] He does so unenthusiastically but resolutely, since puritanical and religious America gives itself as an example of a society in which enlightenment and social pressure serve as guarantees of civil order and bulwarks of political liberty.

What was truly demoralizing, by contrast, was the spectacle of "universal relief and abject groveling that followed the July Revolution."[25] The great political role that Tocqueville had dreamed of playing in the Chamber ended in some minor, if at times rather acidulous, verbal skirmishes with Thiers and Guizot, since he lacked his rivals' oratorical gifts, and the link between thought and action, which can truly be realized only through the eloquence of the rostrum, could not be maintained without those gifts. The *Recollections* offered a melancholy assessment:

The profession of writer and the profession of orator are more harmful to each other than helpful. Nothing resembles a good speech less than a good chapter. I soon noticed this, and I saw clearly that I was counted among the speakers judged to be correct, clever, and sometimes profound but always chilly and consequently powerless. ... Eventually I also discovered that I totally lacked the art necessary to attract and lead a group of people. I have never been able to boast of dexterity except in tête-à-tête conversation and have always found myself uneasy and silent in a crowd.[26]

Whether accidents of genius or genuinely troubling ineptitude, the difficulties that Tocqueville encountered as a public speaker and leader of men, or even of fellow deputies, transformed him in spite of himself into an "observant philosopher"[27] of public life under the July Monarchy. That is why the real duel with Guizot, his leader, took place over *Democracy* and on abstract ground, "for is it not thought, in the most immaterial forms, that has continually roiled the world for the past three centuries, and is not writing still a powerful way of acting?"[28] It is no accident that the theme of abstraction affords Tocqueville the opportunity for a fine flourish when, in the chapter on language, he denounces democratic writers who abuse generic terms: "They will say things like, 'Circumstances require that capacities must govern.' "[29] Here we recognize a statement typical of the wooden language of Reason as wielded by Guizot, the former professor who, after 1830, went from being the theorist of the middle classes during the Restoration to acting as their spokesman. In the political rhetoric of the bourgeois monarchy, Tocqueville encountered words that were like "boxes with a false bottom," abstract words like political *capacities*, which government could define to suit itself, and *equality*, to which Tocqueville intentionally gave the broadest possible definition in the certainty that history would not end with the government of the middle classes, nor equality with civil equality ("It is impossible to imagine that equality will not ultimately enter into the world of politics as it enters into everything else").[30] Thus Tocqueville succeeded in conceptualizing the democratic transition precisely because he refused to immobilize the meaning of notions such as equality, rights, and democracy that were part and parcel of the dynamic process initiated by the French Revolution, to which he did not ascribe the same "sense" as Guizot or even Rémusat.

III. THE NARROW ESCAPE INTO PHILOSOPHY

There is no need to reconsider points that have already been amply discussed in the Tocqueville literature: the need to rethink "the equalization of conditions" in a way different from the *doctrinaires*; the dissection of democracy and its reduction to an ideal-type; and its "reversibility," its propensity to move from equality toward either liberty or despotism.[31] On the theme of Tocqueville as "a physician without patients" because he tried to introduce into France a non-native liberalism based on decentralization and the dynamics of association, I refer the reader to Françoise Mélonio's work on the reception of Tocqueville's thought in France.[32] Hence it will suffice to say this about Tocqueville's political concepts: his decanting of inherited notions, along with the poetics of the "thought portrait" that culminates in the ultimate conception of a "mild" democratic despotism and the use of paradox as a privileged

form of the "impracticable" in the realm of ideas, affords him the
flexibility to incorporate even the unthinkable into his treatise: the
unthinkable of a new revolution, which, though refuted in theory,
continually recurs as a possibility; the unthinkable of History,
which occurs even in the *Recollections*, at a time when he was
clinging to the reassuring image of liberty within order ("I am
tempted to believe that what we call necessary institutions are
often only institutions to which we are accustomed, and that in
matters of social constitution, the range of possibility is far wider
than people living in any given society imagine"[33]); and, above all,
the unthinkable of a supreme disillusionment, which he resisted all
his life, except when writing the *Recollections*: the interruption of
the great project of the Enlightenment (on which Rousseau was the
first to cast doubt) – namely, the education of the individual citizen
as the prerequisite of political liberty.

Tocqueville fought this despair and kept disillusionment at bay
by accepting the need for constraints, pedagogical repetitions, and
efforts at definition, because he never lost sight of his objective: to
take his readers in hand until they were prepared to accept the idea
of democracy, to educate them by patiently explaining the workings
of the democratic system and using commonsense arguments to
induce them to accept his logic. Significantly, these self-imposed
requirements on his writing, which were not so different from the
requirements a scholar would face today in writing for a broad
general public, were set aside when it came time to write *The Old
Regime and the Revolution*. They can be called "democratic" to the
extent that they derived from a "political *Aufklärung*": to enlighten
without asserting superiority, to make knowledge explicit by way of
the "common" language as opposed to the jargon of specialists, and
to take account of the reader and his constraining presence, which
requires a complex deployment of the commonplaces of traditional
eloquence.

It is easy to see, however, how Tocqueville's escapes into philosophy in the second *Democracy* may have cost him a good part of
the audience he so earnestly desired, and how naïve he was to offer
his treatise to the voters of Valognes as a token of his political good
faith. Failure was the result: "I sought to paint the general features
of Democratic Societies, of which no complete model yet exists.
This is where the mind of the ordinary reader escapes my grasp.

Only those well-versed in the search for general and speculative truths care to follow me down such a path."[34] In a way, Tocqueville turned the failure of his rhetoric into a theoretical problem when he drew a contrast between the public's willingness to make do with general ideas and the "contemplation of first causes"[35] that is the concern of true "science," or when he explained in the second *Democracy* that the habits of thought are incompatible with the requirements of action: "Long and learned proofs do not determine how the world is run. Quick assessments of specific facts, daily study of the shifting passions of the multitude, momentary chances and the skill to grasp them – these are the things that decide how affairs are dealt with in democratic societies."[36]

Indeed, all of Tocqueville's work could be re-read as a meditation on this contradiction, on which depends the possibility of a mediation between philosophy and the public, or, what comes to the same thing, an articulation of thought, language, and action within a "democratic" society. This emerges more clearly in the dramatic conclusions of the two volumes of *Democracy*, which dramatize distance:

I am nearing the end of my inquiry. In discussing the destiny of the United States, I have tried thus far to divide my subject into parts so as to study each of them with greater care.

Now I would like to look at everything from a single point of view. What I am going to say will be less detailed but more certain. I shall have a less distinct perception of each object but embrace general facts with greater certainty. I shall be like the traveler who, after passing through the gates of a great city, climbs a nearby hill. As he moves away from the city, the people he has just left vanish from his sight. Their houses blur together. He can no longer see the city's public places. He can barely make out the streets. But his eye takes in the city's contours more easily, and for the first time he apprehends its shape. In just this same way, I have the impression now that the whole future of the English race in the New World is taking shape before me. The details of this vast tableau remain in shadow, but my gaze takes it all in, and I conceive a clear idea of the whole.[37]

In the "general view of the subject" that concludes the second *Democracy*, one finds the same contemplative attitude, now stretched out over several pages of similar solemnity. In both cases, Tocqueville follows the same course toward the "general view," where particular facts are banished in favor of prediction and "final" judgment "the new society that I have sought to describe and want to judge."[38] We touch the outer limits of his reasoning, as he predicts the future of the United States and Europe at the end of the first *Democracy* and strives to "enter into [God's] point of view"[39] in the conclusion to the second. Having achieved absolute mastery of his subject, he has clearly attained a solitude that he experiences as a liberation, and the "I" definitively transcends the limits of "the common sense." The ascent of the traveler at the end of the first *Democracy* can thus be read as an escape: Tocqueville sees himself passing through the walls of the city in order to attain a position from which he can no longer see its "public places," as if he literally needed to free himself from the city's confines in order to conceive a "clear idea of the whole."

IV. THE TOCQUEVILLEAN TEMPTATION AND THE "DIVINE POINT OF VIEW"

Thus the whole question comes down to this: must we read the conclusions of the two volumes of *Democracy*, in which the "I" seems to become hypostasized, as Tocqueville's last word upon achieving the position to which he has aspired, that of a prophet "above the fray?" For there appears to remain no commonality whatsoever between the writer who utters these words and the democratic "host" (*foule*): "I cast my eyes upon this innumerable host of similar beings, among whom no one stands out or stoops down."[40] The symbolic elevation of the "I" that ends the first *Democracy* must indeed be seen as the expression of a distance between the self and the world, or, rather, between the self and a not very enticing democratic society. This withdrawal – a withdrawal of both intellection and aversion – leads Tocqueville to a twofold temptation – of secession and nostalgia – at the end of the second *Democracy*: "The sight of such universal uniformity saddens and chills me, and I am tempted to mourn for the society that is no more."[41]

In each of these conclusions, then, Tocqueville undeniably acknowledges his doubts about democratic equality, which reduces everything and everyone to a level that is not the level of intelligence. Tocqueville turns his back on "concrete" democracy, which is too lackluster for his taste; in the end, he could not become democracy's spiritual savant because democracy, in its everyday detail, struck him as uniform and tedious. Sainte-Beuve was accurate when he criticized Tocqueville for failing to "enliven" his subject in the manner of Montesquieu,[42] and perhaps he also remembered Pascal's great lesson in the *Provinciales*, according to which the worldly art of pleasing is inextricably intertwined in rhetoric with the art of persuading: Tocqueville failed to please his "world" and therefore failed to lead it. Though he worked quite ardently for the public good, he was unable or unwilling to depict democracy as something that could be loved, because he did not love it and did not like the men who made it: "There is but one great purpose in this world ... which is the good of mankind. ... I like man in general, but I repeatedly encounter any number of individuals whose baseness I find repellent. My daily efforts tend to protect me from being overwhelmed by universal contempt for my fellow human beings."[43]

Yet the prophetic position taken in the perorations of *Democracy* is by no means a dramatic presentation of a triumph of thought over stupidity or of the native superiority of the author-thinker over the confused masses. It is the most powerful symbol of Tocqueville's withdrawal, of his distance from both democracy and the democratic *Aufklärung*, and therefore of his own contradiction as monitor. For distance here is not the same as lucidity, total clarity of vision, or the apotheosis of reason. This is the additional element contributed by the "general view of the subject" with which the second *Democracy* ends, and which was not so clearly expressed in the conclusion of the first: "vision grows cloudy," "reason falters,"[44] the limitation of the human point of view becomes apparent:

When the world was full of men both very great and very small, very rich and very poor, very learned and very ignorant, I used to avert my gaze from the latter to focus solely on the former, and they gladdened my eyes, but I know that my pleasure was a consequence of my weakness: it is because I cannot take in everything around me at a single glance that I am allowed to choose in this way among so many objects those that it pleases me to contemplate. This is not true of the Almighty Eternal Being, whose eye necessarily encompasses all things and sees the entire human race and each man distinctly yet simultaneously.[45]

Tocqueville strove to enter into the divine point of view,[46] for God grants *equal* value and *equal* dignity to "each man." But he failed, and there is a certain grandeur in his avowal of failure, because he does not succeed in either experiencing superhuman benevolence or conquering the impenetrable totality.

V. THE *RECOLLECTIONS*, OR THE FAILURE OF PUBLIC SPEECH

The *Recollections*, or the vanity of speaking in the present tense: the empty words of the memoirist writing only for himself, in a Rousseau-like gesture of refusal; the empty words of the July Monarchy and its demoralized eloquence; the inability of republican discourse to constitute, in the literal sense of the word, the regime of the Second Republic. In the opening pages, satire is deployed against the reign of Louis-Philippe, whose speech epitomizes an entire era: a "deluge of commonplaces," clumsy improvisations, and inflated rhetoric, a lack of aptitude for dialogue (Tocqueville suffers the consequences of the prince's deafness in a conversation with him about America), and unforgivable grammatical errors and lapses of taste. "In general, his style on great occasions called to mind the sentimental jargon of the late eighteenth century, reproduced with facile and egregiously incorrect abundance: a mouthful of Jean-Jacques warmed over by a nineteenth-century chef (a prig)."[47] Little is said in these pages about the great orators of July: Guizot, Thiers, and the rest. History has swept them away, nullifying Guizot's rhetoric of "capacities" and Thiers's suspect pleas on behalf of liberty. Only Lamartine remains, and he is treated very harshly in the *Recollections* because Tocqueville had not forgiven him for his February 24 (1848) speech in the Chamber in favor of the republic and against the regency of the Duchess of Orléans. To describe Lamartine, Tocqueville resorts to a cliché made banal by July pamphleteers such as Cormenin in the *Livre des orateurs*, that of a poet astray in politics, whose great, sonorous phrases are aimed "at the popular taste." As the epitome of that very French specialty, "the literary spirit in politics," Lamartine coupled political irresponsibility with writerly individualism, and just as Louis-Philippe's speeches represented the July Monarchy, the poet's eloquent but dangerous lyricism was intimately associated with the revolutionary enthusiasm of the *quarante-huitards*.

The *Recollections* offer an ironic panorama of 1848 in all its rhetorical variety. There is the minister of justice, Hébert, whose rigid judicial manner is ill-suited to the subtleties of deliberative eloquence. The military is represented by General Lamoricière, who works himself up into a frenzy as he harangues his troops during the June uprising. Athanase Coquerel, a priest noted for his eloquence under the July Monarchy, fails his graduation examination at the podium of the Constituent Assembly: "Having been admired for his preaching, he was suddenly transformed into a quite ridiculous political speechmaker."[48] The history of 1848 became the history of a generalized impropriety of public speech – the very same public speech that was supposed to have given form and meaning to the constitutional liberty of which Tocqueville saw himself as the harbinger. The verbal banalities and tired rhetoric of the Chambers under the July Monarchy, which had assembled a collection of "varied and brilliant" talents but condemned them to "quibbling over words,"[49] gave way to the violent contrasts of mixed genres under the republican regime. But when the sublime and the ridiculous come together, as in the hour-by-hour account of the tragic June insurrection as reported to the Assembly by its president, Sénard, the memoirist gleefully accentuates the ridiculousness of the speaker: "Inevitably he added to the courageous qualities he recounted some pompous detail of his own invention, and he expressed the emotion that I believe he truly felt with cavernous sounds, a quaver in his voice, and a tragic catch in his throat that made him, in those very moments, resemble an actor."[50] The rhetoric of 1848 was nothing but a parody of the awful eloquence of the Great Revolution: "The tepid passions of the times were made to speak with the fiery accents of '93."[51] The mixing of genres also affected the language of the Montagnards, as they were called in homage to their illustrious predecessors in the Convention: "For me, this was like discovering a new world. ... The idiom and manner of these Montagnards surprised me so much that it seemed to me that I was seeing them for the first time. They spoke a jargon that was not, strictly speaking, the French of either the ignorant or the literate but partook of the faults of both, for it abounded in obscenities and ambitious expressions."

Yet Tocqueville had previously visited this "new world" and spoken less mockingly of its manners and style. The deputies of the Mountain, who represented the popular "class," expressed themselves in the "democratic language" that Tocqueville himself had defined in *Democracy in America* in 1840, in that new regime of language marked by the mixture of sociolects, unbridled neologism, and hybridization of styles and registers. The event, along with the encounter with the "people," henceforth a presence to be reckoned with in the Assembly, had changed Tocqueville's way of seeing. Instead of the comprehensive sociolinguistics of *Democracy in America*, we now get an ethnological satire, in which political antagonism is no more important than a cultural animadversion intimately connected with a claim to social distinction. In this there is more than the haughtiness of a well-bred aristocrat; there is also the intuition that the old political class, composed of stylistically irreproachable orators, is about to be replaced by tribunes of another kind, among whom Tocqueville cannot count himself. His theoretical treatise on democracy embraced this substitution well before it was confirmed by the concrete presence of his immediate neighbors on the benches of the republican assembly. In the more or less long run, this signified history's negation of the intellectual and elitist liberalism that Tocqueville represented.

The correspondence of later years confirmed this diagnosis:

The political class in France has changed. The one that topples governments in France today, supports them, or allows them to collapse does not read books, cares very little for the thoughts of those who write them, and is quite unaware of the quiet murmur they make above its head. This is the great difference between this and all the other periods of the Revolution that began in 1789 and continues to this day. Until now the people have never played more than a secondary role. Now they have the lead, and that changes the whole spirit of the play and the springs of the action.[52]

Of course, the *Recollections* repeatedly highlight the people's inability to adapt to the customs of parliamentary life (as in the anecdote about the fireman who forces his way to the podium on a tumultuous day of riot only to stand there speechless), as well as the popular hostility to its representatives when they invade the

Chamber: "Let's toss out the sell-outs and take their place!" screams the "rabble" (*populace*) that storms the palace courtyard on February 24.[53] The constitutional monarchy had proved incapable of educating citizens and teaching the French the practical art of political deliberation in accordance with the lessons laid down by *Democracy in America*. The failure of political discourse in the Republic, which culminated in the June tragedy, had a long past. That past, the history of "abstract" and "literary" French political culture and of the difficulty of organizing social dialogue – both legacies of the old regime – would become themes of *The Old Regime and the Revolution*.

Tocqueville's feelings of helplessness, like those of other intellectual liberals incapable of consolidating "the true, the beautiful, and the abstract" in eloquence, were undoubtedly a harbinger of the coming division of labor. In order to portray a "highly colorful" democracy and gain its ear, perhaps one had to learn to love the people as transfigured (and therefore mythologized) by the great Romantics such as Hugo, Michelet, and Sand: these were the new avenues that opened up to literature under the July Monarchy and would lead to the novelistic apotheosis of *Les Misérables*, the book of the People. Another famous liberal would later advocate the separation of the scholar and the politician, in keeping with a new ethic that condemned to obsolescence the old arguments tying thought to action and to rhetoric as the art of persuasion. Tocqueville's reflection on the abstract in *Democracy in America* in a sense worked toward the legitimation of such a separation, and in that sense, Tocqueville's treatise was indeed "a stage in sociological thought."

Pierre Manent has also written of "the assumption of liberty as a value,"[54] which took readers of *Democracy in America* by surprise in *The Old Regime and the Revolution* of 1856: "Do not ask me to analyze this sublime taste," Tocqueville wrote. "One has to feel it. ... There is no way of making it understood to mediocre souls who have never experienced it."[55] Such would be the effect of 1848 on Tocqueville: although he continued to defend the political cause of liberty during the Second Empire, the liberty that *Democracy* sought to accredit as a possible result of collective apprenticeship by way of speech is henceforth also (and perhaps above all) an element of revelation or grace, or else it belongs to the reserved realm of "taste" – both ultimate Tocquevillean formulations of an "Ideal" to which the vulgar have no access. There remains the mystery of an intelligence capable of anticipating things well ahead of his time, down to our own, in fact. This has nothing to do with the conditions of thought and speech at a given point in time. It comes, as in Chateaubriand as well, perhaps, from a lucidity as to his origins (the aristocracy as burden and refuge) and from the aptitude, which is Tocqueville's own, to abstract reality down to its purest outline without betraying it and then, as every writer must, to find the words in which to express it.

NOTES

1 Victor de Laprade, "De la question littéraire," *Revue indépendante*, 10 (10 October 1843), 395.

2 Jules Janin, "Manifeste de la jeune littérature: réponse à M. Nisard," *Revue de Paris*, 2nd series, 1 (1834), 25–26.

3 To be sure, Tocqueville was a "precocious" genius and did not sleep through Guizot's courses on the history of civilization, which he attended during the Restoration. But his letters to family and friends, which can be read in his *Correspondence* (*OC* 14), show that the "July days" took him by surprise.

4 Lucien Jaume, *L'individu effacé ou le paradoxe du libéralisme français* (Paris: Fayard, 1997).

5 Charles de Rémusat, *Passé et présent* (Paris: Ladrange, 1847), 1:17.

6 Germaine de Staël, *De la littérature* (Paris: Garnier-Flammarion, 1991), 66 (originally published in 1800).

7 *Histoire de la civilisation en France depuis la chute de l'Empire Romain* (Paris: Didier [1859] [1829–1833]).

8 Letter to Kergorlay, 4 October 1837, *OC* 13:1, 479.

9 On these notions, see Sylvia Kobi, "Entre pédagogie politique et démagogie populiste," *Mots*, no. 43, 1995, 33–49.

10 Staël, *De la littérature*, 375.

11 Paul Ricœur, *La métaphore vive* (Paris: Editions du Seuil, 1975), 15.

12 Letter to Kergorlay, 26 December 1836, *OC* 13:1, 431.

13 Staël, *De la littérature*, 80.

14 Germaine de Staël, *Considérations sur la Révolution française* (Paris: Tallandier, 1983), 180 (originally published in 1818).

15 *DAII* 1.4, *Œuvres*, P: 530 (trans. Goldhammer), 500.

16 Nisard, "D'un amendement à la définition de la littérature facile," *Revue de Paris*, 2nd series, vol. 2, 1834; Sainte-Beuve, "De la littérature

industrielle," *Revue des deux mondes*, 1 September 1839 (reprinted in Sainte-Beuve, *Pour la critique* [Paris: Folio Essais, 1992]).

17 J.-J. Goblot, *La jeune France libérale: le Globe et son groupe littéraire (1824–1830)* (Paris: Plon, 1995), 567.

18 See George Armstrong Kelly, "Parnassian Liberalism in Nineteenth-Century France," *History of Political Thought* 8 (1987).

19 Françoise Douay-Soublin, "La rhétorique en France au XIXe siècle," *Histoire de la rhétorique dans l'Europe moderne* (Paris: Presses Universitaires de France, 1999), 1160.

20 See Paul Bénichou, *Le sacre de l'écrivain* (Paris: Corti, 1973).

21 Here and in the next paragraph I rely on part 1 of volume II of *Democracy* (1840), which deals with the influence of democracy on "intellectual change."

22 See *DAII* 1.16, and Kenneth Cmiel, *Democratic Eloquence: The Fight over Popular Speech in Nineteenth-Century America* (Berkeley: University of California Press, 1990).

23 *DAII* 1.16, *Œuvres*, P: 579 (trans. Goldhammer), 550.

24 *DAII* 2.8, *Œuvres*, P: 635–636 (trans. Goldhammer), 610.

25 *S* (trans. Lawrence), in *Lettres*, *S*, 755.

26 Ibid., 815.

27 Tocqueville to Kergorlay, 12 August 1839, *OC* 13:2, 64.

28 Tocqueville to Kergorlay, 4 October 1837, *OC* 13:1, 479.

29 *DAII*, *Œuvres*, P: 581 (trans. Goldhammer), 552.

30 *DAI*, *Œuvres*, P: 58 (trans. Goldhammer), 60.

31 See Pierre Rosanvallon, "L'histoire du mot démocratie à l'époque moderne," in *La pensée politique, 1: Situations de la démocratie* (Paris: Gallimard-Seuil, 1993); Raymond Aron, *Les étapes de la pensée sociologique* (Paris: Gallimard, 1990 [1967]); Jean-Claude Lamberti, *Tocqueville et les deux Démocraties* (Paris: Presses Universitaires de France, 1983); and Claude Lefort, *Essais sur le politique: XIXᵉ–XXᵉ siècle* (Paris: Editions du Seuil, 1986).

32 Françoise Mélonio, *Tocqueville et les Français* (Paris: Aubier Histoires, 1993).

33 *S* (trans. Lawrence), quoted in *Lettres*, *S*, 810.

34 To John Stuart Mill, December 1840, *Lettres*, *S*, 470.

35 *DAII*, *Œuvres*, P: 557 (trans. Goldhammer), 528.

36 Ibid., 553–554 (trans. Goldhammer), 524.

37 *DAI*, *Œuvres*, P: 475 (trans. Goldhammer), 470.

38 *DAII*, *Œuvres*, P: 850 (trans. Goldhammer), 831.

39 *DAII*, *Œuvres*, P: 852 (trans. Goldhammer), 833.

40 *DAII*, *Œuvres*, P: 851 (trans. Goldhammer), 832.

41 Ibid.

42 Charles Sainte-Beuve, *Causeries de lundi,* 3rd ed. (Paris: Garnier, 1857–1872), vol. XV, 94–95.
43 Letter to Louis de Kergorlay, November 1833, *OC* 13:1, 345–346.
44 *DAII, Œuvres,* P: 851–852 (trans. Goldhammer), 831.
45 *DA II, Œuvres,* P: 852 (trans. Goldhammer), 832.
46 Ibid.
47 *Lettres,* S, 753.
48 Ibid., 896.
49 Ibid., 754.
50 Ibid., 877–878.
51 Ibid., 808.
52 Letter to Odilon Barrot, 18 July 1856, *Lettres,* S, 1175.
53 *Lettres,* S, 789.
54 Pierre Manent, "Guizot et Tocqueville devant l'ancien et le nouveau," in *Guizot et la culture politique de son temps. Colloque de 1987 de la Fondation Guizot-Val Richer* (Paris: Gallimard, 1991), 154–159.
55 *AR, Œuvres,* P: 195.

8 The Shifting Puzzles of Tocqueville's

The Old Regime and the Revolution

Writing his preface to *The Old Regime and the Revolution* in May and June 1856, Alexis de Tocqueville gave his own view of one of his climactic work's abiding puzzles: "The book I now publish is not a history of the Revolution ... ; it's a study of that Revolution."[1] In keeping with this express rejection of his work as history *per se*, Tocqueville made a concurrent decision to omit from his book the entire edifice of supporting scholarly documentation customary to similar historical works by his contemporaries. He excised, we might say, his book's "scientific" content in the interest of providing what he viewed as a more succinct, more personal, less intimidating, more accessible genre of political and social commentary. He chose pedagogy over history – a choice that readers and scholars of *The Old Regime* have worked assiduously to overturn ever since the book's publication almost 150 years ago.

It was Gustave de Beaumont – himself a prize-winning historian and the reviewer, with his wife, of Tocqueville's final galley-proofs, although not of the outlying texts encompassing his introduction and endnotes – who first sought to build the posthumous case for Tocqueville, the historian. After providing his own view of Tocqueville's historical method in his 1861 introduction to Tocqueville's *Œuvres*, he made the first teasing reference to his friend's extensive reading notes on the French Revolution: "To publish a single volume [of *The Old Regime*], he wrote ten," Beaumont correctly claimed, although he then exaggerated their status as "so many fully developed works."[2] In addition, faced in 1865 with the task of publishing parts of Tocqueville's unfinished sequel, Beaumont artfully reconstructed and inserted within Tocqueville's draft of volume 2, book 1, the very system of historical documentation the author had chosen to omit from volume 1.[3] In 1879, Charles de Grandmaison similarly sought to burnish Tocqueville's historical credentials by recounting in minute detail his first-hand observations of Tocqueville at work in his historical atelier.[4] And in 1925, Antoine Rédier pleaded for the publication of a new edition of *The Old Regime*, volume 1, "enriched by all the notes I found in [Tocqueville's] boxes," thus demonstrating "the scientific value of this book."[5]

It would take some seventy-five additional years for Rédier's call to finally be answered with the publication – first in English (1998) and then in French (2004) – of an annotated edition of *The Old Regime*, volume 1, as the centerpiece of the third volume of the Pléiade collection of Tocqueville's *Œuvres*. This edition of Tocqueville's text was cross-referenced to Tocqueville's writing drafts and the same reading notes whose existence Beaumont and Rédier had trumpeted with such fanfare;[6] it also included a selection of excerpts from Tocqueville's notes that went beyond the smaller sampling edited by André Jardin and published in 1952.[7] In 2003, my own book provided further documentation of Tocqueville's historical inquiries based upon my reading of his complete archives.[8] Scholars have been presented as well with the means to check on the validity of these studies: microfilms of the some 3,700 pages of Tocqueville's archival notes for *The Old Regime*, volume 1, and its sequel, plus his rough drafts and printer's proofs, are currently available for review, with the Tocqueville family's consent, at the Bibliothèque Nationale in Paris.

During 2004, Tocqueville experts have responded enthusiastically to the sudden appearance of this extraordinary new treasure trove. Biancamaria Fontana assesses a number of the qualities of Tocqueville, the historian, as he constructed his "archival tour de force."[9] Bernard Cazes comments on the extent to which Tocqueville "considered the Revolution a fundamentally positive phenomenon," as now evident in the Pléiade edition's presentation of his unfinished sequel.[10] And after noting that "for at least one hundred years after his death few people, and few historians, have regarded and treated Tocqueville as a historian," John Lukacs defiantly asserts that based on the evidence contained in the long-sealed archives, "the recognition of Tocqueville as one of the finest historians in the last 200 years can no longer be eschewed."[11]

This historical deep structure attests to the research and accounts for the design of *The Old Regime*. But in reviewing it, we are faced with a host of new questions. Have old riddles that have long accompanied Tocqueville's text been definitively resolved? What new puzzles greet us as we survey the materials that their author so painstakingly constructed and then deliberately concealed? If a "historical" Tocqueville indeed emerges from his archives, does this new Tocqueville cause us to reassess his historical method, his views on democracy and freedom, or the political message of both his published and intended volumes? After an initial section summarizing the genesis and purpose of *The Old Regime*, I shall examine several of these shifting puzzles in our evolving consideration of Tocqueville's text.

I. THE GENESIS AND PURPOSE OF
THE OLD REGIME AND THE REVOLUTION

The divergent views that have greeted Tocqueville's singular "study of that Revolution" were encapsulated in the lively debate regarding its title that took place among his half dozen closest friends and associates during six weeks in February and March 1856. Two principal choices emerged in this debate, with strong partisans on each side. Jean-Jacques Ampère, Henry Reeve, and Auguste Mignet took what we could call the historian's position, arguing that since the book revealed facts, sources, ideas, and causes that both preceded and explained the Revolution, its title must explicitly capture this developmental and philosophical focus. Beaumont, Jean-Charles Rivet, and the book's editor, Michel Lévy, argued instead simply for "The Revolution" or "The French Revolution." In Lévy's case, this seems to have been pure sales strategy, designed to take advantage of Frenchmen's ever-present fascination with their continuing Revolution. Beaumont's advice, offered near the end of the debate, was more subtle. Of course, as he knew better than anyone else, Tocqueville had dug deeply into the past and produced "absolutely new" findings regarding the Old Regime. But he had done so only to shed light on the French Revolution and their own contemporary era, and the world would only take note of the book on this basis – and on the basis of the identity of its author: "The principal title is your name," he argued. In another example of his prescience, Beaumont urged caution on the author: if you juxtapose "The Old Regime" and "the French Revolution" in one of the suggested titles, you will set up the expectation that you are favoring one over the other.[12]

Tocqueville wavered in his own mind, weighing each of his friends' opinions regarding the polemical, philosophical, and personal uses of history. In doing so, he deliberated about the very concerns that would shape the tone and content of the introduction and endnotes that he would draft later that spring as bookends to the completed historical core of his work. Apparently heeding Reeve's advice to focus on "what constitutes the originality of the book," he finally inserted "The Old Regime and the French Revolution" as his galley-title on March 6.[13] But this was still provisional, especially in light of Beaumont's subsequent recommendations against it ... until Lévy effectively settled the debate by injecting this provisional title into a prospectus which he then mailed to several thousand potential subscribers.

If Tocqueville's title was finally contingent on circumstance, so, too, was the evolution of his book itself, marked as it was with numerous starts and stops, advances and retreats, and twists and turns. As first envisioned at the time of his address to the Académie française in April 1842, and as originally outlined during his convalescent retreat at Sorrento in Italy in 1850–51, Tocqueville set out to write a book on Napoleon and his empire. This was not a surprising choice. Faced in his own time with a pallid version of derivative Napoleonic despotism, Tocqueville sought to study the towering genius of its authentic architect, Bonaparte himself. Tocqueville's best statement of these early views is found in his letter from Sorrento of December 15, 1850, to his cousin, Louis de Kergorlay. There, he set forth his vision of the grandeur of his topic. He also explained how the writing of history could serve as the indispensable catalyst for his meditations on the political forces of his own era. It alone could provide the "solid and continuous base of facts" that Tocqueville could then assess and judge in terms of how these early political facts contributed to contemporary political realities.[14]

Finally released from current political responsibilities by Louis-Napoleon's coup of 1851, Tocqueville launched his Napoleonic studies by first situating his "base" in the period of the Directory immediately preceding the Corsican general's ascent. He analyzed the economic, moral, and spiritual condition of a French people harboring guilt, doubt, and anger about the fate of the Revolution and their roles in it. Consumed by alternate bouts of intense hostility and prolonged apathy, they were disabled as productive citizens and poised to accept a master who could help settle old scores and secure ill-gotten gains. From January to June 1852, Tocqueville read widely on the Directory. Then, in two completed chapters that would remain unpublished during his lifetime, he captured the conflicting passions and public lassitude of the era that paved the way for Napoleon's ascent.[15]

If Tocqueville had been fully satisfied with his portrait of pre-Napoleonic France – "resigning itself, full of terror but at the same time of lethargy, turn[ing] its eyes listlessly from side to side to see if no one would come to its aid"[16] – he never would have written his book on the Old Regime. But plagued by doubts about his projected book's historical subject and genre, and "impelled by the logic of all historical work, which is to proceed backward in time in search of origins,"[17] Tocqueville shifted his study in late July 1852 from the pre-Napoleonic peasant to the pre-Revolutionary one. Undeterred by the isolation of his remote chateau in the far reaches of Normandy, he managed to assemble a disparate set of pre-Revolutionary sources to assist in this new effort: feudist tomes of the mid-1700s; family revenue inventories of 1780; legislative acts, committee reports, and the "records of properties" produced by the Revolutionary assemblies themselves; and local reports of the post-Revolutionary disposition of "*biens d'émigrés.*" He conducted interviews in his own town, sent out questionnaires to neighboring town officials, and considered sending questionnaires seeking to pinpoint patterns of property ownership before and after the Revolution to his erstwhile legislative colleagues situated throughout France. "You would laugh," he wrote a friend, "if you saw a man who has written so much on democracy, surrounded by feudists and poring over old rent rolls or other dusty records." "The boredom that this study causes me," he added, "combined with all the reasons I already had for not loving the Old Regime, ends by making me a real revolutionary."[18]

Tocqueville's 1852 studies of feudal rights and agrarian economics both confirmed and expanded upon earlier theses he had advanced. In his 1836 essay, for example, written for John Stuart Mill's *London and Westminster Review*, he had anticipated his 1852 findings by stating that "at the moment when the revolution broke out, the lands, in a great number of provinces, were already considerably divided."[19] But he had failed to grasp in those early studies the rage of the newly empowered small landholder who found himself subjected to the daily exactions of an archaic feudal system lacking modern justification. Recognizing in his 1852 studies the depths of this seething rural turbulence, even as the weight of the feudal burden declined in absolute terms, Tocqueville grasped a central insight leading to what Lukacs recently dubbed "the Tocqueville effect" in political history: the stability of governments is threatened precisely when they move most actively to ease their people's oppression.[20]

The cumulative thrust of Tocqueville's agrarian studies is captured well in the title he gave to his grand concluding expression of them in *The Old Regime*:

How, Despite the Progress of Civilization, the Condition of the French Peasantry was Sometimes Worse in the Eighteenth Century Than It Had Been in the Thirteenth.[21]

Harking back to his original voyage to America where he famously weighed the pros and cons of the status of the American Indian and the American pioneer, Tocqueville was no cheerleader for the beneficent effects of the progressive march of civilization.[22] To be sure, the French peasant had gained much in civilization's progressive remolding of the French countryside during six centuries. But he had lost much, too, as the French nobility abandoned their ancestral homes for the charms of Parisian society and as the royal government shrewdly stepped into the resulting vacuum, stripping the countryside of local institutions and thereby sapping local freedom and initiative. Tocqueville discovered in his studies – and sought to capture in chapters 1 and 12 of book 2 of *The Old Regime* – the profound ambivalence of the peasant's rising position, especially insofar as it would affect his ability as a citizen to realize his rights and fulfill his responsibilities in the democratic political society to which the Revolution would give birth.

The full scope of Tocqueville's ambitious feudal studies was cut short by acute pleurisy in his lungs contracted on his carriage ride from Normandy back to Paris in early October 1852. He was consigned by doctor's orders to a convalescent retreat that would stretch for twenty months until the end of May 1854, with the latter twelve months of this period spent in sunny Tours, where he and his wife could gain protection from the winds and rain. It was during this Tours segment of his extended convalescence that Tocqueville settled on the subject, genre, and writing style of his projected work of history, although he re-envisioned it only gradually and with his customary authorial angst. Indeed Tocqueville arguably researched and wrote at Tours first drafts of not one but two historical works, presented in *The Old Regime*, volume 1, as his separate but equal books 1 and 2 (with the twenty chapters of book 2 subsequently divided by Tocqueville in his second edition of 1856 into our current books 2 and 3). The two works stand on their own in his finished volume, complete with their own introductions and conclusions; they are integrated within the larger whole principally by Tocqueville's framing introduction and endnotes.

These two books exhibit distinctly different approaches to the writing of history. They are successive steps towards Tocqueville's goal of producing a history blended of facts and ideas – "the mixture of history properly so called with historical philosophy" – that he had articulated so eloquently in his 1850 letter to Kergorlay.[23] Book 1 is weighted toward "historical philosophy." In it, Tocqueville effectively crystallizes ten generations of French social, political, and cultural transition in five short provocative chapters that end by placing the achievements of the French Revolution within the context of Europe as a whole. Apart from the extended literary conceit Tocqueville uses to open and close the book, these chapters are relatively bereft of factual documentation, as evidenced by the fact that he references but three of his seventy-seven endnotes to them. Book 2, on the other hand, is Tocqueville's consummate, mature "mixture" of canvas ("the fabric of facts") and color ("an ensemble of reflections and judgments"),[24] encompassing the full fruit of his four years of archival labors devoted specifically to the Old Regime as well as his almost six years of reflections and experimentation with his preferred historical genre and writing style. The content and style of both books emerged from Tocqueville's interaction with his archival sources, although in quite distinct ways. The essential frames of both books were crafted before Tocqueville left Tours at the end of May 1854.

When Tocqueville first arrived at Tours in June 1853, he was still intent on writing "a small chapter of thirty pages"[25] that would introduce his larger work on Napoleon and his empire. He marshalled his energies at the end of June to write this intro- ductory chapter, sharing his doubts with Ampère about his suc- cess: "If the chapter that I am about to write fails to have some value, I will have lost time and intellectual energy in preparing its elements."[26] The sketches he prepared on or immediately follow- ing June 26, 1853, for this first chapter on the "general physiog- nomy of the Revolution" are noteworthy for several reasons. First of all, we find within them Tocqueville's clearest outline of the five chapters he envisioned for this first volume of his larger Napoleonic book. We see the importance he attributed to his paradoxical findings of the previous year regarding the lessening of the feudal burden and the concomitant intensifying of peasant rage: "The evil was smaller, but as it appeared without justifica- tion, it was tolerated with less patience." We see the emphasis he planned to place on "political liberty" as the critical factor in differentiating despotic France from liberal England, given its role in counteracting the natural tendencies of the English noble, who was "by nature the proudest, the most exclusive, and often the harshest of all nobles." We see his apparent choice at this stage of his studies not to probe either philosophical ideas or adminis- trative centralization as causes of the Revolution, since his out- lines contain no mention of their influence. And we observe all that Tocqueville had gained from his recent readings of Edmund Burke's revolutionary writings, with Burke's influence writ large in the literary conceit that frames his "Order of Ideas" and in the organizing axis of fundamental and accidental revolutionary causes that we watch him construct within it.[27]

The full importance of Tocqueville's Burkean studies to the making of *The Old Regime* will become clearer six months later when he uses this initial outline to draft what by then he has determined will be a separate, detached book on the Old Regime. Despite broad areas of congruity in the two polemicists' approach to French history, Tocqueville chooses to highlight in book 1 the differences in their respective views. Where Burke saw the Revolution as "this strange and hideous beast" that had sprung from the tomb of France's "murdered monarchy" and proceeded to overpower and terrorize the world, Tocqueville emphasizes how his own half-century of historical distance gives him a more dispassionate view of the Revolution's "real meaning ... real character ... and permanent effects."[28] Where Burke identified as fundamental to the Revolution its fanatical irreligion, its anarchic qualities, its propagandistic fervor, and its intended destruction of Europe's Old Constitution, Tocqueville successively dismisses these characteristics in chapters 2, 3, and 4 as "accidental" ones. The organizing motif of his first book culminates in the concluding chapter 5, where Tocqueville dramatically unveils the Revolution's true cause, hidden from the eyes of contemporary observers but only now apparent to those with a proper sense of historical perspective: the democratic leveling of social conditions across all of Europe for ten generations. And where Burke sought to reinstate Europe's old hierarchy of orders as the proper response by civilized men to the Revolution's excesses, Tocqueville argues that that ancient world was fundamentally and irretrievably destroyed.

Despite the development along such promising lines of his original sketches of late June 1853, Tocqueville abandoned this initial drafting effort at the end of the month, unable to resolve to his satisfaction questions of the Revolution's violence, in general, and its "French fury," in particular. "Within this phenomenon," he noted, "there are highly complicated causes that I must research, find again, and analyze."[29] Grandmaison, the Tours archivist, recounts for us the subsequent shift during the summer in Tocqueville's plans for his book, pointing with pride to Tocqueville's description of them to his guests at a dinner at Tours at the end of August:

[Tocqueville] wished to say clearly to Ampère that it was not only in scouring the archives but also in conversing with the archivist that he had settled his ideas – up until this point a bit fluid – and set out the plan of the book that he had decided to detach from his great work and give separately to the public.[30]

Henceforth, all of Tocqueville's labors until June 1856 would be directed to producing this separate work on the Old Regime.

What reasons can we ascertain for Tocqueville's decision? I would suggest three possible "discoveries" in the Tours archives that served as the catalytic converters for his new book. First of all, Tocqueville clearly achieved in the archives a measure of historical truth, or what he would subsequently describe to Grandmaison as a "linking together of rules."[31] On the one hand, to his surprise, he noted on every page of the Old Regime's administrative records the full extent of the royal government's stealthy insinuation within the lives of its subjects, as it sought both to satisfy and control their everyday needs. At the same time, expanding his research during June, July, and August to include the writings of a group of theorists known as "the economists," he studied the extent to which the economists' own proposals expressed a "revolutionary taste for enormous reforms made in one fell swoop," thus reflecting the government's efforts to rationalize all aspects of its citizens' daily lives.[32] Finally, this shift in both governmental practices and emerging opinion toward support for a monolithic, omniscient central power coincided with the leveling of social conditions in Europe as a whole. The latter transition similarly encouraged King, Jacobin Club, Directorial Committee, or Napoleonic emperor to use despotic means to help satisfy society's unslaked appetite for equality. Tocqueville's triage of historical forces, linked at Tours during the summer of 1853, revealed the "rules" that would set the parameters during his lifetime for the French nation's succession of intrusive, volatile, tempestuous, and most often despotic political regimes.

But writing history for Tocqueville went beyond the simple contours of finding and stating historical truth. Truth for Tocqueville must inform modern political consciousness, and it could do so only if it were portrayed in dramatic and riveting fashion. Tocqueville hoped that his discovery of long-neglected source material in the royal archives might help snare the attention of his docile, quiescent fellow citizens, who would then be shocked to witness in the archives' dusty records the origins of their own slide to servitude.

Finally, on a more personal level, Tocqueville found material in the correspondence of the intendants at Tours that stirred his historical imagination and gave him hope that he could avoid his personal demons of self-doubt and despair. "I fall well below the mediocre when I do not take an impassioned pleasure in what I am doing," he had told Kergorlay in 1850.[33] The pervasive hyperactivity of a well-intentioned royal government seeking energetically to preempt all forms of individual initiative by its citizens resonated with Tocqueville's lifelong theoretical understanding of democracy's principal threat: soft despotism. Witnessing with surprise the emergence of this unrecognized precursor of modern "democratic" despotism, Tocqueville could not help but be animated by this fortuitous fusion of historical fact and contemporary political message, conveniently presenting itself at a time when the topic for his new book was still very much in flux.

Throughout the summer and fall 1853, Tocqueville sought to test his emerging "linking together of rules" by making case studies of various eighteenth-century texts that provided telling examples of pre-Revolutionary French opinion. One such set of texts was the writings of the economists, as we have seen, which he continued to study with a mixture of fascination and indignation. Another was those of pre-Revolutionary activists, such as Pierre-François Boncerf, who proposed the redemption of feudal dues in the French countryside.[34] And a third was the cahiers de doléances, those extraordinary snapshots of pre-Revolutionary French opinion drafted in 1789 at the behest of King Louis XVI and forever a monument to his astounding political naïveté. In October 1853, reading an abridged three-volume synopsis "which can be found in all libraries"[35] of the general cahiers of the three orders titled the Résumé Général, Tocqueville sought to discover evidence in pre-Revolutionary public opinion of the varying influence during quite different time periods of his three principal Old Regime "actors": the philosophes and their shorter-term "ideas," the royal government and its longer-term "mores," and the "democratic" social state and its still longer-term "traits" or "tendencies" or "passions" towards equality of conditions in society as a whole. In thus reprising his lifelong fascination with just such an effort to assign priority to the forces that might determine the political fortunes of a nation – be it England, America, Germany, India, or France – Tocqueville sought to identify and isolate the factors that could account for the divergence between liberal and illiberal, free and despotic, governments. But by failing to properly assess the publisher's covert political purposes in this hastily compiled cahiers collection, Tocqueville fell prey to deliberate distortion injected within it.[36]

Tocqueville commenced his definitive drafting of *The Old Regime*, volume 1, on December 2, 1853. In a manner that mirrored the fitful historical evolution of his book, Tocqueville made sudden and dramatic transitions in the course of his writing as well. He wrote his first draft of book 1 during December, using the organizing axis that owed much to his reading of Burke developed in his sketch of June 26, 1853. Two and one-half years later, he would tell Beaumont that "when I wrote these five small chapters [of book 1], I was very pleased with them. They now seem to me the most mediocre and least novel part of my work."[37] Tocqueville's altered verdict stemmed certainly in part from a choice he made at the turn of the year to deliberately refrain from the use or review of his vast archive of reading notes during his drafting efforts for book 2 that would stretch for the next five months from January through May 1854. Only *after* he had completed his initial drafts – having thus forced himself to state and link his general ideas with specificity and precision – did he take two steps that resulted in adding specific facts to them. First, he traveled for three months to Germany where he was able to confirm "by the detail of facts" the validity of general ideas on the European Revolution previously arrived at in his drafts of book 1 "only by abstract reasoning."[38] Second, after settling at Compiègne in the Oise in November 1854, he resumed his work by first constructing a massive index containing almost 3,900 precise references to his "more than one thousand pages" of reading notes.[39] He then used this index to refashion and expand all of book 2 by weaving specific facts within the frames of his previously distilled general judgments on them.

As Tocqueville revisited his facts, he initiated a second strategy designed to add a further level of credibility to his history's emerging arguments: he magnified the presence within his text of his own persona as its intrepid, resourceful, and enterprising archivist. "I found, dated 1757, a royal declaration," he would say on one occasion; "of this course I have noticed a thousand examples," he would add on another.[40] Eighteen months later in May and June 1856, ensconced in Paris where he faced a publisher's looming deadline, he elevated this rhetorical strategy to a form of art when he wrote his work's endnotes and preface. For one goal of these outlying texts became the spotlighting within his work of Alexis de Tocqueville himself as, by turns, master communicator with the "secret" voices of the Old Regime, impartial coroner seeking the truth about that regime's sudden death, caustic critic of contemporary political policies and mores, and fervent advocate for the rebirth of freedom in France. His rhetorical strategy was essential to his pedagogical message in the "study" he now presented. By veiling his sources and personalizing his archival investigations, he sought to enhance his book's clarion call for freedom in France.

Tocqueville's *The Old Regime*, volume 1, was published on June 16, 1856. For the remaining three years of his life, until his death on April 16, 1859, Tocqueville worked on volume 2 in which he sought to "touch the living person" of the Revolution itself.[41] His efforts resulted in an initial draft of his sequel's book 1, written in late 1857 and focused on the passionate eruption in France in 1787 of a powerful thirst for "political freedom" that drove the early resistance to a despotic King and attested to liberty's unique ability to arouse and unite the French nation. The Assembly of Notables in 1787, the Vizille assembly in 1788, and the Estates-General in 1789, described in chapters 3 and 7, all manifested the proud resurgence of this "active passion."[42] In 1858, Tocqueville crossed the threshold of the Revolution itself, examining the pivotal role of liberty in the Constituent Assembly's early activities, culminating in the Night of August 4 and the Declaration of the Rights of Man and the Citizen. He indicated that he planned to conclude book 2 with an explicit statement regarding the meaning of "the principles of '89," with that meaning necessarily based on "democracy ... in the true sense of the word ... [in which] the people take a more or less extensive part in government," and with it "intimately bound to the idea of political liberty."[43] While his studies showed progress on the liberal side, Tocqueville wrestled as well with liberty's immense difficulties in the face of growing class hatreds, anarchy, the idea of "ultrademocratic" universal suffrage,[44] centralized mores (the legacy of volume 1), and the uniquely French "virus" that had created and infected a new race of revolutionaries – "immoderate, violent, radical, desperate, audacious, almost mad, and nonetheless powerful and effective."[45] His studies reached their crescendo in early May 1858 when, in the midst of both scholarly progress and setbacks, he could tell his wife that "it's the first time since the printing of my first book that I feel truly at my work and thinking of it from morning to night."[46] But beset by health problems, he began coughing up blood in June 1858 and was unable during the remaining months of his life to regain the momentum needed to complete his work.

II. OLD MYTHS DISPELLED AND
NEW RIDDLES UNVEILED

The new archival evidence from Tocqueville's preparatory studies for *The Old Regime* allows us to take a fresh look at three abiding myths – "Tocqueville as Seer," "Tocqueville as Closet Aristocrat," and "*The Old Regime* as Lament" – that have dogged Tocqueville and his book since its publication in 1856. While the three myths possess elements of truth about either Tocqueville's historical method, his political and social stance in mid-nineteenth century France, or his principal objective for his book, each is finally distorted in crucial ways. Access to Tocqueville's scholarly materials now permits us to see that.

A. "Tocqueville as Seer" and His Historical Method

A long tradition exists among readers of *The Old Regime* that minimizes the importance, and at times disparages the accuracy or the originality, of his historical research. In part, this stems from the powerful critique shortly after Tocqueville's death by the literary critic Charles-Augustin Sainte-Beuve, who denounced Tocqueville's historical method on several counts. Tocqueville's historical facts in *The Old Regime* were "less novel than the author supposed," Sainte-Beuve charged. His adamant refusal since 1825 to read memoirs and histories of the Revolution "haphazardly and without rhyme or reason (it's the sound method)" accounted for his excruciating levels of doubt and superfluous investigations of topics on which he could already have obtained adequate enlightenment. And his personal, political, and historical rigidity and partisanship led him to start his studies with preconceived concepts as part of "a true *à priori* method ... invariable and inflexible with him," causing him to run roughshod over facts that might then inconveniently interfere. "There's nothing so brutal as a fact," Sainte-Beuve memorably declared. Sainte-Beuve left the final word to his famous anonymous critic: "Tocqueville began to think before having learned anything; which has meant that he sometimes thought falsely."[47] This epigram continues to this day to be recycled as a capsule account of Tocqueville's excessive intuition and flawed erudition.

The notion of Tocqueville as deductive seer received apparent corroboration with the re-publication in the 1860s, first in America and then in France, of his previously unexamined and unattributed 1836 essay for Mill's *Review*. Since the essay appeared to contain the essential lineaments of the chief historical arguments of *The Old Regime*, it placed in further diminished perspective the contribution to his book of his extensive historical research in the 1850s.

More serious readers of Tocqueville's oeuvre – such as George Pierson, Georges Lefebvre, James Schleifer, Seymour Drescher, and François Furet – have countered Sainte-Beuve's claims, even while recognizing the grain of truth that an epigram such as his may contain. Tocqueville did work from an early historical and conceptual prism whose light would shine prospectively on his future years of inquiry. One cannot understand Tocqueville without recognizing this "ensemble of problems conceived so early on,"[48] forged in his private readings, reflections, and educational courses, especially Guizot's lectures of 1828–30. But given these frames, how do we account for the prodigious extent of his continual ruminations and the ways in which he then artfully integrated new findings with existing concepts?

As I indicated in my first section, the new archive casts considerable light on the complex, tortuous, highly self-conscious, developmental nature of this process. We now can state with precision the sources Tocqueville did use (finding that Lefebvre's 1952 list of supposed sources is on occasion in error[49]) and his specific reactions to them. We now know that Tocqueville did not neglect to read modern experts, such as C. Dareste de la Chavanne, Léopold Delisle, and the host of German professors he met at Bonn in 1854. He did not approach his books with advance blueprints, plans, or even conceptual frames: as Drescher has shown for *Democracy in America*, and as we have seen in the first section, important concepts or ideas came to him in the development of his work, often from fortuitous contact with new materials – such as his readings of Burke, the intendants' archives, and Dareste's modern feudal studies – that triggered new avenues of inquiry and new plans and visions for his books. He made mistakes in his research: thus when Furet correctly recognizes the flaws in his *cahiers* conclusions,[50] we can now attribute them to his failure to adequately scrutinize a skewed source rather than to his cavalier substitution of a deductive interpretation for his empirical findings. Finally, and most importantly, Tocqueville's archive reveals layers of historical investigation that both substantiate – often in excessive fashion – and then venture well beyond the conclusions presented in his book.

Uninhibited by artificial boundaries of scholarly discipline or historical dogma, Tocqueville sought to isolate and fix, as we have seen, the respective contributions of philosophical ideas, governmental mores, and egalitarian social conditions in nineteenth century France, all cross-referenced in his historical matrix with considerations of national character, religion, the era's language, economics, political and popular culture, and the eruption of often haphazard political events. Tocqueville's study thus becomes a precocious early investigation of "path dependency" as he sought to calculate the preconditions that could – or could not – make democracy work.[51] Scholars in the future will no longer have to speculate about the supposed insights afforded by his dazzling intuition, but can use Tocqueville's archive to analyze and assess the types of inquiries he conducted and conclusions he drew regarding democracy's ability to take root in evidently infertile soil.

B. "Tocqueville as Closet Aristocrat" and His Democratic Vision

Drawing upon Tocqueville's *Souvenirs*, published in 1893, and on an archival snippet, "My instincts, my opinions," first published by Rédier in 1925,[52] twentieth-century critics of Tocqueville have on occasion resorted to playing a "closet aristocrat" card to seek to discredit his larger democratic vision. Describing one version of such a strategy, even while preparing to dispute it, Richard Herr tells us:

Many democrats have smiled at Tocqueville's wistful recollection of the blessings of aristocracy defending its inferiors against royal tyranny, and have suggested that his own noble blood clouded his normally clear vision.[53]

Superficial critics today continue, all too predictably, to "smile" at Tocqueville's aristocratic "habits of the heart" as evidence of their claims of his purported deficiencies.[54] Sheldon Wolin, however, does not smile at Tocqueville's supposed nostalgia. He argues instead that *The Old Regime* represents an explicit effort by its author to resurrect a utopianized aristocratic past ("*ancienneté*") as "the best practicable realization of the political" or, as he puts it, to launch "a project of political education ... from a reactionary starting point."[55]

Viewed in proper "aristocratic" perspective dating back to the earliest reviews of Tocqueville's book in 1856, Wolin's critique is unprecedented in its bleak portrayal of a Tocqueville who, "close to being a broken man," had arrived at a personal, political, and theoretical dead end by 1851; who returned to his roots, literally and figuratively, in 1854 by finally shifting to a study of the Old Regime; and who then, consistent with the "*mytheoreticus*" he was trying to construct, "grub[bed] in the past in search of sources of political renewal."[56] Wolin's evident predecessor, Lefebvre, anticipated the main lines of Wolin's assertion when he commented on "the profound survival with [Tocqueville] of the traditional nobiliary mentality,"[57] but he qualified his comments in two ways. First, he argued that *The Old Regime* must be read as emerging from Tocqueville's "contradictory tendencies," one tied to his aristocratic milieu and the other to his lifelong rejection of it. Tocqueville articulated most clearly his aristocratic dissidence, Lefebvre reminds us, in his 1836 essay when he rejected "aristocratic liberty" in favor of "the modern, the democratic, and I venture to say the only just notion of liberty" and then proceeded to define such "democratic liberty" as encompassing all men and as necessarily protected by free institutions.[58] Second, Lefebvre consistently marvelled at the ingenuity and depth of Tocqueville's historical research, recognizing its essential role in the making of his book. Wolin – to the detriment of his own argument – makes no such qualifications.

Once again, Tocqueville's archive has much to say about the levels of either nostalgia or reactionary political partisanship that the aspiring author brought to his historical work. Contra Wolin's view, I find Tocqueville in no way engaged in "an act of piety" in his investigations of the Old Regime.[59] His ground-breaking studies in August and September 1852 of the isolation and rage of the French peasant contained scant sympathy for the aristocracy and clergy who had abandoned the peasant to his unholy fate and then continued to extract their feudal dues from him. Reading Edmund Burke in the first half of 1853, Tocqueville repeatedly stressed how Burke was trapped by his own retrospective view seeking to resurrect Europe's Old Constitution and was thus oblivious to "the general character, the universality, the final significance" of the Revolution – the arrival of democratic social conditions.[60]

In his readings, Tocqueville most often operated from a detached historical rather than a partisan political stance, coolly contextualizing Burke's hatred of the Revolution as well as the feudal sympathies he found to his surprise in his readings of modern feudists such as Dareste and Delisle.[61] When Tocqueville did set out in June 1853 to write the opening chapter of what he still saw as his book on Napoleon, he dismissed as "a joke" any claim that a paternalistic government from above would act in the interest of the governed:

We forget that men, kings, or nobles continually fail to do what is in their duty, but rather do what is in their passion and interest. Taken in mass and with a long view, they are good only in exact proportion to the necessity of being so.[62]

Consistent with the beliefs of his lifetime, Tocqueville then argued, as we have noted, that only one means existed to create that "necessity": local political institutions. That Tocqueville finally pushed his book's topic back to the Old Regime during the summer of 1853 was done for reasons of historical accuracy, as we have seen, not for Wolin's presumed political ones based on his sudden awareness in late 1852 of Louis-Napoleon's tightening despotic grip.[63] And when Tocqueville did finally portray in *The Old Regime* the roles of the aristocrats, clergy, and Third Estate in undermining the local liberty and participatory civic culture required by an emerging democracy, he did so with "that type of violence that truth produced in me."[64] The tone and content of Tocqueville's book emerged from his archival studies as they intersected in unexpected ways with the political principles and beliefs to which he had adhered during a lifetime.

In similar fashion, the archive helps us better understand Tocqueville's views of "political liberty." As we would expect in a book that exposes the absence of free institutions as the hidden common denominator in his litany of causes that led to the demise of the Old Regime, Tocqueville relentlessly returned to this topic in his notes. Contra Wolin's assertion, Tocqueville's portrayal of political liberty was not an exclusive, paternalistic one in which he was "intent on appropriating the idea of participatory politics for an inegalitarian ideal."[65] We need look no further than his seventy-seven endnotes for *The Old Regime* to satisfy ourselves on this point, culled as they are directly from his archival notes. In them, Tocqueville provided us with a democratic view of local liberty, not an aristocratic one. We are told in endnote 30 that "the slightest contact of *self-government*" could have sufficed to destroy "the ridiculous and senseless inequality which existed in France at the time of the Revolution," with agricultural societies showing how deliberation and debate about "questions in which the different classes felt themselves interested" could have led to "the rapprochement and mingling of men."[66] Far from presenting a model in which the privileged few exercised their political liberty to exclude the "ignorant demos," as Wolin contends,[67] Tocqueville spotlighted the New England town in endnote 24 and argued that it was precisely "the absence of upper classes" in America that accounted for its political liberty.[68] Freed from their influence, America's republican immigrants could espouse and institute the political equality that in turn galvanized civic vitality, economic prosperity, population growth, and freedom. Throughout his notes, Tocqueville chafed at the propensity of the educated and wealthy classes to negotiate with rather than fight against the blandishments of the central power: in so doing, they chose to purchase their "independence" at the expense of their "liberty," a Faustian trade-off that Tocqueville despised.[69]

Yes, scholars should look at the shifting levels of suffrage in France during Tocqueville's lifetime and calibrate the electoral participation he advocated within the context of his times. Yes, they should evaluate how he responded to the passage of liberalized communal election laws in France on March 21, 1831, twelve days before he sailed with Beaumont for America.[70] And yes, they should examine his support for Cavaignac's emergency sanctions of 1849 that rescinded basic political freedoms throughout France, including those of the press and association, and placed Paris in a state of siege. In each case, Tocqueville should be judged, as all theorists must, on the basis of how he balanced his democratic ideals with his view at each point of time of France's democratic possibilities, given considerations of national stability and security.

C. "The Old Regime as Lament" and Tocqueville's Political Message

Furet's initial essay of 1971 on "De Tocqueville and the Problem of the French Revolution" redefined the ways in which readers would view *The Old Regime*, especially when it became a centerpiece in 1978 to his influential text, *Interpreting the French Revolution*. Furet's early critiques of Tocqueville the historian, harsh as they were, captured important aspects of his historical development, many of which intersect in unexpected ways with our new archival findings. Thus, when Furet emphasized Tocqueville's reversal during twenty years from his analysis that privileged economic and social forces in his 1835–36 writings to his "new emphasis on the autonomy and the primacy of purely political factors" in *The Old Regime*,[71] we can compress that shift in place and time to June 1853 at Tours. When Furet recognized the flaws in Tocqueville's *cahiers* research, as noted earlier, we can provide an explanation for them. When he subsequently sensed Burke's forbidding presence behind Tocqueville's text, we can document it.[72] And when he emphasized that Tocqueville did not regard the "too noble-dominated" view of political liberty contained in book 2, chapter 11, as "suited to survive the advent of democratic institutions, much less to give rise to them," since it was irredeemably tied to privilege,[73] we can attest, as we have just seen, to the congruence of such an observation with Tocqueville's archive.

Furet emphasized a further element of Tocqueville's work, however, which I find less supported by the archive, one that has contributed to a view of *The Old Regime* as "Tocqueville's Lament."[74] For Furet argued that Tocqueville "suffered from a kind of conceptual block" when he came to deal with the Revolution itself, especially its violence, and thus was unable either to understand, incorporate, or escape from the essential revolutionary dynamic.[75] Where Herr previously had focused on Tocqueville's self-description as "ice bound" in his treatment of the Revolution proper, concluding that "evidently something in his constitution reacted against the subject,"[76] Furet found him "imprisoned" within a trap of his own making: by emphasizing his long-term structural account of administrative centralization, Tocqueville removed the possibility of dealing with the radical ideology and rapid societal transformation brought about by the Revolution itself. The two analysts drew different conclusions from their respective assessments, however. In Herr's view, Tocqueville's inability to grasp the Revolution in his proposed volume 2 mirrored his delusions about his true message in volume 1, one to which he had been oblivious: France had no chance to realize its future liberty given the power of its despotic past. His history thus had overwhelmed and counteracted his pedagogy, leading him unknowingly to serve his readers with a "strong dose of opium."[77] Furet's conclusion about volume 2 – further elaborated in his and Françoise Mélonio's introduction to the new Pléiade edition – is ultimately more hopeful, since "the real legacy of this great unfinished work" was "to chart the direction for further research."[78] The dilemma posed by Tocqueville's historical "imprisonment," accentuated we could say by the power of Tocqueville's pedagogy, might still have been resolvable by further historical study.

I agree with Furet's conclusion. But I believe his and Herr's other claims that have contributed to the notion of Tocqueville's "lament" are too strong. Contra Herr's conclusion about volume 1, I find in Tocqueville's archive and correspondence an author fully cognizant of his book's political message, one that he chose to communicate through two carefully calculated and complementary rhetorical strategies. First, he sought to confront the citizens of contemporary France with the true nature of their current servitude. "All of my book has the goal of bringing out the innumerable abuses that condemned the Old Regime to perish," he told Beaumont two months before its publication.[79] The shock of his historical account was intended to prod his fellow citizens to take remedial steps to address their current predicament, since, as he told Francisque de Corcelle five months after publication, "few men would persist in their failings if they could have a clear view of them, see their source, and measure the results of them."[80] Having instructed his fellow-citizens through their reason, Tocqueville then sought to pique either their residual, natural, human dignity or their residual, natural sense of shame, by challenging them to regain their initiative, restore their pride, and win their liberty. "One could say, in a certain sense," Kergorlay quickly recognized, "that the whole book is [contained] in that phrase when you state that the taste for liberty is something that cannot be proven and that this taste consists of loving it for its own sake."[81] Tocqueville intentionally offered no policy pronouncements, no easy formulas, for the reinstatement of liberty in France. With democratic liberty's prospects in decline, he based his future hopes for its revival on a new version of an old passion – "aristocratic" pride. Indeed, as we can see from a review of Tocqueville's writing drafts, he was so committed to the severity of his stark message that he was content to let his chronicle of the Old Regime's abuses stand largely on its own ... all the way until at least June 6, 1856, ten days before his book's publication. Only then, prodded by a friend who argued that "you have made too feeble a defense of the spirit of liberty," did he expand his liberal message by drafting and incoporating in his preface and final chapter several of his book's most famous paeans to liberty.[82]

Contra Furet's assertion of conceptual blockage, I find more fluidity, adaptability, and capacity for change in Tocqueville's approach to the Revolution proper. I do not agree that Tocqueville began his work "with a guiding thread [of administrative centralization] for the long-term continuity of French history," around which he planned to organize his studies.[83] His early studies of 1852 and spring 1853 were more flexible and open to adjustment, based on his archival findings. Indeed, in the spring of 1853, reading Burke, he still saw the Revolution's fundamental causes as "the real weakness of the nobility, envy, vanity in the middle classes, misery, the torments of the feudal system among the lower classes, ignorance – all these were the powerful and ancient causes."[84] Shifting in the summer of 1853 to his studies of administrative centralization, he integrated political and ideological factors into his research, as Furet recognized, even while continuing to examine social and economic forces. Turning in 1857 and 1858 to his studies of the Revolution proper, he focused on all these forces, including the harsh climate, food shortage, and commercial crisis of the winter of 1858, while adding a new emphasis that included the Revolution's actors' conscious and unconscious manipulation of political rhetoric for political gain.

Thus I do not see Tocqueville "imprisoned" in 1858. Rather I see him at a similar stage to where he had been in early summer 1853 and for that matter in spring 1838: he possessed preliminary drafts – still awaiting major rewrites – of parts of a great proposed work, but was still searching for the right combination of historical, artistic, and rhetorical elements that would enable him to resolve its focus and direction. In his planning documents, Tocqueville expressed an awareness of how his new work would deviate from his preceding volume 1, since it involved different types of sources, different public awareness of those sources, a different linkage of concepts, and a different appeal for liberty, this one based, as we have seen, on a proposed *reasoned* defence of the "Principles of '89." Just as readers of *The Old Regime*, volume 1, must determine where they believe Tocqueville finally stood on his historical/pedagogical balance beam, so they must assess from his reading notes and drafts the nature of both historical argument and appeal for freedom that he may have envisioned for his sequel.

III. CONCLUSION

Mirroring similar views expressed by Tocqueville, an unnamed critic in an October 1857 *Edinburgh Review* essay chastised French historians for their failure to produce a true national history.[85] From Guizot to Henri Martin, he claimed, historians had waxed eloquent about the accumulation of power by French absolute monarchs, glorying in the birth of the nation and the liberation of the lower and middle classes from a "superincumbent" aristocracy. But they had failed to see that such royal despotic power finally crushed free institutions. "History cannot be written in perfection without freedom," he proceeded to assert,[86] thereby providing a coda on three levels for the efforts of Tocqueville, the historian, we have examined in this essay.

On a personal level, Tocqueville attempted to write *The Old Regime* during a period when he believed himself to be deprived of freedom, thereby contributing to his bouts of depression and gloom. To be sure, he possessed what the reviewer called "negative freedom," since he was permitted by Louis-Napoleon to circulate his opinions and even publish his book. But what he found lacking – both for himself and the French nation as a whole – were the joys of an "active liberty," for such liberty alone "renders the intellect of the country a participator in public events, and awakens in a people the interest in laws, things, and men, that constitutes political life, and gives birth to political science."[87] To remedy this defect, Tocqueville summoned the passion he needed to investigate the Old Regime's archives and then report his shocking findings to his submissive fellow citizens in the hopes of jolting them to action.

On a historical level, Tocqueville pursued his archival work with the explicit understanding that free men possessed the ability to shape their destinies. He thus operated within the genre and with the spirit he had defined in his chapter, "On Some Tendencies Particular to Historians in Democratic Centuries," in *Democracy in America*, volume 2. In *The Old Regime*, he eschewed both aristocratic history, which privileged the individual actions of a few principal actors, and democratic history, which made great general causes responsible for particular events. Rather he sought to be a historian of a new order, appropriate for the new age of equality, who could comprehend and explain the causes that made possible the "force and independence [of] men united in a social body." His whole archive testifies to his tenacious and ingenious pursuit of "these sorts of fortuitous and secondary causes [that] are infinitely more varied, more hidden, more complicated, less powerful, and consequently more difficult to unravel and follow in times of equality than in centuries of aristocracy."[88]

On a pedagogical level, Tocqueville believed that a historian must not just define and interpret the complicated variables affecting the actions of free men. He must also teach them how to be free. He must deliver a message of his own for freedom properly understood as "active liberty." Perfect history should inspire an understanding of the limits and responsibilities required by perfect freedom. For "no one is less independent," Tocqueville argued in words culled from his archives for *The Old Regime*, "than a free citizen."[89]

NOTES

1   *AR*, 1 (trans. Kahan), 83.
2   Gustave de Beaumont, "Notice sur Alexis de Tocqueville," *OC*, B, 5: 90–91.
3   *OC*, B, 8:55–148.
4   Charles de Grandmaison, "Séjour d'Alexis de Tocqueville en Touraine, préparation du livre sur l'ancien régime, juin 1853–avril 1854," *Le Correspondant* 114, nouvelle série 78 (January–March 1879): 926–49.
5   Antoine Rédier, *Comme disait M. de Tocqueville* ... (Paris: Perrin, 1925), 264–65.
6   "Notes and Variants," ed. Françoise Mélonio, *AR*, 1 (trans. Kahan), 317–434 and *Œuvres*, P 3:1017–94.
7   "Excerpts from Tocqueville's Research Notes," *AR*, 2 (trans. Kahan), 263–373 and *Œuvres*, P 3:317–451; "Notes de Travail," *OC* 2:2, 353–444.
8   Robert T. Gannett, Jr., *Tocqueville Unveiled: The Historian and His Sources for "The Old Regime and the Revolution"* (Chicago: University of Chicago Press, 2003).
9   Biancamaria Fontana, "Old world for new: How Tocqueville moved from America to France," *The Times Literary Supplement*, July 2, 2004), 3–4.
10 Bernard Cazes, "Tocqueville et l'exception française," *La Quinzaine Littéraire* (1–15 avril 2004): 22.
11 John Lukacs, "Unveiling Tocqueville the Historian," *Historically Speaking* (May/June 2004): 10.
12 Beaumont to Tocqueville, 8 March 1856, *OC* 8:3, 377–78.
13 Reeve to Tocqueville, 4 March 1856, *OC* 6:1, 165; Tocqueville to Beaumont, 6 March 1856, *Lettres, S*, 1150.
14 Tocqueville to Kergorlay, 15 December 1850, *Selected Letters* (trans. Toupin and Boesche), 254.
15 "How the Republic Was Ready to Accept a Master" and "How the Nation, While No Longer Republican, Had Remained Revolutionary," *AR*, 2 (trans. Kahan), 191–208 and *Œuvres*, P 3:640–61.
16 Ibid., 208 and 660.
17 François Furet, "Tocqueville," in *A Critical Dictionary of the French Revolution*, eds. François Furet and Mona Ozouf, trans. Arthur Goldhammer (Cambridge: Harvard University Press, 1989), 1022.
18 Tocqueville to Pierre Freslon, 7 September 1852, *Lettres, S*, 1052–53.
19 *Political and Social Condition* (trans. J. S. Mill), 153.
20 Lukacs, "Unveiling Tocqueville the Historian," 11.

21   *AR*, 1 (trans. Kahan), 180.

22   See Ewa Atanassow, *"Fortnight in the Wilderness*: Nature and Civilization" (forthcoming in *Perspectives on Political Science*).

23   Tocqueville to Kergorlay, 15 December 1850, *Selected Letters* (trans. Toupin and Boesche), 256.

24   Ibid., 255–56.

25   Tocqueville to Freslon, 9 June 1853, *Lettres, S*, 1066.

26   Tocqueville to Ampère, 19 June 1853, *OC* 11, 219.

27   *TA*, box 43, folder K, subfile 5 titled, "Initial Outline." This file is divided into two subsections, an "Order of Ideas" (*AR* 2 [trans. Kahan], 263–65 and *Œuvres*, P 3:317–20) and a "26 June 53 sketch" (unpublished). For Tocqueville's list of his five projected chapters at this time, drawn from the "26 June 53 sketch," see the dual references in Françoise Mélonio and François Furet, "Introduction," *AR* 1 (trans. Kahan), 64 and *Œuvres*, P 3:1003, and in "Notes and Variants," *AR*, 2 (trans. Kahan), 375 and *Œuvres*, P 3:1130. For a full discussion of both subsections of this outline, see Gannett, Jr., *Tocqueville Unveiled*, 65–70.

28   *AR* 1 (trans. Kahan), 95.

29   "Order of Ideas," *AR*, 2 (trans. Kahan), 265 and *Œuvres*, P 3:319–20.

30   Grandmaison, "Séjour d'Alexis de Tocqueville," 935–36.

31   Tocqueville to Grandmaison, 9 August 1856, cited in ibid., 946.

32   "Research Notes," *AR* 2 (trans. Kahan), 365 and *Œuvres*, P 3:439.

33   Tocqueville to Kergorlay, 15 December 1850, *Selected Letters* (trans. Toupin and Boesche), 253.

34   *TA*, box 43, folder J, 55–59.

35   *AR*, 1 (trans. Kahan), 287.

36   Gannett, Jr., *Tocqueville Unveiled*, 112–17 and 128–30.

37   Tocqueville to Beaumont, 17 March 1856, *Lettres, S*, 1152.

38   Tocqueville to Beaumont, 16 July 1854, *Lettres, S*, 1102.

39   Tocqueville to Ampère, 12 or 19 November 1854, *OC* 11:260.

40   *AR*, 1 (trans. Kahan), 142, 131.

41   Tocqueville to Montalembert, 10 July 1856, *Lettres, S*, 1173.

42   "Book One: The Outbreak of the Revolution," *AR*, 2 (trans. Kahan), 35 and *Œuvres* P 3:467.

43   "Book Two: Notes Excerpted from Tocqueville's Papers concerning the History of the Revolution," *AR*, 2 (trans. Kahan), 163 and *Œuvres*, P 3:611.

44   *TA*, box 45, folder CC, 39.

45   Tocqueville to Kergorlay, 16 May 1858, *Selected Letters* (trans. Toupin and Boesche), 373.

46   Tocqueville to Mary Mottley, 5 May 1858, *OC* 14, 648.

47 Charles-Augustin Sainte-Beuve, "Œuvres et Correspondance Inédites de M. de Tocqueville," *Moniteur Universel*, 31 December 1860 and 7 January 1861, republished in *Causeries de Lundi* (Paris: Garnier, 1862), 15:96, 104, 116, 98, 105n.

48 François Furet, "The Intellectual Origins of Tocqueville's Thought," *Tocqueville Review* 7 (1985–86): 118.

49 Georges Lefebvre, "Introduction," *OC* 2:1, 18.

50 François Furet, *Interpreting the French Revolution*, trans. Elborg Forster (Cambridge: Cambridge University Press; Paris: Editions de la Maison des Sciences de l'Homme, 1981), 41–45.

51 In *Making Democracy Work: Civic Traditions in Modern Italy* (Princeton: Princeton University Press, 1993), Robert D. Putnam uses *Democracy in America* as the Tocquevillean touchstone for his study. Future such works may find Tocqueville's *The Old Regime* to be his more illuminating model of historical comparative analysis.

52 Rédier, *Comme disait M. de Tocqueville . . .* , 46–48.

53 Richard Herr, *Tocqueville and the Old Regime* (Princeton: Princeton University Press, 1962), 127.

54 See, for example, Garry Wills, "Did Tocqueville 'Get' America?" *The New York Review of Books* (29 April 2004): 56.

55 Sheldon Wolin, *Tocqueville between Two Worlds: The Making of a Political and Theoretical Life* (Princeton: Princeton University Press, 2001), 550, 549.

56 Ibid., 498, 495, 517.

57 Georges Lefebvre, "Introduction," *OC* 2:1, 11.

58 Georges Lefebvre, "À propos de Tocqueville," *Annales Historiques de la Révolution Française* 27, no. 4 (October–December 1955): 317–18; see also, "Introduction," *OC* 2:1, 13.

59 Wolin, *Tocqueville between Two Worlds*, 506.

60 "Notes and Variants," *AR*, 2 (trans. Kahan), 480 and *Œuvres* P 3:1100.

61 *TA*, box 43, folder M, 21 (Burke); folder E, 18 (back side) (Dareste and Delisle).

62 *TA*, box 43, folder K, subfile 5 titled, "Initial Outline," "26 June 53 sketch," 4.

63 Wolin, *Tocqueville between Two Worlds*, 502.

64 Tocqueville to Kergorlay, 28 August 1856, *Lettres, S*, 1194.

65 Wolin, *Tocqueville between Two Worlds*, 528.

66 *AR*, 1 (trans. Kahan), 283. Tocqueville writes "self-government" in English.

67 Wolin, *Tocqueville between Two Worlds*, 559.

68 *AR*, 1 (trans. Kahan), 281.

69 *AR*, *Œuvres*, P 3:290.

70 For my judgment on the importance of this event, see Robert T. Gannett, Jr., "Bowling Ninepins in Tocqueville's Township," *American Political Science Review* 97, no. 1 (February 2003): 4. For an overview of the era's suffrage debates and Tocqueville's place within them, see Alan S. Kahan, *Liberalism in Nineteenth-Century Europe: The Political Culture of Limited Suffrage* (Basingstoke, U.K.: Palgrave Macmillan, 2003).

71 Furet, *Interpreting the French Revolution*, 147.

72 François Furet, "Burke ou la fin d'une seule histoire de l'Europe," *Débat*, no. 39 (March–May 1986): 56–66.

73 Furet, *Interpreting the French Revolution*, 151.

74 See, for example, P. N. Furbank, "Tocqueville's Lament," *The New York Review of Books* (8 April 1999): 49–52.

75 Furet, *Interpreting the French Revolution*, 161–63.

76 Herr, *Tocqueville and the Old Regime*, 102–103.

77 Ibid., 92.

78 Furet, *Interpreting the Revolution*, 163; François Furet and Françoise Mélonio, "Introduction: Tocqueville's Workshop," *AR*, 2 (trans. Kahan), especially 11–19 and *Œuvres*, P 3:lxviii–lxxvii.

79 Tocqueville to Beaumont, 24 April 1856, *Lettres, S*, 1153.

80 Tocqueville to Francisque de Corcelle, 15 November 1856, *OC* 15:2, 186.

81 Kergorlay to Tocqueville, 7 July 1856, *OC* 13:2, 298.

82 Tocqueville's friend was Louis de Loménie. For the "Loménie additions" to his book, see Gannett, Jr., *Tocqueville Unveiled*, 148 and 217 n. 82.

83 Furet, *Interpreting the French Revolution*, 162.

84 "Quatre Jugements sur Burke," *OC* 2:2, 342.

85 "Henri Martin's *History of France*," *Edinburgh Review* 106 (October 1857): 382–407. For Tocqueville's previous comments on Martin's history, see Tocqueville to Nassau W. Senior, conversation of 13 May 1857, *OC* 6:2, 478–79.

86 Ibid., 406, 383.

87 Ibid., 383.

88 *DAII* (trans. Mansfield & Winthrop), 472, 470.

89 *AR, Œuvres*, P 3:290.

9   Tocqueville and Civil Society

I. INTRODUCTION: THE REBIRTH OF CIVIL SOCIETY

Tocqueville's reflections on civil society have proven to be one of his most enduring theoretical legacies. They have also proven to be one of the most contested and promiscuously appropriated. This is especially so in America, where in recent years there has been an explosion of academic and journalistic writing on the topic of civil society. Authors from across the ideological spectrum have turned to Tocqueville for guidance in figuring out how the resources of civil society – the diverse array of political, charitable, educational, religious, neighborhood, and professional associations – might best be deployed in the fight against a wide range of social ills. These include perceived declines in civic engagement and individual responsibility, the loss of trust and a sense of community, and the spread of urban decay, apathy, and selfishness.

Perusing this literature, the casual reader might well conclude that "civil society" has become little more than a feel-good slogan in a time of generalized distrust of (or impatience with) governmental institutions. The core of Tocqueville's idea – civil society as the sphere of intermediary organizations standing between the individual and the state – has been worked and reworked to the point where it is no longer clear where the primary importance of this realm lies. Is it in the moralizing potential of churches, synagogues, and schools? In the ability of the "private sector" to counter-balance or out-perform government bureaucracy?[1] In the pluralism inherent in associational life, the fact that this sphere offers no particular setting for a singular vision of the good life, but rather (in the words of Michael Walzer) a "setting of settings"?[2] Or might it be in the way civil society functions as a "seed-bed" for civic virtue, fostering a sense of citizenship and public life through what Tocqueville called "the habit of association"?

These re-workings result in a confusing picture, one not made any clearer by the fact that when Tocqueville used the phrase "civil society" (société civile) he did so to distinguish a socio-cultural realm of ideas, feelings, and habits (moeurs) from the institutions and practices of government (le monde politique). This distinction frames the respective discussions of Democracy in America's two volumes, the first (1835) focusing on the "political public world," the second (1840) on the attitudes and sustaining moeurs of American democracy. Invoked in the Introduction to Volume 1 and the "Author's Preface" to Volume 2, Tocqueville's "official" separation of political society from civil society promotes a focus on manners and non-political associations – a focus well-suited to the moralizing intentions of many contemporary "neo-Tocquevilleans."

However, it would be a great mistake to see the re-emergence of "civil society" – and the corresponding rise in Tocqueville's theoretical profile – as solely, or even chiefly, the function of specifically American worries and debates. Beyond the chorus praising "membership" and the role of "mediating institutions" in American life, a deeper conceptual sea-change has occurred, one born of very real social and political upheavals that have shaken much of the globe over the last thirty years. These upheavals include the crisis of the welfare state in Western Europe (beginning in the 1970s and continuing to this day); the collapse of state socialism in Eastern Europe and the former Soviet Union; the protracted struggle against right-wing authoritarian regimes in Central and South America; and the gradual abandonment of state-directed programs of modernization in the developing world.[3]

Outside the limited confines of the American debate, "civil society" came to represent a newly born, newly active political and associational life – one without the official sponsorship of the state. It appeared as a marker of broad but fitful democratization, often the result of intense political, struggle. It referred to a diverse array of trade, women's, political and student groups, all of whom were determined to defend not just private but also local and public liberty. It came, in a word, to stand for a decentralized and pluralistic public realm, one capable of advancing society's claims not only against the bureaucratic/authoritarian state, but also against large economic interests (such as multinational corporations). It was outside America that "civil society" recovered, as both concept and reality, the public-political dimension that made it such an important idea for Tocqueville – indeed, his "master idea."

This fact raises a number of questions. First, how is it that "civil society" has such radically different connotations in different parts of the world? Second, why has the "civil society movement" in the United States focused so intently on community, character, and volunteerism rather than dissent, joint action, and the activity of self-government? Third, which broad conception of civil society – the largely non-political one familiar from the American debate, or the self-consciously political one familiar from other parts of the world – is more in line with Tocqueville's theoretical intentions?

The first two questions have elicited a great deal of comment, but fall outside the purview of this chapter.[4] I will focus, instead, on the third. Answering it will demand an exploration of why intermediate organizations – associational life in the broadest sense – loom so large in Tocqueville's view of democracy, its potential pathologies, and its possibilities for freedom. I will begin with a brief consideration of the history of "civil society" in Western political thought, the better to highlight the nature and extent of Tocqueville's theoretical innovation (an innovation often obscured by his "official" distinction between *le monde politique* and *société civile*). I will then consider Tocqueville's discussion of local and political associations in Volume 1 of *DA*. This will provide a broader, more political context for consideration of Volume 2's well-known discussion of "civil associations" (a discussion that provides the point of departure for the American debate on the value of voluntary association).[5] I will conclude by briefly considering the relative valence of public freedom and religious belief in Tocqueville's account of civil society.

I believe that any adequate discussion of "Tocqueville and civil society" must proceed in terms of his overarching theoretical questions. First, are democratic societies fated to be centralized (bureaucratic) non-participatory societies? The example of post-Revolutionary France seemed to point in this direction. Second, how, if at all, can democracy and meaningful decentralization be combined in the modern world?[6] It was the drive to answer these questions that led Tocqueville to focus on the role of intermediate organizations in the first place, and to construe this category in very broad terms indeed. Thus, in Tocqueville's understanding, the "intermediate" sphere of American democracy included (as content or precondition) the following: town meetings, a free press, the separation of church and state, a federal structure of government, political associations and non-political ("civil") associations.[7]

If we want to understand civil society in terms of Tocqueville's political theory, we must see that the central distinction for him is *not* between *société politique* and *société civile*, nor between *political* associations and *non-political* ones. Rather, the crucial distinction is between *local* and *centralized* organizations of power, action, and administration. This broadly Montesquieuian approach to civil society shifts its center of gravity away from the idea of a (seemingly self-contained) realm of manners and mores, and towards the questions of politics, participation, and public life generally. Indeed, as I shall argue, Tocqueville's conception of civil society is one in which the "priority of the political" is very much in evidence – a fact that distinguishes him from both his immediate predecessors (Guizot, Constant, and the *Doctrinaires*) and many of his contemporary appropriators.

II. THE THEORETICAL BACKGROUND

As Hegel – the touchstone for virtually all theoretical discussions of civil society – observed in *The Philosophy of Right*, civil society is "the achievement of the modern world."[8] The idea that *state* and *society* are separate and distinct entities is a relatively recent one in Western political thought, going back only a few centuries. The fact that it comes so naturally to us obscures the long and often painful process by which the spheres of religious belief, market relations, and public opinion gradually emancipated themselves from the state. One need only look back to the ancient Greek notion of a *koinonia politike*, or the feudal Christian idea of a *communitas civilis sive politica*, to see that – for much of our tradition – state and society formed a kind of identity. Functional or "organic" differentiation was recognized early on (most memorably in Plato's *Republic*), as was the idea of political society as a plurality of associations (the famous family/village/polis schema of Aristotle's *Politics*). But it was never doubted that what *we* think of as a relatively independent social sphere inhered, in some way, in a larger, more comprehensive political association (a point of view Hegel tried to revive for the modern age, his stress on social differentiation notwithstanding).

For the longer part of its history, then, the term "civil society" referred to *political* society in this broad, inclusive sense. As late as the 1680s, we find John Locke contrasting "civil society" not with the state, but with the *state of nature*.[9] Civil society was, for Locke, *politically organized* society, a body characterized by a "common established law," a judicature to decide controversies, and a magistrate to "punish Offenders." Where these three elements were lacking, Locke claimed, one remained "in the perfect state of nature."[10] At the same time, however, we find in Locke the beginnings of a systematic distinction between *society* and *government*, the latter being understood as the "trustee" of a collective political power created by a society-forming pact of association (itself designed to remedy the "inconveniences" of the state of nature).[11] It was on the basis of this emergent distinction that Locke famously grounded the right to revolution.[12]

With the Enlightenment, a noticeable shift in the meaning of civil society occurs. This shift has two moments. The first is due to the leading figures of the Scottish Enlightenment (Adam Smith, David Hume, Sir James Steuart, and Adam Ferguson), who delineate a new, essentially economic conception of civil society. Pressing for the separation of economic relations from the state, these thinkers conceived civil society as a more or less self-regulating sphere of interests and markets.[13] The goal was not merely to liberate commercial society from the fetters of the "embedded" economy, but to suggest that the pursuit of self-interest could actually hold society together more efficiently, producing greater freedom and public goods than any political apparatus could. This suggestion received a sharp rebuke from Rousseau, who saw self-interest and "partial associations" as invariably corrupting. Against emergent market society, he reaffirmed the traditional civic republican idea of a "common good" that occupied a moral plane distinct from (and opposed to) that of individual interest.[14]

The second moment of the Enlightenment shift comes with the emergence of what Habermas has called the "bourgeois public sphere" in the course of the eighteenth century.[15] Arising in the coffeehouses, salons, and table societies of the period, a "culture debating public" gradually turned its critical attention to public-political affairs, an arena previously monopolized by the monarchical state. Guided by controversialists such as Diderot and Voltaire and given theoretical articulation by Kant, the "republic of letters" gave birth to a new idea of civil society: the idea of a social space where private persons came together to make public use of their reason.[16] In this sphere, public opinion appeared as a critical, rationalizing force, one that challenged the authoritarian and secretive imperatives of *raison d'état*.

It was Hegel who first brought these two moments at least partly together, giving civil society its first fully modern articulation in political theory. The *Philosophy of Right* famously identifies civil society as a dimension of ethical life, a sphere of difference that "intervenes" between the natural community of the family and the universal (but highly differentiated) moral life of the state.[17]

At first glance, Hegel's concept of civil society seems merely to reiterate that of the Scottish Enlightenment – albeit this time with an emphasis on the socially disintegrative effects of an unconstrained market economy.[18] It is indeed true that Hegel saw civil society as (chiefly) the sphere of "particularity" – that is, as a sphere of more or less universal egoism in which individuals go about pursuing their self-interest.[19] However, Hegel also saw civil society as having an integrative and educative dimension, one that militates against its atomizing, individualistic core.[20] Thus, Hegel's full conception of civil society includes those organs of public authority that regulate and support economic activities. It also includes the main social "estates" or classes (*Stände*), plus professional associations, religious bodies, learned societies, and town councils (a collection that Hegel dubs "the corporation"). The institutions of civil authority protect the welfare and rights of members of civil society, while those of the "corporation" provide a sense of membership, solidarity, and recognition to individuals in an otherwise competitive and egoistic sphere.[21]

Of course, Hegel thought that civil society – the sphere of modern individualism and particularity par excellence – could realize its potential *only* when integrated into the higher (more universal and concrete) ethical life of the state. He worried that the self-seeking "spirit of civil society" would – if given too free a rein – infect the political state, subordinating it to the "free play of interests and the subjective opinions of individual citizens."[22] His solution (such as it was) was to provide a limited role for public opinion, participation, and deliberation, while reserving an expansive one for executive organs, cabinet ministers, and the civil service (the "universal" class).

Yet, despite these flaws, Hegel's concept of civil society successfully articulated a sphere of intermediate interests and associations, filling in the terrain between the particularity of self-interest (on the one hand) and the abstract universality of the state (on the other).[23] Not only that. Hegel also showed how the institutions of civil society (corporations, estates, and municipalities) educated citizens to progressively more general levels of interest. Hegel's idea of civil society thus went a long way towards bridging the apparent abyss between *bourgeois* and *citoyen*, an abyss opened up by Rousseau's vehement critique of the Scots' vision of a commercial society held together by self-interest and an increasingly specialized division of labor.[24]

Tocqueville was barely aware of Hegel, and hardly shared his enthusiasm for the modern, "rational" state (the state created by Louis XIV and "perfected" by the Revolution and Napoleon). However, on the issue of civil society, there is an important but largely overlooked parallel between their works.[25] Both Hegel and Tocqueville focused on the associational middle ground ignored by political economists and civic republicans alike. More to the point, both thinkers were deeply worried about the unchecked spread of modern (what Tocqueville labeled "democratic") individualism. In response, they drew attention to the public dimensions and significance of some of civil society's central institutions. This simultaneous emphasis on civil society's distinctness from *government* and its overlap with *public-political* life is perhaps their greatest shared legacy (less surprising when we recall their mutual debt to Montesquieu).

Two factors enabled Tocqueville to highlight this continuity between civil society and public life in a more profound manner than Hegel. First, there was Tocqueville's deep distaste for the idea of the bureaucratic state as *the* repository of the public good. Second, there was his eye-opening journey to America. When Hegel contemplated America from his Berlin lecture podium in 1830, he saw a country that appeared to be *all* civil society: the young nation lacked, in his view, a developed state and (thus) a meaningful public life.[26] When Tocqueville visited America in 1831–32, he too was struck by the "absence of government" and the spectacle of a society that "goes along by itself."[27] But he also saw that public life had hardly vanished. On the contrary, it had dispersed to a host of local sites and organizations scattered throughout the country.

In America, the Enlightenment's dream of overcoming the state's monopoly on public affairs had been realized, but in a way that neither the *philosophes* nor Hegel could quite have imagined. The centralized state was gone, and public-political life inhabited (to a large extent) the terrain of what we now call social life.[28] This was the great discovery of *Democracy in America*, and the reason why Tocqueville's conception of civil society has proven, ultimately, to be richer and more politically suggestive than Hegel's (his only serious competitor in this regard).

III. CIVIL SOCIETY IN *DEMOCRACY IN AMERICA*

When contemporary social scientists and political commentators turn to Tocqueville on civil society, they invariably cite his declaration that "nothing ... is more deserving of our attention than the intellectual and moral associations of America."[29] It is certainly true that Tocqueville was struck by how the Americans made use of the "means" of voluntary association to achieve an almost comical variety of ends.[30] Yet the reflexive reference to one short chapter in Volume 2 of Tocqueville's masterpiece has had the effect of seriously impairing our grasp of his political conception of civil society and associational life. This can be seen from the fact that Tocqueville's treatment of "civil associations" in Volume 2 is situated in terms of a much broader discussion about how democratic equality fosters individualism, privatism, and the decline of public virtues. Associations – both political and civil – are vital means for combating this tendency, for preserving a robust form of citizenship and public life. Indeed, a case can be made that many of the essentials of Tocqueville's *political* theory of civil society are contained (paradoxically enough) in Volume 1.

In Volume 1 – and again at the beginning of Volume 2 – Tocqueville distinguishes between civil society and the "political world" (*le monde politique*). While fundamental to his theoretical enterprise and the structure of his work, this distinction is also misleading. Like Hegel's apparently clear-cut distinction between civil society and the state, Tocqueville's distinction invites us to place all public-political institutions and activities in one sphere, and all cultural, charitable, business, and social organizations in another. To do so, however, would make a travesty of Tocqueville's central argument about the role of associations *qua* intermediary organizations in American political life. Further, we would be unable to fully grasp his distinctions between *permanent*, *political*, and *civil* associations, or see how these categories map out a social and political space *between* equal individuals and their government. If we want to grasp Tocqueville's idea of civil society, we must conceive it not as a seemingly self-contained realm of mores, habits, and feelings, but rather as a sphere of politically invaluable mediating organizations, a sphere sustained by the "free *moeurs*" these organizations help to create and maintain.

Tocqueville's use of the term "permanent associations" varies according to context. Used with respect to Europe, it refers to the various corporate identities (aristocratic, bourgeois, peasant) that made up the "estates" of the *ancien régime*. One became a member of such an estate by being born into it, and there was very little chance of changing one's place in a social hierarchy composed of such "permanent" associations.[31] In contexts of democratic equality (such as post-Revolutionary France or America), there were no "permanent" associations in this sense. However, in *DAI*, Tocqueville does not drop the term. Rather, he now uses it to refer to local, legally established political entities, such as townships, cities, counties, and other sites of local political administration and participation.[32] These are not "involuntary" in the way that social classes are in an aristocratic society, but neither are they as episodic or as shifting in membership as many voluntary associations.

By "political associations" Tocqueville meant those voluntary groups formed by like-minded individuals intent on advancing a particular political doctrine or opinion, or achieving a specific political goal. Such associations may be small and limited to a single end, or they may be larger and more durable groupings with local chapters and regular meetings. The largest of such groups are political parties that aspire to "rule the state" through the mechanisms of representation and election.[33] Finally, by "civil associations," Tocqueville meant not only "commercial and manufacturing companies," but "associations of a thousand other kinds, religious, moral, serious, futile, general or restricted, enormous or diminutive."[34] Somewhat surprisingly, Tocqueville's notion of civil association also includes the press and newspapers, the latter making possible discussion of political issues by large numbers of people dispersed over great distances.

Merely listing these three types (or levels) of association indicates the *expansive* character of Tocqueville's idea of civil society. It also serves to underline the *priority of the political* in his conception. By construing civil society in loosely Montesquieuian terms – as including virtually every kind of intermediary organization imaginable – Tocqueville signals that he is interested, first and foremost, in the political uses and effects of associational life. Associations serve not only to decentralize administrative and political power; they also enable ordinary citizens to attain a degree of *positive* political freedom it would otherwise be hard to imagine. Associations empower by fostering the habit of joint action amongst the equal, isolated, and privatized individuals of modern democratic societies. They are the primary means by which modern fragmentation and powerlessness are overcome, and "democratic despotism" kept at bay.[35]

I want to take a closer look at each of the three "levels" of associational life that Tocqueville distinguishes, the better to understand his political conception of civil society – a conception that escapes any simple state/society dichotomy.

First there is the level of *permanent association* – the townships, municipalities, and counties that Tocqueville identifies with local administration. From a contemporary standpoint, this represents the most counter-intuitive of Tocqueville's uses of the word "association." Yet it is also the most fundamental. The reason for this is obvious enough. Seen through Tocqueville's Montesquieuian lens, the new democratic world appears bereft of the kind of intermediary powers characteristic of an aristocratic society (noble families, but also guilds, *parlements*, courts, and so on). In America, where such aristocratic institutions simply did not exist, the "permanent associations" of township, city, and county stepped into the breach, occupying a critical part of the terrain between individual and government. Tocqueville clearly saw these "permanent" American associations as highly effective functional substitutes for the old-style *pouvoirs intermédiares* that had hedged in royal power.[36] Indeed, these associations were so successful at dispersing authority that Tocqueville even writes of an "excessive decentralization," one that makes America appear (to European eyes, at least) to be characterized by an utter "absence of government."[37]

What appeared to be an "absence of government" was, in fact, the absence of centralized administration – something made possible by the local authority exercised by the townships. Tocqueville's fascination with this particular form of "permanent association" is well-documented.[38] Dating back to the mid-seventeenth century and imported from the "mother country," the institution of the township had, in Tocqueville's view, an enormous impact on America's political development. The tradition of local administration and political participation it created helped America avoid – at least until the 1830s – the more characteristic pathologies of a "democratic social condition" (hyper-centralized government, majority tyranny, a mass of equal yet powerless individuals). Calling township independence the "life and mainspring of American liberty at the present day," Tocqueville gives a remarkable description of the townships' historical role in fostering a democratic civil society:

The independence of the township was the nucleus round which the local interests, passions, rights, and duties collected and clung. It gave scope to the activity of a real political life, thoroughly democratic and republican. The colonies still recognized the supremacy of the mother country; monarchy was still the law of the state; but the republic was already established in every township.

The towns named their own magistrates of every kind, assessed themselves, and levied their own taxes. In the New England town the law of representation was not adopted; but the affairs of the community were discussed, as at Athens, in the marketplace, by a general assembly of citizens.[39]

This surprising portrait of a Puritan *polis* is revised and expanded in Volume 1's chapter on townships and municipalities. If anything, the basic characteristics of the colonial township have, in Tocqueville's view, grown more pronounced over time. Indeed, he saw the early nineteenth-century township as the concrete instantiation of the American principle of popular sovereignty. It provided a local, participatory form of democracy, one with roots in the colonial town meeting. As a result, it was able to dispense with ruling municipal councils and what Tocqueville calls "the system of representation."[40]

The other outstanding characteristic of the New England township was its *independence* as a political entity. Historically antecedent to both state and federal governments, each township formed, as it were, an "independent nation" jealous of its interests, prerogatives, and capacity for self-government.[41] This independence was most clearly manifest in the township's administrative autonomy and authority – an authority that extended to all aspects of community life (from taxation and education to the maintenance of roads and welfare of the poor) as well as to the enforcement and execution (if not the actual legislation) of the law.[42] Finally, and perhaps most importantly, the township functioned as a "school" for citizenship and public-spiritedness, affording ordinary people not merely the chance to govern themselves, but an insight into the deep continuity between individual and community interests:

The native of New England is attached to his township because it is independent and free: his cooperation in its affairs ensures his attachment to its interests; the well-being it affords him secures his affections; and its welfare is the aim of his ambition and of his future exertions. He takes a part in every occurrence in the place; he practices the art of government in the small sphere within his reach; he accustoms himself to those forms without which liberty can advance only by revolutions. ... [43]

Viewed as a whole, the "permanent associations" of township, municipality, and county create a nexus of local democracy second only to the federal constitution as a bulwark against "administrative despotism" and the threat of majority tyranny.[44] In addition, these associations cultivate a "taste for freedom and the art of being free" at the grass roots level. They create, in other words, an experience and expectation of citizenship *directly opposed* to that fostered by a centralized, administrative state.[45]

Tocqueville's treatment of democratic "permanent" associations does much to scramble his official distinction between civil society and *le monde politique*. The same can be said of his treatment of *political* and *civil* associations, although first impressions suggest otherwise.

In *DAI*, Tocqueville – haunted by the specter of political instability in post-Revolutionary France – offers only a qualified defense of freedom of political association. Presenting American political organizations as a special case of a much broader associative tendency, he is keen to demonstrate how different they are from their European counterparts.[46] In America, "partisans of an opinion" associate mainly to promote a particular political, economic, or social doctrine, and see *persuasion* – not the seizure of power – as their primary task. Through regular discussions and meetings, they articulate their shared opinion more precisely. Through the creation of local chapters or centers, they diffuse it. Should the association become quite large, its members "unite in electoral bodies and choose delegates to represent them in a central assembly."[47] While political associations in Europe can pretend to represent a disenfranchised majority, and remain almost exclusively oriented towards the struggle for power, in America their primary function was to challenge the moral authority of an actually governing majority. Freedom of political association – a somewhat ambiguous blessing in Europe – is, in America, a "necessary guarantee against the tyranny of the majority."[48]

At first glance, this limited (and largely negative) defense of political association seems to confirm the view that, for Tocqueville, the heart and soul of associational life is to be found in the "civil" (social or non-political) arena. Repelled by the dominance of the centralized state and fearful of the violent turbulence born of class-based political struggle, Tocqueville, it seems, can hardly conceal his delight at the energy, peacefulness, and pluralism manifest in American civil society. Applying the "art of association" across the social sphere, the Americans succeed in bringing together – through "artificial" but largely non-political means – what democratic equality effectively tears asunder:

Americans of all ages, all conditions, and all dispositions constantly form associations. They have not only commercial and manufacturing companies, in which all take part, but associations of a thousand other kinds, religious, moral, serious, futile, general or restricted, enormous or diminutive. The Americans make associations to give entertainments, to found seminaries, to build inns, to construct churches, to diffuse books, to send missionaries to the antipodes; in this manner they found hospitals, prisons, and schools. If it is proposed to inculcate some truth or foster some feeling by the encouragement of a great example, they form a society.[49]

Tocqueville's astonished description of the number and variety of voluntary associations in America seems to announce the definitive triumph of society – not only over a self-centered individualism, but over the state and *le monde politique* as well. The "do it yourself" spirit of voluntary ("civil") associations demotes government, politics, and political association itself to an apparently secondary, if not completely peripheral, status. This, at any rate, is how many conservative and communitarian writers have preferred to read Tocqueville, detaching the all important "habit of association" from its roots in politics and public life.

An alternative interpretation of the nature and importance of "civil associations" is suggested the moment we place the passage first cited in its textual context. Tocqueville's description of the spirit of civil association occurs just after his famous analysis of the "atomizing" or socially dissolvent effects of democratic equality. "Aristocracy," he writes, "had made a chain of all the members of the community from the peasant to the king; democracy breaks that chain and severs every link of it."[50] A society in which all are equal may be a society without "natural" hierarchy, but it is also a society without corporate identity and the kind of recognition that goes along with it.

Such a society promotes *individualisme* which, as Tocqueville notes, is something quite different from mere selfishness. It is a "mature and calm feeling," more an "erroneous judgment" than a "depraved passion." It disposes citizens to withdraw from society into the small circle of family and friends, and to imagine that "their whole destiny is in their own hands."[51] The resulting privatization, isolation, and relative powerlessness of democratic individuals saps not only public virtues; it creates an unprecedented opportunity for new forms of despotism. One can speak, in this regard, of a "fatal alliance" between democratic individualism and government centralization (and control) of public life.[52]

Now, Tocqueville clearly thought that *civil* associations have an important role to play in combating the disempowering effects of democratic equality.[53] However, when it comes to avoiding the "administrative despotism" that is the focus of his fears for the future, *non*-political associations turn out to be of limited value. Indeed, as Tocqueville observes, they may even be *encouraged* by governments eager to see popular energies channeled *away* from the political realm.[54] By themselves, "civil" associations fail to teach what Tocqueville considers the basic moral-political lesson: that there is a "close tie that unites private to general interest."[55] Only *public freedom* and *political associations* (of both the "permanent" and more episodic, voluntary kinds) effectively impart this insight, helping thereby to dissolve the abstract opposition between self-interest and the common good. As Tocqueville remarks, "as soon as a man begins to treat of public affairs in public, he begins to perceive that he is not so independent of his fellow men as he first imagined, and that in order to obtain their support he must often lend them his cooperation."[56]

Tocqueville is adamant about the *fundamental* role public freedom and political participation play in combating individualism and avoiding despotism:

The Americans have combated by free institutions the tendency of equality to keep men asunder, and they have subdued it. The legislators of America did not suppose that a general representation of the whole nation would suffice to ward off a disorder at once so natural to the frame of democratic society and so fatal; they also thought it would be well to infuse political life into each portion of the territory in order to multiply to an infinite extent opportunities of acting in concert for all the members of the community and to make them constantly feel their mutual dependence.[57]

Political associations, more than civil ones, reinforce this basic accomplishment of the Founders and of "permanent" associations.

Like local freedom and the "administration of minor affairs," they draw individuals out of their narrow circle of friends and family, teaching them the "art of association" for *public* ends. Along with local freedom, Tocqueville asserts, freedom of political association is the thing most feared by centralizing government. Its very principle challenges the sovereign state's claim to a monopoly of judgment in public matters.[58] In *DAII*, Tocqueville insists that while freedom of *political* association may periodically disturb public tranquillity, this is a relatively small price to pay for the preservation of public liberty – especially when the alternative is the transformation of citizens into a "flock of timid and industrious animals, of which the government is the shepherd."[59]

The idea of a "robust" civil society, separate and distinct from the realm of political affairs, is, then, hardly an end-in-itself for Tocqueville. This point is driven home by his consideration of the relation between political and civil associations (*DAII*, bk. 2, ch. 7). While *DA* gives ample evidence of Tocqueville's acceptance of Guizot's distinction between social condition and political institutions, it by no means supports the currently popular view that "civil" associations are the seed-bed of, or a substitute for, political association and engaged citizenship.[60] In fact, when it comes to learning the fundamentals of the "art of association" (an art essential to the practice of non-docile citizenship), Tocqueville again leaves little doubt as to the priority of political associations. It is they, rather than civil associations, that are the "large free schools" where "all the members of the community go to learn the general theory of association."[61] As Tocqueville explains:

In their political associations, the Americans of all conditions, minds, and ages daily acquire a general taste for association and grow accustomed to the use of it. There they meet together in large numbers, they converse, they listen to one another, and they are mutually stimulated to all sorts of undertakings. They afterwards transfer to civil life the notions they have thus acquired and make them subservient to a thousand purposes.[62]

Tocqueville's insistence on the causal priority of political associations raises the question of why so many "neo-Tocquevilleans" assert the exact contrary. *Civil* associations – churches, clubs, charities, professional and social organizations of all kinds – these, they maintain, are our *real* schools of joint action and civic virtue. One explanation for this otherwise curious inversion is the relative scarcity of spaces of "local freedom" in contemporary society. Where local democracy and self-government are an increasingly dim memory, the hope of many is that civic engagement can be encouraged through more diffuse and generic forms of membership. An alternative explanation is found in the longstanding tendency of liberals and conservatives alike to view commercial associations and the market as the real counter-balance to the state, and religious association as the most important counter-weight to individualism (in the distinctly pejorative sense Tocqueville gives this term).

Tocqueville's emphasis on public liberty and the importance of political participation stands as an effective riposte to recent advocates of membership, trust, and "social capital." As for the idea that political associations are, ultimately, less crucial in the fight against centralization and individualism than either commercial or religious association, I should note the following.

While it is true that Tocqueville thought government intrusion into the economy would constrict liberty and be damaging to the "morals and intellect" of citizens, it is also true that he harbored little love for the commercial or "bourgeois" spirit.[63] Democratic equality creates a society of more or less universal competition and moral isolation, with an unhealthy focus on physical gratification. Left to itself, the self-interest praised by the Scottish economists yields a corrosive materialism, one destructive not only of public virtues, but of public freedom and liberal rights:

When the taste for physical gratification among them [a democratic people] has grown more rapidly than their education and their experience of free institutions, the time will come when men are carried away and lose all self-restraint at the sight of new possessions they are about to obtain. In their intense and exclusive anxiety to make a fortune they lose sight of the close connection that exists between the private fortune of each and the prosperity of all. It is not necessary to do violence to such a people in order to strip them of the rights they enjoy; they themselves willingly loosen their hold. The discharge of political duties appears to them to be a troublesome impediment which diverts them from their occupation and business.[64]

A people driven by competition, self-interest, and the quest for material well-being will fear popular unrest, not authoritarian government. Their desire for public order will be so intense that they will be ready, in Tocqueville's words, to "fling away their freedom at the first disturbance."[65] Thus, Tocqueville thought, Napoleonic despotism was made possible (at least in part) by the cravenness of the French bourgeoisie (a verdict he repeats with even greater disgust at the coming of the Second Empire).[66]

What prevented a similar fate from befalling American democracy was not any supposed link between the "spirit of free enterprise" and that of political freedom. On the contrary, Tocqueville saw everything hinging on the *containment* of the "spirit of civil society" (in Hegel's sense) by a republican-democratic form of civic spirit.[67] The co-presence of these elements on the American scene, and in the American character, led Tocqueville to observe (again, with a certain amount of astonishment), that "an American attends to his private concerns as if he were alone in the world, and the next minute he gives himself up to the common welfare. At one time he seems animated by the most selfish cupidity; at another by the most lively patriotism."[68] Such an energetic double life was possible only so long as traditions of local freedom and political association mediated the drive for material well-being and social advancement.[69] So long as they did, a certain balance or continuity (if not identity) of private and public interest appeared to be commonsensical to the Americans.[70]

But if the unalloyed "spirit of civil society" provides no substitute for the moral achievement wrought by political association (the expansion of narrow self-interest into something far broader in scope), might not the "spirit of religion" overcome the moral isolation created by a democratic social condition? Might not religion help fill the gap left by the demise of "local freedom," demonstrating, in its own way, the "close tie" between individual and community interest? Conservative followers of Tocqueville have been quick to seize upon this idea, drawing support from the strong link he establishes (in *DAI*) between "the spirit of religion" and the "spirit of liberty."

There is little doubt that Tocqueville saw religion as an essential social institution.[71] And there is little doubt that he, like Machiavelli and Rousseau (albeit without their anti-Christian instrumentalism), thought belief was "necessary for the maintenance of republican institutions."[72] But while Tocqueville saw Christianity as underwriting norms of liberal justice and civic equality, he did not think that religious associations, by themselves, could provide anything like a viable substitute for the kind of *public culture* democratic freedom presupposed.[73] The positive contribution he saw religion making in the New World was due, in no small part, to the fact that the Americans had fashioned a "democratic and republican" form of Christianity – one clearly distinct and separate from the state, one at odds with the docility and apolitical worldlessness of both early and orthodox Christianity.[74]

In sum, Tocqueville did not think that civil associations, narrowly construed, could do the moral work of political association and participation.[75] This is not to say that he thought civil association had *no* contribution to make to the public political world. In addition to spreading the habit of association and a spirit of self-reliance (no small achievement), the proliferation of voluntary associations in America challenged the otherwise unfettered dominance of majority feeling and opinion. Tocqueville saw this challenge in terms analogous to those outlined by Madison in *Federalist 10*. By vastly multiplying the number of interests and opinions, civil associations undercut the possibility of any "rule of faction," including that of the majority.[76]

But the proliferation of civil associations also had a more positive contribution to make to *le monde politique*. As Tocqueville explains in *DAII* (bk. 2, ch. 6), "there is a necessary connection between public [civil] associations and newspapers; newspapers make associations, and associations make newspapers ... ."[77] Newspapers serve not only to bring the dispersed but like-minded together, thereby bolstering the judgment of a minority against the "public opinion" of the majority. They "maintain civilization" by informing private individuals every day about public affairs, establishing a diverse, many-voiced public argument and conversation across vast distances. In other words, through the exploitation of freedom of association and of the press, the Americans had created a *de-centered public sphere*: one not dominated by a particular party or city; one free of central government control and – potentially, at least – the dictates of majority opinion. Thus is the *agora* reborn in a society that is no longer face to face and no longer ruled by a single conception of the good life.

Tocqueville's analysis of the close tie between civil associations, newspapers, and the daily experience of citizenship effectively repudiated Rousseau's civic republican dread of "partial" associations, while avoiding the familiar utilitarian conclusion that political life is little more than the clash between conflicting interests and preferences (which need to be effectively "aggregated" at the governmental level). The terrain between individual interests and the "common good" is filled in by ever larger configurations of associational interest. This would approximate our contemporary picture of interest group politics were it not for Tocqueville's repeated stress (parallel to Hegel's) on the political and educational dimensions of associational life, its close tie (through the press and the principle of acting together) to the public realm. The result, in both cases, is a conception of civil society that is intrinsically pluralist – not merely in terms of interests, but also in terms of values.[78] The difference between the two theorists is that while Hegel looks to the corporate bodies of the past (the *Stände*) to embody these values within the "Gothic architecture" of the modern state, Tocqueville looks to voluntary associations and local freedom in the context of a de-centered public sphere.[79]

And it is here that we encounter Tocqueville's greatest theoretical innovation – an innovation we remain blind to as long as we conceive "civil society" in predominantly economic or moralistic terms. What is this innovation? As I indicated earlier, it has little to do with Tocqueville's distinction between *société civile* and *le monde politique*. Nor does it have much to do with his focus, in *DAII*, on the realm of habits, opinions, and *moeurs*. Rather, Tocqueville's unique contribution to the "discourse of civil society" is to be found in his remarkable re-visioning of public-political life as dispersed over a non-state terrain. It is in the realm of "permanent," political and civil associations that citizenship is learned, self-government effected, and debate and argument suffused throughout society. Civil society, comprised of these three levels of association, effectively ends the reign of the sovereign state over public life.

This is not to say that Tocqueville conflates the social and the political (as did the revolutionaries of 1848), or that he wanted republican civic values to penetrate every nook of democratic society (the disastrous ambition of Rousseau and the Jacobins). It is to say that *public freedom, public virtues*, and the "spirit of liberty" remained his guiding passions in a post-Revolutionary world – a world in which peasants, workers, and the bourgeoisie were all too ready to make their accommodation with a centralized, tutelary state. He could not help but view American civil society as a seed-bed for civic virtue and the "habit of association" (the forces opposed to individualism), as well as providing the actual space for (decentralized) political participation. Thus, while retaining and expanding the liberal "art of separation," Tocqueville was able to fashion a concept of civil society that was political at its very core.[80] *Democracy in America* signals the moment, fleeting though it might have been, when *public life* – like economic and religious life before it – slips the confines of the sovereign state and takes on a new, distinctively modern, form.[81]

IV. CONCLUSION

To read Tocqueville on American democracy and civil society is to be reminded of just how far we have come – or, perhaps, of just how far we have fallen. For if Tocqueville demonstrated, through his updating of Montesquieu's *pouvoirs intermédiaires*, the extent to which the public realm could inhabit the space of civil society, our fate has been to see these two spheres separate out once again. What we are left with is the familiar array of economic "special interests" (on the one hand), and the arena of media spectacle (on the other). "Public virtues" now denote little more than the politician's adeptness at the performance of authenticity, or the average citizen's essentially unpolitical willingness to volunteer (for charity, community work, or military duty). "Public life" has been reduced to the moralizing cliché of public service or the unholy cult of celebrity. Nothing could be further from Tocqueville's distinctive brand of liberal republicanism, with its emphasis on limited government, free *moeurs*, and extensive participation in (and attention to) public affairs.

In part, this sad development has to do with the kind of broad cultural shifts described by Hannah Arendt in *The Human Condition* and by Richard Sennett in *The Fall of Public Man*.[82] In part, it has to do with what Habermas calls the "structural transformation" of the public sphere – a transformation wrought by the fusion of corporate capitalism, the bureaucratic state, and a newly "mediatized" public realm. This fusion creates the conditions for a pervasive manipulation and management of public opinion, which loses its critical function and becomes just one more input in "the administered society."[83] But the twilight of public life in America also has roots in a deeply ingrained cultural tendency, one not given much attention by recent theorists of the public realm or by Frankfurt School-inspired critical theory. This is the tendency to view *religion*, not politics or public life, as the only *real* antidote to the pathologies wrought by individualism, materialism, and the unfettered pursuit of self-interest.

Here we need to be clear about Tocqueville's own position. While he drew attention to the "wonderful alliance" between the spirit of religion and the spirit of liberty in the New World, reminding his readers that "it must never be forgotten that religion gave birth to the Anglo-Americans," he did so in order to draw a political lesson.[84] He stressed how Protestant/Puritan/congregationalist beliefs served to cultivate self-reliance, the habit of free association, and the practice of debating and settling collective affairs. He celebrated colonial Protestantism not for its religious content, or even because it would serve as a "countervailing force" against growing materialism and anomie.[85] Rather, he celebrated it as the soil of habits and attitudes characteristic of a *free people* – a people used to managing its own affairs; a people who did not reflexively look to the state for help in resolving, or instruction in administering, public matters.[86]

In contemporary America, this "democratic and republican" form of religion has become yet another dim memory. Tocqueville's attention to the unsuspected civic resources of *specific strains* of seventeenth- and eighteenth-century Anglo-American Christianity has given way to a ubiquitous concern with the individual's "personal relationship with God" – a concern that pervades not only much of contemporary American Protestantism, but Catholicism and non-orthodox Judaism as well. This exclusive focus on subjective belief and a personal relationship with the divine would not have surprised Hegel, who dissected the "law of the heart" and the ethical egomania of romantic Protestantism in his *Phenomenology*.[87] But it would have surprised Tocqueville, who saw the American religion as a great resource in the fight against privatizing individualism, and as "otherworldly" only in the benign sense of reminding a perpetually restless people of matters greater than worldly success.[88]

The point here is that Tocqueville considered religion less for its own sake than for its contribution to the creation of free *moeurs*, non-docile citizens, and the preservation of a public culture. Yet it is precisely this conception of religion as supportive of a publicly oriented culture – as secondary to the value of *public* freedom – that has become most problematic, and indeed most alien, for us.[89] We look to religion to fulfill the spiritual and therapeutic needs of the individual. When religion does enter the public realm, it is usually to cement a misplaced sense of national rectitude (as manifest in the phrase "for God and Country"). Tocqueville, in contrast, sought out those cultural aspects of religion that supported self-reliance, public freedom, and civil equality.

The contemporary American discourse of civil society betrays a similar foreshortening and depoliticization. We are inclined to view this realm in accordance with a strict separation between society and government, *société civile* and *le monde politique*. This allows us to assert the basic Lockean-liberal lesson – that government should serve society, not vice versa – and to count the many blessings of limited government. But it also blinds us to the essential role civil society plays in creating a new kind of space for the public realm, in fostering the "habit of association" and joint action so crucial to public-political life itself. This is, to a large degree, a willful blindness – one born of our desire to be free of the burdens, responsibilities, and argument that characterize public life; one born of our desire to safeguard our *freedom from politics* as best we know how.

Like his liberal predecessor and near-contemporary Benjamin Constant, Tocqueville had no desire to resurrect the myth of ancient collective sovereignty in the modern world.[90] Where popular sovereignty did appear (in the fictional rule of *le peuple* during the French Revolution, or in the "tyranny of majority opinion" threatening America), it was often destructive of freedom. Often, but not always. The lesson of American democracy was that civil society could provide new spaces for, and new forms of, political participation, popular sovereignty, and public freedom; that it could preserve the *moeurs* necessary to self-government in an age of individual powerlessness; and that it could challenge – and, indeed, undercut – the monolith of majority opinion in a democracy. It is an irony of history that the *political* conception of civil society Tocqueville introduced to Europe must now be reintroduced to America – from, of all places, a democratic and secular Europe.

NOTES

1 See Peter L. Berger and Richard John Neuhaus, "To Empower People: From State to Civil Society" in Don Eberly, ed., *The Essential Civil Society Reader* (Lanham, MD: Rowman and Littlefield Publishers, 2000), 143–181.

2 See Michael Walzer, "The Civil Society Argument" in Ronald Beiner, ed., *Theorizing Citizenship* (Albany: State University of New York Press, 1995), 163.

3 See Jean Cohen and Andrew Arato, *Civil Society and Political Theory* (Cambridge: MIT Press, 1992), chapter 1.

4 For a concise critique of the American debate, see John Ehrenberg, *Civil Society: the Critical History of an Idea* (New York: New York University Press, 1999), chapters 8 and 9.

5 On the topic of the role and value of voluntary association in American life, see Amy Gutmann, ed., *Freedom of Association* (Princeton: Princeton University Press, 1998) and Nancy Rosenblum, *Membership and Morals* (Princeton: Princeton University Press, 1997).

6 See the discussion in Larry Siedentop's *Tocqueville* (Oxford: Oxford University Press, 1994), chapter 2.

7 See Ehrenberg, *Civil Society*, 169.

8 G. W. F. Hegel, *Elements of the Philosophy of Right*, trans. Hugh Barr Nisbet (Cambridge: Cambridge University Press, 1991), addition to sec. 182.

9 John Locke, *Two Treatises of Government*, ed. Peter Laslett (Cambridge: Cambridge University Press, 1988), section 87.

10 Ibid., sec. 89.

11 See Peter Laslett's introduction to *Two Treatises*, 113–115.

12 Locke, *Two Treatises*, sec. 222.

13 See Ehrenberg, *Civil Society*, chapter 4.

14 See Jean-Jacques Rousseau, *The Social Contract* in *Political Writings*, trans. and ed. by Frederick Watkins (Madison: University of Wisconsin Press, 1986), bk. II, chapters 3–4. Cf. Lucio Colletti, "Rousseau as a Critic of Civil Society" in Colletti, *From Rousseau to Lenin* (New York: Monthly Review Press, 1971).

15 Jürgen Habermas, *The Structural Transformation of the Public Sphere*, trans. Thomas Burger (Cambridge: MIT Press, 1989).

16 Immanuel Kant, "An Answer to the Question, 'What is Enlightenment'" in Kant, *Political Writings*, ed. Hans Riess (Cambridge: Cambridge University Press, 1971).

17 Hegel, *Elements of the Philosophy of Right*, section 183.

18 Ibid., sections 184, 238–246, 289.

19 Ibid., sections 195, 241; addition to 244.

20 Ibid., sections 187, 289. See Cohen and Arato, *Civil Society and Political Theory*, chapter 2.

21 Ibid., sections 207, 253–256.

22 See Z. A. Pelczynski, "The Hegelian Conception of the State" in Pelczynski, ed., *Hegel's Political Philosophy: Problems and Perspectives* (Cambridge: Cambridge University Press, 1971), 23.

23 Hegel, *Philosophy of Right*, sections 290 and 302.

24 See Jean-Jacques Rousseau, "Discourse on the Origin of Inequality" in Rousseau, *Discourses*, ed. and trans. Roger Masters (New York: St. Martin's Press, 1964). As for Hegel, he retained the distinction between *bourgeois* and *citoyen*, albeit in much softened form. This was made possible, in part, by the dual sense of the adjective *bürgerliche* in German, which has the connotations of both civil or civic (on the one hand) and middle-class or bourgeois (on the other). Hence, for Hegel, the term "civil society" – *bürgerliche Gesellschaft* – already contained individualist and "civic" elements.

25 See, however, Larry Siedentop, *Tocqueville* (Oxford: Oxford University Press, 1994), 58.

26 G. W. F. Hegel, *Die Vernunft in der Geschichte*, ed. J. Hoffmeister (Hamburg: F. Meiner, 1952), 207. See G. A. Kelly's essay "Hegel's America" in Kelly, *Hegel's Retreat from Eleusis* (Princeton: Princeton University Press, 1978), 184–223.

27 Tocqueville, *DAI* (trans. Reeve-Bowen-Bradley), Author's Introduction.

28 A quote from *DAI* (trans. Reeve-Bowen-Bradley, 249; *Œuvres*, P2:278) nicely captures this shift of terrain: " ... the political activity that pervades the United States must be seen in order to be understood. No sooner do you set foot upon American ground than you are stunned by a kind of tumult; a confused clamor is heard on every side, and a thousand simultaneous voices demand the satisfaction of their social wants. Everything is in motion around you; here the people of one quarter of a town are met to decide upon the building of a church; there the election of a representative is going on; a little farther, the delegates of a district are hastening to the town in order to consult upon some

local improvements; in another place, the laborers of a village quit their plows to deliberate upon the project of a road or a public school."

29 *DAII* (trans. Reeve-Bowen-Bradley), 110; *Œuvres*, P2:625.

30 Ibid., 106; *Œuvres*, P2:621.

31 See Siedentop's discussion, *Tocqueville*, 76–77.

32 Tocqueville, *DAI* (trans. Reeve-Bowen-Bradley), 191; *Œuvres*, P2:212.

33 Ibid., p. 192; *Œuvres*, P2:213.

34 *DAII* (trans. Reeve-Bowen-Bradley), 106; *Œuvres*, P 2:621.

35 See Roger Boesche's discussion in his *The Strange Liberalism of Alexis de Tocqueville* (Ithaca: Cornell University Press, 1987), 127.

36 *DAII* (trans. Reeve-Bowen-Bradley), 304; *Œuvres*, P2:822–823. Cf. Alexis de Tocqueville, *AR* (trans. Kahan), 118–119.

37 *DAI* (trans. Reeve-Bowen-Bradley), 70; *Œuvres*, P2:77.

38 Ibid., 61; *Œuvres*, P 65. In *AR*, Tocqueville traces the genealogy of the New England township back to the medieval parish. See Tocqueville, *AR*, 1 (trans. Kahan), 129.

39 *DAI* (trans. Reeve-Bowen-Bradley), 40; *Œuvres*, P 2:44.

40 Ibid., 55–58, 62; *Œuvres*, P 2:60–63, 67.

41 Ibid., 65; *Œuvres*, P2:71.

42 Ibid., 66, 72; *Œuvres*, P2:72, 80.

43 Ibid., 68; *Œuvres*, P2:75.

44 Ibid., 299; *Œuvres*, P2:330.

45 Ibid. Cf. also 319; *Œuvres*, P2:354.

46 Ibid., 191–192; *Œuvres*, P2:212–213.

47 Ibid., 192; *Œuvres*, P2:214.

48 Ibid., 194: *Œuvres*, P2:216. Of course, Tocqueville was hardly an enemy of political association in France or Europe generally. What he feared was the way governmental restrictions served to encourage the growth of demagogic "factions." Political association became "dangerous" when limits on press freedom and the franchise deprived it of its public or deliberative character and the experienced citizen body it demanded. Thus, the July monarchy only made matters worse by imposing such restrictions.

49 *DAII* (trans. Reeve-Bowen-Bradley), 106; *Œuvres*, P2:621.

50 Ibid., 99; *Œuvres*, P2:613–614.

51 Ibid., 98–99; *Œuvres*, P2:612.

52 See Siedentop, *Tocqueville*, 89.

53 See Pierre Manent, *Tocqueville and the Nature of Democracy* (Lanham, MD: Rowman and Littlefield Publishers, Inc., 1996), 25.

54 *DAII* (trans. Reeve-Bowen-Bradley), 118; *Œuvres*, P2:633.

55 Ibid., 104; *Œuvres*, P2:618.

56 Ibid., 102; *Œuvres*, P2:616. I should note that, for Tocqueville, the line between "civil" and political associations is sometimes clear, sometimes not, given the "public" character of the ends often pursued by the former type of association. For a different reading of Tocqueville on associations, one that stresses the *continuity* between political and civil associations, see Boesche, *Strange Liberalism*, 128–129.

57 *DAII* (trans. Reeve-Bowen-Bradley), 103; *Œuvres*, P2:617–618.

58 The burden of Hobbes's *Leviathan* was, of course, to argue precisely for such a monopoly of judgment.

59 *DAII* (trans. Reeve-Bowen-Bradley), 319; *Œuvres*, P2:837. Cf. Boesche, *Strange Liberalism*, 221–225.

60 See Siedentop's discussion, 22–23.

61 *DAII* (trans. Reeve-Bowen-Bradley), 116; *Œuvres*, P2:631.

62 Ibid., 119; *Œuvres*, P 633–634. Cf. Tocqueville's verdict on the French in 1840, delivered in a letter to his mentor Royer-Collard: "I have never seen a country in which the first manifestation of public life, *which is the frequent contact of men among themselves*, is less to be found." (*OC*, 11:89).

63 See Alan Kahan, *Aristocratic Liberalism* (New Brunswick: Transaction Publishers, 2001), 41–46.

64 *DAII* (trans. Reeve-Bowen-Bradley), 141; *Œuvres*, P2:653.

65 Ibid.

66 See *S*, 5–6; *Selected Letters* (trans. Toupin & Boesche), 129. For Tocqueville's general attitude towards the antagonistic relationship between bourgeois "virtues" and political freedom, see the Preface to *AR*, 1 (trans. Kahan) 3–4: "People today are no longer attached to one another by any ties of caste, class, guild, or family, and are all too inclined to be preoccupied with their own private interests, too given to looking out for themselves alone and withdrawing into a narrow individualism where all public virtues are smothered .... In these kinds of societies, where nothing is fixed, everyone is constantly tormented by the fear of falling and by the ambition to rise .... Liberty alone can effectively combat the natural vices of these kinds of societies and prevent them from sliding down the slippery slope where they find themselves. Only freedom can bring citizens out of the isolation in which the very independence of their circumstances has led them to live, can daily force them to mingle, to join together through the need to communicate with one another, persuade each other, and satisfy each other in the conduct of their common affairs. Only freedom can tear people from the worship of Mammon and the petty daily concerns of their personal affairs and teach them to always see and feel the nation above and beside them; only freedom can

substitute higher and stronger passion for the love of material well-being, give rise to greater ambitions than the acquisition of a fortune, and create the atmosphere which allows one to see and judge human vices and virtues."

67 For an account of Tocqueville's distrust of the bourgeoisie, and his reservations about *laissez-faire* economics, see Boesche, *Strange Liberalism*, especially 134–135.

68 *DAII* (trans. Reeve-Bowen-Bradley), 142; *Œuvres*, P2:655.

69 See especially *DAI* (trans. Reeve-Bowen-Bradley), 242–243, 250; *Œuvres*, P2:270–271, 279.

70 See the famous discussion in *DAII* (trans. Reeve-Bowen-Bradley), bk. 2, ch. 7. I should note that, in general, Tocqueville was much less sanguine about the possibility of private and public interest dovetailing (see the passage from *AR* cited in note 60). The general tenor of his discussion of "self-interest, rightly understood" in *DA* is gently ironic: he thinks the Americans invoke self-interest even in the most unlikely times and places, as if a disinterested concern for the public good would somehow tell against them or invite the charge of hypocrisy.

71 See *DAII* (trans. Reeve-Bowen-Bradley), 22–23; *Œuvres*, P2:532–533.

72 See *DAI* (trans. Reeve-Bowen-Bradley), 305–306; *Œuvres*, P2:335–337. See also *DAII* (trans. Reeve-Bowen-Bradley), 22; *Œuvres*, P2:532.

73 Indeed, Tocqueville was well aware that respect for religion and devotion to family could, in the context of bourgeois life, be compatible with the complete abdication of public responsibilities and public life generally. See Boesche, *Strange Liberalism*, 87.

74 See Siedentop's discussion, *Tocqueville*, 63–64. Docility and worldlessness have been the civic republican tradition's standard objections to Christianity. Variations on the theme are to be found in the work of Machiavelli, Rousseau, Hegel, and Arendt.

75 It is in the moralizing potential of political action and citizenship that Rousseau's influence is most strongly felt.

76 See *DAII* (trans. Reeve-Bowen-Bradley), 324; *Œuvres*, P2:843.

77 Ibid., 112; *Œuvres*, P2:627.

78 Boesche is, however, right to question the assimilation of Tocqueville to the kind of liberal pluralism popular among social scientists in the 1950s and early 1960s. See *Strange Liberalism*, 128.

79 See Siedentop's illuminating discussion, *Tocqueville*, 83. For Hegel's pluralism, see Shlomo Avineri's *Hegel's Theory of the Modern State* (Cambridge: Cambridge University Press, 1972), 161–75.

80 Despite the influence of Plato, it is important *not* to read this as a subsumption of society *by* the state; as the return to a pre-modern idea

of "civil society" in which the social achieves integration and order only through a more comprehensive and inclusive *political* order.

81 This point engages Sheldon Wolin's charge that Tocqueville – in his conception of civil society and "intermediary organizations" – is guilty of *ancienneté*: a nostalgic anti-modernism that yearns for the lost world of aristocratic-feudal powers and "freedom." See Sheldon Wolin, *Tocqueville Between Two Worlds: the Making of a Political and Theoretical Life* (Princeton: Princeton University Press, 2001), 450–453. It is important, however, to see that the "young" Tocqueville was capable of looking to the future as well as the past, and of transporting Montesquieu's basic conception into an altogether different terrain – that of modernity.

82 Hannah Arendt, *The Human Condition* (Chicago: University of Chicago Press, 1958); Richard Sennett, *The Fall of Public Man* (New York: Vintage, 1977).

83 See Habermas, *The Structural Transformation of the Public Sphere*, chapters 5 and 6.

84 *DAII* (trans. Reeve-Bowen-Bradley), 6; *Œuvres*, P2:516–517.

85 See, however, *DAII* (trans. Reeve-Bowen-Bradley), 22, where Tocqueville locates the "great utility" of religion in its ability to "inspire diametrically contrary principles" to the atomization, individualism, and love of material gratification promoted by a "democratic social condition."

86 *DAII* (trans. Reeve-Bowen-Bradley), 290; *Œuvres*, P2:809–810.

87 G. W. F. Hegel, *The Phenomenology of Mind*, trans. J. B. Baillie (New York: Harper & Row, 1967), 391–400. See Judith Shklar, *Freedom and Independence* (Cambridge: Cambridge University Press, 1976), chapter 3.

88 See *DAII* (trans. Reeve-Bowen-Bradley), ch. 15. As Cheryl Welch points out, there are some indications in *DAII* that Tocqueville would not be wholly surprised by the trajectory of modern American Protestantism. See her discussion in Welch, *De Tocqueville* (New York: Oxford University Press, 2001), 95–101.

89 This alien quality is perhaps most compactly evident in Tocqueville's declaration (in *AR*, 1 (trans. Kahan)) that "Whoever seeks for anything from freedom but itself is made for slavery" (217). The notion of public freedom as an end in itself has an important twentieth century echo in the work of Hannah Arendt. See Dana R. Villa, *Arendt and Heidegger: The Fate of the Political* (Princeton: Princeton University Press, 1996), chapter 1.

90 See Benjamin Constant, "The Liberty of the Ancients Compared to That of the Moderns" in Constant, *Political Writings*, ed. Biancamaria Fontana (Cambridge: Cambridge University Press, 1988), 309–328.

10 Tocqueville on Threats to Liberty in Democracies

I. INTRODUCTION

This chapter appears in a collective work along with other chapters focused upon such topics as Tocqueville's political philosophy, theory of revolution, and analysis of the *ancien régime*. No doubt their authors will discuss Tocqueville's theories of liberty, and the ways in which equality, revolution, and administrative centralization endanger liberty in modern democracies. Hence, these subjects will be alluded to when relevant to my own concerns, but not discussed in detail. My purpose is to clarify Tocqueville's conceptualizations of modern regimes incompatible with liberty – that is, those governments he classified under the rubrics of "despotism" and "tyranny."

These regime types have played a significant part in political thought since classical antiquity.[1] They may appear to be curious choices of terms for a theorist such as Tocqueville, who insisted on the radical novelty of modern post-revolutionary democracies. Another paradox derives from the fact that Tocqueville conflated the concepts of "despotism" and "tyranny," terms that had been historically distinguished from one another until the late eighteenth century. Despite the variations of meaning in their long histories, and the centrality of different types of "unfreedom" to his own theory, Tocqueville accepted the new tendency to use despotism and tyranny interchangeably to designate all modern types of governments, societies, and practices antithetical to political liberty. Most often, Tocqueville opposed liberty to despotism or tyranny; sometimes he contrasted free governments to absolute governments; less often, anarchy to despotism. Occasionally, when characterizing the history of France between 1789 and the 1850s, he postulated a causal sequence in which revolution produces anarchy, and anarchy, despotism. Since Tocqueville classified regimes in terms of binary oppositions, his characterizations of arrangements contrary or opposite to liberty will be subjected to critical textual analysis, and, when necessary, placed in historical and political context.

Despite his own judgment that "old words such as 'despotism' or 'tyranny' are inadequate," Tocqueville nevertheless continued to apply them to modern regimes systematically denying political liberty to their subjects.[2] Yet there were both continuities and changes in how he deployed these concepts during the three decades of his career as political theorist, politician, and historian. Tocqueville's uses of these terms in *De la démocratie en Amérique* too often have been treated as though they were his last words on this subject rather than his first.[3] While maintaining his repertoire of themes and concepts associated with tyranny, Tocqueville's uses of them depended in part on the theoretical problems that most concerned him at any particular point, in part on his judgment of what was currently at stake in French politics. As Françoise Mélonio has remarked, although Tocqueville's thought seems to be highly abstract, in fact it fed on the alternation between his general system of interpretation, and his close observation and participation in the politics of his time.[4]

Were the concepts of despotism and tyranny adequate to characterize all those practices and regimes Tocqueville identified as incompatible with free government in modern democracies? In order to discriminate and criticize variations in Tocqueville's terminology, his classifications will be located in terms of the family of concepts used by political theorists to designate oppressive regimes that have reduced their subjects to subservience: tyranny, despotism, absolute monarchy, Bonapartism, Caesarism, dictatorship, and totalitarianism.[5] The mode of analysis used here does not assume the semantic transparency of "despotism" or "tyranny."[6] Rather, I consider these terms to be problematic and contested political concepts, the meanings of which shifted according to Tocqueville's political, theoretical, and rhetorical purposes. "Despotism" and "tyranny," like other members of this family, will be treated as what Reinhart Koselleck has called basic political concepts (*Grundbegriffe*) – terms unavoidable in the controversies of actual politics, but always contested in both theory and application.[7]

II. DEMOCRACY AND LIBERTY

Liberty was certainly the political ideal to which Tocqueville was most devoted: "I had conceived the idea of a moderate and orderly liberty, restrained by [religious] belief, mores, and the laws, ... it had become my lifelong passion."[8] Yet, along with democracy, liberty ranks among the most opaque and multivalent concepts in Tocqueville's lexicon.[9] The subject of this chapter, therefore, requires a brief critical treatment of Tocqueville's uses of the concept of political liberty before moving on to the question inseparable from it: what did he mean when he conflated "despotism" and "tyranny" and used them as contraries or opposites of liberty in modern democracies in general, and France in particular?

Tocqueville treated liberty in three different contexts: first, in terms of the benefits produced by the political life of a free government; second, in his distinction between democratic and aristocratic liberty; and third, in his rhetorical inclination to praise liberty as a good in and of itself, a good which can be understood only by those who have experienced it, and the supreme value of which cannot be determined by its consequences. "Liberty is the pleasure of being able to speak, act, and breathe without being constrained, governed only by God and the laws."[10] Indeed, on this view of liberty as a good *sui generis*, liberty cannot be analyzed or explained to those nations or individuals who have never felt "this sublime taste" (*ce gout sublime*). It is the first of these versions – a robust theory of democratic liberty as the genuine political life of a free government – that most often figured as the unspoken theoretical opposite to democratic despotism. I turn, then, to an analysis of what Tocqueville meant by *la vie politique elle-même*.

In a section of the 1835 *Démocratie* entitled "The pervasiveness of political activity in the United States and the influence it exerts on society,"[11] Tocqueville contrasted the benefits produced by the dynamism of general political participation in a country that is free (*pays libre*) to the static quality of life in one that was not. Tocqueville first claimed in the *Démocratie* that democratic republics exceed all others in their energy. The incessant agitation, conflicts, and tumult of democratic political life spill over to civil society, leading indirectly to the prodigious development of industry and commerce. The business of government, whether internal administration or foreign policy, is not conducted as efficiently in free democracies as in absolute regimes dominated by a single person. But democratic political life creates an all-pervasive energy and force that can produce miracles beyond the power of even the most astute despot.

Tocqueville understood that those who prized order and tranquility above liberty would be put off by the never-ending noisy and often unlovely partisan contention he reported in the United States. But, he added, the consequent struggles, the conflicts among individuals, groups, and parties, ought not to be exaggerated and feared as endangering order or leading to revolution. Rather they should be appreciated as the unique contribution of a free political life to the energy and wealth of the society.

A modified version of this analysis recurs in a passage from his 1835 travel notes in England. This time, it is not the nature of democratic republics, but the freedom of English political life that Tocqueville finds responsible for that country's economic dynamism. In England, prosperity had been produced by its free politics and laws:

To live in freedom, it is necessary not to be upset by constant agitation, movement, and danger .... I see the impetus given to the human spirit in England by its political life (*la vie politique*) .... [T]heir laws give the English their courage to seek well-being, their liberty to pursue happiness, their knowledge of the habits requisite to attaining it, and their assurance of enjoying what they have created.[12]

Thus, in the 1835 *Démocratie*, and just after it, during the time that he was writing the 1840 volumes, Tocqueville was developing an argument about the advantages of a genuine political life in a free government. In the 1835 *Démocratie*, he had specified the citizen rights prerequisite to such a free political order in a democratic society: freedom of the press, of association, of forming parties, of religion, and competition between parties. That American political life was so active and varied, he attributed in large part to the immense power of a free press, which "circulates political life throughout every part of this vast territory."[13]

In his parliamentary speeches during the 1840s, Tocqueville deplored the loss of the passion for liberty in France, a passion that had produced the Revolution of 1830: "Instead of the [present] exclusive preoccupation with enjoying material pleasures, there was an active, varied, energetic political life (*une vie politique active, variée, puissante*) ..."[14] But once in power, those who had led the Revolution of 1830 had reversed themselves as early as 1834 by passing legislation sharply limiting those rights essential to liberty in an egalitarian society: freedom of the press, of association, even of religion.[15] In Tocqueville's view, Guizot, Thiers, and Molé were all so obsessed by the fear of revolution that they sought to extinguish political life by encouraging a self-regarding materialism, and by reinforcing governmental centralization so as to discourage popular participation in government, whether national or local. Guizot, exploiting the middle class fear of another revolution, drastically limited the number of those eligible to vote.

This indictment later turned into a theory of revolution, applied by Tocqueville in his *Souvenirs*. There he made a striking analysis in political terms of the reasons for the failure of the July Monarchy and its overthrow by the Revolution of 1848. These Tocqueville attributed in part to the systematic corruption of the legislature by Louis Philippe, but even more to the extinction of political life by Guizot.

In a political world thus composed and led, what was most lacking especially at the end, was political life itself (*la vie politique elle-même*). Such life could hardly emerge ... the people were excluded. As every matter was settled by the members of one class, ... this peculiar homogeneity of position, interests and point of view, which prevailed in what M. Guizot called "the legal country" (*le pays légal*) ... deprived parliamentary debates of all reality ... .[16]

This explanation pointed up the practical consequences of subverting political liberty in a state that claimed to restore civic freedoms.[17] To this analysis, Tocqueville added his indictment of Guizot and Louis Philippe for encouraging the worst predispositions of the type of society they governed: materialism, political apathy, individualism.

To the end of his life, Tocqueville reaffirmed what he would have been willing to call his faith in *la vie politique elle-même*. In this he felt isolated, for he perceived his contemporaries as content with the depoliticized order and tranquility imposed by the absolute government of the Second Empire. This regime encouraged its subjects to enrich themselves and pursue their individual interests, provided only that they abstain from politics.

III: LIBERTY'S OPPOSITES: THE TYPES OF OPPRESSION MENACING MODERN DEMOCRACIES

By the time of Tocqueville's death, he had identified no fewer than five types of oppression threatening *la vie politique elle-même*: legislative despotism; the tyranny of the majority over public opinion; despotic rule on the model of the Caesars; the democratic or administrative despotism of a mild centralized, bureaucratic government; and "imperial" or "military despotism" – that is, what others called Bonapartism, Caesarism, or dictatorship.

A. Legislative Despotism

While writing the *Démocratie*, Tocqueville consulted the entry for "despotism" by Jaucourt, a disciple of Montesquieu, in the *Encyclopédie* of Diderot and D'Alembert. Part of the text Tocqueville copied into his reading notes: "Despotism. Tyrannical, arbitrary, and absolute government of a single man. The principle of despotic states is that a single person governs everything there according to his wishes, having absolutely no laws than those of his caprices. *Encyclopédie*." To this excerpt, Tocqueville added a comment based on his own judgment of the Convention during the French Revolution: "This was written before we saw the despotism of an assembly under the Republic. It is necessary to add 'of a single power.'"[18]

Legislative despotism as a danger to liberty was treated in greater detail when Tocqueville participated in drafting the 1848 Constitution of the Second Republic. He became the advocate of the bicameralist "American model" because of the association of unicameralism with the Terror. Tocqueville here invoked his theory that all political arrangements have some inherent vice. Those playing the classical role of the legislator in founding new governments, as he found himself doing as a member of the constitutional commission, should check rather than encourage the worst tendencies inherent in the type of regime they institute: "The chronic disease fatal to [unicameral] legislatures is their intemperance in lawmaking. The tyranny of this branch consists in its insatiable will to keep making laws .... The [characteristic] disease (lèpre) of democracies is impetuosity, that legislative imprudence which culminates in oppression."[19] Tocqueville called "insupportable tyranny" what he regarded as the inherent tendency of single-chamber legislatures to push the scope of lawmaking ever deeper into previously unregulated areas of private and group life. Here again, Tocqueville used despotism and tyranny interchangeably as opposites or contraries of political liberty.

B. The Tyranny/Despotism of Democratic Majorities that Suppress the Freedoms of Thought and Expression

In both parts of the Démocratie, Tocqueville, when treating regimes, types of society, or movements antithetical to liberty, minimized the effects of fear produced by the use or threat of force. Such means he associated with absolute forms of rule that had existed long before the creation of modern democracy as he defined it. Instead, he emphasized the power of social rather than political or legal sanctions on the exercise of freedom of thought. In the 1835 volumes, nothing depressed Tocqueville more than the suppression by American public opinion of the ideas expressed by critics of democracy, as well as by unpopular individuals and minorities of all kinds. Uncertain about what to call this new form of domination, he sometimes used the term "tyranny of the majority," sometimes "despotism of the majority."

In an arresting paragraph, Tocqueville dramatized the difference between the naked power exercised by pre-revolutionary absolutisms and the ostensibly non-violent means used by the majority in a modern democracy:

> Under the absolute government of one man, despotism tried to reach the soul by striking crudely at the body .... Tyranny in democratic republics ... ignores the body and goes straight for the soul. The master no longer says: You will think as I do or die. He says: You are free not to think as I do. You may keep your life, your property, and everything else. But from this day forth you will be as a stranger among us. ... You will remain among men, but you will forfeit your rights to humanity. Go in peace, I will not take your life, but the life I leave you is worse than death.[20]

Yet, to live in a democracy does not necessarily entail having to accept such abuses. Oppressive majority practices may be mitigated, if not eliminated. This may be done by either political or social means. To them, Tocqueville devoted a chapter (I, ii, 8). What this meant for France was that to reduce administrative centralization would be one political means of mitigating the tyranny of the majority over thought. Another would be guaranteeing freedom of the press and expression.

Tocqueville concluded the 1840 *Démocratie* with a set of recommendations for preserving liberty in democracies. Invoking the classical figure of the legislator, Tocqueville counseled that counter-measures should be taken against the inherent dangers to liberty in democracies:

> set broad but visible and immovable limits on social power; ... grant certain rights to private individuals and guarantee their uncontested enjoyment of those rights, ... reserve what little independence, strength, and originality is left to the individual.[21]

The most effective ways for democracies to prevent unrestrained and extreme actions by majorities against unpopular opinions include such countervailing measures as following established legal forms – that is, procedural due process – and recognizing the rights of individuals and minorities against the social and political power of majorities.

C. "The Tyranny of the Caesars"

But I think that if democratic institutions are not introduced gradually among us [in France], and if all citizens are not provided with those ideas and sentiments that first prepare them for liberty, ... there will be no independence for anyone, ... but an equal tyranny for all. And I foresee that if in time we do not succeed in establishing the peaceful rule of the greatest number, we shall end up sooner or later under the unlimited power of a single person.[22]

The image of imperial Rome was put to very different uses by Tocqueville in the various phases of his thought. Already in the two parts of the *Démocratie*, Tocqueville came to surprisingly divergent conclusions about the applicability of this analogy to modern politics. As already noted, he had ended the 1835 volumes by offering his French readers two alternatives: either a moderated democracy with checks on the government and the participation in politics by all citizens, or else the tyranny of the Caesars, "the unlimited power of a single person."[23] To reject such a moderated democracy would recreate "the terrible centuries of Roman tyranny," in which mores had been corrupted, republican customs destroyed, and the liberty of citizens attacked rather than protected by the law. This was the first of a series of analyses first accepting, then qualifying, and finally rejecting the applicability of the Roman parallel.

The critical editions of the *Démocratie* have identified in the draft manuscript a specific acknowledgment by Tocqueville that he had changed his mind about his striking assertion at the end of the 1835 volume that if rights were not given to all, the only alternative was rule by a single person, the tyranny of the Caesars. He contrasted his rejected conclusion with what he would now say in his famous chapter in the 1840 *Démocratie* on "What Type of Despotism Democratic Nations Have to Fear:"

This picture is both true and original; that given in the first volume is exaggerated, commonplace, trite, and false. The version presented here gives the full originality and profoundity of my idea. What I wrote in my first work was trite and superficial.[24]

In a note to himself found in the critical edition but not the published chapter of the 1840 *Démocratie*, he wrote:

If I wish to impress my readers by my picture of administrative despotism, I must not omit *what we see before our eyes* (Tocqueville's emphasis). A tyranny of the Caesars was a scarecrow which could frighten no one.[25]

Tocqueville now argued that if total domination were ever established in a modern egalitarian society, it would far exceed the degree of control achieved by the Caesars when their power was at its height. That power was at once immense and unchecked, but it was a tyranny that was used against a small part of the population and for limited objectives. Ordinarily, the private life of individuals lay beyond its reach. Thus tyrannical power in antiquity was violent when exercised, but limited in the number of those it affected. The details of both social and individual life went for the most part unregulated. In contrast to even the greatest power achieved in Rome, a modern regime would possess a centralized administration capable of making its will prevail throughout its empire. After eliminating all the obstacles once posed by intermediate groups or civil society, it could codify and make uniform its legislation; it could penetrate both private and social life, regulating even what its subjects thought and believed.[26]

By 1840, then, Tocqueville emphasized the differences rather than the similarities between the power of the Roman Emperors and the unlimited power of a single ruler in a democratic age. Not until the 1850s, in his analysis of the regime of Louis Napoleon, did Tocqueville return to the consideration of modern France in terms of ancient Rome. Because of the seizure of power by Louis-Napoleon and the creation of the Second Empire, Tocqueville then abondoned altogether any comparison to Roman history.

In seeking to legitimate the Second Empire, its apologists followed the lead of Louis-Napoleon, who wrote a book on Julius Caesar arguing that providence produces great men to rescue their countries from chronic civil war and to create at one stroke the new institutions needed to transform societies and lead them into a new era of progress.[27] Earlier attempts to legitimate the regime were phrased for the most part in similarly tendentious theories of "Caesarism." Second Empire apologists stressed the need of a redeeming Caesar and his successors, who had to seize power in order to restore order and replace the structures of a society fallen into anarchy and corruption. As a result of these imperial apologies, Tocqueville began to abandon his earlier interest in making his own analysis of French politics dependent on analogies to Roman history. By 1856, fearing that comparisons between contemporary France and late Republican Rome played into the hands of Louis-Napoleon and his retinue,[28] Tocqueville dismissed such analogies as superficial and intrinsically misleading. In one of his last analyses of Second Empire France, Tocqueville again rejected any comparison to Roman history:

[T]hose who are pleased to believe that we are going to reproduce these vices [of the Roman Empire] on a small scale – all such people I believe to live in books alone and not in the reality of their time. Our nation is not decrepit, but fatigued and frightened by anarchy. ... [W]e are not yet ready for the establishment of a definitive and continuing despotism.[29]

Thus Tocqueville several times altered his comparison between modern France and the "tyranny of the Caesars."

D. Democratic or Administrative Despotism: The Greatest Threat to the Liberty of Democratic Peoples

Thus I think that the type of oppression threatening democratic peoples is unlike anything ever before known. ... I myself have sought a word that would carry precisely the idea I seek to express. But old words such as "despotism" or "tyranny" are inadequate. The thing is new. Since I cannot give it a name, I must seek to define it.[30]

What Tocqueville presented in the 1840 *Démocratie* was not a definition but a thick description of the novel form of despotism he had imagined. In this formulation of what he called "the full originality and profoundity" of his new idea of modern democratic oppression, it became far more compelling than either the image of majority tyranny in America or that of the Caesars. This time, he presented domination, not as exercised by an intolerant majority denying the freedom to form and express opinions, but by a beneficent centralized state apparatus satisfying all the needs of its subjects, who are represented as atomized individuals or families concerned only with their own material well-being. The regime ruling them would be at once absolute, omnipresent, regular in its procedures, detailed in their application, paternal in its anticipation of all its subjects' wants, and non-violent, even mild (*doux*).

By these means, democratic nations could be reduced to nothing more than industrious herds of sheep subservient to their bureaucratic shepherds. Such servitude – ordered, peaceful, benevolent – Tocqueville asserted, is compatible not only with the external forms of liberty, but also with the doctrine of popular sovereignty. What is most remarkable about such a system is not so much the nature of its master as the complete and passive obedience of its subjects. Such docile behavior had been identified by Montesquieu as the distinguishing aspect of despotism. But Montesquieu had attributed this type of obedience to a generalized state of fear on the part of the ruled, who were always threatened by the violence of the despot's agents.

Tocqueville's novelty was to reject the assumption that force or the threat of force would be the spring of the dystopic modern despotism he depicted in this chapter. Rather, its distinguishing feature would be the removal of any desire by its subjects for either individual autonomy or the wish to participate in deliberating or determining policies affecting the common good of the polity. Because political liberty would become incomprehensible, the question of suppressing it would not even arise.

Such a democratic tyranny of the moderns, Tocqueville conjectured, although exercising greater power than that ever attained in antiquity, would not be violent, as in imperial Rome. By removing even the possibility of conceiving liberty as the defining quality of human beings, the regime would degrade those it ruled. But it would not use violence against them. As Tocqueville had argued earlier, in a democratic age when men are approximately equal in their power, wealth, and even in their desires, their *moeurs* become more humane and mild.[31] Even those who rise to power have their desires limited by the type of society in which they live. Such rulers are apt to prefer the role of paternalistic guardians (*tuteurs*) to that of bloody tyrants. Democratic governments may become violent and cruel in exceptional periods of revolutionary effervescence or external dangers. But, Tocqueville predicted, crises and revolutions will become increasingly rare. Yet, in a democratic age, it will be easier for rulers to concentrate all powers in their own hands, and to penetrate more deeply and more regularly into the private lives and even the minds of individuals. One way of legitimating this would be through appropriating the concept of popular sovereignty. By such devices as plebiscites, citizens could be said to have consented to others ruling in their name.

After depicting such a future state of affairs, in which political liberty would have no place, what would Tocqueville call it? In Constant's *De l'esprit de la conquête* (1813), he had suggested that despotism was an antiquated form of domination. What had been created in the Terror and then the First Empire were regimes that penetrated and controlled society far more intensively than ever before. To them, Constant gave the name "usurpation." Their power to mobilize citizens derived from the dynamic revolutionary and democratic energies unleashed for the first time. While "usurpation" used already existing despotic governmental structures, it did so in its own distinctive way, creating an unprecedented form of oppression made possible by demagoguery, propaganda, and mass conscription. Thus, tyrannies and despotisms were, for Constant, static forms of rule that prohibit individual liberty, interdict discussion, and demand passive obedience. But at least they allowed a subject to remain silent. "Usurpation condemns him to speak, it pursues him into the intimate sanctuary of his thought, and forcing him to lie to his conscience, seizes from him the last consolation of the oppressed."[32]

Tocqueville agreed with Constant that the concepts of tyranny and despotism were inadequate to defining the greatest dangers to liberty confronting nineteenth-century democratic societies: "This word 'despotism' is unfortunate because its former sense does not correspond to the new meaning I wish to give it."[33] But Tocqueville did not adopt any of the neologisms such as "usurpation," "Bonapartism," or "Caesarism," offered by other theorists as alternatives to the old terms. When it came to naming any of the threats to liberty he perceived as uniquely modern and democratic, Tocqueville would first admonish himself to coin a word adequate to the new state of affairs, but then, drawing back from doing so, would adapt to his purpose an existing term used in antecedent conditions he had declared to have been superseded. In the 1840 *Démocratie*, after stating that the type of oppression menacing democratic peoples had no precedent in the past, Tocqueville wrote himself a note: "Apply yourself to finding a name [for such oppression]. This is important!" He then settled for sometimes calling it "administrative despotism," sometimes "democratic despotism."[34] When considering the case for using the "old idea" of "military despotism," he noted that the novel element of his own conception was a type of despotism that followed on revolution and "democratic anarchy."[35] Subsequently, when he analyzed the two Napoleonic empires, he called them "military" or "imperial" despotisms.

What were the reasons for Tocqueville's dramatic reversal of his earlier assessment of the dangers to liberty in modern democracies? In another note to himself, dated April 1837, Tocqueville wrote that everything he saw and heard in Paris led him to reevaluate the French political situation.[36] Political liberty was now most menaced not by a potential tyrant, but by the materialism, individualism, and political apathy of the society as a whole. Even the once-revolutionary people displayed profound indifference towards every form of government. As for the middle class, Tocqueville's candid judgment was:

Commerce and industry prosper; that suffices. Their passion for well-being is so imbecilic that they fear even to think about the causes that produce or maintain it.[37]

This cluster of unpolitical values constituted, in Tocqueville's view, the vices (germes de mort) potentially fatal to democratic societies. But one of the enduring elements of Tocqueville's thought was his theory that governments can either reinforce or mitigate the natural tendencies of their type of society and regime. Tocqueville perceived those who led the July Monarchy as deliberately encouraging democratic vices: political apathy, individualism, and materialism. It was these qualities that in the 1840s he saw as the greatest dangers to political liberty in France. But what did this diagnosis have to do with the chapter on the most likely form of despotism in modern democracies that closes the 1840 work? One place to look is in Tocqueville's later applications of such "democratic despotism."

In an 1842 parliamentary speech attacking the government, Tocqueville virtually cited his 1840 chapter. The July Monarchy had devised a subtle strategy for denying political liberty to the democratic society it ruled. By encouraging political apathy, it

opens the way to the dominance of those who control the omnipresent centralized bureaucracy. Bureaucrats then administer all
public matters affecting the general interests of subjects, who now
find no time to participate in politics.[38] Reverting to his prophetic
mode, Tocqueville told his audience that it was this pattern that
prepares a nation to fall under the dominance of a master. As yet he
could not identify any one individual capable of assuming this role.

Well into the 1840s, Tocqueville continued to believe in this
revised version of democratic or administrative despotism as the
greatest danger to liberty. But then a second reevaluation occurred.
As Tocqueville stated in his *Souvenirs*, even before the Revolution
of 1848 and the 1851 coup d'état by Louis-Napoleon, he gave up his
belief that apathy, individualism, and materialism were the principal dangers to liberty for a greater threat:

[M]ore and more the idea took root that we were marching towards a
new revolution. This marked a great change in my thought. The universal
calming down and leveling off that followed the July Revolution made me
suppose, for a long time, that I was destined to live my life in an enervated,
tranquil society.[39]

The new perils he saw stemmed from the indefinite continuation of
the French Revolution and the consequent repetition of the
sequence that had already once produced a Napoleonic empire.
Thus Tocqueville once again significantly altered his diagnosis of
that type of regime democratic nations have most to fear. In the
third decade of his career as political theorist, politician, and historian, Tocqueville increasingly focused on the question of how the
two Empires founded by Napoleon and Louis Bonaparte constituted
a distinctive type of regime, post-revolutionary and post-democratic. This analysis reworked the relationships among those concepts that continued to dominate his thought: democracy, liberty,
revolution, centralization, and equality.

E. The "Imperial Despotism" or "Military Tyranny" of the Two Bonapartes

If an absolute government were ever established in a country with a society
(*état social*) as democratic and as deprived of morality (*démoralisé*) as

France, there would be no conceivable limits upon tyranny. Under Bonaparte we have already seen one excellent specimen of such a regime. ...[40]

In Tocqueville's view, "[t]he French Revolution produced two contradictory currents, which must not be confused: one favorable to liberty; the other, favorable to despotism."[41] Thus its heritage remained ambiguous: two traditions of democracy – one compatible with citizens ruling themselves, while enjoying liberty, the rule of law, and individual rights; the other, characterized by rule in the name of the people by individuals, groups, or parties openly contemptuous of any limitations on popular sovereignty, the ostensible source of the power they exercised.

As early as his 1831 American travel notes, Tocqueville coupled Danton with Napoleon Bonaparte as examples of different types of revolutionaries equally contemptuous of freedom:

When Danton had the throats cut of those unfortunates whose only crime was that of not thinking as he did, was that liberty? When later Robespierre sent Danton to be guillotined because he dared to become his rival, no doubt that was justice, but was it liberty? ... When Bonaparte ... substituted the tyranny of a single person (la tyrannie d'un seul) for the tyranny of factions, was that liberty? ...[42]

Two points made in this entry recur in the Démocratie. The first was Tocqueville's conflation of the Terror and Napoleon Bonaparte as constituting a distinctively French style of despotism born of the Revolution. And in his conclusion to the 1835 Démocratie, Tocqueville repeated the phrase "the tyranny of a single person" (la tyrannie d'un seul) when defining the choice confronting modern egalitarian societies.

Prominent among the significant contributions to the Revolution's illiberal legacy were those Tocqueville attributed in large part to Napoleon: the perfection of a centralized administrative machinery, the codification of a civil law that encouraged individualist self-enrichment but limited freedoms of the press and association, the launching of theoretical justifications for seizing power by force from constitutional governments, the invention of plebiscitary dictatorship as a pseudo-democratic alternative to representative government, and among those who regarded themselves as heirs of the

Revolution, the creation of a tradition of disregard for individual rights and constitutional government. In addition to his innovations, Bonaparte reinforced tendencies developed earlier in what Tocqueville considered the most violent and least defensible periods of the Revolution. As a result of the series of revolutions it had undergone, in which Tocqueville included the period from 1789 to 1815, France now had a distinctive set of post-Revolutionary *political moeurs* (operative practices or political culture).

Many groups accepted the assumptions that violence is normal and acceptable in politics; that representative institutions make strong leadership impossible, that the state may as a matter of course set aside individual or group rights whenever they are found to conflict with the general or national interest as interpreted by those holding power. To these existing revolutionary political *moeurs*, Napoleon added the empire's bureaucratic and legal structures, which effectively excluded citizens and their representatives from deliberating together and from making decisions on any level. Once in power, all successor regimes not only used, but expanded the machinery put into place by the first emperor.

Already in 1831, Tocqueville was coupling Napoleon with the Jacobins as the authors of the revolutionary illiberal tradition: "Bonaparte was the greatest enemy of political liberty, which put obstacles in the way of his program. Bonaparte felt towards liberty that carefully-considered hatred peculiar to his genius, which was at once ambitious and dominating ... ."[43] But it was in 1842 that Tocqueville first created a detailed explanation of how, out of the Revolution, Bonaparte created a regime that, long after the fall of the First Empire, served as a model that permanently endangered democratic liberty in France. The extraordinary success of the *Démocratie* made possible Tocqueville's election in 1842 to *l'Académie française*. He was obliged by its protocol to deliver a eulogy for his predecessor, Jean-Gérard Lacuée, made Comte de Cessac by Napoleon Bonaparte to reward his indispensable services as Minister of War Administration and director general of conscription.[44] In this address, Tocqueville treated the First Empire as a system. Only after 1850 did Tocqueville analyze Bonaparte and the Empire at comparable length. And when he did so, he followed the scheme developed in 1842. Indeed, he attributed to research he had done then the project that became *l'Ancien régime*.

Questions previously raised in both parts of the *Démocratie* about the potential dangers to liberty in democratic society recurred in altered forms when Tocqueville treated the First Empire. Napoleon Bonaparte and his regime were treated as among the worst possible outcomes of the syndrome or pathology diagnosed earlier by Tocqueville. This was caused whenever the government in a democratic type of society chose policies designed to exploit, rather than counteract, individualism, materialism, political apathy, administrative centralization, and the preference of equality to liberty. Above all, it could turn to its advantage the theory of unlimited popular sovereignty. Again, as in the *Démocratie*, Tocqueville here emphasized the dangers of rule built on the worst potentialities of a democratic society.

When dealing with Napoleon Bonaparte, one point of Tocqueville's inquiry was to ask how many of the effects produced by Napoleon were attributable to his own exceptional abilities, and how many to opportunities provided by his period, nation, and the French Revolution. Tocqueville emphasized the revolutionary mobilization of France against its external enemies, but did not minimize the leadership of Napoleon:

The Revolution had brought France to its feet; Napoleon ordered it to march. The Revolution had amassed enormous and unprecedented forces; these he organized and utilized. He produced prodigies, but in an age of prodigies. The person who founded and maintained this Empire was the most extraordinary phenomenon to appear for many centuries. Napoleon was as great as a man without virtue can be.[45]

Tocqueville fully recognized what we, in the wake of Max Weber, now call Bonaparte's charisma. Like Weber, Tocqueville treated this as a form of legitimation. But in a brief but penetrating analysis not irrelevant to twentieth-century experiences with charismatic leaders, Tocqueville pointed out how their compelling personal qualities can be, and have been, used as political excuses by subjects for complicit service to their masters. In words calculated to identify the mechanism and destroy the basis for such servile obedience, Tocqueville wrote of Napoleon Bonaparte: "His singular genius justified and in a sense legitimated [*légitimait*] the extreme dependence of his contemporaries in their own eyes. The hero concealed the despot. It seemed plausible that in obeying him, submission was rendered not to his power, but to the man."[46]

This verdict on Bonaparte derived from Tocqueville's analysis of the dangers to liberty from leaders who use pseudo-democratic theories to legitimate the violent seizure and subsequent abuse of power in a democratic society. It applied both to the Jacobin Committee on Public Safety under Robespierre and to the First Emperor: "Until our time, it had been thought that despotism in any form was odious. Now it has been discovered that there are such things as legitimate tyrannies and holy injustices, provided only that they are done in the name of the people."[47] This passage from the 1835 *Démocratie* had not identified Napoleon as among those exploiting the theory of unlimited popular sovereignty. But here, such abuse in the form of will, popular sovereignty, was explicitly attributed to him:

Although these ideas [of popular sovereignty] originated in [demands for] liberty, they could easily lead to servitude ... Those unlimited powers that had been rightly refused to a king now were conceded to an individual ostensibly representing the nation's sovereignty. Thus Napoleon could say, without much offending public opinion, that he had the right of command over everything because he alone spoke in the name of the people.[48]

From what point of view did Tocqueville criticize the First Empire? First, he restated his conclusion to the 1835 *Démocratie*: political liberty in a democratic society presupposes not only recognizing the individual rights of all citizens, but also encouraging public participation in politics, particularly on the local level. Only by deliberating together can citizens learn the importance of the public interest and respect for the rights of others. In an egalitarian society, political liberty is achieved by mitigating those inherent characteristics of democracy that endanger a free political life. Leaders favoring democratic liberty encourage citizen participation in deliberating on and deciding public policy. Those who, like Napoleon Bonaparte, seek to establish democratic despotism, do so by excluding citizens from this process, and centralizing all decisions and commands in the leader and his agents.

The diffusion of knowledge (*des lumières*) and the division of property has made each of us independent and isolated from the rest. Only interest in public affairs can temporarily unite our minds, and on occasion, our wills. But absolute power would deprive us of this unique setting for deliberating together and acting in common. It chooses to enclose us in that narrow individualism, to which we are already over inclined.[49]

Second, Tocqueville provided his own diagnosis of the blow dealt to liberty in France by Napoleon. Through perfecting the centralized state machinery created by the ancien régime, Napoleon had come closer to total domination of French society than anyone before him. Perceiving the unprecedented opportunities for domination created by a democratic type of society (*état social démocratique*), Napoleon was the first to exploit fully its despotic potential. He found this post-Revolutionary society in a virtual state of anarchy under the Directory in 1799. Already democratized, its individualistic, materialist, and egalitarian nature opened it to his design to monopolize power.

The passages analyzing how Bonaparte accomplished his design to achieve absolute power are among Tocqueville's most important contributions to the theory of the First Empire as a novel type of government. This he depicted as a new form of total domination based on an unprecedented reorganization of government and society. Its power eclipsed anything even dreamed of by absolute monarchs. This government was deliberately designed to exclude political liberty. Despite his claims for its qualitative novelty, Tocqueville called it a despotism:

The emperor without difficulty executed an extraordinary project. At one stroke and on a single plan, he rebuilt the entire fabric of society. He did so in order to make it accommodate absolute power without strain. ... This permitted Napoleon to construct a despotism far more rational and skillfully articulated than any previously attempted. After having promulgated with the same unitary spirit all those laws regulating the relations of citizens with one another and to the state, he was able to create at a single stroke all the powers charged with executing those laws. Thus he could structure all of them so as to constitute a great but simple machine of government. ... The formidable unity of the system, the powerful logic that linked all its parts, left no refuge for liberty.[50]

Finally, in a notable passage, Tocqueville rejected the excuses of those who had failed to resist Napoleon:

In societies with religious faith, or little knowledge, absolute power often constrains men without degrading them. This is because such power is acknowledged as legitimate. ... In our time, this cannot be the case. The eighteenth century and the French Revolution have not left us any moral or honorable ways of submitting to despotism. ... Thus ... when men submit to its laws, they can only despise it and themselves.[51]

Napoleon's regime was illegitimate as well as absolute.

The balance sheet of the First Empire, in Tocqueville's view, showed a series of unprecedented disasters for France. Napoleon had used his genius to restore and to perfect despotism, thus defeating the generous purposes of the Revolution at its inception. His unchecked power had allowed him to squander the lives and fortunes of his subjects in mindless attempts to conquer Europe. Napoleon's most durable achievement had proved permanently harmful to France, for he had perfected the machinery of administrative centralization continued by all successor regimes.

In 1842, Tocqueville's attention to Napoleon and the First Empire had been occasioned by an accident. He had to discuss Cessac, his predecessor in the seat to which he had been elected in l'Académie française. Thus it was not the danger that Napoleon's feat would be repeated that first prompted Tocqueville to analyze the First Empire and its creator. That same year, he had stated that he could not see any potential successor to Napoleon Bonaparte. This was not the case after the coup d'état that overthrew the Second Republic, and led to the creation of a second Bonapartist empire. Both Bonapartes executed military coups that overthrew republican governments, themselves created after great revolutions. Both used plebiscites based on universal manhood suffrage to register ostensible popular approval, first of their use of violence to overthrow freely elected representative institutions, and then of the empires they founded.

Tocqueville diagnosed both Bonapartes and their empires as novel because of their post-democratic and post-revolutionary character. They were post-democratic in claiming that their regimes were legitimate because the people had delegated to them the supreme power to rule directly in the general interest of the nation. They asserted that the people exercised their sovereignty by withdrawing approval for the parliaments they had previously chosen to represent them. Hence, despite the prior use of force, it was argued, voters could and did confer political power on the man who had overthrown the representative institutions of the republic. The regimes were post-revolutionary in that their founders further justified them by reference to their own stances vis-à-vis the great revolutions of 1789 and 1848. Both Bonapartes reassured the beneficiaries of these revolutions that, on the one side, they had nothing to fear from the nobility or the Church, and on the other, that the Empires protected them from radicals or extremists, whether Jacobins, sans-culottes, or socialists.

As François Furet and Françoise Mélonio have written in their volume of the Pléiade edition, Tocqueville after 1851 turned to investigating the genesis of despotism in France. This he envisioned as a three-volume project beginning with the old regime, moving on to the Revolution, and culminating with a volume on Napoleon and his Empire. In Tocqueville's 1853 notes, he explicitly identified Napoleon Bonaparte with "unlimited despotism." Tocqueville then linked the two Empires as embodying "the idea conceived by Napoleon and even more completely realized by his nephew."[52] In sketching the model for his future volume on the first Empire, Tocqueville returned to themes prominent in the *Démocratie* and his French Academy inaugural:

When I come to the Empire, analyze thoroughly its composition: the despotism of a single person raising himself upon a democratic base; the combination best suited for producing the most unlimited despotism, the one best supported by the appearance of being derived from right and sacred interest, that is, of the greatest number; and at the same time, the least responsible.[53]

Tocqueville continued to denounce the two Bonapartes' seizures of power by coup d'état, and their efforts after the fact to legitimate their rule by plebiscite. Tocqueville's notes of the 1850s are explicit, dismissing scornfully such rationalizations as those concocted by Troplong, one of the prominent jurists who rallied to Louis-Napoleon.[54] Thus the use of Caesarist arguments by defenders of

the Second Empire led Tocqueville to attack First Empire rationalizations of the 18th Brumaire, when Napoleon seized power:

[J]urists (*légistes*) create a theory and a philosophy [to justify] power in fact
created by violence and force. Ever since the spread of Roman law, tyrants in all
European nations have found it easier to recruit jurists than hangmen, although
under despots both types flourish. Even the most mediocre usurper has his
legal expert to prove that violence is law; tyranny, order; servitude, progress.[55]

This passage is a bitter indictment of both Bonapartes as engaging in
the cynical manipulation of public opinion by reversing the
meaning of concepts.

Another indictment of this Bonapartist abuse of language came
in the single paragraph about the First Emperor and his Empire in
the introduction to *l'Ancien régime*. There, Tocqueville notes that
Napoleon Bonaparte sought to conceal his regime's suppression of
freedom by fraudulently reversing the meaning of the Revolution's
basic concepts, while claiming at the same time that he was committed to the defense of its legacy:

Popular sovereignty was what this government called the votes of electors who could not inform themselves, deliberate, or choose among
candidates. This government depicted as freely consented taxation, the
assent of assemblies that had been reduced to servitude and silence.
While surrounding itself with the halo of the Revolution's great name,
this regime deprived the nation of self-government, the principal guarantees of law, the rights to think, speak, and write freely, that is, of
everything most precious and noble achieved in 1789.[56]

When *l'Ancien régime* appeared in 1856, no French reader could
have missed the tacit parallelism with Louis-Napoleon and the
Second Empire.[57]

Because of the strict censorship instituted by the Second
Empire, Tocqueville never publicly stigmatized it as the illegitimate and oppressive regime he judged it to be. But in his correspondence and recorded conversation, he called it an "imperial" or
"military" despotism. Writing in the early years of the regime,
which outlasted him by twelve years, he characterized its power as
both absolute and likely to endure until, like its predecessor, it
would be destroyed by an unnecessary war of its own making.

Embodying the violent and illiberal aspects of the Revolution, the Second Empire appealed to all those groups that, sharing this tradition, had supported Napoleon Bonaparte, and now accepted the myth of his greatness and the legitimacy of his family's dynasty:

It is so revolutionary in its origin and traditions, as not to alarm any of the great interests created by the Revolution.

... In a word, it satisfies all the new instincts of a democratic society, excepting only liberty. And it is just these other instincts that it uses to suppress liberty.

... Its origins are not only revolutionary, but military and Napoleonic, which gives it the solid support of the army.

... This regime can use all the procedures of military government to reinstate the traditions of imperial despotism.[58]

In another letter, Tocqueville applied the concept of despotism to the Second Empire by using passages from both parts of the *Démocratie*, his French Academy inaugural, and themes that would reappear in the *l'Ancien régime*:

This is not the end of the French Revolution, but [the return of] one of its forms. While reducing the people to servitude, this government in its laws proclaims the supremacy of popular sovereignty, ... hoping to combine the advantages of absolute rule with the force provided by popular government. ... This is the most absolute despotism ever seen in France.[59]

What the Second Empire had borrowed from democracy in its constitution was limited to the use of the majority principle, but in its worst possible form. For voting took place in the enforced "silence and darkness created by despotism." Those elected under the imposed constitution served in bodies devoid of power; opposition candidates could not address or write to voters, form committees to support their electoral efforts, or travel in their districts.[60] Thus, while Tocqueville in 1842 had attacked the perversion of democratic theory by the first Bonaparte, in the 1850s he added to that indictment the sordid frauds, electoral and otherwise, practiced by the second.

IV. CONCLUSION

Tocqueville's analyses of the greatest dangers to liberty in democracies did not remain constant over his three decades. Although he retained a number of important arguments, he modified some and abandoned still others. Tocqueville's assessments of these dangers can and should serve as one marker for tracing the trajectory of his political, social, and historiographical thought. These cannot be treated apart from the striking transformations of French governments he experienced during his relatively short life, already so affected by the great Revolution into which he was born. Nor was his thought about dangers to political liberty unaffected by what had occurred and was continuing to occur in the United States and United Kingdom, the two other countries that counted most in his comparative analyses.

The 1835 *Démocratie*, while depicting a tyranny of the majority over thought and expression, concluded that there are political and legal means – most notably decentralization and respect for constitutional and legal procedures, as well as guarantees of individual rights – for minimizing such constraints. At that time, Tocqueville's qualified optimism about combining liberty with democracy led him to construct the choice he offered his compatriots between "the tyranny of the Caesars" and a carefully balanced constitutional government recognizing the rights of all.

By the time he finished the 1840 *Démocratie*, Tocqueville had been first a candidate for, and then a member of, the Chamber of Deputies. There he experienced what politics meant in a society where individualism, apathy, materialism, and indifference to the welfare of others were actively encouraged by the government led by Guizot and Louis Philippe. Discarding "the tyranny of the Caesars" – that "scarecrow" of violent domination he had invoked in 1835 – he now replaced it by the dystopia of a paternal state reducing its citizens to sheep incapable of even conceiving the possibility of governing themselves. After insisting that the type of oppression menacing democratic peoples had no precedent in the past, Tocqueville settled for calling it sometimes "administrative despotism," sometimes "democratic despotism."

As the July Monarchy continued into the 1840s, Tocqueville began to see still other consequences of its leaders' successful annihilation of liberty understood as general participation in a genuine political life. The consequent corruption and isolation of the dominant elites, as well as the revival of revolutionary activism and the first appearance of socialism in the excluded lower classes, caused Tocqueville once again to abandon his earlier diagnoses of the greatest danger to liberty in his society. Even before 1848, Tocqueville revised the perceptions of risk successively articulated in the two *Démocraties*. Now he saw all of them superseded as the greatest danger to liberty by the reappearance of the French Revolution. In this threat, he included all the changes of government over the sixty years following 1789, including the First Empire. With the reappearance of that revolutionary tradition opposed to individual rights, representative government, and any constitutional limitations of national sovereignty, Tocqueville realized that his hopes for political liberty in France could no longer be sustained. "While one great revolution may be able to found a nation's liberty, several successive revolutions make the enjoyment of an ordered liberty impossible for a long time."[61]

Although Tocqueville was not altogether surprised by the second Napoleonic empire, he did not join other leading theorists in conceptualizing it as a qualitatively new form of government produced in the wake of revolution and democratization. Novel but contested terms were proposed for this type of regime. Even the names of the "isms" meant to designate it provoked controversy. Contemporaries had to choose among such neologisms as "Bonapartism," "Caesarism," "Napoleonism," and "Imperialism."[62] Once again, Tocqueville chose to retain the pre-revolutionary concepts of despotism and tyranny, modified by such adjectives as "military" or "imperial."

When it came to naming any of the threats to liberty he perceived as uniquely modern and democratic, Tocqueville first admonished himself to coin a word adequate to this new type of modern oppression. Then, drawing back from doing so, he adapted to his purpose an existing term coined to designate types of society and regimes he had declared to have become obsolete. Why did he continue applying these ancient terms to distinctively modern practices? How justifiable was his decision? When Tocqueville explained his distaste for neologisms and innovative uses of existing words, he argued that they endanger the language by making uncertain the meaning of ideas. "[G]ood language is impossible

without clear terms."[63] Was Tocqueville's political theory clarified
by his retaining and extending the concepts of despotism and tyranny to all the dangers to liberty he diagnosed as inherent in
modern democracies?

These two terms, long distinguished, had by the end of the
eighteenth century become conflated, though in eighteenth-century
France the preferred term for every disliked aspect of absolute monarchy had been *despotisme*. Because of the intensity of political
conflict, the concept of despotism came to carry a bewildering
number of senses.[64] This produced what has been called "the whiting
out of meaning."[65] That is, by the time Tocqueville began to write,
the word *despotisme* was at once so omnipresent and contested that
it no longer conveyed any single distinctive sense. Conflating the
concepts of despotism and tyranny reduced them to vague synonyms
suggesting little more than any government incompatible with
political liberty, however defined. Readers of Tocqueville should be
aware that his decision to continue using the concepts of despotism
and tyranny in such undifferentiated forms may have contributed to
blunting the edge of many of his valuable analyses, thus sometimes
reducing what is most original in them to apparent platitudes. For-
tunately, Tocqueville, by his thick descriptions of actual and potential dangers to liberty in democracies, often compensated for the lack
of precision in his definitions and political language.

NOTES

1   The most comprehensive historical studies of the concepts of tyranny and
     despotism are Mario Turchetti, *Tyrannie et tyrannicide de l'antiquité à nos
     jours* (Paris, 2001) and Hella Mandt, "Tyrannis, Despotie," in *Geschichtliche
     Grundbegriffe*, eds., Brunner, Conze, Koselleck, 6, 651–706. The most
     extensive treatments to date of the concept of despotism are the essays
     contained in *Dispotismo*, ed. Domenico Felice (2 vols; Naples, 2001). Shorter
     Treatments in English Include Richard Koebner, "Despot and Despotism:
     Vicissitudes of a Political Term," *Journal of the Warburg and Courtauld
     Institute*, 14 (1951): 272–302, and Melvin Richter, "The History of the
     Concept of Despotism," in the *Dictionary of the History of Ideas* (New York,
     1973), II, 1–20.
2   *DAII* (Nolla), 265.
3   The most thorough analysis confined to the *Démocratie* is James
     Schleifer, *The Making of Tocqueville's Democracy in America* (Chapel

Hill, 1980), 173–87. However, like Françoise Mélonio, Schleifer fails to indicate just how contested and variable in meaning the concepts of despotism and tyranny have been. Mélonio adds socialism to the catalogue of dangers in her "Tocqueville et le despotisme moderne," *Revue Française d'Histoire des Idées Politiques* 6 (1997): 339–54.

4 Françoise Mélonio "Tocqueville et le despotisme moderne," 340.

5 See my "A family of political concepts: Tyranny, despotism, Bonapartism, Caesarism, dictatorship, 1750–1917," *European Journal of Political Theory*, forthcoming. It has been convincingly argued by Raymond Aron, *Essai sur les libertés* (Paris, 1965), 143–44, and Martin Malia, *Journal of Democracy* 11 no. 1 (2000): 179–86, that Tocqueville did not and could not have anticipated twentieth-century totalitarianism.

6 See the discussion of "semantic transparency" in Douglas Howland, *Translating the West* (Honolulu, 2002), 18–25.

7 "As distinguished from concepts in general, a basic concept ... is an inescapable, irreplaceable part of the political and social vocabulary. Only after a concept has attained this status does it become crystallized in a single word or term such as 'revolution,' 'state,' 'civil society,' or 'democracy.' Basic concepts combine manifold experiences and expectations in such a way that they become indispensable to any formulation of the most urgent issues of any given time. [T]hey are always both controversial and contested." Reinhart Koselleck, in *The Meaning of Historical Terms and Concepts, New Studies on Begriffsgeschichte*, eds. Hartmut Lehmann and Melvin Richter (Washington, DC: German Historical Institute, 1996), 64.

8 *Lettres, S, Oeuvres,* P 3, 779.

9 I have attempted to chart changes in his concept of democracy in "Guizot and Tocqueville on Democracy: From a Type of Society to a Political Regime," *History of European Ideas* 30 (2004), 61–82; see also Pierre Rosanvallon, "The History of the Word 'Democracy' in France," *Journal of Democracy* 6 (1995): 140–54.

10 *AR, Œuvres,* P 3, 195; *AR,* 1 (trans. Kahan), 237.

11 *DAI* (Nolla), 189–92; *DAI* (trans. Goldhammer), 277–82.

12 *OC* 6:2, 91; *Œuvres* P 1, 513–14; *Journeys to E and I*, 116.

13 *DAI* (Nolla), 144.

14 *OC* 3:2, 134.

15 Letter V to the editor of *Le siécle*, 14 January 1843, *OC*, 3:2, 113.

16 *OC* 12:35 *S* (trans. Lawrence), 110.

17 Tocqueville's formulation, as given later, should be compared with "the neo-roman theory of free states" as described in Quentin Skinner, *Liberty before Liberalism* (Cambridge, 1998), 1–100. However, Skinner's schema does not fit Tocqueville. He believed that even in

absolute states, some, if members of privileged groups, could enjoy liberty. And he also made participation in public affairs by citizens into a defining quality of modern democratic liberty.

18 Schleifer, *The Making of Tocqueville's "Democracy in America,"* 173.
19 The transcript of the commission's proceedings has been published as *Genesi di una constituzione*, ed. Piero Craveri (Naples, 1985). The passage cited is from Tocqueville's remarks at the session of May 25, 1848, Craveri, 131.
20 *DAI* (trans. Goldhammer), 294.
21 *DAII* (trans. Goldhammer), 826–29.
22 *DAI, OC,* 330.
23 *DAI, OC,* 330. This passage is explicated in Tocqueville's letter to Kergorlay, n.d., *OC,* 13:1, 373: "[W]e are being swept along by our laws and moeurs towards a virtually complete equality of conditions. This being the case, I can see nothing between a democratic government (and by these words, I mean not a republic but a type of society (*état de société*) in which everyone more or less takes part in [public] affairs, and uncontrolled government by a single person. ... This I do not want."
24 *Œuvres* P 2, 837, 1177.
25 *DAII* (Nolla), 270, note x.
26 *DAII* (Nolla), 263–64.
27 Emperor Napoleon III, *History of Julius Caesar* (2 vols; New York, 1865–66), 1, vii.
28 Tocqueville to Reeve, 16 April 1856, *OC,* 5:1, 167; Tocqueville to Ampère, 17 January 1856, *OC* 11, 305.
29 Tocqueville to Beaumont, 27 February 1858, *OC* 8:3, 543–44.
30 *DAII* (Nolla), 265. Both *le despotisme administratif* and *le despotisme démocratique* are used on page 268 to characterize this type of government, to which Tocqueville had refused to give a name just a few pages before.
31 *DAI, OC* 1:2, 145–48.
32 Constant, *Œuvres,* ed. Rollin (Paris, 1957), 1004–05.
33 *DAII* (Nolla), 263, note b.
34 The note to himself is in *DAII* (Nolla), 265, note e (1); "administrative despotism" and "democratic despotism" occur in the same paragraph of the printed version of the text, *DAII* (Nolla), 268.
35 *DAII* (Nolla), 264, note d.
36 *DAII* (Nolla), 269, note t.
37 *OC* 13:1, 416–17.
38 *OC* 3:2, 198, note 2.
39 *OC* 12, 35. The translation is from *S,* 11.

40 Tocqueville to Kergorlay, end of January 1835, *OC* 13:1, 373.

41 *DAI* (Nolla), 79.

42 *Œuvres* P 1, 191.

43 *Œuvres* P 1, 190–91. Twenty years later, after the establishment of the Second Empire, Tocqueville repeated the same judgment: "The revolution continued its course, but liberty soon was the loser. For 'revolution' and 'liberty' are two words which historians must strictly distinguish. The First Consul, who in his own way personified and continued the French Revolution, was nevertheless among the greatest enemies ever known of human liberty." OC 16, 234, note 6a. For a discussion of the extent to which this hostility to Bonaparte was registered in the *Démocratie*, see my "Tocqueville, Napoleon, and Bonapartism," in *Reconsidering Tocqueville's Democracy in America*, ed. E. Eisenstadt (New Brunswick, 1988), 110–45.

44 Cessac had carried through what Isser Woloch has called the most surprising triumph of the Napoleonic regime, by successfully supplying its imperial master with the 400,000 young men he needed every year for his omnivorous armies. *The New Regime. Transformations of the French Civic Order, 1789–1820s* (New York, 1994), 424.

45 *OC* 16, 263.

46 *OC* 16, 264.

47 *DAI* (Nolla), 302.

48 *OC* 16, 262.

49 *OC* 16, 266.

50 *OC* 16, 264–65.

51 *OC* 16, 265–66.

52 *OC* 2:2, 319.

53 *Œuvres*, P 3: 702; *AR*, 2 (trans. Kahan), 247.

54 *OC* 2:2, 319; Tocqueville to Ampère, 27 December 1855, *OC* 11, 305.

55 *OC* 2:2, 319.

56 *AR*, OC 2:1, 72.

57 For an extended treatment of this topos, see James Boyd White, *When Words Lose Their Meaning* (Chicago, 1984); for 'l'abus des mots,' Sophia Rosenfeld, *A Revolution in Language* (Stanford, 2001); Ulrich Ricken, "*Réflexions du XVIIIe siècle sur 'l'abus des mots*," Mots 4 (1982): 29–45.

58 "*Note pour le Comte de Chambord*," 14 January 1852, OC 3:3, 466.

59 Letter to Francis Leiber, August 4 1852, *OC* 7:144–45.

60 Letter to Monckton Milnes, 9 February 1852, *DAII* (Nolla), 269, note t.

61 *S* (trans. Lawrence), 65.

62 See my "Tocqueville and French Nineteenth-Century Conceptualizations of the Two Bonapartes and their Empires," in *Dictatorship in*

History and Theory, eds. Peter Baehr and Melvin Richter (Cambridge: Cambridge University Press, 2004), 83–102.

63 *DAII* (trans. Goldhammer), 550. Some critics of Tocqueville's terminology may see an unintended irony in his manuscript marginal note on this paragraph, which ends with the call for clear terms: "To cut, I think." *DAII* (Nolla), 70, note g.

64 See my *"Le concept de despotisme et l'abus des mots,"* in *Dix-huitième siècle* 34 (2002): 373–88.

65 Professor Koselleck has called attention to just such a loss of meaning as the concept of crisis came to be grossly overused. See his conclusion to the article on *Krise* in *Geschichtliche Grundbegriffe*, eds. Brunner, Conze, Koselleck, 3, 647–50.

11 Tocqueville on Democratic Religious Experience

Rather than entering into a discussion of the frequently asked questions – "Was Tocqueville himself a believer," "Did he think Christianity was true or useful (or both)," and so on – I will consider whether we can conclude from *Democracy in America* that there is such a thing as democratic religious experience? To put the question somewhat differently, do the "conditions of social equality" about which Tocqueville wrote occasion modes of religious experience that are historically novel, relatively coherent, and distinguishable from what might be called aristocratic religious experience?

In order to investigate this thought, I will rely on Tocqueville's historical schema in *Democracy in America*, first, to illuminate what I will here call "the fable of liberalism," within which, it is often presumed, religion and democracy are immiscible, and second, to provide an account of certain developments within Christianity in the modern period that Tocqueville intimates can be explained by the emergence of democratic social conditions. My concern, among other issues, will be the emergence of an impulse toward fundamentalism, which I suggest is a necessary development in the democratic age; the increasing claims of unmediated personal religious experience and the decreased importance of religious formalities, which I take to be related phenomena; the appearance of radical claims about the depth of sin; and the crisis of authority in the churches. All of these developments can be seen in the democratic age. My thesis here is that the analysis Tocqueville offers in *Democracy in America* allows us to comprehend them in a unified manner.

I. "THE FABLE OF LIBERALISM"

Near the end of *Democracy in America*, Tocqueville tells us that the people about whom he has written are like two "distinct [kinds] of humanity."[1] By this he means that the aristocratic and democratic ages, respectively, can each be understood in terms of the preeminence of a "type" of person. The thesis of his book, as we know, is that we now live on the threshold of the democratic age,[2] and that the democratic "type" will soon prevail.

To be sure, Tocqueville is rather ambivalent about the emergence of this new "type" of human being, yet we cannot go back to the aristocratic past, he tells us. To do so would be, in his words, "to fight against God Himself."[3] We are told, in fact, that we are caught up in a grand providential plan, and that human responsibility in history now requires that we act with a view to the limits and possibilities set forth by that plan.[4] Since my thesis about what I am here calling "democratic modes of religious experience" is predicated on the contours of the account Tocqueville gives of this providential plan, let me here first rehearse that account – not in the form of a theology of history but rather in terms of a salutary tale that can be called, fittingly, the "fable of liberalism." The tale is not, of course, originally Tocqueville's, and for that reason I will cite other authors who have contributed to its development along the way. Tocqueville's iteration of the fable of liberalism is, however, the grandest of all those who have contributed to it, and for that reason I will present it as if in his own voice. When I turn to the subject of democratic religious experience, the brilliance of his own contribution to this fable will become apparent. My thesis here is that while the "fable of liberalism" suggests that religion will be an archaism in the democratic age, Tocqueville's iteration of it offers the rather remarkable claim that religious experience changes form in the democratic age, but does not dissipate. All that in due course, however.

*   *   *

Our genealogy, so the fable of liberalism begins, is marked by two distinct epochs. The first, "the aristocratic age," corresponds to a past that is either rapidly receding from view or irretrievably lost, and that is known to us through the recorded deeds of men who evinced grandeur of soul that can no longer be fancied, let alone produced. Here, loyalty, honor, virtue, manliness, and, above all, great longings held sway in the souls of a few. Here, too, pettiness, destitution, and squalor overwhelmed the lives of the many. In this first epoch, society was a relatively well-understood hierarchy, even if not a well-ordered one, purportedly corresponding to nature itself, in which the bonds of affection were prescribed by the rank into which one was born. Authority was vested in men and not in abstract principles, and formality and protocol were, for the nobility (and not only for them), the "decent drapery of life."[5] Landed property was the basis of wealth, the consequence of which was the curious elevation of both prudential knowledge and military valor: the former, because the leisure alone afforded to a landed class could give rise to it; the latter, because there was no overarching power to secure the boundaries of landed property itself. The privileged knowledge of the aristocracy, and its incessant warfare, constituted the defining features of the epoch.

Where the warrant for the first epoch was the legacy of the past, the warrant for the second epoch, "the democratic age," is the promise of the future, a future not under the guardianship of a few great men, but rather the possession of nations, or even of humanity as a whole. The aristocrat was a steward who vouchsafed the mortal patterns inherited from his fathers; the human being of the present moment, however, labors alone – or perhaps guided by the beneficent hand of an invisible God – not in order to imitate the fathers but rather to innovate.[6]

Let us add that nature itself offers no guide to human beings in this second epoch, for it, too, arose out of a series of contingent events that could have been otherwise – whether by God's hand or not, we cannot say.[7] Gone, therefore, is nature's familiarity and humanity's easy confidence about a natural order into which it has been placed, and to which its faculties correspond. Here, loyalty can mean little, for it depends on organic union, which is illusory; honor can mean little, for it depends on rank, which affronts modern sensitivities; virtue can mean little, for it depends on character, which takes too much time and effort to develop; manliness can mean little, for it depends on the prospect for violence, which has been eliminated; great longing can mean little, for it depends on an emptiness of soul, the awareness of which has been buried by a glut of goods or made the object of therapy.

Where nature offers no comprehensive guide, humanity is thrown back on its own resources, upon its "reason," which is now understood, not in its unity as communion with God, but in its dissevered, disenchanted, aspects: subjectively, as self-interest; objectively, as science. The multiple and nuanced possibilities of human excellence that emerged in the first, enchanted epoch have here receded and been replaced by the monolith of reason – not incidentally, at the very moment that multiple social ranks collapse and give way to the univocal aspiration for "well-being," which is the very hallmark of social equality.[8]

Yet this forlorn situation of humanity without aristocratic bearings is not without recompense. Reason so delimited attains its proper object. In its subjective, self-interested, aspect, the self-referentiality of reason invites the development of reflective judgment, private conscience, and, above all, individual responsibility. In its objective, scientific aspect, it invites the development of a generalized method of inquiry for the purpose of understanding and transforming the natural world, so that well-being may be secured for humanity as a whole.

Not only does reason attain its proper object in this second epoch, but also, in finally finding it, humanity need no longer indulge and exhaust itself endlessly in the passions of war. The calmer and tamer disposition of reason that is both cause and consequence of commerce triumphs as humanity is finally able to make a productive purchase on the natural world. "Commerce cures destructive prejudices, and it is an almost general rule that everywhere there are gentle mores, there is commerce and everywhere there is commerce, there are gentle mores."[9] The height to which humanity may ascend through reason is lower than the height to which the aristocratic man may ascend through glory, but in its general availability and advantage to all constitutes reason's superiority. Glory is the purview of a few aristocratic men; reason is the purview of humanity as a whole. On the battlefields, a few great men emerge; in the market place, humanity as a whole benefits. The taming of man, and the advent of universal commerce for humanity, is to be the achievement of the second epoch. Here, moneymaking supplants the aristocratic longing for glory. A world exhausted by war chooses a tamer course.

We have finally reached the age of commerce, an age that must necessarily replace that of war, as the age of war was bound to precede it. War and commerce are only two different means to achieve the same end, that of possessing what is desired. Commerce is ... an attempt to obtain by mutual agreement what one can no longer hope to obtain through violence .... War then comes before commerce. The former is all savage impulse, the latter civilized calculation. It is clear that the more the commercial tendency prevails, the weaker must the tendency to war become.[10]

The taming of humanity that occurs in this second epoch is a consequence of more than just the victory of reason over glory, however. The collapse of multiple social ranks carries with it the burden and promise of human relations without predicates. The chasm between nations, social ranks, generations, and between men and women is, if not bridged, then at least bridgeable in principle, since differences between them have no durable foundation in nature.[11] Where the first epoch is characterized by rank and the "pathos of distance," the second epoch is characterized by social equality and "fellow feeling."[12] Here, each human being is close enough to every other so that all suffering is noticed, and mutual sympathy is possible. Reason and commerce tame the passion for glory, and render life orderly; but it is sympathy that finally softens humanity. In the second epoch – and this is one of its most wholesome achievements – concern and solicitude become possible.

The accomplishments and future potentialities of the second epoch are not grand, but they are decent. Commerce cannot produce great men, but it can yield well-being for all. Sympathy and concern are no doubt pale affections in comparison to loyalty of the sort that rank inspires; but with loyalty comes cruelty as well, and the advantage of the paler affections is shown by this very conjunction.

*   *   *

The contours of this fable are recognizable in the theory of modernization told in one form or another in classrooms and in foreign policy bureaus of every democratic nation around the globe. Unmodified, the fable intimates that the religious impulse, like the longing for honor and glory that characterizes the aristocratic age, will dissipate as the moral vocabulary of self-interest comes to prevail. Let us turn our attention, however, to Tocqueville's nuanced assessment of religion in the democratic age. There we will find ample evidence that this is not, in fact, the fate of religion.

While it is certainly the case that the *Democracy in America* is suffused with observations about what (more generously) could be called the "great leveling" or (less generously) the coming mediocrity of the democratic age,[13] Tocqueville's writing about the nature of religious experience cannot be said to align in any simple way with his general assessment of the mediocre democratic character and temperament of the future. True, there are any number of passages in which he worries that religion in the democratic age will lose its magisterial quality, as it is reconfigured by democratic man's incessant, misplaced drive to overcome "differences" – the grandest of all being the difference between God the Creator and God's Creation.[14] But as with all ideas Tocquevillean, there are countervailing tendencies, which we would do well to bear in mind if we wish to have a complete understanding of the character of religious experience in the democratic age. On the one hand, Tocqueville thought that religious experience would, like everything else in the democratic age, become tame and self-referential.[15] On the other hand, however, he intimated that the social conditions of the democratic age make new forms of religious experience possible or, if not simply possible, then prevalent. This insight suggests an important modification to the fable of liberalism, the contours of which I have just outlined.

II. THE IMPULSE TOWARDS FUNDAMENTALISM

Is religion in the democratic age an anachronism, as any number of Enlightenment thinkers have suggested? While writers throughout history have noted that religion is a perennial aspect of human life,[16] a prominent strand of Enlightenment thought presumes (historically) that modernity involves the movement from enchantment to disenchantment, and (normatively) that in the face of this historical truth, if religion is embraced, it is because individuals lack the strength of character to live in a world without God.[17] To this claim, Tocqueville replies: "Eighteenth-century philosophers had a very simple explanation for the gradual weakening of beliefs. Religious zeal, they said, was bound to die down as enlightenment and freedom spread. It is tiresome that the facts do not fit this theory at all."[18]

Tocqueville writes about the persistance of the religious impluse against the background of the disintegration of Christianity in Europe. The reason for that disintegration cannot occupy us here, except to say that it occurred because of the European Churches' inability to disentangle themselves from political power during the age of aristocracy. Tocqueville's observations of religious practice in the United States, which lacked an aristocratic past, led him to conclude that the supposition of any number of European Enlightenment thinkers about the fate of religion in the democratic age must be turned around: the United States "anomaly" is actually paradigmatic, and the Europe of his own day is anomalous. Disbelief, Tocqueville says, is an (historical) accident; faith is the only permanent condition of mankind.[19]

If religion is to make an appearance in the democratic age, what are the impulses that will animate it, and what are the forms religion is likely to take? The title of this section gives us some indication of what is to be expected – namely, an impulse toward fundamentalism. The term, "Fundamentalist," emerged at the dawn of the twentieth century, as a consequence of the 1917 publication of a multi-volume series entitled *The Fundamentals*.[20] By the locution, "impulse towards fundamentalism," I intend to identify neither the Fundamentalist sect nor the twentieth-century Neo-Evangelical, Pentecostal, and Charismatic sects that are also animated, more or less, by the impulse to establish the "fundamentals" of Christian living. Rather, I am concerned with the animating impulse that predates the advent of any and all of these sects. I am interested in the impulse itself, and in the reason why that impulse emerges with great force in the democratic age.

To be sure, one source of this impulse is to be found in the Puritans themselves, whose criminal codes, Tocqueville says, were occasionally "taken word for word from Deuteronomy, Exodus, and Leviticus."[21] But path-dependency arguments alone do not get us to the heart of the matter. There are several other factors involved. The first and foremost of these is material prosperity, which is not so much a source of the impulse behind certain religious sects as the force behind religion itself. The Puritans may have been the prototype for what followed, but unless we can first understand why the material prosperity that developed in the United States did not overpower any and all religious sentiment, we will be baffled not only by the durability of religion but also by its periodic reinvigoration. Why does this happen?

In the United States, Tocqueville argues, material prosperity is a great temptation, which makes citizens periodically forget all else. Yet elsewhere, he says that material prosperity can also lead to religious zeal.[22] Man has both a material and spiritual nature; the more he throws himself into one aspect of his existence the more the other makes its demands felt. It is not an accident, on this reading, that in the United States – the land where material prosperity is loved more than anywhere else – there should be periodic and enthusiastic revivals of religion. In Tocqueville's words:

I should be surprised if, among a people uniquely preoccupied with prosperity, mysticism did not soon make progress. It is said that the emperor's persecutions and the massacres in the amphitheaters peopled the deserts of the Thebaid; I should rather hold Roman luxury and Greek Epicureanism responsible.[23]

"The short space of sixty years can never shut in the whole of a man's imagination,"[24] Tocqueville says. The world may captivate man's attention, but only for so long. The "instinctive sense of another life without difficulty"[25] makes itself known, and in proportion (if only periodically) to the effort to hide amidst abundance. The experience of the United States, in a word, confirms the proposition that materialism is a threat to spiritual health, and that it can be a goad to it.

Materialism, then, is not necessarily an obstacle to the vibrancy of religion. But let us turn to a more interesting aspect of Tocqueville's thinking about democratic modes of religious experience – namely, to the "social conditions of equality" which are at the heart of his understanding of the democratic age. These, we can educe, also contribute to the fundamentalist impulse. I will consider two aspects of these social conditions: first, the contingent character of experience that it elicits, and second, the epistemological prejudice that emerges because of such contingency.

With respect to the contingent nature of human experience in the democratic age, consider, as an exemplar, the thought of Thomas Hobbes. Whatever else may be said about Hobbes's assessment of the state of nature, its depiction of the exposure and contingency associated with the condition of equality accords well with the experience of the democratic age. For Hobbes, there is no Finis Ultimis, no Summum Bonum, to which we may readily accede; instead there is only "perpetual and restless desire of power after power, that ceaseth only in death."[26] We may wish to attenuate the language somewhat, but the fact remains that the experience of the contingency of the world occupies and haunts the democratic imagination. Tocqueville agrees.

In such a world, as I intimated in my outline of the fable of liberalism, the idea of a stable human nature becomes less and less thinkable, and democratic man searches restlessly, now here, now there, for a place of repose – to no avail. Under such circumstances, Tocqueville writes, the need for simple, intelligible, injunctions of the sort that religion supplies[27] will make itself felt. Thus, in the United States, the land of continual social upheaval, there is a perennial return, not to the philosophers, but rather to the "plain and simple meaning" of Scripture. These occasional but deeply transforming reorientations towards Scripture have been followed by periods of worldly accommodation – after which, again, the complexities of worldly life become too much to integrate, and Scripture finds its way once more into the inner recesses of the human heart. The history of the mainline Protestant Churches certainly evinces this pattern, and there is no reason to expect that this pattern will not continue long into the future.[28]

The matter of the contingency wrought by the emergence of social equality, however, does not fully account for the efflorescence of the fundamentalist impulse. A second factor that must be borne in mind is what could be called the epistemological prejudice that attends the emergent conditions of social equality. This prejudice, which we see already beginning to form in both the

Enlightenment thought of Descartes and the Protestant thought of Luther,[29] involves the desire to strip away the mystifications of knowledge, the desire to find the "clear and simple" truth of the matter, whatever it may happen to be.

The religious expression of this desire is scriptural literalism. In Tocqueville's estimation, it is neither an accident nor an anachronism that scriptural literalism emerges in the democratic age. Scriptural literalism is a response to the problem of complexity, a need to find the plain and simple meaning of things when the exigencies of life provide scant time to dwell on the nuances and mysteries that are evident enough – provided there is adequate leisure time to notice them. In the democratic age, when such subtleties appear through the lens of impatience to be little more than mystifications, literal interpretations will always be appealing. "Men living [in democratic] times are impatient with figures of speech; symbols appear to them as childish artifices used to hide or dress up truths which could more easily be shown to them naked and in broad daylight."[30] Democratic man senses himself to be thrust into a contingent world, and is without the inclination to consider anything other than the plain facts of the matter. Having limited time to solve the manifold problems that daily come into view, the hermeneutic principle relied upon is likely to be straightforward and self-evident.

On this reading, the varying sects of fundamentalism may wax and wane as political forces, but it would be a mistake to see in these oscillations a battle between purported "democratic impulses," on the one hand, and archaic "religious impulses," on the other.[31] Whatever the other grounds for the incompatibility of Fundamentalist Christianity and modern democracy may be, the two are in accord with respect to their epistemological prejudice in favor of literalism. Said otherwise, the impulse towards fundamentalism is a religious articulation of the democratic age. Notwithstanding its occasionally sharp opposition to the secular world, the impulse towards fundamentalism accords with the democratic epistemological prejudice in favor of simplicity and plain meaning. Far from being anti-modern, this impulse is only fully plausible within the democratic age itself.

III. UNMEDIATED PERSONAL RELIGIOUS
EXPERIENCE AND THE DIMINISHED IMPORTANCE
OF RELIGIOUS FORMALITIES

The impulse towards fundamentalism is one important aspect of democratic religious experience. Another is that religious experience is unmediated and direct – that is, without need for mortal mediaries. It is, in a word, comparatively unbounded[32] by the strictures of tradition and authority that characterized religion in the aristocratic age. The possibility of unmediated religious experience is corroborated by mystics of all ages, yet Tocqueville seems to suggest that the conditions of social equality conspire to make this the dominant religious sentiment of the democratic age. How might this be so?

Interestingly enough, Tocqueville's most sustained treatment of the prospect for unmediated character of religious experience occurs at the end of a provocative chapter entitled "The Sources of Poetic Inspiration." Its subject is the changing character of art as the aristocratic age gives way to the democratic age. At first blush, it is odd that he should conclude this chapter with a set of observations about the character of religious experience in the democratic age. Yet it makes sense in light of what could be called his "general theory of mediation" – namely, that as the aristocratic age gives way to the democratic age, mediation of all forms becomes less and less thinkable. In his words:

> The idea of secondary powers, between the sovereign and his subjects, was natural to the imagination of aristocratic peoples .... Opposite reasons naturally banish such an idea from the minds of men in ages of equality.[33]

For political scientists, especially in the post-World War II period, the central theme of *Democracy in America* is the importance of, and prospect for, political mediation between the solitary citizen and the powerful state.[34] Yet here, in his chapter on art, the concern is quite different. In the aristocratic age, beauty is mediated by and through the well-established idioms – largely classical or biblical – that have been handed down, generation to generation. As we enter the democratic age, however, the very idea of mediation comes into question, the consequence of which, for art, is that the inherited idioms through which beauty has been mediated cease to hold sway over the democratic imagination – hence, for Tocqueville, a crisis in the visual arts, which was confirmed by developments at the end of the nineteenth century.

Dubiety about mediated forms of Beauty in the democratic age clearly worried Tocqueville, but the chapter in which we find this concern does not end with the collapse of art into solipsism. Rather, Tocqueville there raises the prospect that the object of man's longing may shift away from art – and towards God. Thus, while art in the aristocratic mode of modifications on inherited idioms may no longer be possible in the democratic age, the very suspicion of mediated forms generated in the democratic age grants a new possibility in the domain of religion – namely, direct and unmediated experience of God.

Just when every man, raising his eyes above his country, begins to see mankind at large, God shows himself more clearly to human perception in full and entire majesty. In democratic ages faith in positive religions may waver, and belief in intermediary agents, by whatever names they are called, may grow dim, yet men are disposed to conceive a much more vast conception of divinity itself, and God's intervention in human affairs appears in a new and brighter light.[35]

It could be argued that this is scant evidence on which to base a rather broad claim about the prevalence of unmediated religious experience in the democratic age. There is evidence in other portions of *Democracy in America*, however, that corroborates this claim, the most explicit being Tocqueville's veiled warning to the Roman Catholic Church about dressing religion up in formalities that no longer comport with democratic man's need for direct religious experience:

[I]n a time of equality nothing is more repugnant to the human spirit than the idea of submitting to formalities. Men living in such times are impatient with figures of speech; symbols appear to them as childish artifices used to dress up or hide truths which could be more naturally shown to them naked and in broad daylight. Ceremonies leave them cold, and their natural tendency is to attach but secondary importance to the details of worship.[36]

The abandonment of inherited forms is a central feature of the democratic age.[37] This has implications for more than just the Roman Catholic Church, however. In the democratic age, the link between what is venerable and what is old is broken.[38] Without such a link, democratic man is thrown back upon himself. Impatient to negotiate his way through a contingent world, he has little time for ideas and experiences that are not self-evident, simple, and direct. In the realm of religion, this means that there will likely be a palpable movement away from the formalisms of the church in favor of the direct evidence of divine intervention, at the personal level.

While the fable of liberalism would seem to suggest the contrary, Tocqueville's reading of the affinities between religion and democracy leads us to expect that claims about direct divine illumination will become a cornerstone of religious experience in the democratic age. Democracy and "spiritual enthusiasm" go hand in hand. The dubiety about mediation is the cornerstone on which democratic experience, in general, and religious experience, in particular, stand in the democratic age.

IV. THE ADVENT OF RADICAL NOTIONS OF ORIGINAL SIN

I am going to be more speculative here than I have been so far, in part because Tocqueville himself has very little to say about sin in *Democracy in America*. True, he writes extensively about the Puritans in the opening passages, but his intention there is not to illuminate their theology of human depravity, which was quite austere, but rather to point out the need for religion to bound the imagination of the self, so that it may exercise its political freedom well.[39] His intention seems less to defend Puritan religious views than to attack Enlightenment philosophical views.[40]

There is, nevertheless, a puzzle about the idea of sin in the democratic age to which Tocqueville's analysis can be addressed, notwithstanding his own silence on the matter: why is it that radical doctrines of the depravity of humankind emerge with such force at the dawn of the democratic age – say, in the form of the attraction of Luther or of Calvin to Pauline Christianity? To put the matter otherwise, why do the Epistles of Paul, largely contained by

Roman Catholic theology up until the sixteenth century,[41] explode onto the scene at the dawn of the Democratic age? Invoking Tocqueville's terms, in what manner do conditions of social equality contribute to the emergence of more radical doctrines of human depravity at the beginning of the democratic age?

A large part of the answer to this question emerges in Tocqueville's chapter on what could be called the moral vocabulary of the democratic age – that is, in his chapter on "self interest rightly understood."[42] There, and elsewhere, Tocqueville does not go so far as to say that the moral vocabulary of virtue found in the aristocratic age is entirely absent, but he does say that in the democratic age, self-interest rather than virtue prevails – and this because in the democratic age, man intimates that he is cut off from both nature and a stable social order. Isolated and alone, he finds the language of self-interest more congenial to his existential situation. "No power on earth can prevent increasing equality from turning men's minds to look toward the useful or disposing each citizen from getting wrapped up in himself."[43]

Tocqueville seems to have understood here that there can be no moral vocabulary of virtue without an intact understanding of nature. Theologically, the Roman Catholic Church maintains the view to this day that while sin disrupted human nature, the original communion between God and His highest creature was not wholly sundered. That is, in the experience of sin, man is not entirely cut off from God. Yet Tocqueville did not think that this understanding could possibly hold sway in the democratic age – not so much because it is false, but because it does not comport well with what human experience discloses in that age. The "conditions of social equality" that are the hallmark of the age of democracy suggest to democratic man that he is, in fact, cut off, delinked[44] from his world. Under such conditions, is it any wonder that theologians should conclude that the right understanding of man's relation to God involved a radical reading of the doctrine of original sin, of man being radically cut off from God? The breakdown of seemingly eternal social relations founded in nature itself during the long dominant aristocratic age threw the very idea of nature into question. The theological manifestation of this breakdown – which appeared under the guise of a "recovery" of the original Christian teaching – was a doctrine of original sin that denied that an intact "nature" survived Adam's fall.[45] On Tocqueville's reading, I believe, this radical doctrine would have only become broadly thinkable in the event of social upheavals on the scale that brought the aristocratic age to a close.

While no one cause can be singled out as the source of the demise of aristocracy, the precursors to capitalism about which Weber wrote in *The Protestant Ethic and the Spirit of Capitalism* – commerce involving "free labor," double entry book-keeping, protection of contracts and so on – were clearly at the heart of the transformation. Tocqueville saw this as well. "While kings were ruining themselves in great enterprises and nobles wearing each other out in private wars, the commoners were growing rich by trade."[46] The preeminent location of this transformation was in the cities of Europe. And it was there that the Reformers, armed with their message of the radical depravity of man, first took hold.[47] Tocqueville no doubt would have understood the connection: the social disruption caused by nascent capitalism was coincident with the emergence of radical doctrines of the sinfulness of man. Both presuppose the experience of man cut off from nature, on his own and naked; both confirm that man lives in a post-Edenic world.

Should this correlation not be spurious, we can expect that as the pressure of markets and the demand for global free trade impinges upon those relatively intact enclaves where the idea of a stable nature still prevails, we will not only see the disruption of the aristocratic honor cultures that still reign in many parts of the world, as the fable of liberalism would predict,[48] but also a shift in those parts of the world with a post-Colonial legacy of Christianity away from Roman Catholic understandings of sin to the more radical understandings of the sort offered by the Reformed Churches. Evidence suggests that this shift is already underway in Latin America,[49] and elsewhere,[50] as a Tocquevillean reading of events there would predict.

Unrefined renditions of the fable of liberalism have no room for an analysis that links religion and modernity,[51] yet Tocqueville's more nuanced understanding of the character of democratic experience points in this direction. As the vestiges of aristocracy vanish and honor is supplanted by self-interest, the experience of being cut off and delinked that is a necessary precondition for market self-interest to thrive also yields radical religious formulations of the doctrine of original sin in those nations with a strong Christian heritage, whether by diffusion or by conquest. Said otherwise, religious denominations that emphasize man's radical sinfulness will find an especially hospitable home in nations where money[52] – the single measure left in the democratic age – comes to prevail. In the United States, this is true already. Not surprisingly, "post-materialist" Europe[53] shows little evidence of such a linkage. It is in the developing world, however, where Tocqueville's insights are most illuminating. Instead of the dissipation of religion, we see particularly stringent formulations of the doctrine of original sin, which are manifestly opposed to the self-understanding that now prevails among the secular elites in North America and elsewhere.[54]

V. THE CRISIS OF AUTHORITY IN THE CHURCHES

Thus far I have suggested that the impulse towards fundamentalism, unmediated religious experience, and a radical notion of human depravity are attributes that comport with democratic experience, by which is meant the sort of experience generated by conditions of social equality. A fourth attribute, borne out by the evidence, is the crisis of authority in the Churches. Here again I recur to Hobbes. Written at the dawn of the democratic age, Hobbes's *Leviathan* is instructive more for the problem it identifies than for the resolution it offers. And what is that problem? Much of the debate about the *Leviathan* has been inattentive to the territory Hobbes traverses in his consideration of the authority of the Church. In brief, his antagonists are the Roman Catholics, who he claims are guilty of what might be called "false universalism," and the Reformers, who he claims are guilty of what might be called "radical particularism."[55] On Hobbes's reading, the problem with the Roman Church was that it claimed universal jurisdiction before the End Time.[56] When Christ comes again in glory, the Universal Church will appear, but not until then.[57] On the other hand, while the Reformed Church may have been correct in denying authority to the Pope, the effect of the controversy between them undermined the authority of both, for now the word of God was in the hands of the people. "After the Bible was translated into English, every man, nay, every boy and wench, that could read English, thought they spoke with God Almighty, and understood what He said."[58] Hobbes's resolution of this dilemma was to accord to the sovereign of each nation the right to interpret Scripture. Each nation should, in effect, have a Pope – or, even more apt, a Moses, under whom political and religious authority is unified.

To be sure, the resolution at which Hobbes arrives is anachronistic. Yet what he did see, plainly, was the nature of the crisis of authority that the democratic age would evince: the destruction of mediational sites of authority and the emergence of a bifurcated arrangement in which authority is simultaneously vested in the solitary individual and in a purportedly universal community. We have already seen, in Tocqueville's *Democracy in America*, how conditions of social equality break the links between persons and encourage the self-referential language of self-interest. Yet equality also generates opposite tendencies as well:

> In times of equality men, being so like each other, have no confidence in others, but this same likeness leads them to place almost unlimited confidence in the judgment of the public .... The same equality which makes him independent of each separate citizen leaves him isolated and defenseless in the face of the majority.[59]

In the democratic age, authority does not disappear; it gets relocated. This relocation of authority has implications for religion in the democratic age, which I will consider here.

Tocqueville, himself nominally a Roman Catholic, thought that Protestantism could not long prevail because man cannot long endure the isolation it engenders.[60] Protestantism tends to decompose into a form of solipsism in which the method and object of love cease to correspond. While Tocqueville doesn't fully develop this latter thought, a critique of Protestantism that accords with a long-standing body of literature on the subject emerges in conjunction with his observations about the problem of authority in democracy.[61] Hegel, himself a Lutheran, understood the difficulty: many Protestants have recently gone over to the Roman Catholic Church because they found their inner life worthless. They had grasped at something fixed, at a support, an authority, even if it was not exactly the stability of thought which they caught.[62] And elsewhere: "[t]he self-tormenting disposition [of Protestantism] in the present day has induced many persons to enter the Catholic pale, that they might exchange this inward uncertainty for a formal broad certainty based upon the imposing totality of the Church."[63] Notwithstanding these difficulties, Hegel staunchly defended Protestantism:

Each individual [came to enjoy] the right of deriving instruction for himself from [the Bible], and of directing his conscience in accordance with it. [Because of the Reformation] we see a vast change in the principle by which man's religious life is guided: the whole system of Tradition, the whole fabric of the Church becomes problematical, and its authority is subverted.[64]

In our own day, we are able to see this phenomenon in the proliferation of sects within Protestantism and, just as importantly, in the proliferation of translations of the Bible. The age of democracy, which privileges the authority of each individual, will only cause this phenomenon to increase, and with it the dissipation of Protestantism.[65]

According to Tocqueville, the longing for an escape from this dissipating situation, in which the authority of subject is at once absolute and socially insignificant, leads the soul invariably towards the Roman Catholic Church. Catholics may have been resigning their faith because of the unholy alliance between Church and worldly powers in Tocqueville's Europe, but when Protestants reached the abyss of independence and impotence, they would be drawn back towards the Roman Church – in his day and in our own. For this reason, Tocqueville was able to say: "Our grandchildren will tend more and more to be divided clearly between those who have completely abandoned Christianity and those who have returned to the Church of Rome."[66]

On this reading, it is not by accident that we are now entering into what has been called "the Catholic Moment." Without detracting from the respects in which the (largely Protestant) phenomena I have considered in this chapter genuinely accord with democratic experience, it is not self-evident that Protestantism can withstand the withering critique Hobbes long ago leveled and Tocqueville later corroborated. Should it be able to draw anew upon the covenantal tradition inaugurated by Judaism and carried forward by the Puritans, then perhaps there is hope that Protestantism yet has resources upon which it can draw. Short of that, the strength of "the Catholic Moment" will likely continue unabated. To be sure, this is a massive counter argument against the claims I have made in Sections II–IV of this chapter. If Tocqueville is correct, however, in his claim that authority in the democratic age is located in two distinct sites, then both the forces I considered in Sections II–IV, which militate towards distinctly Protestant modes of religious experience, and the strengthening of the Roman Catholic Church, briefly discussed here in Section V, are to be expected. This seeming contradiction, which points to the fortification of both the Protestant and Roman Catholic Church in the democratic age, does not indicate a contradiction in Tocqueville's thought. Rather, it is the consequence of the contradictions inherent in the nature of the democratic experience that Tocqueville analyzes.

VI. CONCLUSION

In its colloquial form, the fable of liberalism offers little understanding of either the enduring strength of Christianity or the forms that it takes. Tocqueville, himself perhaps the most prophetic architect of that fable in the nineteenth century, was well aware that the democratic age would not witness the decline of religion, but that religious understanding would be altered by the conditions of social equality. While he is known within the field of political science as a thinker for whom freedom could only be saved by the mediational forms of civil association and local government,[67] his theory of mediation is far more generalizable than has been recognized. Thought, too, is mediated – by the social conditions in which the thinker finds himself. With respect to religion, this means that as conditions of social equality emerge, religious understanding will be mediated by those social conditions. Here, I have pointed out the multiple facets and trajectories that such mediated understanding may evince. Religion, like authority, does not disappear in the democratic age; it merely changes shape. In that light, we would do well to modify the fable of liberalism in accordance with the insights that a more complete reading of Tocqueville provides – in part for the purpose of fidelity to Tocqueville, but even more importantly because the risk of misunderstanding the place of religion in the twenty-first century has political consequences the outlines of which we can already begin to see.

NOTES

1   *DAII* (trans. Lawrence), Part IV, Ch. 8, 704. All future references to *DAI* and *DAII* are to this edition.

2   Always worth bearing in mind is Tocqueville's claim (in *DAII*, Part III, Ch. 21, 642) that we live in what could be called the "transitional age" between aristocracy and democracy. We do not yet live at the end of history; we are not yet "the last man."

3   *DAI*, Author's Introduction, 12.

4   See *DAII*, Part IV, Ch. 8, 705.

5   This was Samuel Johnson's phrase, but Burke adopted it to describe the caustic assault on aristocratic sensibilities wrought by the French Revolution. In his words, "But now all is to be changed. All the pleasing illusions, which made power gentle and obedience liberal, which harmonized the different shades of life, and which, by a bland assimilation, incorporated into politics the sentiments that beautify and soften private society, are to be dissolved by this new conquering empire of light and reason. All the decent drapery of life is to be rudely torn off. All the superadded ideas, furnished from the wardrobe of a moral imagination, which the heart owns, and the understanding ratifies, as necessary to cover the defects of our naked, shivering nature, and to raise it to dignity in our own estimation, are to be exploded as a ridiculous, absurd, and antiquated fashion" (Edmund Burke, *Reflections on the Revolution in France*, J. C. D. Clarke, ed. [Stanford, CA: Stanford University Press, 2001], 239).

6   See Bernard Mandeville, *The Fable of the Bees* (Indianapolis, IN: Liberty Classics, 1988), Part II, Dialogue vi, 284 [335]: CLEO. "Man, as I have hinted before, *naturally loves to imitate* what he sees others do, which is the reason that savage people all do the same thing: this hinders them from meliorating their condition" (emphasis added). The editor of Smith's *Wealth of Nations* cites the passage immediately before this one in Mandeville's *Fable* as the possible basis for Smith's locution, "the division of labor" (see Adam Smith, *Wealth of Nations* [Chicago: University of Chicago Press, 1976], Vol. I, Bk. I, Ch. I, 7). Marx's response to Smith is that bourgeois civilization reproduces itself in its "own image" ("Communist Manifesto," in *Marx-Engels*

Reader, 477). Bourgeois civilization destroys one form of imitation, only to introduce another.

7 Adam Smith, whom I will allude to again shortly, was not prepared to go this far. See Adam Smith, *The Theory of Moral Sentiments,* D. D. Raphael and A. L. Macfie, eds. (Indianapolis, IN: Liberty Classics, 1982), Part VI, Sec. II, Ch. III, 235: "This universal benevolence, how noble and generous soever, can be the source of no solid happiness to any man who is not thoroughly convinced that all the inhabitants of the universe, the meanest as well as the greatest, are under the immediate care and protection of that great, benevolent, and all-wise Being, who directs all the movements of nature; and who is determined, by his own unalterable perfections, to maintain in it, at all times, the greatest possible quantity of happiness. To this universal benevolence, on the contrary, *the very suspicion of a fatherless world, must be the most melancholy of all reflections;* from the thought that all the unknown regions of infinite and incomprehensible space may be filled with nothing but endless misery and wretchedness. All the splendour of the highest prosperity can never enlighten the gloom with which so dreadful an idea must necessarily over-shadow the imagination; nor, in a wise and virtuous man, can all the sorrow of the most afflicting adversity ever dry up the joy which necessarily springs from the habitual and thorough conviction of the truth of the contrary system" (emphasis added).

8 The collapse of multiple social ranks into one corresponds to the collapse of multiple, *socially embodied,* measures into the single measure of disembodied public reason, without social rank. Rawls's project, which begins from the vantage point of a "veil of ignorance" (John Rawls, *Theory of Justice* [Cambridge: Harvard University Press, 1971], Part One, Ch. 1, §3, 12), and out of which citizens without a socially constituted history emerge, is a resume of a social order without rank.

9 Montesquieu, *The Spirit of the Laws,* Anne M. Cohler, Basia Carolyn Miller, and Harrold Samuel Stone, eds. (Cambridge: Cambridge University Press, 1989), Part 4, Bk. 20, Ch. 1, 338.

10 Benjamin Constant, "The Spirit of Conquest and Usurpation," in *Political Writings,* Biamcamaria Fontana, ed. (Cambridge: Cambridge University Press, 1988), Part I, Ch. 2, 53.

11 See Thomas Hobbes, *Leviathan,* Edwin Curley, ed. [Indianapolis, IN: Hackett Publishing Co., 1994], Part I, Ch. XIII, ¶2, 75: "For Prudence is but experience, which equal time equally bestows on all men in those things they equally apply themselves unto." See also Smith, *Wealth of Nations,* Vol. I, Bk. I, Ch. II, 18: "The difference of natural talents in

different men is, in reality, much less than we are aware of; and the very different genius which appears to distinguish men of different professions, when grown up to maturity, is not upon many occasions so much the cause, as the effect of the division of labor."

12 See Smith, *Theory of Moral Sentiments*, Part I, Sec. I, Ch. I, ¶¶2–3, 8–9: "By our imagination we place ourselves in [another man's] situation, we conceive ourselves enduring all the same torments, we enter as it were his body, and become in some measure the same person with him .... His agonies, when they are brought home to ourselves, when we have thus adopted and made them our own, begin at last to affect us .... [T]his is the source of our fellow-feeling for the misery of others."

13 See also Friedrich Nietzsche, *The Genealogy of Morals*, Walter Kaufman, trans. (New York: Random House, 1967), First Essay, §9, 36: "The 'redemption' of the human race (from 'the masters,' that is) is going forward: everything is visibly becoming Judiazed, Christianized, mob-ized (what do the words matter!)."

14 See *DAII*, Part I, Ch. 7, 451: "[In the age of democracy] the concept of unity becomes an obsession."

15 For an early twentieth-century warning about the coming collapse of orthodox Christianity in America and its supercession by liberal Christianity, see J. Gresham Machen, *Christianity and Liberalism* (Grand Rapids, MI: Wm. B. Eerdmans Publishing Co., 1923).

16 "[The seeds of religion]," Hobbes says, "can never be abolished out of human nature" (Thomas Hobbes, *Leviathan*, Edwin Curley, ed. [Indianapolis, IN: Hackett Publishing Co., 1994], Part I, Ch. 12, ¶23, 71). See also Tocqueville, *DAI*, Part II, Ch. 9, 297: "faith is the only permanent state of mankind." In more biological terms, following Hans Blumenberg (*Work on Myth*, Robert M. Wallace, trans. [Cambridge, MA: MIT Press, 1985]), the achievement of upright posture so extended the horizon from which reality "can come at one" (5) that it became necessary for the imagination to arrest the "existential anxiety" (6) that ensued when the human being nakedly faced the unoccupied, unnamed, horizon. Myth fills that horizon and arrests anxiety. On this reading myth is a permanent need of human beings, diminished perhaps, but never overcome, by the machinations of logos which would tame "the world." Tocqueville, too, seems to have recognized this need of "the human spirit never [to see] an unlimited field before itself" (*DAI*, Part II, Ch. 2, 292).

17 Notwithstanding his anti-Enlightenment sentiments, Freud, in the twentieth century, shared this notion with many other Enlightenment thinkers. See Sigmund Freud, *Civilization and Its Discontents*, James

Strachey, ed. (New York: W. W. Norton & Co., 1989), Ch. 2, 22, *passim*, where he reluctantly resigns himself to the fact that most human beings will be unable to face reality and so remain in the perpetual childhood that monotheistic religion countenances.

18 *DAI*, Part II, Ch. 9, 295.

19 *DAI*, Part II, Ch. 9, 297.

20 *The Fundamentals: A Testimony to the Truth*, R. A. Torrey, ed. (Los Angeles: Bible Institute of Los Angeles, 1917).

21 *DAI*, Part I, Ch. 2, 41.

22 The contrary idea that material satisfaction permanently closes off a transcendent dimension of human experience is to be found in any number of thinkers. Think, for example, of Marcuse, who construed the problem of modernity as one in which the future is arrested because capitalism "delivers the goods." His deepest worry was that in advanced capitalist society, "the space for the transcending historical practice ... is being barred by a society ... that has its raison d'être in the accomplishments of its overpowering productivity" (Herbert Marcuse, *One-Dimensional Man* [Boston: Beacon Press, 1964], 23, emphasis added). Consider also Nietzsche: "[O]ur modern, noisy, time-consuming industriousness, proud of itself, stupidly proud, educates and prepares people, more than anything else does, precisely for 'unbelief'" (Friedrich Nietzsche, *Beyond Good and Evil*, Walter Kaufman, trans. [New York: Vintage Books, 1966], Part III, §58, 69). But see Tocqueville, *DAI*, Part II, Ch. 7, 254–56; Vol. II, Part III, Ch. 21, 645.

23 *DAII*, Part II, Ch. 12, 535. Cf. G. W. F. Hegel, *The Philosophy of History*, J. Sibree, trans. (New York: Dover Publications, 1956), Part III, Sec. III, Ch. 2, 318–19.

24 *DAI*, Part II, Ch. 9, 296.

25 *DAI*, Part II, Ch. 9, 300.

26 Hobbes, *Leviathan*, Part I, Ch. XI, 57–58, ¶¶ 1–2.

27 Here is the basis of Tocqueville's profound difference with J. S. Mill, for whom all matters must be, in principle, open to critical inquiry. For counterpoint to Mill's argument in "On Liberty," see *DAII*, Part I, Ch. 5, 443.

28 See Roger Finke and Rodney Stark, *The Churching of America, 1776–1990: Winners and Losers in Our Religious Economy* (New Brunswick, NJ: Rutgers University Press, 1992).

29 See *DAII*, Part I, Ch. 1, 430–31.

30 *DAII*, Part I, Ch. 5, 447. See also Martin Luther, "Lectures on Isaiah," in *Luther's Works*, Helmut T. Lehmann, ed. (Philadelphia: Fortress Press, 1967), Vol. 16, 327: "[F]aith must be built on the basis of history,

and we ought to stay with it alone and not so easily slip into allegories ..." Nietzsche would later hold Luther responsible for the democratic prejudice for which he had such contempt. See Nietzsche, *On the Genealogy of Morals*, First Essay, §16, 54.

31 Cf. Anthony Giddens, *Runaway World* (New York: Routledge, 2002).

32 *DAII*, Part II, Ch. 12, 534. Tocqueville's locution, "enthusiastic forms of spirituality," which is in the title of this chapter, is meant to capture this unbounded, irruptive, aspect of American religious experience.

33 *DAII*, Part IV, Ch. 2, 668.

34 See *DAII*, Part II, Ch. 5, 515: "Feelings and ideas are renewed, the heart enlarged, and the understanding developed only by the reciprocal action of men, one upon another."

35 *DAII*, Part I, Ch. 17, 486.

36 *DAII*, Part I, Ch. 5, 446.

37 Again, see footnote 5, for how this idea plays out in the realm of political economy.

38 See *DAII*, Part I, Ch. 1, 429: "To escape from imposed systems, the yoke of habit, family maxims, class prejudices, and to a certain extent national prejudices as well, to treat tradition as valuable for information only ... – such are what I would call the principal characteristics of the American philosophical method."

39 See *DAI*, Part I, Ch. 9, 292: "Religion, which never intervenes directly in the governance of American society, should therefore be considered the first of their political institutions, for although it did not give them the taste for liberty, it singularly facilitates their use thereof."

40 See *DAI*, Part I, Ch. 9, 294: "I am informed that on the other side of the ocean freedom and human happiness lack nothing but Spinoza's belief in the eternity of the world or Cabanis' contention that thought is a secretion of the brain. To this I have really no answer to give, except that those who talk like that have never been in America, and have never seen either religious peoples or free ones."

41 See also St. Augustine, *The Trinity*, Edmund Hill, trans. (New York: New City Press, 1991), Bk. IV, Ch. 1, §2, 153: "[W]e were exiled from this unchanging joy, *yet not so broken and cut off from it* that we stopped seeking eternity, truth, and happiness even in this changeable time-bound situation of ours" (emphasis added).

42 See *DAII*, Part II, Ch. 8, 525–28.

43 *DAII*, Part II, Ch. 8, 527.

44 See *DAII*, Part II, Ch. 4, 510: "Equality puts men side by side without a common link to hold them firm."

45 See, for example, Luther, "Lectures on Genesis," in *Luther's Works*, Vol. 1, 55–68. With respect to Genesis 1:26 ("in our image, after our likeness," etc.), he concludes that "since the loss of this image through sin we cannot understand it to any extent" (61), and that "not only do we have no experience of [this likeness to God], but we continually experience the opposite; and so we hear nothing but bare words" (63).

46 *DA*, Author's Introduction, 10.

47 See Max Weber, *The Protestant Ethic and the Spirit of Capitalism*, Talcott Parsons, trans. (London: G. Allen & Unwin, 1930), Ch. 1, 36: "A number of those sections of the old Empire which were most highly developed economically and most favored by natural resources and situation, in particular a majority of the wealthy towns, went over to Protestantism in the sixteenth century." See also Karl Marx, "The Grundrisse," in *The Marx Engels Reader*, Richard Tucker, ed. (New York: W. W. Norton & Co., 1978), 224: "Only in the eighteenth century, in 'civil society,' do the various forms of social connectedness confront the individual as a mere means toward private purposes, as external necessity." Elsewhere, Marx credits Luther with providing the individualist ethic necessary for inaugurating capitalism.

48 Tocqueville seems to have understood that one possible reaction to the destruction of aristocratic honor cultures is the attempt to reenchant the world. See *DAI*, Part II, Ch. 6, 236: "What can be done is such a condition? Retreat. But nations do not return to the feelings of their youth any more than men return to the innocent tastes of their infancy."

49 See David Martin, *Tongues of Fire* (Oxford: Basil Blackwell, 1990).

50 See Philip Jenkins, *The Next Christendom: the Coming of Global Christianity* (Oxford: Oxford University Press, 2003).

51 See Albert O. Hirschman, *The Passions and the Interests* (Princeton: Princeton University Press, 1977).

52 See *DAII*, Part III, Ch. 17, 615: "In aristocratic nations, money is the key to the satisfaction of but a few of the vast array of possible desires; in democracies it is the key to them all."

53 See Ronald Inglehart, *Culture Shift in Advanced Industrial Society* (Princeton: Princeton University Press, 1990).

54 Of interest in this regard is the still-festering controversy within the Anglican Communion over the American Episcopal Church's decision on August 6, 2003, to ordain as Bishop of New Hampshire, Gene Robinson, who himself does not follow the long-standing teaching on marriage to which a vast majority of those within the Anglican Communion in the developing world adhere.

55 So formulated, the pairing with which Hobbes is concerned has a secular and contemporary equivalent in the debate about the inadequacy of both globalism and identity politics. See, for example, Benjamin Barber, *Jihad vs. McWorld: How Globalism and Tribalism Are Reshaping the World* (New York: Ballantine Books, 1996).

56 In this regard, see Pierre Manent, *The City of Man* (Princeton: Princeton University Press, 1998), for the claim that the Roman Catholic Church today is the collective "beautiful soul" about which Hegel wrote in *The Phenomenology of Spirit*, which hovers over the world but never enters into it because it is without political clout.

57 See Hobbes, *Leviathan*, Part III, Ch. 38, 335–36; also ibid., Ch. 41, 353.

58 Thomas Hobbes, *Behemoth*, Ferdinand Tönnies, ed. (Chicago: University of Chicago Press, 1990), Dialogue I, 21.

59 *DAII*, Part I, Ch. 2, 435.

60 *DAI*, Part II, Ch. 9, 288: "In general [Protestantism] orients men much less toward equality than toward independence." See also Hobbes, *Leviathan*, Part II, Ch. 26, ¶41, 188: "In a commonwealth, a subject that has no certain and assured revelation to himself concerning the will of God, is to obey as such, the command of the commonwealth, *for if men were at liberty, to take for God's commandments, their own dreams and fancies, or the dreams and fancies of private men; scarce two men would agree upon what is God's commandment*" (emphasis added).

61 See, for example, Friedrich Schleiermacher, *On Religion: Speeches to Its Cultured Despisers*, Richard Crouter, trans. (Cambridge: Cambridge University Press, 1988), Second and Third Speeches, 96–161; G. W. F. Hegel, *Phenomenology of Spirit*, A. V. Miller, trans. (New York: Oxford University Press, 1977), §658, 399–400; Karl Barth's Introductory Essay in Feuerbach, *The Essence of Christianity*, xix; Ernst Troeltsch, *Protestantism and Progress* (Philadelphia: Fortress Press, 1986), 95–99; Weber, *The Protestant Ethic and the Spirit of Capitalism*, 180–83; Robert Bellah, *Habits of the Heart* (New York: Harper & Row, 1985), 243–48, *passim*.

62 G. W. F. Hegel, *Philosophy of Right*, T. M. Knox, trans. (Oxford: Oxford University Press, 1967), Addition to §141, 258–59.

63 Hegel, *Philosophy of History*, Part IV, Sec. III, Ch. 1, 425.

64 Hegel, *Philosophy of History*, Part IV, Sec. III, Ch. 1, 418.

65 If Hegel is correct about the character of Protestantism, the insight that subjectivity is the inner kernel of Christianity will evaporate into shining either as the authority of that very subjectivity destroys its own foundation. Perhaps this is what Nietzsche had in mind in his compact formulation at the end of the *Genealogy of Morals* (Third Essay, §27,

160): "[T]wo thousand years of training in truthfulness ... finally forbids itself the *lie involved in the belief in God"* (emphasis in original).

66   *DAII*, Part I, Ch. 6, 451.

67   See Robert D. Putnam, *Making Democracy Work: Civic Traditions in Modern Italy* (Princeton: Princeton University Press, 1993).

12 Tocqueville on Fraternity and Fratricide

Near the end of his classic essay "Two Concepts of Liberty," Isaiah Berlin struggled to deal with a verbal confusion that allegedly confounded negative liberty not with his famous concept of positive liberty but with "her sisters, equality and fraternity."[1] These, Berlin argued, are less matters of freedom than of status. For example, when members of groups denied both freedom and respect long for the emancipation of their entire nation or race or religious brotherhood, they often confuse liberty with the recognition of fraternity. Such longings, however labeled, are certainly no less explosive in the twenty-first century than they were fifty years ago. I read Tocqueville – interpreted by Berlin as well as many others primarily as a brilliant theorist of the tensions between liberty and equality – for insight into the perplexing relationship between liberty and fraternity. Here, as elsewhere, his struggles for clarity about democracy's contrary tendencies, his ambivalence, and his uneasy compromises in some ways mirror our own.

Tocqueville believed and feared that the modern world was moving not only toward equality but toward sameness – that "variety [was] vanishing from the human species."[2] Hence the distinctive ties that bind particular peoples called for analysis and evaluation. We see his attention to such ties not only in *Democracy in America* – with its seminal treatment of the different fates of Europeans, Africans, and Amerindians in the New World – but also in his political writings on European colonial slavery, imperial conquest, and the nationality question within Europe.[3] In this chapter, I use "fraternity" to describe the community of ideas and practices – as opposed to interests – that, according to Tocqueville, separates one people from another. It may seem that employing the term in this way distorts the French understanding of *fraternité*, with its connotations of world brotherhood, and unfairly foists a word onto Tocqueville that he deliberately avoided. Indeed, although *fraternité* was used to connote affective political solidarity within the boundary of the nation during the radical years of the French Revolution, it was even then thought to be in some sense coeval with humanity. By the 1830s and 1840s, *fraternité* most often evoked the universalistic bonds of kinship favored by Christians and socialists, an expansive syncretistic imagery re-politicized in 1848.[4] Tocqueville, of course, was a critic both of Jacobinism and of sentimental Christian republicanism and socialism. He shunned the word *fraternité*, preferring to speak of the ties of fellowship among *concitoyens* or of shared ideas, practices, and sentiments.

The terms "fraternity" and "fratricide," then, are mine not Tocqueville's, heuristic not historical. I use them nevertheless because they capture important elements of Tocqueville's discussion of peoples in the democratic age. Under the pressures of the democratic revolution, ties of internal membership and mutual loyalty come to have an important relationship to liberty. Yet these ties may foster exclusionary identities in which the majority refuses to fraternize with subordinated groups, or in which subordinated peoples create reactive fraternal identities. Moreover, the charged cognate "fratricide" captures Tocqueville's revulsion at the notion of intentionally destroying fellow human beings who are potential *concitoyens* – that is, deliberately "smothering" part of the "great human family."[5]

After briefly reviewing the interrelated historical forces that Tocqueville assumes are both homogenizing the world and privileging Europe, I turn to his writings on contact and conflict among particular peoples, and explore three possible outcomes of such collisions: fratricide, fraternity from above, and domination without fellowship. These three scenarios, I argue, structure Tocqueville's understanding of the different fates of separate human communities in a world increasingly marked both by an awareness of a common humanity and an emerging European hegemony. By reconstructing these alternatives in his writings, and recognizing that they appear to him to exhaust the universe of possibilities, we can make sense of what may appear to be conflicting accounts of Europe's expansion into new worlds. I argue that Tocqueville's views on European imperialism are ultimately contradictory, but not because he employs different moral frameworks for America, the West Indies, or North Africa. On the contrary, the elements of his analyses are remarkably similar, though his ironical register may shift. He contradicts himself, rather, in neglecting to apply fully his own insights about the potential despotism of states, the instability of interest, and the power of *ressentiment*.

I. A LINKED TRIAD: DEMOCRACY, HUMANITY, CIVILIZATION

It has often been noted that the advent of democracy – equality of social condition, with the strong egalitarian passions and the weaker taste for liberty that this equal condition engenders – forms both the providential backdrop and the obsessive subject of Tocqueville's theorizing about society and politics. To understand his discussion of fraternity and fratricide, however, we must recognize the extent to which Tocqueville's narrative of the inexorable rise of a democratic social condition is inflected by two other notions: humanity and civilization. His complex attitudes towards these linked universalizing tendencies – democracy, humanity, civilization – underlie his accounts of relationships among peoples.

Democracy, Tocqueville tells us in many contexts, entails the claims of *humanité* because equality must have some referent, some dimension on which all are equal. That dimension is our common membership in the human race: "[m]en in each country, deviating more and more from the ideas and sentiments peculiar to a caste, occupation, or family, are simultaneously converging on something more nearly derived from the constitution of man, which is everywhere the same."[6] Democracy in this sense represents the providential unfolding of Christian ideals of universality and equal fellowship, and for this reason Tocqueville resolved to welcome it. Indeed, his faith in the compatibility between religion and democracy fueled his hope that in a democratic future people would both recognize each other as fellows (*semblables*) and also exercise the free will implicit in the Christian notion of responsibility for one's soul. As people become more alike – Tocqueville uses the verbs *se confondre, s'assimiler, s'amalgamer* – each person potentially is freed to act as an independent moral agent. Because it is universal, this democratically inflected notion of liberty can be thought of as more just than limited notions of aristocratic freedom.[7]

If Tocqueville recognizes and valorizes the ideal of universal human freedom, a just world in which all claim liberty only on the basis of absolute equality, he is nonetheless acutely sensitive to the dark aspects of the equalizing and homogenizing forces in the modern world. These forces unleash a dangerous dynamic, in which surrender to individualism and materialism may lead eventually to new forms of despotism. The threats to liberty posed by uniformity, then, caused him to focus both on the ineradicability and the potential benefits of particularity and plurality. Different peoples or nations – Tocqueville uses the terms interchangeably – exhibit a wide variety of customs, distinct "physiognomies" that persist through time.[8] Centripetal forces tend to limit the acknowledgement of social ties (and thus the recognition of strong normative obligations) to those within the nation's boundaries. And, on Tocqueville's view, this limitation is no bad thing, for a theory of justice rooted solely in duties to humanity can have but a feeble purchase on the human imagination.

At first glance it seems that those moralists, above all among the Christians, who apparently forget duty to country in order to think only of humanity, who forget the fellow-citizen [le concitoyen] for the fellow-man [le prochain], it seems, I say, that they are right. It is in fact by taking a detour that we discover that they are wrong. Man, as God has created him (I don't know why), becomes less devoted as the object of his affections becomes larger. His heart needs the particular, it needs to limit the object of its affections in order to grasp the object in a firm and lasting embrace.[9]

Only a very few are capable of viewing the human species with more than "a distant, uncertain, and cold gaze,"[10] since identification with others grows weaker as it is extended.

It is not only foolish to long for world community, but also dangerous. Discrete states, whose members claim a common historical heritage, feel some attachment to territory, and recognize each other's claims to equal citizenship are, for Tocqueville, the *sine qua non* of modern liberty because they provide the only viable contexts for mutual trust, joint action, and rising above self. The stubborn human propensity towards narrower fraternal loyalties provides a crucial counterweight to the dangers of unfettered democracy. Tocqueville's ultimate hope was that individuals "well directed by reason and morality" could serve humanity as a whole by loving and valuing their particular fragment of humanity (*patrie particulière*).[11] Since earlier forms of spontaneous or instinctive local patriotism were rapidly decaying, democratic peoples had to be schooled to love the *patrie* in a new way, to develop another, more rational form of patriotism: " ... less generous, less ardent perhaps, but more fruitful and durable. This second form of patriotism is born of enlightenment. It develops with the aid of laws, grows with the exercise of rights, and eventually comes to be bound up in a way with personal interest."[12] Tocqueville values this newly cultivated "considered patriotism," which makes use of the tendencies of democracy rather than struggling futilely against them, precisely because it helps to stave off the pernicious effects of equality.

There are two consistent threads, then, in Tocqueville's discussions of the particular fraternal ties that bind nations or peoples: one relating to fact and one to value. First, human nature is such that neither discrete peoples nor the historical patterns of interaction among them (mutual influence, competition, conflict, conquest, domination) will vanish completely. Second, we ought not to wish for the disappearance of healthy patriotic sentiments; civic fraternity serves liberty, and thereby gains a certain moral standing.[13] Tocqueville does not, however, assign transcendental value to nations or sub-groups of humanity in themselves. As Rémusat once remarked, Tocqueville's "cast of mind inclined him to consider the constitutional rather than the patriotic aspect of politics."[14] Nations are merely historical legacies or constructs – imagined communities, to echo Benedict Anderson's influential phrase – without any transcendental moral claims on the allegiance of their members. When Tocqueville himself imagines the possible outcomes of collisions between such historically constructed communities, the force inherent in "civilization" becomes decisive.

It was perhaps J. S. Mill who first observed that Tocqueville confounded democracy's effects with the growth of civilization and all the tendencies of modern commercial society.[15] The beliefs that peoples become enlightened at different rates, that enlightenment

entails economic and social development, that development brings
power, and that the power of civilized nations seduces the less
civilized underlie Tocqueville's discussion of relations among
European nations, and dominate his understanding of Europe's
colonial diaspora.[16] In these assumptions, Tocqueville reflected a
widely accepted theory that all peoples pass through the stages of
hunting-gathering, herding, and agriculture before arriving at civilization. Adopting contemporary usage, Tocqueville often referred
to hunter-gatherers as savage, while conflating pastoral and agricultural stages as barbaric or imperfectly civilized.[17] His understanding of the dynamic of progress internal to the final stage –
civilization – was indebted to his "teacher and guide" François
Guizot, and to his constant companion, Rousseau.[18]

From Guizot, Tocqueville absorbed a rich narrative of fifteen
centuries of European civilization beginning with the fall of Rome
and accelerating in his own time. Guizot's initial lecture in *The
History of Civilization in Europe* traces the interrelation of two
processes: first, the perfection of civil life, the increasing production
and more equitable distribution "of the means of giving strength
and happiness to society," and second, the perfection of man's
internal faculties, his sentiments and ideas, regenerated by the
spread of Christianity and the growth of reason. Though Guizot
warned his listeners "not to give ourselves up too much to the idea
of our happiness and amelioration, or we may fall into two grave
dangers, pride and indolence," he nevertheless believed that material, intellectual, and moral progress had synergistically combined
in Europe to assure its world dominance.[19] Tocqueville's notion of
the rise of European democracy cannot be severed from this elite
liberal discourse about the inevitable prevalence of the norms of
civility and contract, and the spread of enlightenment. He did not
doubt that civilization definitively transformed the pattern of confrontation and conflict among nations by privileging the European
powers: " ... in this matter the choice is no longer ours to make.
The European population has arrived; civilized and Christian
society has been founded."[20] If Europe had reached a dominating
plateau, however, Tocqueville hesitated to cede it the moral high
ground.

Like his other guide Rousseau, Tocqueville judged that European
civilization harbored the potential for despotism. He distrusted

both the individualism and materialism associated with the rise of civil society and democracy and the moral valence of enlightenment, which could inadvertently further despotic tendencies. Therefore, although Tocqueville cast his lot with the future – with the possibility of democratic liberty, the ideal of *humanité*, the benefits of civilization, and the hegemony of Europe – he was afflicted with permanent double vision. His acute sense of the moral and spiritual dangers associated with the uncontrolled tendencies of democracy and civilization, and of the damage that could be wreaked by the deliberate embrace of such abstractions, pushed him continually to ironical second sight, especially in considering the results for the "great human family" of Europe's expansion into new worlds.

When Tocqueville, in prophetic mode, takes the long view, he foresees a leveling not only of individuals but of nations or peoples: "it is not only the members of a single nation who become more alike. Nations themselves grow more similar until they seem, in the eye of the beholder, to merge into one vast democracy, each citizen of which is a people."[21] Yet some will not survive their contact with civilization, and thus will not live to take up the status of citizen-nations. The ghosts of dead peoples haunt Tocqueville's work: images of extinction in which communities, once imagined, have no one left to imagine or even remember them. These cases of vanishing peoples occupy an ethically grey area in which ironies abound. On the one hand, Tocqueville was convinced that the collision between civilized and less-civilized peoples inevitably and even providentially favored the former. Thus, like an Olympian impartial spectator, he sometimes appears to proclaim that extinction is over-determined and therefore unresponsive to human choice. On the other hand, Tocqueville, as always, resists the lure of determinism. Even though a people may seem to be disappearing because of a deadly combination of particular and general causes, he nevertheless condemns the impulse to hasten a people's death rather than attempt its rescue. Those who deliberately intend, cruelly hasten, or hypocritically mask the extinction of peoples are guilty of tearing the fabric of humanity. In these cases, the coroner's verdict is murder, not death by natural causes. Given Tocqueville's religious conviction of the essential oneness of the human community, of the injunction to preserve human life, and of the duties of Christian charity, these instances of social fratricide are inevitably judged to be both evil and unjust.

II. FRATRICIDE

Let me review the ways in which inevitability, intentionality, and responsibility come together in three accounts of fratricide: the alleged fates of emancipated slaves and Indians in the United States, and the potential threat to Arabs and Berbers in Algeria. The first two are "distressing nightmares" associated with Tocqueville's famous American journey; the third is an analogous French *cauchemar*, repressed and denied, but disturbing and recurrent.

A. American Nightmares

Tocqueville and his fellow traveler in America, Gustave de Beaumont, were associated throughout their legislative careers with the question of how to emancipate slaves in the West Indies. They judged the institution of black chattel slavery to be the clearest of moral evils, an "accursed seed" that had unexpectedly flourished in democratic soil.[22] Slavery was anachronistic, economically less productive than free labor, and thus eventually doomed to retreat "in the face of enlightenment born of experience."[23] Yet, for them both, the true evil of modern slavery, especially in the United States, was the complex legacy of racial antipathy and exclusion that apparently prevented the assimilation of ex-slaves into the civic polity.[24] Tocqueville and Beaumont describe a political situation in which peoples of different races cannot be blended or fused (they consistently use the verb *se confondre*) but remain at once intermingled and separate.[25] Indeed, African freedmen in the North are isolated, prevented from exercising civil and political rights, economically exploited, and socially starved – a misery empirically confirmed in their relatively high mortality rate.[26] Africans are allegedly "disappearing from all the northern states."[27] In the South, where there were large African populations, emancipation would lead to a race war that could mean the expulsion of whites. What are the reasons given for these apocalyptic judgments about post-emancipation America?

In the accounts given by Tocqueville and Beaumont, a complex mixture of particular and general causes appears to doom racial integration in the Northern states. Among the particular factors are qualities of the English national character (the English recoil from mixing their blood with that of other races) and the specific anxieties of a post-colonial people. Anglo-Americans exhibit a tenacious pride in their origins; indeed, political emancipation led to stronger rather than weaker cultural identification with the mother country.[28] The general tendencies of both civilization and democracy intensify the propensity to shun or disdain other races. Economically unprofitable in the more developed North, many slaves were exported to the Southern states. Since their numbers were not replenished by emigration of freedmen from the South, the Northern population of Africans was shrinking. According to Tocqueville, these small populations would be impossible to assimilate. It is true that Africans came originally from agricultural societies, which "take" to civilization more easily than hunters or shepherds. But first the dehumanizing aspects of slavery (forced deportation and degradation) had to be overcome through education and socialization.

It is precisely this "apprenticeship in freedom" which is denied to ex-slaves, for the effects of democracy itself foster racial exclusion. Tocqueville notes that it takes generations to erase caste markers, even when there are no visible signs to demarcate descendants. Paradoxically, the social psychological effects of equality intensify these difficulties. Pride of origin "is markedly increased ... by the individual pride born of democratic liberty." If all one has is one's citizen status, the notion of fraternizing with former slaves becomes abhorrent. "Racial prejudice seems to me stronger in the states that have abolished slavery than in those where slavery still exists, and nowhere is intolerance greater than in states where servitude was unknown."[29] Because democratic equality leads to generalized anxiety about status, it increases the psychological propensity to validate one's worth by depressing the status of others and preventing them from sharing in the existing social state.

The dilemma presented by emancipation was different in the Southern states; there it seemed to threaten race war. Tocqueville assumes that there is no obvious place to which freed Southern slaves can emigrate. Schemes of gradual emancipation would never be implemented by whites because of fears of black majority power;

moreover, such schemes would cause resentment among slaves who remained in bondage while others were freed. African slaves, then, would have to be emancipated en masse, and would *ipso facto* become the majority before learning to exercise freedom responsibly. Like the French peasant in the eighteenth century, however, the Southern slave would seize the occasion to retaliate against former masters: "there is no way to prevent him from learning enough to appreciate the extent of his afflictions and conceive a vague idea of the remedy. More than that, a singular principle of relative justice lies deep within the human heart."[30] Thus, Tocqueville argues, "[i]f we assume that Whites and emancipated Negroes are to occupy the same land and face each other as foreign peoples, it is easy to see that the future holds only two prospects: either Negroes or Whites must blend altogether [*se confondre*] or they must separate."[31] A key element here is the presumed lack of outside support from the North for the Southern white minority. If the federation were to be dissolved, Tocqueville believed that the strength of Southern blacks (superior numbers and the emergence of a self-conscious reactionary fraternity) would lead to a black victory, leaving them dominant and unrestrained in a land "apparently destined by Providence to be theirs."[32]

Tocqueville's exaggerated racial scenarios are warnings about the fusion of majority opinion and majority power in situations, where one cannot count on internalized mores or outside pressure to restrain majorities from exceeding moral limits. In those situations, one can expect only "unprecedented atrocity, which by itself reveals some profound perturbation in the laws of humanity."[33] Both Tocqueville and Beaumont frequently allude to the foiled designs of nature in America. The spontaneous human desire for contact with others should naturally result in shared *sociabilité* and legal intermarriage. Anything else, says the Frenchman Ludovic in Beaumont's *Marie*, seems to "go against nature's laws."[34] Yet, in America, the half-caste or mulatto, who should be a natural link between peoples, has been relegated to pariah status.[35] Tocqueville begins and ends the discussion of the three races in America with vivid anecdotes of "the order of nature overturned:" examples of the spontaneous feelings of sociability being denatured by artificial taboos.[36] Thus, while Tocqueville presents the failure to integrate the races in America as the consequence of a *conjoncture* of particular and general forces, it is not necessarily an *unintended* consequence. Indeed, it is sustained by a deliberate refusal of fraternity that – Tocqueville warns – will in the long run lead to instability and national dissolution.

The failure of European Americans even to attempt to assimilate disappearing peoples also lends an accusatory note to Tocqueville's requiem for American Indian tribes – a parallel narrative whose elegiac tone is deepened by his identification with their aristocratic pride.[37] Over-determined by a fateful mix of the particular and the general, the extinction of Indians has become irreversible. For all that, Indian "removal" is also a consequence of deliberate choice and murderous intent, elements that make it a fratricide.

As in the case of Africans, Tocqueville takes note of particular barriers to the fusion of peoples. English patterns of immigration to the New World – unlike those of the Spanish and French – brought families, not single adventurers or trappers. Hence, interbreeding with native peoples was severely reduced.[38] Moreover, the typical Englishman – as in his relationships with blacks – carefully avoided mixing his blood with the "blood of barbarians."[39] These barriers were worsened by general causes; indeed, living peacefully "side by side" is impossible in a situation of great disparities of civilization or social state. Tocqueville thought it particularly difficult for hunters who had yet to be tamed and disciplined by a sedentary economic life to adapt to civilization; contact with more advanced civilizations tended to cause such societies to disintegrate.[40] Economic trade, even without bad faith, disadvantaged Indians, who became dependent on whites as the spread of European agricultural settlement progressively destroyed their environment (and thus the source of what they had to offer in trade). Natives were forced to relocate, and in doing so, to lose their social identity. "Already these migrants had no homeland, and soon they ceased to constitute a people."[41] If they did not move, they became a "small colony of unwanted aliens in the midst of a numerous and dominating people."[42] Even if Indians tried to civilize themselves, they could not do so fast enough when in uncontrolled competition with a more advanced people. The highly intelligent Cherokees, for example, attempted but failed to assimilate economically. But most Indians did not even try to join the majority culture because of the psychology implicit in their social state. The notion of civilized labor revolted Indians – as it had repelled European aristocratic barbarians – and they clung to their way of life as a matter of honor. Unlike the Europeans, however, they had the misfortune to be conquered, rather than to conquer.[43]

Among their conquerors, in contrast, competition and the profit-motive had become the life-blood of the most complete democracy in the world; to labor and profit thereby were badges of honor, and these transplanted Europeans "traffic in everything, not excepting morality and religion." With no outside restraints, this "cold and implacable egoism" had led to hypocritical trespassing of the moral strictures (against theft and fraud) implicit in all recognizably human communities.[44] By using civilized notions of the rule of law – "with marvelous ease, quietly, legally, philanthropically, without bloodshed, without violating a single one of the great principles of morality in the eyes of the world" – the Americans engaged in what we would now call "ethnic cleansing."[45] Private greed colluded with legislative tyranny at both the state and federal levels to achieve "complete expulsion."[46] Indeed, "these savages did not simply retreat; they were destroyed."[47] Towards Indians, as towards freed Africans, Americans exhibit the particular arrogance arising from a democratic majority's lack of accountability.[48] Tocqueville expressed both awe at the single-minded energy with which European settlers raced towards the frontier, and criticism of the overreaching hubris of manifest destiny.[49]

The tragedy of the collisions of peoples in America results from a combination of a particular history of colonization, the peculiar national character of English colonials, and the general tendencies of human nature in civilized democratic times. What most excited Tocqueville's condemnation was not the consequent denial to peoples of the right to self-determination (he recognizes no such right), but rather the deliberate surrender to "interest and pride" on the part of the European settlers, a surrender that led to a reckless trespassing of the bounds of civilized humanity for which they must bear some responsibility. Tocqueville believed that these American failures were perhaps inevitable, since there was no countervailing force, either from another people or from a higher authority: "an entire people cannot rise, as it were, above itself."[50] Because of the lack of an inhibiting power, Europeans in the New World had forsaken nature and humanity and were impelled toward tyrannical excesses.[51] In America, these tendencies had grown to such unmanageable proportions that it sometimes seemed to Tocqueville and Beaumont that there was no alternative but to bear witness to the spectacle of man's inhumanity to man, fatefully unwinding to a dreadful conclusion. But this tone serves only to reinforce rhetorically the implicit reminder: it is too late for them, but not – *à Dieu ne plaise!* – for us.

B. A Repressed Nightmare for the French

Despite Tocqueville's determination that the French must not repeat American policies towards the Indians, one can glimpse in his subsequent writings on the French conquest of Algeria a recurrent fear that they would be charged with a similar fratricide. As in America, what disturbed him was not European colonization, but rather the conduct of the war and the peace. He tried to repress his dread that the French would be held responsible for exterminating the Arab and Berber peoples because of the reckless brutality of the army and the deliberate violation of property rights and breach of promises by the civil administration. Indeed, an attentive reading of Tocqueville's writings on Algeria reveals his dismay that the French were surrendering to a "flood of violence and injustices" that might both destroy all sense of moral limits in the perpetrators and lead to the extinction of North African peoples.[52] Such a surrender was particularly dangerous, since French democracy had already shown a taste for terror in the Revolution.

The question of whether the French were engaging in policies that would lead to expelling or exterminating the native inhabitants of North Africa was a central issue in debates over the Algerian war. The anti-imperialist critic Amedée Desjobert explicitly quoted Tocqueville's *Democracy in America* in support of his argument that French policies were exterminating the indigenous population, even if no one explicitly intended this result, and thus the French were imitating rather than avoiding the American example.[53] Because Tocqueville believed that the French were committed by interest and honor not to abandon the Algerian campaign, and because he hoped that a colonizing project could potentially revive French patriotism and invigorate free *moeurs* at home, he let himself be temporarily seduced by fatalism. He speculated that the

French might be powerless to prevent the disappearance of the Arabs; the "Arab element," like the African freedmen or Indians in America, "is becoming more and more isolated, and little by little it is dissolving."[54] After the conquest was complete, he denied even the wish: "above all I do not want to exterminate them."[55]

The lesson of America, then, was not that democratic peoples must inevitably become criminals. Scenarios of fratricide were "American without being democratic"; other nations (and above all, France) might yet escape these evils. Beyond the solace that could be taken from their different particular circumstances, European nations might learn from the American experience to recognize and counteract the dangerous general proclivities of democracy and civilization: the tendency of self-interest to become avarice, of pride to become arrogance, and of democratic rule to become majority tyranny. Tocqueville would attempt to apply these lessons of self-control in the cases about which he was most concerned: France's sugar colonies and its newly acquired empire in North Africa.

The essence of Tocqueville's hope to control and moderate European collisions with less-advanced civilizations can be glimpsed in his comment that a despot might succeed in mixing peoples in America, or in the contrast (made also by Beaumont) between the different patterns of racial integration in Protestant and Catholic churches.[56] Because Protestant ministers are elected, they come under the sway of tyranny of majority opinion. Hence Protestant congregations replicate the patterns of exclusion characteristic of the society in which they are embedded. Catholic priests, however, impose law, rather than conforming to it. Under the benevolent despotism of the priest who preaches the equality of Christian souls, an integrated religious confraternity may emerge. The political analogue of this religious example is state-created fraternity.

III. FRATERNITY FROM ABOVE

The counter-type to fratricidal scenarios of deliberate isolation and extermination is the deliberate fusion of different populations into a new whole. Such societies foster a common political identity that permits the flowering of democratic sociability; their members share enough mutual recognition to inspire trust and participation in a common life. The precipitating causes of such fusions are, Tocqueville assumes, the same as the causes of extinctions: contact and conquest. What makes Tocqueville's vision of fraternity the opposite of fratricide is neither the absence of political force nor any presumed parity of influence between peoples. Indeed, political force is necessary to create fraternity, and one people or nation will dominate. What distinguishes the positive image of new "fraternities" from the negative image of fratricide is the relatively unresisted nature of the amalgamation (achieved by self-restraint on the part of the powerful and voluntary acculturation on the part of the weak) and the gradual emergence of a sense of shared fate. None of Tocqueville's accounts of successfully fused communities are purely spontaneous and voluntary; all involve the maintenance – long or very long – of a tutelary power that holds the collectivity together while a process of assimilation occurs, a power that enables peoples to mix "in such a way as to derive the same benefits from the state of society."[57]

Considered apart from the failed fraternization with Africans and Indians, the society of white Anglo-Americans, dominated by the North, is perhaps the closest approximation to a new people founded spontaneously through voluntary contact. Tocqueville describes a society absorptive enough to assimilate other European peoples while undergoing some change itself. "As Americans mingle, they assimilate. Differences created by climate, origin, and institutions diminish. Everyone comes closer and closer to a common type .... This constant emigration from North to South significantly favors the fusion of all provincial characters into one national character."[58] Yet there are also powerful political forces holding the Americans together. Society undergoes a period of nation-building under the common imperative of republican institutions that require repeated acts of cooperation. Eventually patriotism *réfléchi* emerges as a kind of learned response: "what was calculation becomes instinct, and by dint of working for the good of one's fellow citizens, one ultimately acquires the habit of serving them, along with a taste for doing so."[59]

A more apt example for European expansion, however, was Europe's own evolution. Very close to the surface here are Guizot's lectures on the history of France – a forced mixture of peoples that spawned a new and greater civilization. The key element in all of these cases of new peoples who must share geographic and social space is long interaction under steady political pressure. In his own time, Tocqueville held out the hope that political control – if the elite is far-seeing and exercises good judgment – could initiate processes of enforced fraternization that would maintain peace and rule of law and allow imitation, borrowing, and mutual interest to percolate.

A. Caribbean Hopes

It is this model of fraternity enforced from above that underlies Tocqueville's hopes for the post-emancipation societies of the French Caribbean, countering his pessimistic predictions of extermination or race war in the United States. In 1845, Tocqueville rose to speak in the Chamber in support of yet another modest proposal to begin to dismantle slavery in the sugar colonies. Against an opponent who charged Tocqueville with inconsistency by citing *Democracy in America* on the horrors that would follow slave emancipation in the American South, Tocqueville insisted that he had not changed his views. "[I]t is precisely because I thought that then, and still think it today, that I believe that the necessary prelude to any kind of emancipation is first to place the state in a superior and dominant position." If the French state exerts the proper force, it can impose itself between planters and ex-slaves and "force the two refractory elements to combine themselves in some way in order to form one and the same people."[60] Control by the metropole will prevent planters from imposing a racial despotism over ex-slaves and ex-slaves from rising up against their erstwhile masters.

It has often been noted, sometimes reproachfully, that Tocqueville's case for the emancipation of French colonial slaves was economic and political rather than moral. It is quite true that Tocqueville's writings on emancipation do not press the moral case. But that was a considered strategic decision. By the 1840s, even the planter lobby conceded the moral case against slavery; yet it was quite successful in preying on elite fears about the consequences of emancipation for French industry and for the peace and prosperity of the colonies. Thus the key questions were all pragmatic: how to convince all parties that immediate emancipation was in their interest and how to manage the transition. Tocqueville was convinced that slavery was morally evil and economically unfeasible. His concern was to devise a scheme that would allow the planters to keep producing sugar, turn ex-slaves into free workers, and manage the transition by restraining the planters. During the period of transition, the state would assume heightened political and economic control.[61] Since Tocqueville also seems to have thought that the particular fear of race-mixing was less marked in the French national character, he hoped that the deadly combination of particular and general causes that doomed American race relations could be avoided in the French colonies.[62]

The question of the inherent attractiveness of the European plantation economy was central to debates over slave emancipation in the sugar colonies. It was assumed – by Tocqueville as well as many others – that Christianizing and educating the ex-slaves would accelerate assimilation by transforming their psychology, and that freedmen would then be drawn voluntarily into a modern economic order as they came to see their proper self-interest in working for wages. The experience of British emancipation in the West Indies had indicated that ex-slaves preferred inefficient small holdings to working on plantations or in sugar refineries, but Tocqueville did not find this objection fatal to his plans for post-emancipation plantation society. His *Report on Slavery* (1839) entertained the possibility – and his later newspaper articles on the topic made the explicit recommendation – that ex-slaves be forced by the state to remain on the plantations by being denied the opportunity to purchase land for a transitional period, until they could be transformed into workers who would choose (had no choice but) to remain.[63]

B. Algerian Dreams

Fraternity from above was also Tocqueville's initial vision for Algeria, a hopeful projection that formed an exact counter-type to the Americans' interaction with the indigenous populations. Unlike the doomed American Indians, who could not civilize themselves up to a level that would allow them to "insist on their land rights and be assimilated by their conquerors,"[64] the Arabs and

Berbers – so Tocqueville argued – might integrate themselves peacefully into a new civilization. Tocqueville's first writings on France's colonial confrontation with the indigenous population in North Africa foresee a new people, formed under the benevolent eye of the state.[65] On this view, the French, by buying land legally, could establish themselves next to the Arabs "without causing them to suffer." In this way, populations will gradually become "intermixed" (entremêlées). But, as in America, to be intermixed but not "blended" into a common identity leads to tyranny or instability. "[I]t is not at all enough for the French to place themselves next to the Arabs if they do not manage to establish durable ties with them and finally to form a single people from the two races."[66] They must advance from being entremêlés to being confondus.

In his first writings on Algeria, Tocqueville examines both particular factors (religion and civil customs) and general ones (level of civilization) in order to argue for the likelihood of such a fusion of peoples. He notes that Islam is not an insurmountable barrier, and attempts to find points of contact between the French and Arab national characters.[67] Most important, general factors also favor French efforts. The Arabs, he argues, are not wholly wedded to pastoral life, but could easily be induced to become sedentary and agricultural – that is, more civilized. Already, Tocqueville argued in 1837, there was desire for contact on both sides (such as eagerness to learn each other's languages). These desires suggested that the French were not exclusionary and that the Arabs were gravitating into the magnetic orbit of a more powerful culture. Unlike in America, therefore, there did not seem to be that fateful confluence of forces militating against the emergence of fraternity between conquerors and indigenous populations. Or, as Tocqueville hopefully phrases it, "God is not stopping it."[68] What might prevent the outcome of amalgamation were all-too-human deficiencies, and Tocqueville warned the French about failing to reign in the greed and arrogance that he had deplored in America.

In Democracy in America, Tocqueville chided the Americans for ignoring the wisdom of George Washington, who had argued that because the settlers were more enlightened and powerful than the Indians, it was "a matter of honor to treat them with kindness and even generosity."[69] In his Second Letter on Algeria, Tocqueville is the French Washington: "we are more enlightened and stronger than the Arabs, and it is up to us to yield at first, up to a certain point, to their habits and prejudices."[70] But whereas the American majority had nothing to restrain its willful injustice, the French civil administration and army in Algeria could be guided, so Tocqueville hoped, by a benign metropolitan government, which would allow them "safely to negotiate the transitional period that elapses before two peoples of different civilizations can manage to refound themselves as a single whole."[71] He concluded that "time, perseverance, ability, and justice" would eventually conciliate native populations and resign them to the French presence.[72] This initial vision of a French Algeria was not precisely a *mission civilicatrice*, although Tocqueville did assume that the French would necessarily "exercise an almost invincible influence on small and fairly barbarous peoples."[73] Indeed, enforced fraternity in the Caribbean and North Africa were plausible only to the extent that European-dominated economy and civilization would gradually detach less-advanced peoples from their backward social state by the promise of economic development and increased access to material goods.

C. Hopes and Dreams Deferred

A central feature of the success of any modern democratic people, according to Tocqueville, was its ability to manage the tensions of economic competition and the inequalities of class. He was acutely sensitive both to the susceptibility of the European working classes to destructive egalitarian visions, and to the failure of the bourgeoisie to recognize that its long-term self-interest lay in schemes of social cooperation and political expansiveness. The relationship between living *ensemble* and living with a division of labor – between living as civic equals and as class unequals – was the problem of modern democratic Europe. In the case of the French Caribbean, or the initially idealized vision of French Algeria dominated by the interests of French colonists, Tocqueville's tenuous vision of a society being re-founded as one people even as it progressed to a higher material level of civilization and became more democratic was strained to the breaking point.

At a minimum, this vision of enforced fraternity involved the transformation of ex-masters and ex-slaves, colonists and colonized. It implied a certain openness on the part of the propertied classes to competitors and workers of all races and to assimilation and intermarriage. It had to assume that the *métis* would become the norm, rather than the scorned outcast depicted in Beaumont's *Marie*. Even in Europe, however, there were disquieting and inconvenient signs of the difficulty of fraternity from above. In the late 1840s, Tocqueville favored a social program designed to create solidarity with the lower classes that would allow the French to overcome the political divisiveness of class. He foresaw a new role for the state in equalizing tax burdens, establishing institutions such as free schools and mutual aid societies, and mitigating the worst effects of industrial inequality.[74] Yet Tocqueville came to despair over the refusal of the middle classes to shoulder its responsibility to integrate and educate the popular classes, thus allowing society to drift towards revolution. He also came to believe that the resentment of the French lower classes would follow a sterile revolutionary script that ended in despotism rather than a free republic. Together, these failures would deliver France to new forms of "unfreedom" rather than to a new form of political liberty.

Tocqueville never refined his portrait of enforced fraternity in the West Indies, where a past of rigid racial exclusion and a future of class divisions aligned with existing cultural and racial ones would seem to doom his notion of state-sponsored assimilation. And he explicitly repudiated this vision for North Africa. His first visit to Algeria forced Tocqueville to abandon the hope of enforced fraternity between French and *indigènes* – "the fusion of these two populations is a chimera that people dream of only when they have not been to these places" – and to sketch out a model of long-term domination.[75]

IV. DOMINATION WITHOUT FELLOWSHIP

Thus far we have considered two Tocquevillean models of the outcome of collisions between "civilized" and "less-civilized" peoples in the democratic age: the first – fratricide – was morally repugnant, the second – fraternity from above – empirically implausible. We are left with his third alternative: domination without fellowship, a society characterized by "tranquil possession" in which two peoples live "side by side," held together by an outside power that restrains its own nationals from lawless brutality and that polices the subordinate population without attempting to create a common political life between the two. It is instructive to begin a consideration of domination without fellowship by examining a potential variant of the type: English rule in Ireland.

The seventeenth-century English pacification of Ireland, in Tocqueville's account, is an example of an advanced civilization imposing itself on one "semi-barbarous."[76] Without outside pressure to restrain the conquerors, indeed with every reason to think that the mother country would support them in acts of tyranny, the English aristocracy exploited the conquered population economically and isolated them socially. The result was "the most detestable society imaginable."[77] No moral ties united the two peoples; indeed, political opinion, religious belief, race, and the gulf in material circumstances rendered them strangers to each other, "even enemies."[78] Things had come to such a pass that Christianity itself – a natural force for joining people together in equality – had become an apparently ineradicable source of mutual hatred.

The parallel between Ireland and the American South did not escape either Tocqueville or Beaumont.[79] They had to struggle to avoid the conclusion that social wounds cut so deep that the situation could not be repaired by human action. Because oppression had triggered an implacable reactive resentment and distrust, peaceful amalgamation was a chimera. Yet in Ireland, unlike in America, there was at least the possibility of pressure from above. At several points in his notes on Ireland, Tocqueville queries whether the situation might yet be improved by a temporary English dictatorship "exercised in a firm and enlightened manner."[80] Indeed, the only solution appeared to be more centralization and direction from London. Despite the belief that the divisions between conqueror and conquered were too deep to be adjudicated, and despite skepticism over the possibility of dismantling the political, social, and religious barriers that prevented fraternity in Ireland, this mechanism seemed the only avenue to be pursued.[81]

The Irish case might seem to indicate that peoples who live "side by side" in a situation of great inequality resulting from a history of unrestrained greed and violence not only could not be blended into one people, but must eventually separate. The inability of Tocqueville and Beaumont to envision voluntary divestment on the part of a great power, however, left them clinging to the notion of using the force of the English state to manage the highly unstable and volatile Irish situation.[82] If it was impossible for Beaumont to argue that France's great rival would or should give up its domination over a sympathetically portrayed Catholic people, it was unthinkable for Tocqueville to envision France itself abandoning a "barbarous" territory that she had spilled so much blood to subdue. Hence, after Tocqueville's first visit to Algeria in 1841, when he realized that his initial vision of enforced fraternity failed to take into account implacable Arab resistance ("a promised land, if one didn't have to farm with gun in hand"[83]), he began to envision neither assimilation nor separation, but rather domination without fellowship. For guidance in constructing this model, he turned to British rule in India, a case that he mined for *arcana imperii*.

After the French victory in North Africa was assured, Tocqueville wrote two parliamentary reports on what France should do to secure the peace, reports that reflect his study of the English organization of its conquest of India.[84] Since it would be impossible to destroy the "blind hatred created and sustained by foreign domination,"[85] the first rule of domination without fellowship was to "remain strong." The conquered could not be treated as "fellow citizens" or "equals."[86] Tocqueville argues that after a brutal colonial war against an indigenous force with impressive leadership, leadership that had for the first time created nationalist sentiment in Algeria through the use of Islam, North Africa would need a strong hand. Yet he hoped to weaken indigenous hatred through "good government," through helping the Arabs rebuild institutions that were destroyed by the French, and through a power "that guides them, not only toward our interest, but in theirs."[87] Hence Tocqueville warns that the French must resist forcing populations to move, must carefully monitor property transactions, and in general must "take care that it is not the same for us" as it was for the Europeans in North America. Otherwise, Algeria would become "a closed field, a walled arena, where the two peoples would have to fight without mercy, and where one of the two would have to die."[88]

How will the indigenous peoples be conciliated if they are not assimilated? Tocqueville here falls back on the notion of a stabilized *modus vivendi*: mutual interest under a rubric set out by the conquerors. The French cannot form a bond "through the community of ideas and practices, but we may hope to do so through the community of interests."[89] The French, that is, can buy indigenous goods and employ indigenous manpower. "The European needs the Arab to make his lands valuable; the Arab needs the European to obtain a high salary."[90] Tocqueville proposes a great increase in European colonization, and an initial (in his own eyes illegal) one-time seizure of Arab lands for this purpose.[91] Domination without fellowship presupposes that prolonged contact with an advanced power, even under a "strong hand," will promote a voluntary alignment with its interests. Yet it is difficult to believe that power alone, or a forceful administration of civil justice that policed an economy run primarily for the interests of the colonizers and that denied the Arabs political rights, could achieve a fruitful peace.

In retrospect, the vulnerability of his vision seems obvious, and it is Tocqueville himself who helps us to see the flaws. He had long argued that interest alone cannot generate lasting association; such communities cannot hold out against the tendencies of the strong to exploit the weak and even to exclude them from the bounds of humanity, a scenario made more likely by the legacy of a brutal war. It is unclear why the French state will exercise the far-sighted restraint that Tocqueville believes is necessary to prevent this outcome – that is, why this imperialist project is not likely to be a democratic version of the aristocratic Irish disaster.

Moreover, Tocqueville displays a clear sense of the effects of repression on oppressed peoples. In Ireland, Catholic emancipation will eventually mean retaliatory oppression of Protestants. According to Tocqueville, even African ex-slaves and Indians, to whom he denies a future, exhibit a consciousness of oppression that will stir them to revolt. They will adopt the language of the rights of man, form ideologies of resistance, and produce new leaders. These aspirations are still-born only because the groups are isolated and socially vulnerable. In the case of those faced with French imperial rule, Tocqueville clearly recognizes a sort of febrile reactive nationalism. Aspirations towards German unity were created indirectly by Napoleon, and – more ominously in his view – Algerian nationalism was stimulated by the war and defeat. Abd-el-Kadr was not merely a traditional religious marabout, but one who learned military and administrative strategy from the Turks and the French, and brilliantly mobilized religion for political purposes. It would be foolish to "believe that this power, after having shone for a moment, will fade like so many others."[92] It is Tocqueville, after all, who makes vivid in the *Old Regime* the dangers implicit in a caste society, a society in which the upper classes do not even recognize the humanity of those below them, and thus are blind to the threats posed by resentment and distrust. It is he who allows us to understand the chilling import of Governor-General Jules Cambon's warning to the French Senate in 1894. French policy in Algeria, in Cambon's view, had reduced the native population to "a sort of human dust on which we have no influence and in which movements take place which are to us unknown."[93]

V. CONCLUSION

Tocqueville's notion of modern liberty requires a sense of attachment to fellow citizens in which the warmth of considered patriotism counters the chilling uniformity of individualism and the cold greed of materialism. Fraternal feeling and group loyalty will supply the motivation to live a self-determining existence, and will help channel the restless energies of civilized men. Within Europe, Tocqueville hopes that the great powers will live in peace, regulated by a balance of power and common recognition of the international norms of civilized nations. Yet the rapid emergence of Europe as both increasingly democratic and civilized changes the nature of its contact and competition with the rest of the world. Ever-increasing equality and economic growth in Europe involves, as far as Tocqueville can see, European world domination.

Although the patriotism of less "advanced" peoples sporadically elicits Tocqueville's admiration, because actions that go beyond self always engage his moral sensibilities, he nevertheless does not valorize struggles against the imposition of modernity by peoples who mobilize on the basis of ethnicity, culture, or religion, either in Europe or beyond it. It is not that the Irish, central Europeans, ex-slaves, Amerindians, peoples of India, or indigenous North Africans are less deserving of national self-determination than the dominant groups among the civilized great powers. They are simply victims of incomprehensible chance, having lost the historical lottery for an independent place in the sun. Although it is a crime to push them further into the shade – or into an early grave – the only realistic alternatives to such cruelty are long periods of forced fraternity, and perhaps even longer periods of dominance without fellowship. In the very long run, less advanced peoples, if not obliterated by the uncontrolled consequences of the rise of European civilization and democracy, may arrive at a free way of life by merging their identities into larger political states. But such outcomes, according to Tocqueville, depend on wisdom and self-restraint on the part of the strong and rational calculation on the part of the weak. Both are rare. Indeed, his optimism in this regard rests – paradoxically – on social processes about which he himself is deeply skeptical.

Tocqueville's writings on the necessary conditions for establishing liberty in European democracies focus on the need to combat new forms of centralized state tyranny made possible by the surrender to individualism and materialism (a world ruled by self-interest) or by revolutionary upheaval (a world of anarchy that triggers a turn to despotism). These threats arise from an inability to combat the vicious tendencies (*germes de mort*) of democracy and civilization, and he warns repeatedly that they may have permanently infected French political culture. Yet when Tocqueville confronts the results of European expansion, and especially French expansion, these reasons for despair become occasions for hope.

A theorist who sees the growth of unrepresentative state bureaucracies and the usurpations of military despots as among the greatest threats to a culture of freedom, Tocqueville nevertheless proposes to counter the criminal eruptions of democratic xenophobia, exclusionary racism, and retaliatory nationalism with long periods of unaccountable imperial tutelage. He overestimates the neutrality and benignity of the state both in his model of fraternity from above, in which even-handed state power promotes the natural processes of contact and sociability, and in the model of domination without fellowship, which makes the state a permanent referee among hostile groups, even as it shores up the power of a conquering people. It is clear from his writings on Algeria that this far-sightedness on the part of the state, in his own view, had yet to make a real appearance. The conquest was fostering deadly bureaucratization and creating demagogic military leaders who could emerge to threaten the republic at home.

A theorist who distrusts unrestricted economic development, who fears atomizing *individualisme*, and who believes that "durable ties" cannot result from interest but only from communities of attachment, Tocqueville nevertheless eventually rests his hope for the viability of enforced fraternity and domination without fellowship solely on perceptions of mutual interest. Ex-slaves in the West Indies will be drawn into a modern economy through perceptions of interest alone, and Arab and Berber peoples will eventually be placated by the profit to be gained in "commercial ties."

Finally, Tocqueville, a theorist who will soon paint the French *Old Regime* as a society in which the remnants of formalized caste inequality cannot withstand the explosive emergence of democratic universalism, despite a relatively benevolent and reform-minded central administration, nevertheless puts his trust in permanent political containment. His classic account of the French Revolution subtly analyzes how collective *mentalités* emerge in history: how people in a caste society can "live side by side forever, without ever knowing each other,"[94] how *ressentiment* can constitute a revolutionary time bomb, and how political ideologies (a feverish collective dreaming akin to religious enthusiasm) may overtake reality and for a while completely replace it. Yet, in the context of European expansion, Tocqueville hopes to prevent or defuse these explosive new fraternities by a combination of severity and pacification, by taking the perilous path – as he will later put it in the *Old Regime* – of exchanging "the role of sovereign for that of guardian."[95]

NOTES

1   "Two Concepts of Liberty," in *Four Essays on Liberty* (London: Oxford University Press, 1969), 154. My use of the term fraternity parallels Berlin's: "solidarity, fraternity, mutual understanding, the need for association on equal terms" (158).

2   *DAII* (trans. Goldhammer), 723, Cf. *Ibid.*, 832. [Subsequent citations from *DAI* or *DAII* without attribution are from the Goldhammer translation.]

3   In this chapter, I do not consider Tocqueville's writings on nationalism in Europe in 1848, but I believe that my analysis would hold for those cases as well. To be sure he saw these matters through the prism of French national interest, but his skepticism about the "springtime of peoples," about aspirations for German unity, and about the break-up of the Austrian Empire suggests that his ideal was a system of liberal states that would grant individuals (not ethnic peoples) civil and political freedoms within their borders; and would create new political identities that could inspire "considered patriotism." This is a version of what I call "fraternity from above." On these writings, see Françoise Mélonio, "Nations et Nationalismes," *La Revue Tocqueville/The Tocqueville Review* 18: 1 (1997), 67–71. On Tocqueville's discussion of "civic virtue and international society," see also David Clinton, *Tocqueville, Lieber, and Bagehot: Liberalism Confronts the World* (New York: Palgrave Macmillan, 2003), 17–43.

4   See Lynn Hunt, *The Family Romance of the French Revolution* (Berkeley, CA: University of California Press, 1992), 12–14, and especially Mona Ozouf, "Liberty, Equality, Fraternity," *Realms of Memory, Vol. 3: Symbols*, trans. Arthur Goldhammer (New York: Columbia University Press, 1992), 77–114. On Tocqueville's avoidance of the term fraternity, see Laura Janara, *Democracy Growing Up: Authority, Autonomy, and Passion in Tocqueville's Democracy in America* (Albany, NY: State University of New York Press, 2002), 75–76.

5   Tocqueville evokes the image of putting a people in a "death grip:" *les y étreindre et les y étouffer* ("Second Report on Algeria," *OC* 3:1, 329); cf. *T on Slavery and Empire* (trans. Pitts), 146. The phrase "great human family" is from "Fortnight in the Wilderness," (trans. Pierson), G. W. Pierson, *Tocqueville in America* (Baltimore: John Hopkins University Press, 1938 [1996]), 274. [All subsequent citations to Tocqueville's writings on Algeria are from the Pitts translation.]

6   *DAII*, 723. See also *DAII*, 779–780, note 1.

7   Perhaps the clearest articulation of this ideal of a just liberty derived from membership in the human race ("the modern notion, the democratic notion, and I dare say the just notion of liberty") appears in Tocqueville's 1836 sketch "L'état social et politique de la France," *Œuvres*, P3:36–37. See also *DAII*, 833: "Equality is less lofty, perhaps, but more just, and its justice is the source of its grandeur and beauty. I am doing my best to enter into this point of view, which is that of the Lord, and trying to consider and judge human affairs from this perspective."

8 *DAI*, 31. Cf. his comments in "Fortnight in the Wilderness" (trans. Pierson), 270–275.

9 *AR*, 2 (trans. Kahan), 262; Cf. his letter to Sophie Swetchine of 20 October 1856, *OC* 15:2, 296, in which he urges priests to remind Christians that they also belong to "these great human associations that God has doubtless established to make the ties among individuals more visible and lively, associations which are called peoples and whose territory is called la Patrie."

10 *AR*, 2 (trans. Kahan), 262.

11 Ibid.

12 *DAI*, 269–270; see also *DAI*, 76, 105–107 and *DAII*, 631–632.

13 As Françoise Mélonio has argued, for Tocqueville the worth of different national inheritances is to be judged by whether they favor the growth of democratic liberty – a universal, not particular concept: "Nations et Nationalismes," 64–65.

14 Charles de Rémusat, *Mémoires de ma vie*, 5 vols. (Paris: Plon, 1960) 3: 449.

15 "Tocqueville on Democracy in America (Vol. II)," in *Essays on Politics and Culture*, ed. Gertrude Himmelfarb (Gloucester, MA: Peter Smith, 1973), 257.

16 On the different levels of civilization among Europeans see *DAI*, 384–385, note 19; Tocqueville speculates that Swiss federalism is difficult because of the differing levels of civilization of the cantons, *DAI* (Nolla), 282 note t and "Voyage en Suisse (1836)," *Œuvres*, P 1:631.

17 Matthew Mancini did a content analysis of Tocqueville's and Beaumont's usage of this terminology in their published writings on race and found that "though the savagery-barbarism nomenclature by no means represents an absolute, clear-cut distinction for Tocqueville, he does use them with surprising consistency." "Political Economy and Cultural Theory in Tocqueville's Abolitionism," *Slavery & Abolition* 10: 2 (September 1989), 154.

18 The phrase "teacher and guide" is from André Jardin, *Tocqueville (1805–1859): A Biography*, trans. Lydia Davis with Robert Hemenway (London: Peter Haliban, 1988), 81. For a discussion of the recent literature on Guizot and Tocqueville, see my "Tocqueville's Resistance to the Social," *History of European Ideas* 30 (2004), 96–106. For the influence of Rousseau, see a letter of 10 November 1836, *OC* 13: 1, 418, "There are three men with whom I live a bit every day: they are Pascal, Montesquieu, and Rousseau."

19 Trans. William Hazlitt (London: Penguin, 1997), 16–17, 19.

20 "First Report on Algeria," 130. See also his letter to Henry Reeve, 12 April 1840, *OC* 6:1, 58. Cf. a much later letter to Gobineau, 13

November 1855, *OC* 9, 243: "[The Europeans] will be in another hundred years the transformers of the globe that they inhabit and the masters of their species. Nothing is more clearly announced in advance by Providence. If they are often, I admit it, great knaves, they are at any rate knaves to whom God has given force and power, and whom He has manifestly put for a time at the head of the human race."

21 *DAII*, 558.

22 *DAI*, 393. Seymour Drescher's judgment about the unconflicted nature of Tocqueville's commitment to slave emancipation is exact: "Rarely did liberty, equality, and religion so clearly converge in Tocqueville's perception," *Dilemmas of Democracy: Tocqueville and Modernization* (Pittsburgh: University of Pittsburgh Press, 1968), 190.

23 *DAI*, 402.

24 See also an alternate text in *DAI* (Nolla), 262 note d, in which Tocqueville observes that although destroying millions of Indians in the New World was an atrocious evil, it was less wounding to humanity than the legacy of slavery.

25 *DAI*, 366, 392, 395, 396, 410. Arthur Goldhammer's translation of *se confondre* as "blended" rather than "intermingled" captures the distinction that Tocqueville maintains throughout his discussions of the results of contact and conflict among peoples. Peoples who are intermingled or intermixed (*entremêlés*), or who live side by side (*côte à côte*), retain their distinctiveness and remain separate and potentially isolated. If two peoples are *confondus* or *assimilés*, however, they lose their particular identities and become merged in a new one. See his "Translator's Note," in *DA* (trans. Goldhammer), 876.

26 *DAI*, 405.

27 *DAI*, 406.

28 *DAI*, 411–412.

29 *DAI*, 395, 412. See also *DAI* (Nolla), 263, note f and 264, note n. This theme comes out even more strongly in Beaumont's *Marie or, Slavery in the United States*, trans. Barbara Chapman (Baltimore: Johns Hopkins University Press, 1999), 63, 74. Tocqueville also speculated that racism – the idea that the "invisible influence of race" condemns "some to freedom and others to servitude" – was a "natural vice of the human mind" in democratic times because it was materialist. See an unpublished draft in *TA* (Beinecke), quoted in James Schleifer, *The Making of Tocqueville's Democracy in America* (Indianapolis: Liberty Fund, 2000), 91. This notion is later pursued in his 1853 correspondence with Arthur de Gobineau, *OC* 9, 201–206. For an insightful discussion of the psychological link between U.S. racism and the general tendencies of democracy, see Laura Janara, "Brothers and Others: U.S.

Genealogy, Democracy, and Racism," *Political Theory* 32: 6 (December 2004), 788–793.

30 *DAI*, 410.

31 *DAI*, 410, cf. 416.

32 *DAI*, 413. See also Tocqueville's comments on the emergence of black "outrage at being deprived of nearly all the rights of citizens" (*DAI*, 416), an outrage that will inevitably produce "future leaders" (*DAI*, 417). Or the alternate text: "The blacks are a foreign nation that was conquered, and to which one gives a nationality and means of resistance by freeing them, or even enlightening them." *DAI* (Nolla), 277, note j. These attitudes about the danger to white society were widespread at the time in both American and French writers. See William B. Cohen, *The French Encounter with Africans: White Response to Blacks, 1530–1880* (Bloomington: Indiana University Press, 2003 [1980]), 194–195.

33 *DAI*, 417. It is sometimes argued that the same "subterranean anxiety and yearning for predictable structure" underlie Tocqueville's accounts of female and racial exclusions from the public sphere. Janara, "Brothers and Others," 779. See also her *Democracy Growing Up*, 167. It would take a longer discussion to sort out this comparison, but it is important to emphasize that these two narratives – how democracy becomes gendered and how it becomes racialized – serve entirely different purposes in Tocqueville's texts. The first invites praise for the way that Americans counter the dangerous tendencies of their social state, achieving an exemplary balance of empowerment and self-restraint leading to democratic stability. And the heroic agents are women themselves. The second elicits condemnation for the way in which Americans indulge the worst instincts of their social state, exceeding moral limits and eventually provoking violent instability. And the villains are those who thwart nature by denying the agency of racialized others. For a good statement of the contrast between sexual and racial dominance in Tocqueville, see Margaret Kohn, "Tocqueville and Beaumont on Race and Slavery," *Polity* 35: 2 (Winter 2002), footnote 16.

34 *Marie*, 62. The novel indicts American society as unnatural for allowing members allegedly of different races to come into contact, but not to fuse together (*se confondre*) (pp. 63, 66, 189, 215, 238). On the central importance of the notion of miscegenation and intermarriage to French nineteenth-century monogenists and the abolitionist tradition, see Claude Blankaert, "Of Monstrous Métis? Hybridity, Fear of Miscegenation, and Patriotism from Buffon to Paul Broca," *The Color of Liberty: Histories of Race in France*, ed. Sue Peabody and Tyler Stovall (Durham, NC: Duke University Press, 2003), 44–48.

35 *DAI* 380, 411.

36 In the opening scene, Tocqueville uses an encounter between an African woman, an Indian woman, and a European child to make vivid "perverted" social relations: "and nature, in striving to bring them together, made the vast distance that prejudices and laws had placed between them even more striking." *DAI* 370. In the closing scene, a Southern white man suffers agonies in seeing his own mulatto children pass into slavery: thus "nature avenges herself for the wounds inflicted by laws." *DAI*, 418.

37 In "Brothers and Others," Laura Janara recasts the commonplace observation that Toqueville treats the Indians as aristocrats and slaves as a people fallen into hebetude. She argues that Tocqueville – like others at the time – fraternalizes relations between Europeans and Indians, but dehumanizes ex-slaves, turning them into unassimilable others. This reading, however, ignores Tocqueville's many references to *les noirs* as a "partie de l'espèce humaine" ("Report on Slavery," *OC* 3:1, 125) or "nos sembables" (Ibid., 110–111). Or in *DA* itself: "Free Negroes ... find themselves in a position vis-à-vis Europeans analogous to that of native Americans." *DAI*, 405; they resemble a "small, poor, nomadic tribe." *DAI*, 406. Tocqueville does not maintain the position that the hebetudinous effects of slavery are irreversible and make ex-slaves unassimilable.

38 *DAI* (Nolla), 261, note a.

39 *DAI*, 381.

40 *DAI*, 369. The Indians in South America had already reached the agricultural stage; if they had not, they also would have been destroyed in the Spanish conquest. *DAI*, 391.

41 *DAI*, 374.

42 *DAI*, 385.

43 *DAI*, 379.

44 The phrases are from "Fortnight in the Wilderness," 244, 235.

45 *DAI*, 391. Tocqueville contrasts this hypocritical use of justice to the more honest method of the sword. He struggles with the same dilemma of the relative moral "demerits" of fraud and force in Algeria. See "Essay on Algeria," 85, 87.

46 *DAI*, 387.

47 *DAI*, 371. In an alternate text, he expressed this distinction clearly. Referring to state and federal policy towards Cherokees and Creeks, he notes "what comes first is an unconscious and as it were involuntary action of one race on the other, but often joined to it is the actual and intentional action of governments." *DAI* (Nolla), 249, note h.

48 *DAI*, 382.

49 Cf. *DAI*, 437: "There is something providential about this gradual and steady progress of the European race toward the Rocky Mountains: it is like a human flood, rising steadily and daily driven on by the hand of God" to his later comments in a letter to Sedgwick deploring "this spirit of conquest, and even a bit of rapine, [that] has appeared among you for some years. It is not a sign of good health in a people which already has more territories than it can fill." Letter of 4 December 1852, *OC* 7, 146–147.

50 *DAI*, 411. Cf. *DAI* (Nolla), 273, note a: "Of all governments, those that have the least power over mores are free governments."

51 *DAI*, 392.

52 "Notes on Algeria," 70. For an analysis of how these repressed fears lead to rhetorical evasions, see my "Colonial Violence and the Rhetoric of Evasion: Tocqueville on Algeria," *Political Theory* 13:2 (April 2003).

53 *La question d'Alger: politique, colonisation, commerce* (Paris: P. Dufart, 1837), 63–65.

54 "Essay on Algeria," 111.

55 "Intervention in the Debate over Special Funding" (1846), 118. In a letter to Corcelle (1 December 1846, *OC* 15: 1, 224), he notes that even to "wish for" the disappearance of the Arabs is cruel and absurd. Yet he also confesses that his mind is troubled and hesitates when confronted with the question of "what should be done so that the two races enter into contact with one another."

56 *DAI*, 411: "A despot who managed to reduce both the Americans and their former slaves to the same state of subservience might succeed in mixing them . . . ." For the contrast of Protestant to Catholic churches, see *Marie*, 75–79, 126 and DAI (Nolla), 264, note e. The theme of cultural and biological homogenization of the races as facilitated by a specifically Catholic form of Christianity was widespread in the French philanthropic movement. On this, see Alyssa Goldstein Sepinwall," Eliminating Race, Eliminating Difference: Blacks, Jews, and the Abbé Grégoire," *The Color of Liberty*, 29–37.

57 *DAI*, 412.

58 *DAI*, 444.

59 *DAII*, 594. Tocqueville, however, did worry about the influx of foreigners who lacked civic habits. See letters to Beaumont 6 August 1854, *OC* 8:3, 228–229 and letter to Sedgwick, 14 October 1856, *OC* 7, 182. He also thought it an open question whether the reflective patriotism attached to individual states could be solidly transferred to the Union, *DAI*, 424.

60 "Intervention dans la discussion de la loi sur le régime des esclaves dans les colonies" (30 May 1845), *OC* 3:1, 114.

61 "Report on Slavery (1839)," *OC* 3:1, 75–77.

62 See his contrast of the English and French character in "Fortnight in the Wilderness," 272–273; also *DAI*, 381.

63 The 1843 articles in *Le siècle* dropped the notion of a state-controlled period of transition that would moralize freed slaves after emancipation (a proposal that had not been able to generate much support) and endorsed the scheme of simultaneous emancipation endorsed by the Broglie Report. Thus Tocqueville was left in the position of putting even more hope in the salutary influence of a restrictive land law.

64 *DAI*, 382.

65 See "First and Second Letters on Algeria (1837), 5–26.

66 "Second Letter on Algeria," 25.

67 See Welch, "Colonial Violence," 242–243. Tocqueville is later less sanguine about the compatibility of Islam with free democracy.

68 "Second Letter on Algeria," 26.

69 *DAI*, 386.

70 "Second Letter on Algeria," 23.

71 Ibid., 24.

72 Ibid., 24.

73 Ibid., 22.

74 For recent discussions in the Tocqueville literature see Eric Keslassy. *Le libéralisme de Tocqueville à l'épreuve du paupérisme* (Paris: L'Harmattan, 2000), esp. 201–262; Michael Drolet, *Tocqueville, Democracy and Social Reform* (London: Palgrave Macmillan, 2003), 135–201. See also the classic discussion in Seymour Drescher, *Dilemmas of Democracy*.

75 "Essay on Algeria," 111.

76 *Œuvres*, P 1: 531, 555

77 *Œuvres*, P 1:556.

78 Ibid., 521.

79 "And how have these two nations reached situations so sad and so similar? – By the same roads – by a primary act of violence, followed by a long course of injustice." Beaumont, *Ireland: Social, Political, and Religious*, 2 vols., ed. W.C. Taylor (London: Richard Bentley, 1839), 2: 351.

80 *Œuvres*, P 1: 523, 548, 553–554.

81 Beaumont, *Ireland*, 2: 214. The aristocratic social state of England and Ireland complicates the comparison to democratic imperialist ventures. Beaumont acknowledges that the English parliament, impregnated with particularistic aristocratic political *moeurs* and suspicious of democratic universalism, would be hard put to act as a benevolent third party. It would have to dismantle its vicious sister aristocracy,

even while acting as a neutral arbiter between the democratic passions of the Irish middle classes and the aristocratic prejudices of Ireland's Protestant rulers.

82 "What nation would consent to its own dismemberment? Does not every power, whose territory is diminished, appear to be on the decline?" Beaumont, *Ireland*, 2: 325.

83 "Notes on Algeria," 37.

84 "Ébauches d'un ouvrage sur l'Inde," *OC* 3:1, 444–550. Tocqueville admired the indirect but firm rule the English adopted in India, but disdained the moral smugness of their official reports in which, he argued, they pretend to act out of "principle" or for the "good of the indigenous people," when in fact they are motivated by "des passions interessées" (505).

85 "First Report on Algeria," 145.

86 Ibid., 141.

87 Ibid., 142.

88 Ibid., 146. He adds that for the French (who have been forewarned) to destroy the *indigènes* would be "a thousand times less excusable" than for earlier conquerors.

89 Ibid., 145.

90 Ibid.,

91 Ibid., 149, 163.

92 "Essay on Algeria," 67.

93 Quoted in William B. Quandt, *Revolution and Political Leadership: Algeria, 1954–1968* (Cambridge, MA: MIT Press, 1969), 5.

94 *AR* (trans. Kahan), 190.

95 Ibid., 124.

13 Tocqueville and the French

Translated by Arthur Goldhammer

"Since you're here, Monsieur de Tocqueville, I'd like you to tell me a little about America," said Louis-Philippe, the king of France, in 1848.[1] For 150 years, the French have enjoyed discussing America with Tocqueville; the Americans, too. In America, as in France, Tocqueville is best known as the author of a single book, *Democracy in America*, which is read as a textbook on the political constitution of the United States. The French see Tocqueville as the apologist for a foreign model: "That American," his adversaries call him.[2] For Americans, Tocqueville is an honorary citizen, who reinforces their idea of their own exceptionalism.

The Americanization of Tocqueville is evident from the fact that the remark for which Tocqueville is best known in the United States is apocryphal. Presidents from Eisenhower to Reagan and Clinton have repeated what Tocqueville is supposed to have said but never did: "America is great because America is good. When America ceases to be good, she will cease to be great."[3] Though falsely attributed to Tocqueville, the saying is instructive nonetheless. Like other, genuine quotations, but in a more obvious way, it aims to reinforce an American identity based on moral values and said to derive from an initial promise to which the nation is urged to remain faithful or perish. The invocation of Tocqueville expresses the "manifest destiny" of the American Union, which becomes more manifest, apparently, when admired by Europeans. Hence, in the United States, Tocqueville is rarely read in a comparative perspective or as a French author, despite a number of notable books devoted to his work, and his historical works (*Souvenirs, L'Ancien Régime et la Révolution*) attract little interest outside a small circle of specialists.[4] The wider American public has no interest in

Tocqueville as a French thinker embedded in a particular history of his own and intelligible in terms of his situation in a French debate. Or, rather, the fact that he is French and an aristocrat matters only insofar as it enhances the value of his praise, coming as it does from an aristocratic convert to American democracy and a son of the great revolutionary nation discovering a sister revolution in which the end of history is being played out. Tocqueville is thus invoked as evidence of a transfer of knowledge and power from old Europe to the New World. He is part of the "French heritage," along with the Québecois, the Marquis de Lafayette, Major Charles Pierre L'Enfant (the designer of Washington, DC), and Bartholdi (the sculptor of the Statue of Liberty).[5]

The Americanization of Tocqueville, which deserves full credit for having assured the survival of his work, nevertheless leads to a bias in its interpretation: although Tocqueville worried about the judgment of the American audience, he did not write primarily for it. His purpose was to derive from American political experience a lesson for Europeans – that is, for societies just emerging, or about to emerge, from absolutism. Tocqueville saw himself as the thinker of the democratic transition, and unless we keep that objective in mind, we cannot understand what ties his various works together. *Democracy in America* offers Europeans an image of their possible future; *The Old Regime and the Revolution*, for which the title "Democracy in France" had been contemplated, deals with the survival of absolutist culture in continental Europe and the way in which it complicated the establishment of liberal democracy.[6]

The purpose of this chapter is to show that Tocqueville's thought gains in stature if we take account of his roots in French culture. The vigor of Tocqueville's interpretation of the United States stems from his comparative approach. The purpose of *Democracy in America* is not to describe the American Constitution or mores but to draw from them lessons for other democracies by way of a constant comparison with Europe and, above all, with France. For "it is one of the singular infirmities of the human mind that it cannot judge objects or see them clearly and in full daylight unless it places them alongside other objects."[7]

Tocqueville's relation to French tradition has two dimensions, political and literary, and both must be taken into account in interpreting his work.

Political: For Tocqueville, writing was a propædeutic to action. "What we must develop in ourselves is the political man," he wrote his friend Beaumont in 1828. The journey to America was intended to "alert the public to your existence and attract the attention of the parties."[8] *The Old Regime* was written in 1856 to invigorate the liberal spirit in the despotic Second Empire. Tocqueville's work was thus always engaged with the conflicting opinions of his times and always had a pragmatic goal.

Literary: Tocqueville belongs to a line of "eloquent" writers that runs from Pascal and Bossuet in the seventeenth century to Rousseau in the eighteenth and Madame de Staël, Chateaubriand, and Guizot in the early nineteenth. Drawing on these models, he invented a new language for democracy.

I. THE POLITICAL PURPOSE

Tocqueville's political plans played the primary role in the inception of both *Democracy in America* and *The Old Regime and the Revolution*. Scholarly and theoretical concerns were secondary. Both works use words to influence people. The goal is to clear a path for the future legislator – the future French legislator – whose mission is to bring the Revolution to an end and establish a well-regulated democracy.

Tocqueville owed this political goal to his personal history. What distinguished him in his own eyes was the accident of his birth: "Aristocracy was already dead when my life began, and Democracy did not yet exist. Hence my instinct could not pull me blindly toward one or the other."[9] Tocqueville was thus convinced of belonging to a transitional generation from which he derived a special theoretical lucidity. He never knew his great-grandfather, the magistrate Malesherbes, who first protected the *philosophes* of the Enlightenment and then defended King Louis XVI before the Convention, for which he was guillotined. Tocqueville was determined not to fall short of the virtues of his ancestors. To be sure, he did not believe that a return to aristocracy was possible, and refused to use his noble titles: "De-countify me, please," he wrote to his friend Beaumont. Yet he was brought up in the memory of aristocracy and with a taste for the aristocratic way of life, which is why he judged democracy to be mediocre. If aristocracy died before

Tocqueville was born, democracy had not yet begun to live, or, rather, the democracy that did exist was infantile and revolutionary: it was a "monster splattered with blood and mud, clad in rags, and accompanied by loud disputations straight out of Antiquity."[10] On his travels as well as in his 1835 work, he said exactly the same thing that Guizot was saying: "The true task of our era is to purge the principles of 1789 of any alloy of anarchy."[11] In other words, Tocqueville, while still quite young, found in his historical situation the theoretical question to which he would devote all his work, and it was a question that he shared with his contemporaries: How to accommodate democracy in such a way as to encourage respect for individual rights, the religion of law, and genuine and effective liberty? The revolutionary experience thus gave a new dimension to a search for individual guarantees that can be traced back to the eighteenth century and to the work of Montesquieu in particular.

From very early on, even before the end of the Restoration, Tocqueville sought the answer to this political question in a philosophy of history whose broad outlines he took from his contemporaries. The goal was to bring the Revolution to an end, to use a formula derived from the Revolution itself, and to that end what was sought was if not a model then at least an example in the comparative history of Western countries.

The project of *Democracy in America* was closely related to the French historiography and political debates of the 1820s and 1830s. Tocqueville was heir to what has been called a new regime of historicity. For him, as for his contemporaries, history had a direction: it was moving inexorably toward democracy. All societies were caught up in this movement. Hence one could look elsewhere in Europe or in that extension of Europe, the United States, for hints to the future of France. The liberals of the Restoration (1815–1830) tried to read the future of France in the history of England, which had already served as a model for Montesquieu and Voltaire in the eighteenth century. The parallel between the Stuarts and the Bourbons, which dates from the middle of the seventeenth century, became a commonplace during the Restoration. To write about Cromwell, as Victor Hugo did, was to write about revolutionary France.

Tocqueville learned his English history primarily from Guizot. At the Sorbonne in 1828–1829, he was one of many young students who attended Guizot's lectures on the history of European civilization, in which England played the leading role. Guizot glorified the English Revolution of 1688, which deposed James II in favor of his daughter Mary and his son-in-law William of Orange, a Protestant and a Dutch *stathouder*. For Guizot, this represented a victory of free institutions over monarchical despotism, an emancipation of the individual, and a reconciliation of all the constitutive elements of English society: aristocracy, monarchy, and democracy. In England, Guizot wrote, "the victor was always obliged to tolerate the existence of his rivals and to give each his due."[12] England invented mixed government: "The essence of liberty is the simultaneous expression and influence of all interests, all rights, all forces, and all elements of society."[13] From this English model, Guizot drew the lesson that France ought to rest its regime on the middle classes, which offered access to the aristocracy above while welcoming meritorious offspring of the popular classes below.

The overthrow of the legitimate monarchy in 1830 gave new pertinence to the parallel between the English Revolutions and the history of France. The comparison of 1688 with 1830 gave legitimacy to the revolution of 1830 and also seemed to justify the conclusion that no further revolution was possible: 1830 completed 1789 as 1688 had completed 1640. Louis-Philippe was the French William of Orange. Tocqueville inherited this historical schema, and his work was built on his early rejection of it.

Although a student of Guizot, Tocqueville was also the descendant of an aristocratic family decimated by the Revolution, hence he had no sympathy for bourgeois rule. "Does anyone think that democracy, having destroyed feudalism and vanquished kings, will be daunted by the bourgeois and the rich?"[14] Tocqueville's originality thus lay in revising the parallel between English and French history, rejecting the view that the English past could be read as a prefiguration of the French present. There is no clearer evidence of this than the two parallel descriptions he gave of the French and English Revolutions. The first of these, probably written in 1833, was entitled "similarity and dissimilarity of the revolutions of 1640 and 1789," and the second, from 1842, was identified as "notes on the revolutions of 1688 and 1830."[15] To be sure, he concedes that "a rather broad analogy" exists between the two histories. Louis-Philippe, the bourgeois king, can be seen as an avatar of William of Orange, "secretive, selfish, devoid of morality, contemptuous of men and leading them as though they were worthy of contempt,"[16] but the English revolution took place in a country that remained "profoundly aristocratic and mon-archical."[17] Nothing like this was true in a France that was already democratic. The English experience belonged to the past and was misleading anyone who thought it contained a lesson for the future of the French. When Tocqueville defined political science before the Académie des Sciences Morales on April 3, 1852, he had Guizot and the Doctrinaires in mind: "The very study of history, which often illuminates the realm of present facts, sometimes obscures it. How often have we encountered among us people whose minds, shrouded in shadows of such learning, saw 1640 in 1789 and 1688 in 1830, and who, always one revolution behind, wished to administer to the latter a treatment appropriate to the former, rather like those learned physicians who, being well-versed in the old maladies of the human body but ever ignorant of the specific new ill from which their patient was suffering, rarely failed to kill him with erudition!"[18]

Tocqueville was thus in many respects an heir of the Restoration historians. From them he took the idea of a universal (or at least occidental) course of civilization, the comparative method of doing history, the desire to make history a propædeutic of politics, and a philosophical manner of structuring history in terms of what were then called "idées mères," or hypotheses. He changed the focus of the question, however, and therefore the field of study. Guizot, like Mme de Staël, had studied the history of civilization, by which he meant the progress of enlightenment and technology. Tocqueville studied the ineluctable progress of democracy. This did not neces-sarily imply progress in enlightenment, since he envisioned two possible evolutions for democracy – toward enlightenment or toward barbarism. What mattered for him was the sentiment of equality, which, more than progress in science in technology, determines the course of history. As for the field of study, America was still for Guizot what it had been for Joseph de Maistre, an "infant in diapers."[19] It was still a relatively underdeveloped country with a democratic social form and a republican political form suitable only to a very young nation. By contrast, Tocqueville looked to the United States for instruction, not as to the childhood of societies but as to their future. America was thus an incomparable laboratory for an intellectual adventure: to investigate democracy in gestation.

The audacity of this move needs to be appreciated. Tocqueville owed almost nothing to the small band of contemporaries who admired the United States. Though he was Chateaubriand's nephew by marriage, and his traveling companion Beaumont was a distant relative of Lafayette, his thought owed nothing to either Chateaubriand's journey or the small republican coterie gathered around Lafayette. In 1825, he was critical of Chateaubriand's display of enthusiasm for the America of which Lafayette was then making a triumphal tour: "The genius should have taken as his only task to show us the difference that exists between [the American republic] and us, and not to abuse us with a misleading resemblance." What changed Tocqueville's view was thus the revolution of 1830 and its precursors of 1828–1829. He went to the United States in search of a resemblance he could not see in 1825, a resemblance between two egalitarian societies, one (France) still revolutionary and intentionally despotic, the other (the United States) respectful of the law though not always exempt from the tyranny of the majority. Through an exploration of this new American terrain and unprecedented American experiment with democracy, Tocqueville thus rediscovered a problem first posed by eighteenth-century liberalism: What guarantees does the individual require? This was a question that had been asked first by Montesquieu and by Tocqueville's great-grandfather Malesherbes and then, earlier in the nineteenth century, by Benjamin Constant and Mme de Staël.

Clearly, Tocqueville's book had what it took to have an impact on French history in terms not only of its practical political implications but also of its deep reflection on French identity. As we have seen, the author's political concerns were intimately related to his intellectual project. In 1835, Tocqueville drafted for the Chamber of Deputies a note on the powers of the President of the United States in order to help resolve a diplomatic conflict with President Jackson. On June 22 of that same year, he explained the rules of secret balloting in France and the United States to the British Parliament, which had undertaken an investigation of voting fraud.[20] Between 1839 and 1848, he took part in any number of parliamentary debates in which comparative reflection on France and the United States played a key role (concerning, for instance, colonial issues and freedom of religion and teaching). In 1848, he participated in drafting the constitution of the Second Republic, even as his book figured centrally in debates about the pertinence of the American republic as a model for France. As a "public intellectual," Tocqueville saw himself as a man of action as much as a speculative thinker. This was by no means an exceptional case among the thinkers of his time. The fact that Tocqueville was never a leading deputy or a good minister and never served as a party leader demonstrates his lack of skill in the game of back-scratching flattery and deal-making. Yet the purpose of his thinking was always to have an influence on French policy, and at this he was partially successful.

At first sight, *The Old Regime and the Revolution* (1856) seems to be a work of pure scholarship without a political purpose, yet its objective was no different from that of *Democracy in America*. For Tocqueville, history was the continuation of politics by other means, at a time when the Second Empire had condemned him to retirement. What Tocqueville was looking for was "an important subject in political literature." "At bottom, the only things that interest me or the public are contemporary subjects. The spectacle of the world today is so impressive and striking that no one attaches much value to historical curiosities of the sort with which feckless scholarly societies content themselves."[21] Thus the questions Tocqueville asked himself had not changed: Why did the democratic transition in France take a revolutionary form? How can liberty be guaranteed in an egalitarian society? "Why did quite analogous principles and similar political theories" lead the United States to a peaceful democracy and France to recurrent revolutions?[22]

The answer looked to the *longue durée*: in the history of France, there was one and only one guilty party. The kings of France had sought only to divide their subjects in order to reign more absolutely. To place the seed of the enduring French taste for servitude in the Old Regime was a bold thesis. It explained why one revolution after another ended in despotism, first with Napoleon, then with Napoleon III. By illuminating the past, it made emancipation from it possible. *The Old Regime* is a book about the identity of France and, more broadly, of continental Europe, scarred by absolutism and struggling to establish liberal democracies.

The entirety of Tocqueville's work is thus a reflection on the management of the democratic transition. Knowing this, we can see at once why the fate of that work in France and indeed all of Europe has been so strange. It was pondered seriously until the 1880s – that is, until the French republic was stabilized. After that, it ceased to be of more than historical interest, and only rarely aroused the curiosity even of professional historians. Political liberalism faded, it was believed, because it had been too successful, because it had no further demands to make, no glaring abuses to denounce. From 1880 until World War II, republican France believed it had reached safe harbor. It took the experience of the war and of totalitarianism to put the question of guarantees of liberty back on the table and to raise new questions about the republican and democratic tradition.[23] Tocqueville began to be read again in France in the 1960s. The revival of interest in his work coincided with the revival of interest in other liberals such as Benjamin Constant, and was one of any number of signs of a resurgence of liberal thought.[24] What stands out in this revival is that Tocqueville's works are read not as historical texts but as analyses of the world we still live in, as contributions to political thought to which we turn for understanding of the present, not of the past. To reread Tocqueville today is to discover a penetrating reflection on the tension between two aspects of the modern idea of emancipation: the desire for individual autonomy and universal participation in the exercise of power – or, to put it slightly differently, liberalism and political democracy, individual and citizen.

This ahistorical reading of the work has sometimes led to the assertion that liberalism's recent "vogue" in France marked the sudden conversion of the French to the cause of liberty after centuries of erring ways and voluntary servitude, as if liberal theory were an import from the English-speaking countries and as if the concern with liberty were a matter of concern only to a tiny minority[25] whose cherished liberty was in any case threatened by the emergence of a new Moloch in Brussels. The truth is precisely the reverse, that it is Tocqueville's historical involvement in the French tradition that has made his work perennial, for it has gone hand in hand with the broad movement of the past two centuries that has made the demand for equal dignity for all individuals the common reference of the societies in which we live. Its strength lies in its willingness to confront the difficulties of the present. It does not offer an atemporal doctrine of democracy. It does not succumb to the illusion of detaching itself from its time or from the society it inhabits or from a particular historical situation. Yet this does not mean that readers remote from that time cannot hear what it has to say, even though they are often unaware of the historical context in which Tocqueville wrote.

II. BETWEEN ESSAY AND MORAL TREATISE: TOCQUEVILLE IN FRENCH LITERATURE

Tocqueville's writing is inseparable from the political goal he set himself. The objective is to describe, but in order to judge, and to instigate a salutary shock: "I am not, please God, one of those people who believe that the malady from which we are suffering is incurable," he wrote in a variant text of *The Old Regime and the Revolution*.[26] The whole œuvre is presented as offering a helping hand to a people in danger. This accounts for the frequent appeals to the reader: "Have, then, of the future the salutary fear that keeps one alert and ready for battle, and not the limp, lazy terror that strikes the heart and saps its energy."[27]

This mode of writing surprises those who want to turn Tocqueville into a sociologist, given the degree to which sociology now distinguishes sharply between analysis, normative discourse, and moral discourse. This aspect of Tocqueville's style has thus been seen as archaic. It is nevertheless a mistake to read Tocqueville as a precursor of Max Weber. His originality was to take the old tradition of eloquence and with it to invent a new language for democracy, to adapt the commonplaces of the classical writers to describe a novel world. The essential difficulty of reading and translating Tocqueville's work is precisely to take into account this classical dimension of a work that abounds with allusions to ancient writers, to the moralists and preachers of the seventeenth and eighteenth centuries, and to the *philosophes* of the Enlightenment, and that plays constantly with cultural familiarity.[28] To replace the œuvre in literature, to determine the literary genre to which it belongs, is to make interpretation possible.

Tocqueville adapted to democracy an old theme of the ancient and classical moralists, *homo viator,* "man is a voyager." The preface to the 1835 *Democracy* and the grand conclusion to the *Democracy* of 1840 dramatically orchestrate this theme, which Tocqueville probably took primarily from the seventeenth-century Jansenists Pascal and La Rochefoucauld. "Where are we headed, then? No one can say ... "(*DAI,* 7). Pascal tried to persuade libertines and atheists of the need to wager on the existence of God by showing them that they were "embarked," as Tocqueville describes himself: "Immersed in a rapidly flowing stream, we stubbornly fix our eyes on the few pieces of debris still visible on the shore, while the current carries us away and propels us backward into the abyss" (*DAI,* 8).[29] With this old theme, however, Tocqueville tried to describe the new world. If, as moralists reiterated before Tocqueville, we must brave the perils of the "crossing," the crossing in question is no longer, or at any rate not primarily, of this world by men en route to eternity; it is rather the crossing of the democratic world, or, as we would say today, the democratic transition. Tocqueville thus offered a secularized, historicized version of the discourse of the ancient and classical (that is, seventeenth-century) writers, because for him the theme of *homo viator* characterized not so much human experience in general as the historical situation of democratic man. Indeed, one prominent feature of democracy is that its meaning is elusive, that everything is unstable.

The instability of which I speak affects the individual as much as society. Tocqueville belongs to a line of moralists such as Montaigne in the sixteenth century and Pascal in the seventeenth who do not believe in a stable form of being. To escape the prison of the self was for him an intimate experience: "Here you see me whole, the most incomplete and incoherent of all the members of a species that is itself the most incoherent and incomplete of all the species ever created; weaker than all my fellow men in some respects, as strong as any of them in some others. Badly put together, ill-assorted in my various parts, and by my very constitution incapable of ever attaining the happiness I seek."[30] Tocqueville was clearly tired of being himself. Vague anxiety and restless desires were for him a "chronic disease."[31] Yet that intimate affliction was not an individual malady but a historical one. Anxiety, a metaphysical ill, is aggravated in democratic man. Not everyone is conscious of it, but all are afflicted by it. The eighteenth century had placed excessive confidence in the perfectibility of man. The nineteenth century – exhibiting the tell-tale signs of the democratic disease – succumbed to despair at the sight of man's incapacity to satisfy his vast desires. Tocqueville thus expressed the modern malaise in a language inherited from the moralists and using their anthropological categories.

From the moralists he also took his wish to help man "achieve the kind of grandeur and happiness that is appropriate to him"[32] by way of a discourse that moves incessantly back and forth between analysis of man's "misery" and analysis of his grandeur. It comes as no surprise to discover that his contemporaries saw him as "a kind of political Pascal": "In reading him, every page reminds you of those melancholy words of Pascal that he more than anyone had the right to use as his motto: 'I castigate equally those who choose to praise man, those who choose to blame him, and those who choose to amuse him, and I can approve only of those whose quest is accompanied by moans.' "[33] If democratic man rises up, Tocqueville knocks him down, but having knocked him down, he raises him up again in a perfectly Pascalian dialectic. For one must look at "the other side of the painting," and having demonstrated the instability and mediocrity of democracy, one must also show its grandeur. No social regime is as favorable as democracy to sublimity of thought: "Nothing is more admirable or powerful, in my view, than a great orator debating great affairs in a democratic assembly. Since no class is ever represented there by men bound to defend its interests, speakers invariably address the nation as a whole, and it is in the name of the nation as a whole that they speak. This enlarges their ideas and elevates their language." (DAII, 605) Democratic eloquence, because it is addressed to all men, who are everywhere the same, moves the "human race." Democratic man is thus seen to be man in the fullness of his nature, stripped of everything that disfigures him, of all artifices stemming from differences of rank or age – like man in a state of nature in Rousseau's Discourse on the Origin of Inequality. Thus we can say that it was in the discourse on democracy that moralistic discourse found its true generality, that democracy created the historical situation in which it became possible to rise to the point of view of man in general. Classical writers thought they were talking about human nature, but only the philosopher of democracy could truly achieve the generality that the absence of a feeling of similarity placed beyond the reach of the greatest philosophers of antiquity as well as the writers of the classical age in France.

Thus one finds in Tocqueville a whole range of echoes of the moral literature. Take, for example, his analysis of religious sentiment, which is too often read solely in terms of the disenchantment of the contemporary world. For Tocqueville, God was a hidden God, even an absent God. Yet the fact that he never had evidence of the divine did not prevent him from affirming that the desire for God is bound up with man's very sense of incompleteness. Even within democracies, which are by their very nature inclined toward materialism, a need for the infinite survives, a need made manifest to the traveler by the "follies" associated with the Great Awakening (he had been dumbfounded by the Quakers). "Man did not bestow upon himself the taste for the infinite and the love of what is immortal. These sublime instincts were not born of a caprice of his will. Their fixed foundation lies in man's nature. They exist in spite of his efforts. He can hinder and deform but not destroy them. The soul has needs that must be satisfied, and no matter what pains one takes to distract it from itself, it soon grows bored, anxious, and agitated among the pleasures of the senses." (DAII, 647) Everything in this passage is rooted in a literary tradition: not only the inherited vocabulary (soul, boredom, anxiety, pleasures of the senses) but also the reference to human nature. Tocqueville deals with this human nature on two levels, because he looks beyond all social regimes to their "fixed foundation" in human nature, and because democracy is the regime in which that nature reveals itself in its purest form.

This analysis of democracy, as the regime in which human nature expresses itself in its primordial simplicity, also shaped the reformist mission of the moralist and legislator, the former laying the groundwork for the latter. Tocqueville recovered the Aristotelian ideal of prudence. There is no advantage in fighting the spirit of one's time and country. Yet the necessary art of accommodation implies no renunciation of will. The writer, the moralist, and the legislator set themselves the task of guiding democratic man through the long voyages of the democratic transition. "The legislator is like a navigator on the high seas. He can steer the vessel on which he sails, but he cannot alter its construction, raise the wind, or stop the ocean from swelling beneath his feet" (*DAI*, 185). What was the best way to speak to democracy without allowing oneself to be blindly led by it? How could one influence the will of others to modify their practice? By means of a decentering. One can say of Tocqueville what his friend Kergorlay said, "that he is obviously a student of our great writers of the seventeenth century, but a student who put the weapon that his masters placed in his hands to an entirely new use."[34]Like the writers of the classics, he aimed to write common sense, the mostly widely shared thing in the world (as Descartes called it). Yet at the same time he took his distance in order to judge the world as an outsider.

For Tocqueville, the quality common to all great writers is common sense: "Study all the writers bequeathed to us by the age of Louis XIV, that of Louis XV, and the great writers from the beginning of our own era such as Mme de Staël and Chateaubriand, and you will find that common sense is the basis of all their work."[35] Common sense is the art of presenting only a clear, simple point of view, as well as the art of engaging in conversation with the commonplaces of one's time. Tocqueville knew the danger of cliché, yet by political vocation he avoided originality and tried to say better and more systematically what others had anticipated. The resulting community of language was what enabled him to introduce new ideas to his readers. The democratic regime thus gave new meaning to what the moralists of the seventeenth century had undertaken. Like Pascal, Tocqueville could write: "Let no one say that I wrote nothing new. The arrangement of subjects is new. In tennis, both players use the - same ball, but one places it better than the other."[36] Hence the modern reader often has the disarming feeling that what he finds in Tocqueville he has already read somewhere else, even though originality is the central aesthetic value of literary modernity.

To place the ball better is to place oneself where it is not. The moralist is an eccentric, as Louis van Delft makes clear: "The moralist never blends completely into the crowd. To some degree at least he is always decentered and finds himself either above the multitude or to one side of it: he remains on the human level but never exactly where others are. He is akin to an outsider."[37]

Tocqueville placed himself precisely in the position of outsider in a democratic world that denied otherness. The democratic literature practiced by Tocqueville therefore radicalized the eccentricity of moral literature: the moralist is both in the world and outside it; the democratic moralist is in the democratic world but outside it. Tocqueville turned his social background into his destiny as a writer. He was not a writer who laid claim to aristocracy, not even the aristocracy of the mind. He wrote from within democracy, but the shadow cast by family memories of times gone by ensured that he would enjoy the privilege of distance.

This historical distance was coupled with geographical distance. Tocqueville's so-called comparativism was intended to liberate his mind. He was a man between worlds: between America and Europe and, within Europe, between France, England, and Germany. The spectacle of the world nourished his independence of mind. Like the classical moralists an observer, Tocqueville nevertheless worked harder than they did at maintaining his distance, because it is the character of democracy to abolish all differences and to destroy independence of thought. Geographical comparativism is apt to offer nothing more than variants of democracy, given the degree to which every nation follows the same road to ultimate uniformity, each in its own way and at its own pace. The historical distance between aristocracy and democracy seems to fall apart before the eyes of the observer, for aristocracy exists in Tocqueville's text only as a mythical epoch. The historical ages of aristocracy are already permeated with democracy: Milton is both an aristocratic and democratic poet, and even Bossuet's *Discourse on Universal History* seems tailored to the democratic taste for generalities.[38] Democracy is inescapable ... In the midst of universal confusion, the moralist must achieve a radical distance if he is to find his way, and the only radical distance that will do is that of the divine, the wholly-other. Tocqueville resorts to this, however, only in the ultimate chapter of his work ("General View of the Subject"), in order to put an end to the vacillation of his thinking: "My vision grows cloudy and my reason falters" (*DAII*, 850).

Thus it is primarily through an effort of style that Tocqueville succeeds in establishing his distance and forcing the reader to judge the world of which he is a part. He uses all the tropes of distance in order to disabuse the reader of the deceptive evidence of democracy.

The irony that obliges the reader to step back and humbles the powerful is an emancipatory irony. The use of paradox is also a way of emancipating the reader by showing him that his prejudices are inconsistent with one another. Seeking to make manifest what Pascal called the "contrarieties" of man, Tocqueville proceeds by way of antitheses and distinguos. This was noted long ago by the great nineteenth-century literary critic Sainte-Beuve: "No thinker ever raised so many objections in advance or argued with himself more before setting to work: all the *buts, ifs*, and *fors* that can enter a thoughtful mind he conjured with beforehand and weighed carefully in his balance."[39] Tocqueville's drafts show that he himself worried about being thought "far-fetched" or "lapsing into the improbable and paradoxical and seeming to spin out a phantasmagoria."[40] Indeed, his thinking was often given to oxymoron: in *Democracy in America*, independence turns out to be a form of servitude, whereas in *The Old Regime*, "there is nothing less independent than a free citizen." The oxymoron is of course the figure of thought that best expresses the effort to see "the other side of the canvas," just as in Pascal's *Pensées* the purpose of paradox is to show how contrary effects proceed from a single cause, thereby forcing the reader to loosen his grip on the present.

The elimination of the picturesque and the move toward generality are also tropes of distance, and Tocqueville of course has more in common with literature than with sociological writing. That is what made him seem old-fashioned to late-nineteenth-century social scientists. Boutmy, a typical representative of the political science of the time, reacted to Tocqueville's classicism by criticizing him "for disposing [of the facts] before writing. He shakes them off as a traveler shakes the dust from his boots before entering a drawing room." For Boutmy, this demonstrated Tocqueville's "classical" cast of mind, for which "observations about individuals or limited to one place and one point in time ... do not in themselves count as proofs. They are only indications or examples, means of discovering, classifying, and occasionally of *illustrating* – which must always be done soberly – the real points of the argument. This rests essentially on a series of important physical and historical causes together with their psychological effects and on the consequences and manifestations of those effects in the human soul and in society."[41] In fact, Tocqueville does eliminate everything that might particularize his text: picturesque memories from his travels, contemporary allusions, indications of his reading. The *saynètes* (dramatic encapsulations) in *Democracy in America* turn the text into a sort of reprise of the *Caractères* of La Bruyère, which Tocqueville studied in high school.[42] *The Old Regime and the Revolution* conceals the sources on which it draws so as to focus all attention on a few central ideas. This pruning away of all facts offended the sociologists and positivist historians of the late nineteenth century. It is still disconcerting today. Yet it is this move toward generality that enables generation after generation to read a work that has detached itself from its time.

If judged by the standards of logic or social science, Tocqueville's work may therefore seem outdated. *Democracy in America* contains no rigorous definition of equality or liberty. Its method of generalization is odd, and the text is given to dissimulation of its sources. The impeccable architecture of the major sections seems to crumble chapter by chapter into fragments, corrections, and incessant repetitions, which represent so many approaches to a brand new reality for which no words lay ready to hand. Tocqueville therefore does not belong to the archeology of the social sciences. His writing is much more a kind of hermeneutics. To describe the new world, Tocqueville turned back to the ancient practice of deciphering "signs of the times." The literature professor Villemain saw this as long ago as 1840:[43] "He makes the same use of America as the Church does of sacred history when it seeks in each narrative of the past a figure or image of the present or the future." That is why the quest remains incomplete: each of Tocqueville's works is a rewriting of the previous one, because the deciphering of the future through the signs of the present and traces of the past must always be begun anew. The initial purpose of *The Old Regime* was to offer "a set of reflections and observations of the present time, a free judgment of our modern societies, and a forecast of their probable future,"[44] which was identical to the project of 1835.

One might argue that Tocqueville's "classical" writing makes no difference to the comprehension of his political thought, that the ideas, which are eternal, can be separated from the literary form, which is dated and intimately associated with European, and more particularly French, culture. Nothing could be farther from the truth.

Owing to its classical style, *Democracy in America*, like *The Old Regime*, is the very embodiment of prudence, which was the essence of Tocqueville's political program. It contains nothing to encourage romantic effusions of sensibility or imagination. Tocqueville ventured to tame democratic man, adopting his prejudices in order to force him to yield to his, Tocqueville's, arguments. In doing so, he quite consciously ran the risk of writing tediously or lapsing into platitude. Raymond Aron called attention to the colorlessness of Tocqueville's style. Indeed, his writing, by deliberately resisting enthusiasms and muting rhetorical effects, can seem to lack charm in much the same way that American women, according to Tocqueville, lack allure for being more reasonable than they ought to be. Platitude is an even worse affliction. In both the United States and France, Tocqueville's work is a favorite source for anthologies on the theme of "morality in action," although the most effective of the moralistic dicta attributed to him are apocryphal. It is the fate of every writer to be abandoned to the mediocrity of his readers, against whom he is helpless, but Tocqueville embraced this fate from the outset by seeking to dissolve his thought in a sampling of "crude commonplaces" that he thought might serve the cause of liberty. Tocqueville's literary eloquence, his classical rhetoric, was intended to serve deliberative democracy, the only defense against despotism. The conception of politics as a space for argument is undeniably a modern one. Tocqueville developed it, however, in a specific historical situation and within the venerable literary tradition of the treatise or essay. Tellingly, the only example he cites of the democratic communication of which he dreamed lay in Greek Antiquity, glorified in Plutarch's *Lives*: "In this text soldiers speak to their generals constantly and quite freely, and generals eagerly listen to what their soldiers have to say and respond to them. They lead by word and example far more than by coercion and punishment. They seem to have been companions as much as commanders" (*DAII*, 799; Goldhammer translation, 778). In other words, the "sort of familiar confraternity" that Tocqueville sees as providing a model for a disciplined society of free men accustomed to treating one another as equals could be conceived only as a myth, transposed to the very beginning of history, as if the combination of equality with liberty could be imagined only in an extra-historical context, in terms of heroic fantasies passed down through generation after generation of academic culture.

Here we touch on what makes Tocqueville's work distinctive for today's interpreter. He wrote for the French, or at any rate for the Europeans of his time: "I passionately desired a free Europe," he wrote to a friend in 1856.[45] His work, dialogical in form, continually makes room for a figural interlocutor, usually represented as an adversary but equipped with the same classical culture as Tocqueville and involved in the same controversies as to the form of the political regime, the decadence of literature, the threat of pantheism, and so on. Few works seem as closely tied to the historical situation of a nation, or to a literary tradition, whose conservatory was the Académie Française, of which Tocqueville became a member while still very young, in 1842. Yet from 1835 to the present, Tocqueville has been regarded by the French as an eccentric thinker, uninvolved in the fractiousness of the political parties, dismissed as too American, and more useful as a critic of democracy than as a father of the republic. Thus, more than that of any other writer on politics, his work demonstrates the difficulty of interpreting political literature: it is inseparable from its historical context but at the same time irreducible to it, and even sufficiently detachable from the circumstances of its inception as to open itself up to endless new readings.

NOTES

1   *Souvenirs, Œuvres*, P 3, 730.
2   Barbey d'Aurevilly, *Le Pays*, 22 January 1861.
3   The quote was taken from a 1941 book on religion and the American dream. Eleven years later, Eisenhower attributed it to a great French thinker. Then, in 1982, Reagan attributed it to Tocqueville, as did Clinton in 1994 and 1995 and Pat Buchanan when he announced his presidential candidacy in 1996. In speech after speech, Tocqueville is invoked as a Solomon of democracy, lending nobility to some piece of collective wisdom. See John J. Pitney, Jr., "The Tocqueville Fraud," *The Weekly Standard*, 13 November 1995.
4   Some recent works have sought brilliantly to challenge this decontextualization. See especially Cheryl Welch, *De Tocqueville* (Oxford: Oxford University Press, 2001), and Oliver Zunz and Alan Kahan, eds., *The Tocqueville Reader: A Life in Letters and Politics* (Oxford: Blackwell, 2002).

5 This is the list of Frenchmen presented to the Senate on June 24, 2002, as part of a resolution proposed by Senator Robert Smith of New Hampshire proclaiming "French Heritage Month." Paradoxically, therefore, the major interest for historians of the American reading of Tocqueville is not so much what it can teach us about cultural exchanges between the two continents as what it reveals about the problematic image that Americans have had of themselves for the past 150 years.

6 See letter to Sedgwick, 14 October 1856, OC, 7, 182: "A book on the French Revolution can never arouse as much interest in America as in Europe, moreover. The French Revolution is a considerable part of the special history of each of the continental nations, and it is impossible to speak of it without obliging them to look back on themselves." The reception of Tocqueville in Europe since 1835 has been characterized by a concern with how democracy can be accommodated in light of the American experience. Hence Tocqueville is read only in periods when Europe looks toward the United States: until about 1880 and after World War II. He is often read, moreover, as though the issue were how to import American experience into France.

7 Letter of 30 July 1854 to Freslon, Lettres, S, 1107.

8 Letter of 4 November 1830 to Charles Stoffels, Lettres, S, 159.

9 Letter to Reeve, 22 March 1837, Lettres, S, 377.

10 Travel notebooks from the journey to America, 12 January 1832, Œuvres, P 1, 191.

11 Speech of 14 March 1838.

12 Guizot, Histoire de la civilisation en Europe, 14th edition (Paris: Hachette, 1985), 288.

13 Ibid.

14 DAI, Œuvres, P 7.

15 See Mélanges, OC, 16, 558–561.

16 Mélanges, OC, 16, 561.

17 Ibid., 560.

18 Mélanges, OC, 16, 231.

19 Joseph de Maistre, Considérations sur la France, 1797 (Brussels: Editions Complexe, 1988), 61.

20 These two documents are published in OC, 16.

21 Tocqueville-Kergorlay correspondence, OC 13:2, 230–231.

22 "Considérations sur la Révolution," Œuvres, P 3: 612.

23 See my Tocqueville et les Français (Paris: Aubier, 1993; English translation: Tocqueville and the French (Charlottesville, VA: University Press of Virginia, 1998).

24 See, for example, in the generation that rediscovered Tocqueville, the work of Raymond Aron, François Furet, Claude Lefort, Raymond Boudon, and Michel Crozier.

25 See Tony Judt, *Past Imperfect: French Intellectuals, 1944–1956* (Berkeley: University of California Press, 1992).

26 *Œuvres*, P 2, 47.

27 *Œuvres*, P 2, 849.

28 See Arthur Goldhammer, "Translating Tocqueville: the Constraints of Classicism," *Tocqueville Review / La Revue Tocqueville*, vol. 25, no. 1 (2004), 165–190, and included in a substantially different version in this volume.

29 On the central character of this theme in the work of the moralists, see Louis Van Delft, *Le moraliste classique. Essai de définition et de typologie* (Paris: Droz, 1982), 176–191. See, for example, Pierre Nicole, *Essais de morale*, quoted on 177 : "We float upon the sea of this world at the whim of our passions, which carry us now this way, now that, like a vessel without sails and without a pilot." Van Delft deplores the inflation of the term moralist and its application to writers like Tocqueville (13). Nevertheless, his typology applies admirably to Tocqueville's writing.

30 Letter to his wife, 26 December 1837, *Lettres, S*, 400.

31 Letter to Sophie Swetchine, 11 February 1857, *Lettres, S*, 24.

32 *Œuvres*, P: 2, 853.

33 Jules Levallois, *L'opinion nationale*, 5 May 1861.

34 "Etude littéraire sur Alexis de Tocqueville," *Le Correspondant*, April 1861, reprinted in *OC*, 13:2, 361.

35 Letter to Charles Stöffels, 31 July 1834, *Lettres, S*, 302.

36 Pascal, *Pensées*, ed. P. Sellier (Paris: Classiques Garnier, 1993), *Pensées*, 575, 409. See Tocqueville's letter to Royer-Collard, 20 August 1837, *Lettres, S*, 13 : "I find it difficult to write about certain ideas that no one else has yet dealt with, but what is far more difficult is to restate completely, reasonably, and with some measure of novelty a great many things that others have already hinted at or crudely represented."

37 Van Delft, *Le moralisite classique*, 297.

38 See chap. 1 "of some sources of poetry in democratic nations." Draft. "What is more poetic than Bossuet's *Discourse on Universal History*."

39 Sainte-Beuve, *Nouveaux lundis*, vol. 10, 1868, 320–321.

40 See Laurence Guellec, *Tocqueville et les langages de la démocratie* (Paris: Honoré Champion, 2004), 354.

41 Emile Boutmy, *Eléments d'une psychologie du peuple américain: la nation, la patrie, l'état, la religion* (Paris: Colin, 1912[1902]), 11–13.

42 Example: "An American, instead of dancing joyously in the public square in his hours of leisure as many people of similar occupation still do throughout much of Europe, may retire to his private sanctum to drink alone. Such a man will savor two pleasures at once: while thinking about business he can become decently inebriated in familial seclusion." (*DAII*, 736); Goldhammer translation, 715. In French, the passage begins "il y a tel américain ... ," and this formula, "il y a tel," recurs frequently.

43 *Journal des Savants*, 1840.

44 Letter to Kergorlay, 15 December 1850, *Lettres, S*, 702.

45 Letter to F. Lieber, 1 September 1856, *OC*, 7:179.

14   Tocqueville and the Americans

Democracy in America as Read in Nineteenth-Century America

I. A SLOW BEGINNING

Volume I of *Democracy in America* was published in France in January 1835 to immediate acclaim.[1] In England, Henry Reeve translated it promptly, and it was published during the same year. But an American edition, the first requirement for broad circulation in the United States, had to wait until 1838.[2]

A great difficulty in getting this initial installment of Alexis de Tocqueville's book to the American literary market was the sorry state of French-American relations. According to Tocqueville's friend Jared Sparks, *Democracy in America* could not have come out at a worse time. Sparks was a Unitarian minister ordained by William Ellery Channing, former proprietor and editor of the *North American Review*, soon-to-be Harvard's first history professor, and a New England Whig. Sparks had an interest in the book's appearance as he had had extensive conversations with Tocqueville and suggested to him two of the volume's driving ideas – the tyranny of the majority and the importance of the New England town as the point of departure for American democracy (on which he wrote a long disquisition for Tocqueville's personal use). On June 6, 1837, Sparks wrote to Tocqueville: "I am vexed and mortified that an edition of your 'Démocratie' has not yet been published in America. ... The work came out [in France] just at the time of the unfortunate 'Indemnity Controversy,' and then General Jackson's war spirit began to stir up in the people a hostile feeling towards France. Hence little interest was felt for a book by a French writer."[3]

France and the United States had long been at odds over reparations for French seizure of American ships and cargoes during the

Napoleonic blockade of the continent. The issue had lingered, and the French had paid scant attention to it for years. But when Andrew Jackson became President in 1829, he made it a point of national honor to have the French pay, and sent William Cabell Rives as minister to France to resolve the matter. Rives signed a treaty in 1831 that obligated the French government to make good on its obligations. When the French Chamber repeatedly refused to appropriate the necessary funds, Jackson appointed his Secretary of State, Edward Livingston, as minister to France in 1833 and charged him with settling the affair, but this effort proved equally unsuccessful. Frustrated (and hoping to divert attention from the censure he had received from the Senate for removing federal deposits from the Bank of the United States), Jackson resorted to threats of "reprisals" including "seizure" of French property in December 1834. With the French demanding an apology for Jackson's intemperate remarks and the Americans pressing for their money, American-French relations came to a complete impasse. Although nobody wanted war, there was serious talk of it, and formal diplomatic relations were suspended in late 1835 (after *Democracy* appeared in France). With Jackson toning down his rhetoric, the French Chamber finally consented to allocate the monies Louis-Philippe had promised long ago. The British then conveyed the news to the Americans in February 1836, and the French government paid 59 cents for every dollar claimed shortly thereafter.[4]

Although Livingston failed to achieve an early settlement with the French government, he did succeed in returning home in 1835 with a copy of Tocqueville's *Democracy in America*, which contained a glowing acknowledgment of the minister's role in the making of the book. The acknowledgment was significant. During his voyage, Tocqueville had met with about 200 Americans and recorded their conversations meticulously in notebooks and letters, but he refused on principle to acknowledge any of them, with the exception of Livingston, for fear of revealing the source of his misgivings and causing friends "embarrassment and chagrin."[5]

There were legitimate reasons for singling out the older American minister. Livingston was fluent in French, which he spoke with his wife, the young widow of a wealthy planter from Santo Domingo. Livingston had done a number of favors for Tocqueville and Beaumont, arranging for them to attend sessions of Congress, to collect official records, and to meet the President. As an authority on prison reform (the official reason for Tocqueville's and Gustave de Beaumont's visit to the United States), he is quoted several times in their 1832 report on the American penitentiary system, but we do not know whether he personally gave Tocqueville the benefit of his experience. Tocqueville left no record of an interview with Livingston on the topic. Nor is there any evidence that Livingston influenced the writing of *Democracy in America*, except perhaps indirectly in a single note on the introduction of the Anglo-American jury system in newly acquired French Louisiana. Livingston had spent part of his career there and had rewritten its penal code.[6]

Tocqueville's motive for acknowledging Livingston in this mysterious footnote may well have been that he counted on the elder statesman to promote the book in America in the midst of Andrew Jackson's anti-French rhetoric. Although Tocqueville had met other statesmen in America besides Livingston – including John Quincy Adams and Daniel Webster – he was in no position to ask them for a favor. Unfortunately, Livingston, who died shortly after his return to the United States, showed no intention of playing in America the role that Chateaubriand was playing so effectively in France, introducing the book and its author in all the right places.

Sparks pointed to a second reason for the lack of American interest in *Democracy in America*. The British reviews that greeted its publication predictably dwelled on the negative aspects of American democracy. "Our newspapers," Sparks wrote, "have been filled with extracts from the English reviews, containing the parts of your work most objectionable to American readers; that is, your remarks on the defects of Democratic institutions."[7] Nassau Senior, the British economist who was revising the poor laws when Tocqueville visited him in 1833, advised Tocqueville upon receiving *Democracy in America* not to expect much from England, a country where "there is great difficulty in getting a review of any book requiring much thought."[8] One of the exceptions among the British reviewers was John Stuart Mill, who "greatly rejoice[d]" at the book's "appearance in an English dress," but Mill, who wrote anonymously, was still a few years away from becoming a major intellectual figure.[9]

Under these circumstances, *Democracy in America* barely circulated in the United States after its French and British publication. In Boston, one might have expected Francis Lieber to prepare an American edition. The young German political exile, wounded in the battles following Waterloo and editor of the first *Encyclopedia Americana*, had already translated the prison report. But Tocqueville had been displeased with Lieber's attempt to turn the report into a plea for the Pennsylvania system of complete isolation of inmates.[10] Jared Sparks tried to promote an American edition, but his discussions with a Boston publisher (while Tocqueville was clearing the way for a French edition of Sparks's volume on Gouverneur Morris) were unfruitful.[11]

Help finally came from John C. Spencer, arguably the second most important informant for *Democracy*, whom Tocqueville had met in New York. Spencer was a distinguished Whig lawyer (although a Jacksonian early on), New York State legislator, former U.S. Congressman, and future Secretary of War and Treasury Secretary in the Tyler administration. Spencer had invited Tocqueville and Beaumont to visit him at his Canandaigua home in upstate New York, close to the Auburn penitentiary where the two commissioners had stopped for a long study. Beaumont credited Spencer with being their first valuable source, a man with whom they held wide-ranging conversations on constitutional issues, the judiciary, the press, and religion in America.[12] This dialogue continued for years. Tocqueville and Spencer were still carrying on a correspondence on bicameralism in 1849, when Tocqueville was on the constitutional committee for the Second Republic.[13]

Spencer convinced a New York publishing house to hijack the British translation. Americans did not respect international copyright laws until the 1890s and rarely paid royalties to foreign authors – and indeed Tocqueville never earned money from the American editions of his book.[14] Spencer wrote a preface and some explanatory notes. Volume 1 came out in 1838, almost four years after the French edition. Volume 2 appeared in 1840, shortly after its French and British publication. With the two volumes available, and the French-American storm a thing of the past, an American debate on *Democracy in America* could begin in earnest.

II. THE INITIAL RECEPTION: DOES TOCQUEVILLE REALLY LIKE US?

A. Tocqueville's Theory

Tocqueville once wrote to the Russian mystic and Parisian society figure Madame Swetchine, "Long practice has taught me that the success of a book is much more due to the ideas the reader already has in mind than to what the author writes."[15] Tocqueville's first American readers certainly proved him right. They did not seem to share Tocqueville's deep anxiety about the difficult association of equality with liberty.

We know Tocqueville's main proposition. He expressed it very concisely: "One can imagine," he wrote, "an extreme point at which liberty and equality touch and become one. Suppose that all citizens take part in government and that each has an equal right to do so. Since no man will then be different from his fellow men, no one will be able to exercise a tyrannical power. Men will be perfectly free, because they will all be entirely equal, and they will all be perfectly equal because they will be entirely free. This is the ideal toward which democratic peoples tend."[16] In an ideal society, then, liberty and equality are one and the same. If you are really everybody's equal, you are free. If you are free, you are everybody's equal. But in the actual world, people desire equality so much that they are willing to sacrifice their political liberty for it. Tocqueville argued that new forms of despotism (such as that of public opinion) had to be feared as much as absolutism because they reduced the range of individual possibilities. They promoted equality in powerlessness – the enemy of freedom. This is why one had to work constantly at keeping liberty alive.

Tocqueville further explained that because Americans had a long practice of political liberty, they were better equipped than the French to manage the increasing equality of conditions. The French were in disarray because they had had no apprenticeship of liberty under the absolute monarchy. Without knowing any better, the French repeatedly resorted to despotism in the hope of maintaining the equality of conditions acquired during the Revolution.

Ever ambivalent, Tocqueville did not always help his case. He often argued opposite sides of these issues, tilting the balance only slightly one way or the other. In reading him, you come to appreciate the power of his conclusions, because he persists in making them in the face of very real misgivings. Many who read Tocqueville concentrated on these often extensive misgivings, turning the book into an indictment of both democracy and America, to Tocqueville's dismay. Potential misreadings caused by his method were compounded by translation, that enemy of ambiguity, as the correspondence between British translator Henry Reeve and Tocqueville makes abundantly clear. In one letter, Tocqueville reproached Reeve for making him too much a foe of monarchy; in another, too much one of democracy.[17] Tocqueville knew that he was going to be often misunderstood. He wrote to his friend Kergorlay, shortly before publication, "The best thing that can happen to me is if no one read my book."[18]

B. The Essential Goodness of Democracy and of Americans

The difficulties posed by Tocqueville's method and the inherent problems of translating a theoretical work were impediments to Americans' understanding Tocqueville, but they paled in the face of the preconceptions they brought to their reading. When American readers finally turned to *Democracy in America*, they seemed temperamentally handicapped to engage its main proposition. They preferred the Tocqueville who wrote that "nothing is more unproductive for the human mind than an abstract idea."[19] Americans treated the book as though it reflected only on their character. Insecure about their national identity, they looked to Tocqueville for approval. They read *Democracy* as an opportunity for them to comment on "Democracy" and "Americans" rather than on the theories Tocqueville brought to either subject.[20]

I. THE PROVIDENTIAL MARCH OF DEMOCRACY. Tocqueville's initial American readers found much to applaud. They approved of his insistence on Providence as the source of democracy. A reviewer for *The Knickerbocker* spoke for many in writing: "As M. de Tocqueville more than intimates, it was not man, but God, that made America. It is one of the results of a high and inscrutable Providence."[21] Another noted in *The American Museum of Science*,

Literature, and the Arts that American democracy made a significant advance toward the ultimate goal of blending "man's free agency with heavenly influences."[22]

We know Tocqueville had serious misgivings about the Providence he insisted on. He had lost faith when reading the eighteenth-century *philosophes* in his father's library as a teenager. But Tocqueville's personal faith was not of concern to American readers. Nor was the obvious fact that the providential metaphor had been used for centuries to justify the divine rights of despots. Americans were interested primarily in their own history.

Following Sparks's advice, Tocqueville began his examination at the point of departure, with the Puritans. "M. de Tocqueville finds the germ of our social condition in the history of the settlers of New England; where, in fact, every intelligent traveler has been forced to look for some of the best elements of the American character" writes a reviewer for *The American Quarterly Review*.[23] Edward Everett, a Congressman and ex-Harvard professor, who had introduced Tocqueville to John Quincy Adams in Boston, praised Tocqueville in *The North American Review* for recognizing "the necessity of commencing his inquiries" from the "municipal corporations," in particular the New England towns, and the "separate States" rather than from the Federal government down, and for showing the power of local civil society in preventing the "curse of centralization."[24]

Tocqueville recorded the view that a providential America expanded out from the community, by reproducing itself throughout a vast continent. Had Tocqueville visited America a generation earlier, he might have been caught in Jefferson's anxiety over the acceptance of republicanism and apprenticeship of liberty beyond the bonds of the original Confederation. How to assimilate foreigners and "others" to American republicanism was much debated during the Louisiana Purchase. But such anxieties were gone – at least temporarily. Democracy was to progress providentially throughout the continent, through assimilation or destruction, whatever the case may be.

Yet Tocqueville was genuinely torn on the topic of how much destruction Providence thought permissible. Although the Jacksonian *U.S. Magazine, and Democratic Review* gave *Democracy in America* a lot of space, Tocqueville, in my view, could not have embraced uncritically editor O'Sullivan's concept of "manifest destiny," a term O'Sullivan coined in 1845 to justify American expansion. In observing the removal of Choctaw Indians, Tocqueville had felt a deep resentment toward the American policy of race extinction under the guise of treaties. He remarked that "to destroy human beings with greater respect for the laws of humanity would be impossible."[25] Tocqueville did not believe in the superiority of one race over another. But he had no qualms about asserting the superiority of one civilization over another, and accepted the consequences. This is why he also supported the French conquest of Algeria. Tocqueville was a non-racist colonialist who was apprehensive of the excesses of expansionism.[26] American reviewers, however, preferred to read Tocqueville as justifying the Indian genocide. In the opinion of The American Quarterly Review, Tocqueville described it as "the consequence of an irreversible law, as much beyond our means of control as the encroachments of the ocean," but the reviewer added defensively, "On this topic, as on that of the Negroes, we ask no advice from Europeans."[27]

2. RELIGION IN AMERICA. The first wave of American reviewers also reacted positively to Tocqueville's assessment of religion's positive influence on democracy. While The United States Magazine and Democratic Review pointed out that religion "has no direct tendency to maintain the democratic form of the government, or to prevent its change to a different one," it agreed with Tocqueville that religion's "present office is to cooperate with our excellent institutions in diffusing virtue and happiness among the people."[28]

But at the same time, all reviewers objected to Tocqueville's prediction that Catholicism would grow here as a religion of the masses while elites turned toward pantheism. They found this prediction "very much overstrained," even "absurd."[29]

3. AMERICANS: GRATEFUL AND GRATIFIED. Fed up by the antagonism of the British, Americans were, on the whole, thrilled to find a foreign visitor liking them. The reviewer for The New-Yorker, a Whig paper founded and edited by Horace Greeley, contrasted Tocqueville to "the great majority" of travelers to America who "have been scavengers in by-places, ransacking every corner where

scandal could be found, and looking to bar-rooms and grog-shops for an explanation of our social system."[30] Even Jackson's partner, Thomas Hart Benton, senator from Missouri (who wrote a little later), distinguished Tocqueville from "the riffraff of European writers who come here to pick up the gossip of the highways, to sell it in Europe for American history, and to requite with defamation the hospitalities of our houses." "Old Bullion Benton," renowned for his advocacy of Jacksonian hard money positions, reserved his criticism to correcting Tocqueville's "errors" on Jacksonian policy.[31]

By and large, Americans were so insatiable for praise that they did not just welcome it; they insisted on it. This annoyed Tocqueville, irritated as he was by American conceit. "America is therefore a land of liberty," Tocqueville wrote, "where, in order not to offend anyone, a foreigner must not speak freely about individuals or the state, the people or the government, public or private enterprises, indeed about anything he finds there, except perhaps the climate and soil. In fact, one encounters Americans prepared to defend even the latter two things as though they had had a hand in making them."[32]

As Tocqueville had anticipated, American reviewers were often on the defensive. Several objected to Tocqueville's claim that democracies do not foster great writers. Others were indignant about his assertion (inspired by Jefferson) that American laws were unstable as a consequence of democracy.[33] But *Democracy* was met with most criticism when reviewers of all political persuasions turned against Tocqueville's theory of the tyranny of the majority. The notion that the spread of equality might endanger freedom is something that Americans of the 1830s and 1840s were not willing to consider as part of their history, even though some of them had given Tocqueville the idea in the first place.

C. The Rejection of Tocqueville's Theory of the Tyranny of the Majority

The heart of Tocqueville's American experience was his encounter with New England, as George Pierson has correctly argued.[34] Tocqueville felt a deep sense of kinship with New England elites, ex-federalists and proto-Whig politicians who had not reconciled themselves to Andrew Jackson's presidential victory of 1828. These

New Englanders were well-bred members of the elite who believed that it was their job to lead and were struggling with an American version of Tocqueville's personal aristocratic dilemma. How, they asked, could power have shifted from educated, cultured people like themselves to a group of Jacksonian adventurers? They formed a close-knit group around the towering figures of Daniel Webster and Edward Everett, the Unitarian church, and Harvard. Tocqueville met many of them, and they remained Tocqueville's friends and supporters as his reputation grew. Principal among them, as we have seen, was Jared Sparks, who had instilled the theory of the tyranny of the majority in Tocqueville's mind by telling him that "the political dogma of this country is that the majority is always right."[35]

After seeing these views reflected in Tocqueville's prose, however, the New Englanders retreated from this position. They joined other critics in denying that there had ever been a tyranny of the majority in the United States.[36] Tocqueville seems to have crossed a line when he wrote, "I know of no country where there is in general less independence of mind and true freedom of discussion than in America."[37]

Tocqueville formulated his views on the tyranny of the majority as a contribution to the theory of democratic societies. Emphasizing his disagreement with Rousseau (without mentioning him by name), he wrote, "There are those who have made so bold as to insist that a people, insofar as it deals with matters of interest to itself alone, cannot overstep the bounds of justice and reason entirely, hence that there is no reason to be afraid of bestowing all power on the majority that represents that people. But to speak thus is to speak the language of a slave."[38] To counter Rousseau, Tocqueville relied on Madison's reflections on minority rights, the overbearing majority, and public opinion.

Self-referential American reviewers did not comment on this opposition between Rousseau and Madison in *Democracy in America*. Even though both Sparks and Everett were engaged in extensive dialogue with Madison at the time of Tocqueville's visit, they did not appreciate his comparative treatment. Sparks merely complained that Tocqueville had just made too much of his remarks, while Everett argued that Tocqueville had misrepresented both Madison and Jefferson.[39] Spencer, in the notes to his edition of

Democracy in America, added that Tocqueville was criticizing, not Americans in general, but only the Jacksonians and the "tyranny of party."[40]

The Jacksonians, not surprisingly, were loudest. This section of *Democracy* gave Benton the opportunity to denounce the "book learning" of the "enlightened classes" and, in making his position absolutely clear, substituting the "tyranny of the majority" with "the intelligence of the masses."[41] Other voices echoed the same feeling: "We are not aware, that any more perfect state of society has yet been invented, than the rule of the majority" wrote *The Knickerbocker*.[42] "What citizen has M. de Tocqueville ever seen who has suffered ostracism for his opinions? If distinguished men will stake their reputation upon false and untenable theories, they cannot expect employment; but they are never forced to retreat into silence by the tyranny of those who think differently," added *The American Quarterly Review*.[43]

Tocqueville, who had anticipated the critique, dropped the term "tyranny of the majority" in the second volume but did not abandon this essential objection to democracy.

A related question Tocqueville asked was whether an aristocracy could survive under the threat of a tyranny of the majority. This generated a small debate over the existence of an aristocracy in the United States. Tocqueville himself tried to locate an American aristocracy, variously in lawyers, slave owners, and new industrialists accumulating excessive wealth. Some reviewers argued that Tocqueville was hunting "a shadow," for "there is no such element."[44] Democrats pointed to "the owners of accumulated wealth," served by the lawyers, whom Tocqueville had singled out as the closest to an aristocratic body for their conservative influence. Southern Democrats denounced New England elites, while New England elites pointed to slave owners.[45]

D. The Missing Parts

Such was the range of discussion in the first ten years – much was missing. To deny the possibility of a tyranny of the majority, as most American reviewers did, was at best to disagree with Tocqueville's theory of the difficult relationship between liberty and equality and at worst to disregard it. In either case, reviewers in effect ignored Tocqueville's claim that he was developing "a political science" for a world "totally new."[46]

American reviewers missed much else. They discussed only in passing Tocqueville's powerful analysis of the new concept of individualism and his equally powerful discussion of self-interest properly understood – Tocqueville's brilliant way of arguing that America could be great even if its people were not.[47] Only one reviewer, from the South, credited Tocqueville for his notion that "the democratic principle" had "produced a greater love of the *bien-être* than of the *bien*."[48] But on this very point, Whig political economist Henry Carey, the staunchest advocate of the American tariff, faulted Tocqueville for attributing comfort to the democratic principle rather than to Whig economics.[49]

Other Tocquevillean themes were skipped. It was Tocqueville's genius to capture Americans' commitment both to individualism and to community and to highlight voluntarism as the mechanism for their mutual reinforcement. Tocqueville did it with such brilliance that he helped later Americans make sense of their own practice. The first reviewers were not interested, however, because they did not recognize Tocqueville's proposition that democracy was threatened by the tyranny of the majority, so they tended to dismiss his assertion that associations provided a counterbalance to that threat. There was little sustained discussion of voluntary associations and associative life, outside the reviewers' discussion of local government or religion promoting a decentralized civil society. Tocqueville's specific views of national character were only touched on in these reviews.[50] His analysis of federalism was mentioned briefly, with only one magazine citing Tocqueville on the danger to states' rights posed by the federal judiciary.[51] While his analysis of local self-government was much emphasized, there was no significant mention of the jury, that "free school" of democracy.[52]

Although much of the second volume of *Democracy* is on American mores, or habits of the heart, it surprisingly elicited few independent comments, except perhaps when it came to women. Tocqueville gave American women full credit for elevating the morals of the country. "If someone were to ask me what I think is primarily responsible for the singular prosperity and growing power of this people," Tocqueville wrote, "I would answer that it is the superiority of their women."[53] American women were predictably pleased and pithily answered: "De Tocqueville deserves the thanks of American women for his warm and bold tribute to their worth" wrote *Godey's Lady's Book, and Ladies American Magazine*.[54] None approved more effusively of Tocqueville's understanding of the division of labor between American men and women, and the latter's "voluntary surrender" to their husbands than Catharine Beecher, in the widely read *A Treatise on Domestic Economy for the Use of Young Ladies at Home, and at School* she published in 1842.

One wishes that Beecher had used Tocqueville's argument to reflect on her own formidable program of promoting women's education and their "equal interest in all social and civil concerns," rather than to confirm the beauty of self sacrifice. Historians have pointed to the large role that women such as Beecher have played in the great associational movement of the Benevolent Empire (including Bible societies, charities, and do-good associations of all sorts). They have further pointed out that voluntarism, as influenced by educated women, was an important moral counterpoint to the self-serving search for profit on the part of individualistic males.[55] They have shown ways in which disfranchised but determined women relied on voluntary associations to participate in politics. On all this, Tocqueville provided little guidance.

III. TOCQUEVILLE BECOMES RELEVANT

The initial reaction to Tocqueville, which focused almost exclusively on his ability to reflect back to Americans their image of their political system and country, soon became too limited. Americans at mid-century broadened their reading of Tocqueville, and the Civil War shed new light on the work.

A. Tocqueville as Statesman

By the 1840s, Tocqueville was becoming increasingly well-known and respected as a famous author who was also active in politics. The American press reported on his speeches in the French Chamber on prison reform and the abolition of slavery in the French colonies.[56] In June 1849, Tocqueville became foreign minister of the

Second Republic, a post he would hold for only five months. It is remarkable that Tocqueville's brief foreign ministry should have been embroiled in a serious diplomatic incident with the United States. Secretary of State John Clayton asked the French government to recall Guillaume Tell Poussin, the French minister to Washington, for having used offensive language in demanding the censure of an American Navy commander. (The commander had rescued a French boat in the Gulf of Mexico but detained it for a few days in a vain hope for an award for salvage.)[57] Tocqueville actually disliked Poussin, whose 1841 *Considérations sur le principe démocratique qui régit l'union américaine et de la possibilité de son application à d'autres états* had presented an overly rosy picture of American race relations while refuting Tocqueville's *Democracy*. As Poussin put it, "I do not share in any way M. de Tocqueville's fears. My own experience of the facts he mentions, my knowledge of the country he has understood well, yet without fully appreciating the full array of its resources, and my own intimate convictions based on having lived in the United States for fifteen years, amply support my opposing his views on slavery."[58] Reiterating the attack two years later, Poussin saw no reason, "contrary to authors who have written on this subject," to fear "any struggle between the white and black population of the southern portion of the Union."[59]

Tocqueville moreover disapproved of Poussin's conduct. But a comedy of errors ensued. Clayton, not sure whether Tocqueville would actually recall Poussin, dismissed him under instructions from Zachary Taylor. This made it impossible for Tocqueville officially to receive the new American minister, who was none other than William Cabell Rives, the diplomat who had negotiated the 1831 indemnity treaty for Jackson, but was now returning for a second appointment in Paris. In the 1830s, Rives was a Jacksonian; in 1849, he had become a prominent member of the Whig party. The dispute was resolved, and Rives installed as minister, only after Louis-Napoleon's change of heart abruptly put an end to the Barrot ministry and hence to Tocqueville's brief tenure as foreign minister. Thus Tocqueville was twice in his lifetime personally caught in the middle of grave disruptions of formal French-American diplomatic relations, and the irony was certainly not lost on him.

Tocqueville's reputation as a towering intellectual figure would only grow in France with his retirement from politics after Louis-Napoleon's coup. The generation of Americans coming to power in the 1850s also came to admire Tocqueville. Among them was Charles Sumner, who as a young reformer had learned much from Tocqueville on penitentiaries and the penal system.[60] Summer toured Europe in 1857 while recovering from injuries sustained when he was assaulted in the Senate after his "crime against Kansas" speech. He visited Tocqueville in Paris and also stayed at Tocqueville's home in Normandy.[61] The two became close friends. Sumner was fond of quoting Tocqueville to the effect that life "is serious business, to be entered upon with courage in the spirit of self sacrifice."[62]

Sumner was also a close friend of Francis Lieber, with whom Tocqueville had remained in touch all these years despite his reservations about Lieber's handling of his prison report. Lieber had taken a teaching position at the University of South Carolina, where he had made his reputation as the author of *Political Ethics* (1838) and his classic work *On Civil Liberty and Civil Government* (1853).[63] In 1856, he took a position at Columbia University and had the college dedicate it to history *and* political science. The creation of the chair did much to establish the academic field of political science. German idealism aside, there were great similarities between Tocqueville's and Lieber's political science. Their thoughts followed the parallel routes of endorsing political rights while remaining apprehensive of the abuses of majority rule and egalitarian leveling. Lieber believed in a system of "checks, guarantees, and self-government" to protect "American liberty" from "democratic absolutism."[64] In the American colleges of the 1850s, Lieber was read, not Tocqueville.[65] But when Tocqueville's *The Old Regime and the Revolution* appeared in 1857, the two authors were frequently compared.[66]

With Lieber in his influential chair at Columbia, American political science changed. The conditions were right for Tocqueville to come into his own. After Tocqueville's untimely death, at 53, in 1859, Beaumont's publication of a selection of Tocqueville's works led to a widespread critical reappraisal of Tocqueville in the United States. Americans were more receptive to ideas they had found offensive earlier, especially if they were reading John Stuart Mill, whose *On Liberty*, which appeared as Tocqueville was dying, owed much to Tocqueville's theory of the "tyranny of the majority." Beaumont's publication contained several of Tocqueville letters to Mill, which revealed something of the depth of their intellectual exchange.[67]

B. The American Civil War: The New Political Science Comes of Age

Although the intellectual seeds had been sown for a reappraisal of Tocqueville, it was the Civil War that motivated a close reading of his work. Mobilization put extraordinary power into the hands of the state, and the fight over the Union and slavery highlighted the tension between liberty and equality that is at the heart of Tocqueville's work. The war took Tocqueville's "political science" – his discussion of the relation between liberty and equality – from the realm of theory to practice.

Among Boston Brahmins, whose elders had supported Tocqueville, was Francis Bowen, Harvard philosophy professor and long-time editor of the *North American Review*. In the 1850s, Bowen found ammunition in Tocqueville to argue that "national prosperity" resulted primarily from the moral character of Americans as embedded in their institutions.[68] Then Bowen went one step further. He completely revised the Reeve translation of *Democracy in America*. His 1862 edition, together with Beaumont's publications, set the stage for a Tocqueville revival.[69] Until the 1860s, most reviews had dealt with Tocqueville's text mostly as a high-class piece of reporting on the United States. In the 1860s, the national soul searching provoked by the Civil War led to a more profound reading of *Democracy in America*. Perhaps it made a small difference that some of Tocqueville's more ardent promoters were formulating the conduct of the conflict. Senator Sumner was among the abolitionists. Lieber volunteered to set down the rules of war. His text became Lincoln's General Orders 100, a classic codification of military engagement.[70]

Foremost among the new interpreters was Charles Eliot Norton, who had met Tocqueville in Paris in 1850 when only twenty-three. Norton's uncle, George Ticknor, a prominent literary scholar, was a friend of Adolphe de Circourt's, an intellectual and man of the world then instructing Tocqueville on German topics for the preparation of Tocqueville's *Old Regime*. Madame de Circourt maintained an active literary salon in Paris. The young Norton, still engaged in business, had no inkling when meeting Tocqueville that he was encountering a future mentor. He was also still a long way from being admired for his literary work on Dante (Lieber would call one of his translations "exquisite") and becoming the first American professor of art history at Harvard.[71]

The Civil War radicalized Norton and accelerated his transition from the counting house to a full-time life of the intellect. Norton had originally believed that liberty demanded respect for all laws, even bad ones, until such time as they could be replaced. This proved defective in a country intent on keeping slavery. With the war, Norton opened up to the world and felt, like Oliver Wendell Holmes, Sr., the young historian Francis Parkman (a close friend), and others, the urgency of a broadly shared civil culture. Like his family friend Francis Bowen, Norton found a rationale for part of this view in Tocqueville.

But unlike Jared Sparks, his other family friend, who had taught him history at Harvard, Norton had had no part in the creation of *Democracy*. He read Tocqueville anew in 1861. Prompted by Beaumont's edition of new texts, Norton wrote an essay reappraising Tocqueville for *The Atlantic Monthly*. He beautifully recounted Tocqueville's life and works, and for the first time in the United States, to my knowledge, dwelled on Tocqueville's interpretive system and underscored the need for Americans to reconcile liberty with equality.

As Norton saw it, Americans may have led the way in Tocqueville's day. But this was no longer the case. Analyzing Tocqueville, Norton wrote: "It was plain that the dominating principle in the modern development of society was that of democratic equality; and this being the case, the question of prime importance presenting itself for solution was, How is liberty to be reconciled with equality and saved from the inevitable dangers to which it is exposed? Or in other words, can equality, which smoothes the way for the establishment of a despotism, either of an individual or of the mob, by dividing men and reducing the mass to a common level, be made to promote and secure liberty?"[72]

In the midst of the war, Norton continued to pursue the theme. Around him, Norton advanced not just a "new science of politics" but "a science of ideal politics" that would give Americans "a truer sense of what was meant by American principles," to make "them recognize the rights of man," to impress on them "the responsibilities and duties that are involved in our immense privileges," thus developing "in them faith in liberty and equality as principles of universal education."[73]

Norton also took inspiration from a letter Tocqueville had written to Madame Swetchine (published by Beaumont) in which Tocqueville argued that public virtue should take precedence over private virtue, for the education not only of men but also of women. Women also fought the war. Here was a prescription for the times.

Norton's efforts to revive Tocqueville were echoed in a number of New England journals during the Civil War years. *Democracy in America* became a lens through which to view the causes of secession and the future of the Union. The reviewer for *The Christian Examiner* pointed to Tocqueville's discussion of the New England towns to argue that democracy existed only in New England and thus the South's secession could not be blamed on democracy. He went on to complain that English conservatives adopted Tocqueville's tyranny of the majority to account for the war – in this case, the common people's obsession against the tariff – therefore using Tocqueville to justify their arguments about the failings of democracy.[74] At the same time, there was a more critical discussion of Tocqueville's treatment of American federalism. A reviewer pointed out in the pages of *The North American Review* that Tocqueville had failed to predict the significant rise of the Federal government.[75]

In the hands of New Englanders, the chapter on race finally took on the meaning Tocqueville had intended. Tocqueville had cleverly separated his discussion of "Indians and Negroes" from his discussion of democracy and of the Union by saving it for the last chapter of Volume I. As he put it: "Although Indians and Negroes have come up frequently in the course of this work, I have yet to pause to show how these two races stand in relation to the democratic people I have been describing." But Tocqueville intended for the chapter on the three races to point to "the dangers that threaten the confederation" and explore "the prospects for the confederation's survival."[76] As the slavery debate heated up in the 1850s, Tocqueville was cited by abolitionists on the one hand and by advocates of colonization schemes for sending blacks to Africa on the other. The *Christian Examiner and Religious Miscellany* mentioned that Tocqueville saw slavery to be a great danger to the preservation of the Union.[77] Tocqueville's "Testimony against Slavery" was published in *The Liberty Bell*.[78] Also, *The African Repository* cited Tocqueville's positive discussion of the Liberia project.[79] With the danger becoming apparent for everybody to see, and the race issue defining the future of democracy, the relevancy and power of Tocqueville's analysis became obvious.[80] An extended lament, coming as expected from the South, wished Tocqueville had seen American history as a "gigantic and degrading tyranny" where "every thing truly great and noble tended to wither under its deadly shade; while every thing essentially mean and malignant was made to flourish."[81]

Tocqueville became thus central to American discourse because the animating question raised by his work – of reconciling equality and liberty – had finally come to the fore in the country where it was the most relevant. When Tocqueville had been in America in 1831–32, it seemed to him that the two qualities could be consistent on American soil, as opposed to France. Now the Civil War was calling it all into question, and the importance of Tocqueville's essential theory was finally being grasped by his American readership. This was a giant step forward.

In the years following the Civil War, Sumner did much to cement Tocqueville's reputation as a visionary. Sumner included a chapter on Tocqueville in his last book, *Prophetic Voices Concerning America* (1874).[82] He listed among Tocqueville's famous prophecies the 1848 revolution in France, the role of slavery in breaking the Union, and the ultimate unity of the American people as "something entirely new in the world, the implications of which imagination itself cannot grasp."[83] But the ultimate unity of Gilded Age America just could not be built on Tocquevillean principles as understood by Boston Brahmins. The America that had simultaneously inspired and required Tocqueville was about to disappear.

C. Cracks in the System

Even if New England's "immortal glory" was that "of having destroyed slavery" as Mill put it, the Brahmin interpretation of

Tocqueville's liberty-equality paradigm could not survive the reconstruction of America.[84] Once the war was over, Americans stopped finding in Tocqueville the mirror of their concerns.

A new America was emergent already in the war years. Norton, who co-edited the *North American Review*, turned to his New York friend Edwin L. Godkin, whom he had helped launch the *Nation*, to comment on the Bowen edition. In writing for the *North American* in 1865, the Irish-American editor felt none of his Bostonian friend's aristocratic dilemma. To Godkin, neither democracy nor the life of the mind had anything to fear from mass immigration or Western expansion.[85] Tocqueville seemed already less relevant even before the age of robber barons and huge working classes.

That the New England insistence on the currency of Tocqueville would be shortlived is not surprising, given the tenor of the Gilded Age. Nowhere is it more evident than in Henry Adams's relation to Tocqueville. Adams, like his fellow Brahmins, came under the influence of Tocqueville's views and methods in philosophy professor Bowen's class in the late 1850s. But it is only when in England in 1863 – when serving as private secretary to his father whom Abraham Lincoln had appointed minister to the Court of St. James – that Adams discovered a close personal tie to Tocqueville.[86] Henry wrote to his brother Charles Francis, "I have learned to think de Tocqueville my model and I study his life and works as the gospel of my private religion."[87] Adams's realization coincided with that of Norton, with whom he would be closely associated.

Henry Adams found much in Tocqueville to emulate and admire: a confirmation in the primacy of New England, a remarkable ambivalence towards most things, and a yearning for the wisdom of elites. But while Tocqueville tilted the balance towards hope, Adams gave into nostalgia. He ignored Tocqueville's embrace of modernity, choosing to resist every inch of the capitalist system "which ruthlessly stamped out the life of the class into which Adams was born."[88] In 1837, John Quincy Adams had asked Tocqueville to remove from *Democracy in America* a brief passage condemning the spoils in his administration. The former president could not have predicted that Tocqueville would become, in his grandson's eyes, the "high priest" of the dying Adams' faith.[89]

The Tocqueville who remained discussed in the late nineteenth century could neither guide the present, as Godkin pointed out, nor sustain a lost world, as Adams would have liked. Daniel Coit Gilman, president of the new Johns Hopkins University and an influential figure of an expanding American higher education, stressed Tocqueville's hopeful vision of self-government and mobility in an 1898 preface to a new edition of *Democracy*, while recognizing the corporate power and inequality generated by new wealth.[90] But despite the effort, Tocqueville became more relevant to scholars than to citizens at large. Hopkins was one of the American centers of a new, more professionalized academic life that began with earning a Ph.D. It is at the Hopkins history seminar, led by Herbert Baxter Adams, that the visiting Lord Bryce naively argued that he held the key to political science, compared with the inductive and emotion-laden methods of the Frenchman.[91] A more fitting tribute to Tocqueville was Professor Adams's publication, in the *Johns Hopkins University Studies in Historical and Political Science*, of the correspondence between Sparks and Tocqueville – a historical text that had become appropriately suitable for the new methods of documentary editing.[92] The 1896 appearance of Tocqueville's posthumous *Recollections* of the 1848 revolution in France confirmed the famous visitor's status as a historical figure.[93] Thus Tocqueville's nineteenth-century odyssey came to a close.

IV. EPILOGUE

In 1861, Charles Norton thought that Tocqueville had "reached the summit of his fame as an author," but it was only the beginning of a long career of interpretations and reinterpretations still going strong.[94] If the nineteenth-century reception of *Democracy in America* is any guide, Tocqueville's formulations need only to coincide with a perceived threat to reach their full force.

Early in the twentieth century, Tocqueville's influence receded. The Progressives had little use for his work in their criticism of capitalism and rhetoric of social conflict. They neglected it even as some of them dusted off Madison's "Federalist 10" to devise a new theory of interest-group politics. But the eclipse was short-lived. When the Progressives' countervailing powers blossomed into the New Deal, and an enlarged state was perceived as a Leviathan, Tocqueville returned as the theoretician of independent voluntary associations for "a nation of joiners"[95] Tocqueville is still with us, mostly in that capacity.

APPENDIX: SELECTED NINETEENTH-CENTURY AMERICAN REVIEWS OF ALEXIS DE TOCQUEVILLE'S WORK

1833

Lieber, Francis. Introduction to *On the Penitentiary System in the United States and its Application in France*, by Gustave de Beaumont and Alexis de Tocqueville. Philadelphia: Carey, Lea and Blanchard, 1833: v–xxxv.

"De Beaumont and de Tocqueville on the Penitentiary System." Review of *On the Penitentiary System of the U.S. and its Application in France*, by Gustave de Beaumont and Alexis de Tocqueville. *The North American Review* 37, no. 80 (July 1833): 117–38.

1835

"Tocqueville's American Democracy." Review of *De la démocratie en Amérique*, by Alexis de Tocqueville. *Southern Literary Messenger* 1, no. 10 (June 1835): 596.

Review of *Democracy in America*, by Alexis de Tocqueville. Cincinnati Mirror, and *Western Gazette of Literature, Science, and the Arts* 4, no. 37 (July 11, 1835): 294.

"Original Gossip and Table-Talk." *The New-York Mirror, a Weekly Gazette of Literature and the Fine Arts* 13, no. 36 (March 5, 1836): 282.

Review of *Democracy in America*, by Alexis de Tocqueville. *The American Quarterly Review* 19 (March and June 1836): 124–66.

Everett, Edward. "De Tocqueville's Democracy in America." Review of *De la Démocratie en Amérique*, by Alexis de Tocqueville. *The North American Review* 43, no. 92 (July 1836): 178–206.

Everett, Edward. Letter to Sir Robert Peel, 29 March 1837. In *Sir Robert Peel From His Private Papers*, edited by Charles Stuart Parker. Vol. 2. London: John Murray, 1899:333–35.

Tocqueville, Alexis de. "Intelligence of the American People." *The American Magazine of Useful and Entertaining Knowledge* 3, no. 8 (May 1837): 306 [excerpt from Tocqueville].

"Retrospective View of the State of European Politics, Especially of Germany, Since the Last Congress of Vienna." *The United States Magazine, and Democratic Review* 1, no. 1 (October 1837): 123–42.

"Republicanism." *The American Monthly Magazine* 10 (November 1837): 430–31 [mention].

Review of *Democracy in America*, by Alexis de Tocqueville. *The American Monthly Magazine* 10 (December 1837): 599–600.

"European Views of American Democracy." Part 1. *The United States Magazine, and Democratic Review* 1 (1837): 91–107.

1838

"European Views of American Democracy." Part 2. *The United States Magazine, and Democratic Review* 2 (1838): 337–56.

Spencer, John C. Introduction to *Democracy in America*, by Alexis de Tocqueville. New York: Adlard and Saunders; George Dearborn & Co, 1838): v–xi.

Review of *Democracy in America*, by Alexis de Tocqueville. *The New-Yorker* 5, no. 12 (June 9, 1838): 189.

R., S. S. Review of *Democracy in America*, by Alexis de Tocqueville. *Oasis; a Monthly Magazine Devoted to Literature, Science and the Arts* 1, no. 11 (June 30, 1838): 168–69.

Review of *Democracy in America*, by Alexis de Tocqueville. *The Knickerbocker: or, New York Monthly Magazine* 12, no. 3 (September 1838): 256–60.

Review of *Democracy in America*, by Alexis de Tocqueville. *The American Monthly Magazine* 12 (October 1838): 377–81 [reprint of Spencer's Introduction to *Democracy in America* as an anonymous review].

Review of *Democracy in America*, by Alexis de Tocqueville. *The New-Yorker* 6, no. 3 (October 6, 1838): 45.

Review of *Democracy in America*, by Alexis de Tocqueville. *Common School Assistant; a Monthly Paper, for the Improvement of Common School Education* 3, no. 12 (December 1838): 96.

T., P. Review of *Democracy in America*, by Alexis de Tocqueville. *The American Museum of Science, Literature, and the Arts* 1, no. 4 (December 1838): 385–89, 484–94.

S., O. "Three Views of Democracy: Sismondi – Heeren – De Tocqueville." *The Western Messenger; Devoted to Religion, Life, and Literature* 6, no. 2 (December 1838): 110–14.

1839

"De Tocqueville's Opinions." *Common School Assistant; a Monthly Paper, for the Improvement of Common School Education* 4, no. 1 (January 1839): 4 [excerpts].

"Appendix." *The United States Magazine, and Democratic Review* 5, no. 13 (January 1839): 97–98 [mention].

"Appendix. Speech of Charles J. Ingersoll." *The United States Magazine, and Democratic Review* 5, no. 13 (January 1839): 99–144 [mention].

"Democracy in America." *The National Magazine and Republican Review* 1, no. 3 (March 1839): 219–25.

"Abolition of Slavery in the French Colonies." *The New-Yorker* 8, no. 9 (November 16, 1839): 142 [mention].

1840

Carey, Henry C. "Review. M. de Tocqueville." Chap. 8 of vol. 3, *Principles of Political Economy* (Philadelphia, 1840), 231–50.

Review of *Democracy in America: Part the Second*, by Alexis de Tocqueville. *The Merchants' Magazine and Commercial Review* 3 (1840): 443.

"English and French Travelers in America." Review of *Democracy in America*, by Alexis de Tocqueville. *The New York Review* 6 (1840): 142–69.

"De Tocqueville's Democracy in America." Review of *Democracy in America*, by Alexis de Tocqueville. *The New York Review* 7 (1840): 233–48.

"Literary Intelligence." *The New-Yorker* 9, no. 3 (April 4, 1840): 45.

"Social Influence of Democracy." Review of *Democracy in America*, by Alexis de Tocqueville. Parts 1, 2. *The New-Yorker* 9, no. 10 (May 23, 1840): 145–46; no. 11 (May 30, 1840): 161–62.

"Literary Intelligence." *The New-Yorker* 9, no. 15 (June 27, 1840): 237.

Review of *Democracy in America*, by Alexis de Tocqueville. *Godey's Lady's Book, and Ladies' American Magazine* 21 (July 1840): 48.

"The Pardoning Power in America." *The New-Yorker* 9, no. 19 (July 25, 1840): 301 [mention].

Review of "De la Démocratie en Amérique." *The Christian Examiner and Religious Miscellany* 29 (September 1840): 105–7.

"Literary Intelligence." *The New-Yorker* 9, no. 26 (September 12, 1840): 414.

Review of *Democracy in America: Part II: The Social Influence of Democracy*, by Alexis de Tocqueville. *The New-Yorker* 10, no. 2 (September 26, 1840): 29.

Review of *Democracy in America – Part the Second*, by Alexis de Tocqueville. *The Ladies' Companion, a Monthly Magazine; Devoted to Literature and the Fine Arts* 14 (November 1840): 48.

1841

Camp, George Sidney. *The Alleged "Tyranny of the Majority" in America.* Chap. 1 of part 2 in *Democracy* (New York: Harper and Brothers, 1841).

"Catholicism." *The Boston Quarterly Review* 4 (1841): 320–38.

Review of *Democracy in America*, by Alexis de Tocqueville. *The New-Yorker* 10, no. 22 (February 13, 1841): 350.

"Poussin on Democracy in America." *The North American Review* 52 (April 1841): 529–33.

Review of *Democracy in America*, by Alexis de Tocqueville. *The New-Yorker* 11, no. 8 (May 8, 1841): 125.

Review of *Democracy in America*, by Alexis de Tocqueville. *The Methodist Quarterly Review* 1, no. 21 (July 1841): 412–29.

"Literary Intelligence." *The United States Magazine, and Democratic Review* 9, no. 38 (August 1841): 200–202 [mention].

1842

"Mr. Camp's *Democracy*." Review of Democracy, by George Sidney Camp. *The United States Magazine, and Democratic Review* 10, no. 44 (February 1842): 122–28 [mention].

1843

Review of *Democracy in America*, by Alexis de Tocqueville. *The Southern Quarterly Review* 4, no. 7 (July 1843): 61–75.

1847

"Alexander Vattemare's Mission to the United States, and the French Department of Commerce." *The Merchants' Magazine and Commercial Review* 17, no. 2 (1847): 146–50.

"De Tocqueville." *The United States Magazine, and Democratic Review* 21, no. 110 (August 1847): 115–23.

1848

"The French Republic." *The United States Magazine, and Democratic Review* 23, no. 121 (July 1848): 61–73 [mention].

1849

"Primogeniture and Entail." *The United States Magazine, and Democratic Review* 25, no. 133 (July 1849): 17–27 [mention].

"Flogging in the Navy." Part 2. *The United States Magazine, and Democratic Review* 25, no. 135 (September 1849): 225–42 [mention].

1851

"American Institutions and Their Influence." Review of *Democracy in America*, by Alexis de Tocqueville. *The American Whig Review* 13 (1851): 382.

1853

B.,E. H. "Political Philosophy of South-Carolina." Review of *Democracy in America*, by Alexis de Tocqueville. *The Southern Quarterly Review* 7, no. 13 (January 1853): 120–40.

G.,M. R. H. "Calhoun on Government." Review of *A Disquisition on Government, and a Discourse on the Constitution of the United States*, by John C. Calhoun. *The Southern Quarterly Review* 7, no. 14 (April 1853): 333–79 [mention].

1854

Allen, Joseph Henry. "Prospects of American Slavery." *The Christian Examiner and Religious Miscellany* 57 (1854): 220–44.

Benton, Thomas Hart. *Thirty Years View.* 1. New York: D. Appleton and Co., 1854.

1856

Tocqueville, Alexis de. "Testimony Against Slavery." *The Liberty Bell. By Friends of Freedom 14* (1856): 29–30.

Review of *The Old Regime and the Revolution*, by Alexis de Tocqueville. *The Universalist Quarterly and General Review* 13 (October 1856): 428–29.

"De Tocqueville on the Causes of the French Revolution." Review of *The Old Regime and the Revolution*, by Alexis de Tocqueville. *Putnam's Monthly Magazine of American Literature, Science, and Art 8*, no. 47 (November 1856): 471–82.

1857

"America and Africa." *The African Repository 33* (January 1857): 12–13 [mention].

1858

"Writers on Political Science." Review of *The Old Regime and the Revolution*, by Alexis de Tocqueville, and *On Civil Liberty and Self Government*, by Francis Lieber. *The Biblical Repertory and Princeton Review* 30 (1858): 621–45.

"Annual Meeting of the American Colonization Society." *The African Repository* 34 (February 1858): 33–44 [mention].

"Miscellany." *The Historical Magazine, and Notes and Queries Concerning the Antiquities, History and Biography of America 2*, no. 2 (February 1858): 64 [letter from Tocqueville].

1859

Review of *On Civil Liberty and Self-Government*, by Francis Lieber. *The Biblical Repertory and Princeton Review* 31 (1859): 620–22 [mention].

"M. de Tocqueville." *New York Times* (May 11, 1859): 2.

"Recollections of de Tocqueville." *New York Times* (August 9, 1859): 2.

"Recollections of de Tocqueville." *National Era 13*, no. 659 (August 18, 1859): 129.

1860

"Feudalism in America." *DeBow's Review and Industrial Resources, Statistics, etc. Devoted to Commerce, Agriculture, Manufactures 3*, no. 6 (June 1860): 615–24 [mention].

1861

Norton, Charles E."Alexis de Tocqueville." *The Atlantic Monthly* 8 (1861): 551–57.

"Alexis de Tocqueville's Opinion of the English Mind." *New York Times* (August 10, 1861): 4.

Review of *The Old Regime and the Revolution,* by Alexis de Tocqueville. *The North American Review* 93, no. 193 (October 1861): 391–417.

1862

Review of *Memoirs, Letters, and Remains of Alexis de Tocqueville. The American Theological Review* 4 (1862): 748.

Review of *Memoir, Letters, and Remains of Alexis de Tocqueville. The Christian Examiner* 72 (1862): 297–300.

Palmer, R. "Alexis de Tocqueville." *Review of Memoirs, Letters, and Remains of Alexis de Tocqueville. The New Englander* 21 (1862): 669–94.

Bowen, Francis. *Introduction to Democracy in America,* by Alexis de Tocqueville. Translated by Henry Reeve and revised by Francis Bowen (Cambridge: Sever and Francis, 1862): iii–xiv.

Smith, C. C. "Alexis de Tocqueville." *The Christian Examiner* 73 (1862): 381–402.

"De Tocqueville on Democratic Discipline." *New York Times* (January 17, 1862): 4.

Review of *Memoirs, Letters and Remains of Alexis de Tocqueville. The Universalist Quarterly and General Review* 19 (April 1862): 216–17.

Towle, G. M. "Alexis de Tocqueville." Review of *Memoir, Letters, and Remains of Alexis de Tocqueville. The North American Review* 95, no. 196 (July 1862): 138–63.

"De Tocqueville." Review of *Memoir, Letters, and Remains of Alexis de Tocqueville. New York Times* (July 4, 1862): 2.

"New Publications." *American Publishers' Circular and Literary Gazette* 8, no. 10 (November 1, 1862): 116–17.

1863

"Democracy on Trial." *The Christian Examiner* 74 (1863): 262–94.

"The War." *The Biblical Repertory and Princeton Review* 35 (1863): 140–69 [mention].

1864

Canoll, John W. Henry. "The Authorship of *Democracy in America*." *The Historical Magazine, and Notes and Queries Concerning the Antiquities, History, and Biography of America* 8, no. 10 (October 1864): 332–33.

1865

Godkin, Edwin Lawrence. "Aristocratic Opinions of Democracy." Review of *Democracy in America*, by Alexis de Tocqueville. *The North American Review* 100, no. 206 (January 1865): 194–232.

1866

Brooks, E. "The Error of de Tocqueville." Review of *Œuvres Complètes d'Alexis de Tocqueville*. *North American Review* 102, no. 211 (April 1866): 321–34.

1867

Bledsoe, Albert Taylor. "De Tocqueville on the Sovereignty of the People." *The Southern Review* 1 (1867): 302–52.

1870

"American Institutions." Review of *Democracy in America*, by Alexis de Tocqueville. *The Biblical Repertory and Princeton Review* 42 (1870): 167.

1874

"Prophetic Voices." Review of *Prophetic Voices Concerning America*, by Charles Sumner. *The Literary World; a Monthly Review of Current Literature* 5, no. 1 (June 1, 1874): 3–4 [mention].

1875

"Lafayette, de Tocqueville, and Ampère." *New York Times* (October 10, 1875): 3.

1880

Robinson, W. C. "Alexis de Tocqueville." *Catholic World* 32 (1880): 157–66.

1881

"In Memory of Charles Sumner." *New York Times* (March 28, 1881): 3 [mention].

1890

Abbott, Lyman. "Industrial Democracy." *Forum* (August 1890): 658–69 [mention].

1893

"De Tocqueville's Memoirs." Review of *Souvenirs de Alexis de Tocqueville. The Atlantic Monthly* 72 (1893): 120–25.

"De Tocqueville Memoirs." Review of *Souvenirs de Alexis de Tocqueville*, by Alexis de Tocqueville. *New York Times* (April 2, 1893): 19.

1897

"De Tocqueville." *Review of The Recollections of Alexis de Tocqueville, edited by the Comte de Tocqueville. The Literary World; a Monthly Review of Current Literature* 28, no. 9 (May 1, 1897): 141–42.

"The Memoirs of Count de Tocqueville." Review of *The Recollections of Alexis de Tocqueville*, edited by the Comte de Tocqueville. *The Dial; a Semi-monthly Journal of Literary Criticism, Discussion, and Information* 22, no. 261 (May 1, 1897): 287.

"De Tocqueville and the Third Napoleon." Review of *The Recollections of Alexis de Tocqueville*, edited by the Comte de Tocqueville. *Overland Monthly and Out West Magazine* 29, no. 174 (June 1897): 652–53.

Dunning Wm. A. Review of *The Recollections of Alexis de Tocqueville*, edited by the Comte de Tocqueville. *Political Science Quarterly* 12, no. 2 (June 1897): 319–21.

1898

Adams, Herbert Baxter. "Jared Sparks and Alexis de Tocqueville." *Johns Hopkins University Studies in Historical and Political Science* 16, no. 12 (1898): 563–611.

Gilman, Daniel Coit. 1898 Introduction to *Democracy in America*, by Alexis de Tocqueville. New York: Century Co., 1898: v–xlvi.

Blind, Karl. "Alexis de Tocqueville's *Recollections* and Self-Revelations." Review of *The Recollections of Alexis de Tocqueville*, edited by the Comte de Tocqueville. *Forum* [24, no. 6] (February 1898): 744–60.

Gilman, Daniel Coit. "Alexis de Tocqueville and His Book on America – Sixty Years After." *Century Illustrated Magazine* 56, no. 5 (September 1898): 703–15.

"*Democracy in America* in New Setting." *The Dial; a Semi-monthly Journal of Literary Criticism, Discussion, and Information* 25, no. 297 (November 1, 1898): 307–8.

Shaw, Albert. "De Tocqueville." *New York Times* (December 10, 1898): BR844.

1899

Morgan, John T. Introduction to *Democracy in America*, by Alexis de Tocqueville. New York: The Colonial Press, 1899: iii–viii.

Ingalls, John J. Introduction to *Democracy in America*, by Alexis de Tocqueville. New York: The Colonial Press, 1899: ix–xi.

"De Tocqueville." *New York Times* (January 21, 1899): BR41.

"Russia, England, and America." *New York Times* (July 2, 1899): 16 [mention].

1900

Stanton, Elizabeth Cady. "Progress of the American Woman." *The North American Review* 171, no. 529 (December 1900): 904–7 [mention].

NOTES

I would like to thank Brian Bolin for exemplary research assistance, and my friends Nicolas Barreyre, James Burnett, Charles Feigenoff, Arthur Gold-hammer, Michael Holt, Maurice Kriegel, Dorothy Ross, John Stagg, James Turner, and Cheryl Welch for their precious suggestions. I have also benefited from stimulating discussions in the Fall of 2004 with students in my "Reading Alexis de Tocqueville" class at the University of Virginia, and the Tocqueville seminar led by Seth Cotlar at Willamette University.

1   For biographical information, see André Jardin, *Tocqueville: A Biography, 1805–1859*, trans. Lydia Davis with Robert Hemenway (New York: Farrar, Straus & Giroux, Inc., 1988) and my chronology in *DA* (trans. Goldhammer), 878–906.

2 Alexis de Tocqueville, *Democracy in America*, trans. Henry Reeve, with an original preface and notes by John C. Spencer (New York: Adlard and Saunders; George Dearborn & Co, 1838).

3 Herbert Baxter Adams, "Jared Sparks and Alexis de Tocqueville," *Johns Hopkins University Studies in Historical and Political Science* Ser. 16, no. 12 (December 1898): 601.

4 John M. Belohlavek, *Let the Eagle Soar!; The Foreign Policy of Andrew Jackson* (Lincoln: University of Nebraska Press, 1985), 90–126.

5 *DAI* (trans. Goldhammer), 16, and note 2, also on 16.

6 William B. Hatcher, *Edward Livingston, Jeffersonian Republican and Jacksonian Democrat* (Baton Rouge: Louisiana University Press, 1940), 419–47.

7 Adams, "Jared Sparks and Alexis de Tocqueville," 601; Sparks's opinion is echoed in American reviews: "The English, at first, were lavish of their praise of the 'great commentator' on our government and institutions, but when a close examination of the work convinced them that it was not a censure on democracy in general and on American democracy in particular, they denied the correctness of their first judgment and denounced the book as visionary, dull, obscure; and we have regretted to see some of these depreciating criticisms republished in America in advance of the appearance of the essay itself, which will by no means occasion such estimates in the minds of intelligent and candid men." *The New-Yorker* 10, no. 2 (September 26, 1840): 29.

8 N.W. Senior to Tocqueville, 13 February 1835, *OC* 6:2, 66; Tocqueville to H. Reeve, 5 June 1846, *OC* 6:1, 33; in that last letter, Tocqueville comments on Senior's pessimism for the book.

9 *London Review* 1 (October 1835): 129 [also *Westminster Review* XXX], signed only with the letter A. Mill's review was reprinted by Theodore Foster in New York in 1836 in Volume IV of *Foster's Cabinet Miscellany: A series of Publications on Various Subjects from the Latest and Most Approved Writers*. Phillips Bradley, in his introduction to *DA* (trans. Reeve-Bowen-Bradley), xli, sees the reprint as part of an effort to counter negative reviews.

10 Tocqueville to Beaumont, 1 November 1833, *OC* 8:1, 137, and George Wilson Pierson, *Tocqueville in America* (1938; reprint, Baltimore: Johns Hopkins University Press, 1996), 705–77; Frank Freidel, *Francis Lieber, Nineteenth-Century Liberal* (Baton Rouge: Louisiana University Press, 1947).

11 Tocqueville to J. Sparks, 14 February 1837, *OC* 7, 63–64.

12 Gustave de Beaumont, *Lettres d'Amérique, 1831–1832* (Paris: Presses Universitaires de France, 1973), 98.

13 J. C. Spencer to Tocqueville, June 10, 1848, *TA* (Beinecke).

14 An initial effort to negotiate a royalty agreement with Tocqueville failed; see Tocqueville to J. C. Spencer, 20 September 1838 and 12 September 1839, *OC* 7, 70–72, 77–80.

15 Tocqueville to Madame Swetchine, 7 January 1856, *OC* 15:2, 269.

16 *DAII* (trans. Goldhammer), 581.

17 Tocqueville to Henry Reeve; compare 5 June 1836, *OC* 6:1, 34 to 15 September 1839, *OC* 6:1, 48.

18 Tocqueville to Kergorlay (early) 1835, *OC* 13:1, 374.

19 *DAII* (trans. Goldhammer), 726.

20 For nineteenth-century American reviews, see, in addition to the Appendix to this chapter, the (shorter) list established by Phillips Bradley in appendix IV of *DA* (trans. Reeve-Bowen-Bradley), 2: 392–401, and the (less reliable) one by S. Karin Amos, *Alexis de Tocqueville and the American National Identity: The Reception of "De la démocratie en Amérique" in the United States in the Nineteenth Century* (Frankfurt am Main: Peter Lang, 1995), 276–80. *Poole's Index to Periodical Literature* Vol. 1, Part 2, K-Z, 1802–1881 (Gloucester, MA: Peter Smith, 1963) identifies some of the reviewers who published anonymously.

21 *The Knickerbocker: or, New York Monthly Magazine* 12, no. 3 (September 1838): 257; the reviewer notes on 260 Tocqueville's comparison of Russia with the United States at the end of volume one, so frequently quoted during the Cold War.

22 1, no. 4 (December 1838): 488; another reviewer wrote: "Deep, immutable and of infinite power are the influences which have formed and which must preserve our institutions, and no insight that cannot recognize these is sufficient to read our national character." *The New-Yorker* 11, no. 8 (May 8, 1841): 125.

23 19 (March and June 1836): 135.

24 43, no. 92 (July 1836): 198–99; Tocqueville told H. Reeve of his pleasure at reading this review, so afraid was he of having made mistakes in his description of American institutions, Tocqueville to H. Reeve, 21 September 1836, *OC* 6:1, 36.

25 *DAI* (trans. Goldhammer), 391.

26 Tocqueville to T. Sedgwick, 4 December 1852, *OC* 7, 146–47; Tocqueville to J. Sparks, 11 December 1852, *OC* 7, 148–49.

27 19 (March and June 1836): 156–58; another reviewer writes that the United States is proof of "the law of civilization" (civilization always spreads from East to West) and of "the mission of the present predominant race in the world." *The New York Review* 6 (January 1840): 157.

28 "European Views of American Democracy," part 2, 2 (1838): 351.

29 "De la démocratie en Amérique," *The Christian Examiner* 29, 3rd ser.
11 (September 1840): 106; *The New-Yorker* 9 (1840): 145. The *Boston Quarterly Review* 4 (July 1841): 323, 326, concurred, pointing to Tocqueville's "native prejudice in favor of the pomp and power, if not the principles of the Romish church." Also in the same article: "the 'individualism,' which De Tocqueville so clearly discerns in the United States; that strong confidence in self, or reliance upon one's own exertion and resources, is precisely the antipodal principle of a tyrannical Catholicism."

30 11 (1841): 125; or "After having seen our country, its institutions and manners, misrepresented by traveler after traveler – superficial observers for the most part, who were unable to take in the whole of such a subject, and bad digesters of what little they did pick up – we have now before us the production of an intelligent man who had an eye to mark, a judgment keen to discriminate, and a mind truly philosophical, in so far as freedom from prejudice and great general-izing powers may warrant that epithet." *The American Museum of Science, Literature, and the Arts* 1, no. 4 (December 1838): 385.

31 Thomas Hart Benton, *Thirty Years' View; or A History of the Working of the American Government for Thirty Years, from 1820 to 1850*, vol. 1 (New York, 1854), 114.

32 *DAI* (trans. Goldhammer), 271; on the conceit of Americans, see also T. to Beaumont, 1 November 1833, *OC* 8:1, 137.

33 *Methodist Quarterly Review* 1, no. 21 (July 1841): 426, 429, in an otherwise favorable review primarily of Volume 2.

34 Pierson, *Tocqueville in America*, 347–454.

35 *Journey to America* (trans. Lawrence), 59.

36 In this, they contrasted sharply with the British reviewers, who used Tocqueville's tyranny of the majority as ammunition against democ-racy; see Edward Everett to Sir Robert Peel, 29 March 1837, in *Sir Robert Peel from his Private Papers*, ed. Charles Stuart Parker, vol. 2 (London, 1899), 333–35; and Bradley's introduction to *DA* (trans. Reeve-Bowen-Bradley), note 49, p. xxxix.

37 *DAI* (trans. Goldhammer), 293.

38 *DAI* (trans. Goldhammer), 288; on this point, see Jean-Claude Lamberti, "Two Ways of Conceiving the Republic," in *Interpreting Tocqueville's "Democracy in America,"* ed. Ken Masugi (Savage, MD.: Rowman & Littlefield Publishers, Inc., 1991), 7.

39 Sparks to G. Poussin, 1 February 1841, in Adams, "Jared Sparks and Alexis de Tocqueville," 605; see also H. B. Adams, *The Life and*

Writings of Jared Sparks, 2 vols. (Boston, 1893), 208–35, "Everett to Peel."

40 Tocqueville, *Democracy*, with notes by John C. Spencer, 452.

41 Benton, *Thirty Years' View*, 113, 227–228.

42 12, no. 3 (September 1838): 259.

43 19 (March and June 1836): 153.

44 Ibid., 142

45 Southern Democrats pointed out: "In Boston and Philadelphia there is a class in the upper ranks of society, which to say the least, views democracy with a dissatisfied feeling, and which considers that the well being of the whole would be promoted, by the diminution of the political influence of the inferior ranks of society." *The Southern Quarterly Review* 4, no. 7 (July 1843): 71.

46 *DAI* (trans. Goldhammer), 7.

47 Two reviewers had something substantial to say on individualism. In *The Boston Quarterly Review* 4 (1841): 323, the author discusses the paradoxical trend toward a "general assimilation of character and belief" that arises out of the increasing individualism of the democratic age. In *The North American Review* 52 (April 1841): 532, the reviewer of Poussin's volume (see note 57) argues that Tocqueville is wrong to predict that individualism increases in the democratic age because democracy gives rise to party politics, which puts people in close combination. He was the first reviewer to argue that Tocqueville missed significant aspects of party politics.

48 *The Southern Quarterly Review* 4, no. 7 (July 1843): 66–67.

49 Henry C. Carey, *Principles of Political Economy*, vol. 3 (Philadelphia, 1840), 231–250; on Carey, see Daniel Walker Howe, *The Political Culture of the Whigs* (Chicago: University of Chicago Press, 1979), 118–112; on Carey and Tocqueville, see Dorothy Ross, *The Origins of American Social Science* (New York: Cambridge University Press, 1991), 44.

50 A few reviewers noted Montesquieu's work but did not address his influence on Tocqueville's treatment of national character. National character, when mentioned, was discussed superficially; see, for example, "Original Gossip and Table Talk," *The New-York Mirror* 13, no. 36 (March 5, 1836): 282, or *Merchants' Magazine* 3 (1840): 443.

51 "Appendix," *The United States Magazine, and Democratic Review* 5, no. 13 (January 1839): 97–98, and "Appendix. Speech of Charles J. Ingersoll." *The United States Magazine, and Democratic Review* 5, no. 13 (January 1839): 99–144.

52 *DAI* (trans. Goldhammer), 316.

53 *DAII* (trans. Goldhammer), 708.

54 July 1840, 21; see also "Democracy in America – Part the Second," *Ladies's Companion: A Monthly Magazine* 14 (1841): 48, "Proud should we be of the evidence of such a writer, that proves the daughters of America, to be purer in moral principles, and more proficient in domestic relations, than any other country in the world."

55 Beecher, *Domestic Economy* (Boston, 1842), 27; on Beecher, see Kathryn Kish Sklar, *Catharine Beecher: A Study in American Domesticity* (New Haven: Yale University Press, 1973); on civil society, see Kathleen D. McCarthy, *American Creed: Philanthropy and the Rise of Civil Society, 1700–1865* (Chicago: University of Chicago Press, 2003).

56 On Tocqueville and the abolition of slavery, see *Niles' National Register*, May 20, 1843, 178.

57 Mary Wilhelmine Williams, "John Middleton Clayton," in *The American Secretaries of State and their Diplomacy*, ed. Samuel Flagg Bemis (New York: Alfred A. Knopf, 1928), 19–31.

58 (Paris, 1841), 173; for an American review of the French edition, attempting to arbitrate between Tocqueville and Poussin, see *The North American Review* 52, 111 (April 1841): 529–33.

59 Guillaume Tell Poussin, *The United States: Its Power and Progress*, first American edition from the third French edition (Philadelphia, 1851), 424; first published in France in 1843.

60 Their correspondence begins in 1838, *OC*, 7, 69–70; see also David Herbert Donald, *Charles Sumner and the Coming of the Civil War* (Chicago: University of Chicago Press, 1960), 121, 123, 328.

61 *OC* 7, 198n, 208n, 217n.

62 "In memory of Charles Sumner," *New York Times*, March 28, 1881, 3. During his American travels, Tocqueville jotted down in his notebook on 14 October 1831 that life "is a serious duty imposed upon us." *Journey to America* (trans. Lawrence), 155.

63 In discussing self government, Lieber quoted Tocqueville's July 8, 1851, speech to the French Chamber on the evil of French centralization, *On Civil Liberty and Self Government* (Philadelphia, 1853), I: 275. In later editions, Lieber added notes on Tocqueville's *Old Regime* (Philadelphia, 1877), 186, 254.

64 Idem, *On Civil Liberty*, I: 172–73, 277; see also George M. Fredrickson, *The Inner Civil War: Northern Intellectuals and the Crisis of the Union* (1965; reprint, Urbana: University of Illinois Press, 1993), 24.

65 Ross, *Origins of American Social Science*, 40–42.

66 "Writers on Political Science," review of *The Old Regime and the Revolution*, by Alexis de Tocqueville, and *On Civil Liberty and Self*

Government, by Francis Lieber, *The Biblical Repertory and Princeton Review* 30, no. 4 (October 1858): 621–45.

67 Gustave de Beaumont, ed. *Œuvres et correspondence inédites d'Alexis de Tocqueville* 2 vols. (Paris, 1861); translated as *Memoir, Letters, and Remains of Alexis de Tocqueville,* 2 vols. (Boston, 1862); in reviewing the translation, Ray Palmer noted Tocqueville's idea of combining liberty and equality, "Alexis de Tocqueville," *The New Englander* 21 (1862): 680; C. C. Smith pointed out that Tocqueville confided in Mill his disappointment at the French reception of the second volume of *Democracy,* "Alexis de Tocqueville." *The Christian Examiner* 73, 5th ser., 11 (November 1862): 394–95.

68 In his *Principles of Political Economy Applied to the Condition, the Resources, and the Institutions of the American People* (Boston, 1856), 503, on Tocqueville and the laws of inheritance.

69 2 vols. (Cambridge, 1862); Bowen omitted a few notes and simplified others, which Phillips Bradley later restored in *DA* (trans. Reeve-Bowen-Bradley).

70 Freidel, *Lieber,* 323–41; David Clinton, *Tocqueville, Lieber, and Bagehot: Liberalism Confronts the World* (New York: Palgrave Macmillan, 2003), 63–71.

71 James Turner, *The Liberal Education of Charles Eliot Norton* (Baltimore: Johns Hopkins University Press, 1999), esp. 85–99, 218.

72 8 (1861): 553; Norton ends the paragraph by noting that "for the study of this question, and of others naturally connected with it, the United States afforded opportunities nowhere else to be found."

73 Turner, *Liberal Education,* 184, quoting from Norton's correspondence to Frederick Law Olmsted and Jonathan Baxter Harrison in 1863 and 1864.

74 "Democracy on Trial," *The Christian Examiner* 74, 5th ser., 12 (1863): 271–73, 281.

75 E. Brooks, "The Error of de Tocqueville," *The North American Review* 102, no. 211 (April 1866): 324–329.

76 *DAI* (trans. Goldhammer), 365.

77 Joseph Henry Allen, "Prospects of American Slavery," *The Christian Examiner and Religious Miscellany* 57, 4th ser., 22 (1854): 220–21.

78 Alexis de Tocqueville, "Testimony against Slavery," *The Liberty Bell. By Friends of Freedom* 14 (1856): 29–30.

79 "America and Africa," 33 (January 1, 1857): 12.

80 In announcing the new Bowen edition, the *American Publishers' Circular and Literary Gazette,* November 1, 1862, 10, pointed to the significance of Tocqueville's discussion of the three races "in the present state of our affairs."

81 Albert Taylor Bledsoe, "De Tocqueville on the Sovereignty of the People." *The Southern Review* 1 (1867): 302–52.

82 Boston: Lee and Shepard, 1874.

83 Ibid., 164; Sumner translated this passage from the conclusion of volume 1 of *Democracy in America* using the 1864 (14th) French edition.

84 J. S. Mill to E. L. Godkin, in response to Godkin's review of the Bowen edition (see note 83) in Hugh S. R. Elliot, ed., *The Letters of John Stuart Mill* (New York: Longmans, Green and Co, 1910), 2: 35.

85 Edwin Lawrence Godkin, "Aristocratic Opinions of Democracy," *The North American Review* 100, no. 206 (January 1865): 202–205, 208, 222–24.

86 Ernest Samuels, *The Young Henry Adams* (Cambridge: Harvard University Press, 1948), 24–25, 136–40; Adams developed a similar affinity towards John Stuart Mill.

87 H. Adams to C. F. Adams, Jr., May 1, 1863, in Worthington Chauncey Ford, ed., *A Cycle of Adams Letters, 1861–1865* (Boston: Houghton Mifflin Co., 1920), 1: 282.

88 Henry Adams, *The Education of Henry Adams: An Autobiography* (1918), Library of America (New York: Viking, 1983), 1035; On Tocqueville's lasting influence on Adams's writings, see J. C. Levenson, *The Mind and Art of Henry Adams* (Stanford: Stanford University Press, 1957), 126–27, 146–47.

89 H. A. to C. F. A., May 1, 1863, in Ford, ed. *A Cycle* 1: 281.

90 Daniel Coit Gilman, Introduction to *Democracy in America*, by Alexis de Tocqueville (New York, 1898), xxix, xxxii; and idem, "Alexis de Tocqueville and His Book On America – Sixty Years After," *Century Illustrated Magazine* 56, no. 5 (September 1898): 710–11; the two texts significantly overlap.

91 See James Bryce, "The Predictions of Hamilton and de Tocqueville," *Johns Hopkins University Studies in Historical and Political Science* 5, no. 9 (September 1887): 347–49, 351–53.

92 Adams, "Jared Sparks and Alexis de Tocqueville."

93 The French edition appeared in 1893.

94 Norton, *Atlantic Monthly*, 555.

95 Pierson conceived of his monumental work during the New Deal and published it in 1938. Arthur M. Schlesinger captured the theme in his "Biography of a Nation of Joiners," *American Historical Review*, 50 (October 1944): 1–25.

BIBLIOGRAPHY

Adams, Henry. *The Education of Henry Adams: An Autobiography (1918).* Library of America. New York: Viking, 1983.

Adams, Herbert Baxter. "Jared Sparks and Alexis de Tocqueville." *Johns Hopkins University Studies in Historical and Political Science,* Ser. 16, no. 12 (December 1898).

The Life and Writings of Jared Sparks, 2 vols. Boston, 1893.

Allen, Barbara. *Tocqueville, Covenant, and the Democratic Revolution: Harmonizing Earth with Heaven.* Lanham, MD: Lexington Books, 2005.

Allen, Joseph Henry. "Prospects of American Slavery." *The Christian Examiner and Religious Miscellany* 57, 4th ser., 22 (1854).

Amos, S. Karin. *Alexis de Tocqueville and the American National Identity: The Reception of "De la démocratie en Amérique" in the United States in the Nineteenth Century.* Frankfurt am Main: Peter Lang, 1995.

Antoine, Agnès. *L'impensé de la démocratie: Tocqueville, la citoyenneté, et la religion.* Paris: Fayard, 2003.

Arendt, Hannah. *The Human Condition.* Chicago: University of Chicago Press, 1958.

Aristotle. *Nicomachean Ethics.* Translated by Martin Ostwald. Upper Saddle River, NJ: Prentice Hall, 1962.

The Politics. Translated by Carnes Lord. Chicago: University of Chicago Press, 1984.

Aron, Raymond. *Essai sur les libertés.* Paris: Calmann-Levy, 1965.

Les ètapes de la pensée sociologique. Paris: Gallimard, 1990 [1967].

Main Currents in Sociological Thought. New Brunswick, NJ: Transaction Publishers, 1998.

Atanassow, Ewa. "*Fortnight in the Wilderness*: Nature and Civilization." In *Perspectives on Political Science.* (forthcoming).

Audier, Serge. *Tocqueville retrouvé: genèse et enjeux du renouveau tocquevillien français,* Paris: Vrin-EHESS, 2004.

Augustin, Charles. *Pour la critique.* Paris: Folio Essais, 1992.

Aurevilly, Barbey de. *Le Pays.* 22 January 1861.

Avineri, Shlomo. *Hegel's Theory of the Modern State.* Cambridge: Cambridge University Press, 1972.

Barber, Benjamin. *Jihad vs. McWorld: How Globalism and Tribalism Are Reshaping the World.* New York: Ballantine Books, 1996.

Barth, Karl. "Introductory Essay." In Ludwig Feuerbach, *The Essence of Christianity.* New York: Harper, 1957.

Beaumont, Gustave de. *Ireland: Social, Political, and Religious.* 2 vols. Edited by W. C. Taylor. London: Richard Bentley, 1839.

"La Russie et les États Unis sous le rapport économique." *Revue des deux mondes,* Ser. 2, 5 (1854).

Lettres d'Amérique, 1831–1832. Paris: Presses Universitaires de France, 1973.

Marie or, Slavery in the United States. Translated by Barbara Chapman. Baltimore, MD: The Johns Hopkins University Press, 1999.

Œuvres et correspondence inédites d'Alexis de Tocqueville. 2 vols. Paris, 1861. Translated as *Memoir, Letters, and Remains of Alexis de Tocqueville.* 2 vols. Boston, 1862.

Beecher, Catherine. *A Treatise on Domestic Economy.* Boston, MA: Marsh, Capen, Lyon, and Webb, 1841.

Bellah, Robert. *Habits of the Heart.* New York: Harper & Row, 1985.

Belohlavek, John M. *Let the Eagle Soar! The Foreign Policy of Andrew Jackson.* Lincoln, NE: University of Nebraska Press, 1985.

Bénichou, Paul. *Le Sacre de l'écrivain.* Paris: Corti, 1973.

Benoît, Jean-Louis. *Comprendre Tocqueville.* Paris: Colin, 2004.

Tocqueville Moraliste. Paris: Champion, 2004.

Tocqueville: un destin paradoxal. Paris: Bayard, 2005.

Benton, Thomas Hart. *Thirty Years' View; or A History of the Working of the American Government for Thirty Years, from 1820 to 1850.* Vol. 1. New York: D. Appleton and Co. 1854.

Berger, Peter L., and Richard John Neuhaus. "To Empower People: From State to Civil Society." In *The Essential Civil Society Reader,* edited by Don Eberly. Lanham, MD: Rowman & Littlefield Publishers, 2000.

Berlin, Isaiah. *Freedom and Its Betrayal: Six Enemies of Human Liberty.* Princeton, NJ: Princeton University Press, 2002.

"Two Concepts of Liberty." In *Four Essays on Liberty.* London: Oxford University Press, 1969.

Blankaert, Claude. "Of Monstrous Métis? Hybridity, Fear of Miscegenation, and Patriotism from Buffon to Paul Broca." In *The Color of Liberty:*

Histories of Race in France, edited by Sue Peabody and Tyler Stovall. Durham, NC: Duke University Press, 2003.

Bledsoe, Albert Taylor. "De Tocqueville on the Sovereignty of the People." *The Southern Review* 1 (1867).

Blumenberg, Hans. *Work on Myth*. Translated by Robert M. Wallace. Cambridge, MA: MIT Press, 1985.

Boesche, Roger. *The Strange Liberalism of Alexis de Tocqueville*. Ithaca, NY: Cornell University Press, 1987.

Bossuet, Jacques-Bénign. *Discourse on Universal History*. Translated by Elborg Forster. Edited by Orest Ranum. Chicago: The University of Chicago Press, 1976.

Boudon, Raymond. "The logic of relative frustration." In *Rational Choice*, edited by J. Elster. Oxford: Blackwell, 1986.

Tocqueville aujourd'hui. Paris: Jacob, 2005.

Boutmy, Emile. *Eléments d'une psychologie du peuple américain: la nation, la patrie, l'état, la religion*. Paris: Colin, 1912 [1902].

Bowen, Francis. *Principles of Political Economy Applied to the Condition, the Resources, and the Institutions of the American People*. Boston, 1856.

Brooks, E. "The Error of de Tocqueville." *The North American Review* 102, no. 211 (April 1866).

Brunner, Otto. *Geschichtliche Grundbegriffe; Historiches Lexikon zur Politisch-Sozialen Sprache in Deutschland*. Edited by Brunner, Conze, Koselleck. Stuttgart: Klett-Cotta, 1982.

Bryce, James. "The Predictions of Hamilton and de Tocqueville." *Johns Hopkins University Studies in Historical and Political Science* 5, no. 9 (September 1887).

Burke, Edmund. *Reflections on the Revolution in France*. Edited by J. C. D. Clarke. Stanford, CA: Stanford University Press, 2001.

Caeser, James W. *Liberal Democracy and Political Science*. Baltimore, MD: Johns Hopkins University Press, 1990.

Carey, Henry C. *Principles of Political Economy*. Vol. 3. Philadelphia, 1840.

Cazes, Bernard. "Tocqueville et l'exception française." *La Quinzaine Littéraire* 1–15 (April 2004).

Clinton, David. *Tocqueville, Lieber, and Bagehot: Liberalism Confronts the World*. New York: Palgrave Macmillan, 2003.

Cmiel, Kenneth. *Democratic Eloquence: The Fight over Popular Speech in Nineteenth-Century America*. Berkeley, CA: University of California Press, 1990.

Cohen, Jean, and Andrew Arato. *Civil Society and Political Theory*. Cambridge, MA: MIT Press, 1992.

Cohen, William B. *The French Encounter with Africans: White Response to Blacks, 1530–1880*. Bloomington, IN: Indiana University Press, 2003 [1980].

Colletti, Lucio. *From Rousseau to Lenin.* New York: Monthly Review Press, 1971.

Cosentino, Andrew J, Françoise, Mélonio, and James Schleifer, *A Passion for Liberty: Alexis de Tocqueville on Democracy and Revolution.* Washington, DC: Library of Congress, 1989.

Constant, Benjamin. *Oeuvres.* Edited by Alfred Roulin. Paris: Gallimard: 1957.

"The Liberty of the Ancients Compared to That of the Moderns." In Constant, *Political Writings,* edited by Fontana. Cambridge: Cambridge University Press, 1988.

"The Spirit of Conquest and Usurpation." In Constant, *Political Writings,* edited by Fontana. Cambridge: Cambridge University Press, 1988.

Conway, Stephan. *The British Isles and the War of American Independence.* New York: Oxford University Press, 2000.

Craiutu, Aurelian. Liberalism Under Siege: The Political Thought of the French Doctrinaires. Lanham, MD: Lexington Books, 2003.

"Tocqueville's Paradoxical Moderation." The Review of Politics 67.4 (Fall 2005).

Craiutu, Aurelian, and Jeremy Jennings. "The Third Democracy: Tocqueville's Views of America after 1840." American Political Science Review 98.3 (August 2004).

Craveri, Piero. *Genesi di una constituzione.* Naples, 1985.

Desjobert, Amedée. *La question d'Alger: politique, colonisation, commerce.* Paris: P. Dufart, 1837.

Diaz, José-Luis, and Françoise Mélonio, eds. *Tocqueville et la littérature.* Paris: Presses de l'Université Paris-Sorbonne, 2004.

Donald, David Herbert. *Charles Sumner and the Coming of the Civil War.* Chicago: University of Chicago Press, 1960.

Douay-Soublin, Françoise. "La rhétorique en France au XIXe siècle." In *Histoire de la rhétorique dans l'Europe moderne.* Paris: Presses Universitaires de France, 1999.

Drescher, Seymour. *Alexis de Tocqueville: Memoir on Pauperism.* Chicago: Ivan R. Dee, 1997.

Dilemmas of Democracy: Tocqueville and Modernization. Pittsburgh: University of Pittsburgh Press: 1968.

Tocqueville and Beaumont on Social Reform. New York: Harper and Row, 1968.

Tocqueville and England. Cambridge, MA: Harvard University Press, 1964.

"Tocqueville's Two Démocraties." *Journal of the History of Ideas* 25 (April–June 1964).

Drolet, Michael. *Tocqueville, Democracy and Social Reform*. London: Palgrave, 2003.

Droz, Joseph. *Histoire du règne de Louis XIV pendant les années où l'on pouvait prévenir ou diriger la Révolution française*. Paris: Renouard 1860.

Ehrenberg, John. *Civil Society: the Critical History of an Idea*. New York: New York University Press, 1999.

Eisenstadt, A. S., ed. "More than America: Comparison and Synthesis in *Democracy in America*." In *Reconsidering Tocqueville's Democracy in America*. New Brunswick, NJ: Rutgers, 1988.

Elliot, Hugh S. R., ed. *The Letters of John Stuart Mill*. New York: Longmans, Green and Co., 1910.

Elster, Jon. *Alchemies of the Mind: Rationality and the Emotions*. Cambridge: Cambridge University Press, 1999.

Closing the Books: Transitional Justice in Historical Perspective. Cambridge: Cambridge University Press, 2004.

"Crossvoting." *Journal of Political Philosophy* (forthcoming).

Explaining Technical Change. Cambridge: Cambridge University Press, 1983.

Political Psychology. Cambridge: Cambridge University Press, 1993.

Ulysess Unbound: Studies in Rationality, Precommitment, and Constraints. Cambridge: Cambridge University Press, 2000.

Emperor Napoleon III, *History of Julius Caesar*. 2 vols. New York, 1865–66.

Fehrenbacher, Don E. *The Slaveholding Republic: An Account of the United States Government's Relations to Slavery*. New York: Oxford University Press, 2001.

Felice, Domenico, ed. *Dispotismo*. 2 vols. Naples: Liguori, 2001.

Finke, Roger, and Rodney Stark. *The Churching of America, 1776–1990: Winners and Losers in Our Religious Economy*. New Brunswick, NJ: Rutgers University Press, 1992.

Fontana, Biancamaria. "Old world for new: How Tocqueville moved from America to France." *The Times Literary Supplement* (2 July 2004).

Ford, Worthington Chauncey, ed. *A Cycle of Adams Letters, 1861–1865*. Boston: Houghton Mifflin Co., 1920.

Forment, Carlos A. *Democracy in Latin America*. Chicago: University of Chicago Press, 2003.

Foster, Theodore. *Foster's Cabinet Miscellany: A Series of Publications on Various Subjects from the Latest and Most Approved Writers*. New York: Theodore Foster, 1836–1837.

Fredrickson, George M. *The Inner Civil War: Northern Intellectuals and the Crisis of the Union*. Urbana: University of Illinois Press, 1993 [1965].

Freidel, Frank. *Francis Lieber, Nineteenth-Century Liberal.* Baton Rouge: Louisiana University Press, 1947.

Freud, Sigmund. *Civilization and Its Discontents.* Edited by James Strachey. New York: W. W. Norton & Co., 1989.

Furbank, P. N. "Tocqueville's Lament." *The New York Review of Books* (8 April 1999).

Furet, François. "Burke ou la fin d'une seule histoire de l'Europe." *Débat,* no. 39 (March–May 1986).

Interpreting the French Revolution. Translated by Elborg Forster. Cambridge: Cambridge University Press; Paris: Editions de la Maison des Sciences de l'Homme, 1981.

"Naissance d'un paradigme: Tocqueville et le voyage en Amérique (1825–1831)." *Annales* 39:2 (March–April 1984).

"The Intellectual Origins of Tocqueville's Thought." *Tocqueville Review* 7 (1985–86).

"Tocqueville." In *A Critical Dictionary of the French Revolution,* edited by François Furet and Mona Ozouf, translated by Arthur Goldhammer. Cambridge, MA: Harvard University Press, 1989.

Gannett, Robert T., Jr. "Bowling Ninepins in Tocqueville's Township." *American Political Science Review* 97, no. 1 (February 2003).

Tocqueville Unveiled: The Historian and His Sources for "The Old Regime and the Revolution." Chicago: University of Chicago Press, 2003.

Giddens, Anthony. *Runaway World.* New York: Routledge, 2002.

Gilman, Daniel Coit. "Introduction." In *Democracy in America.* New York, 1898.

Goblot, J-J. *La Jeune France libérale: le Globe et son groupe littéraire (1824–1830).* Paris: Plon, 1995.

Godkin, Edwin Lawrence. "Aristocratic Opinions of Democracy." *The North American Review* 100, no. 206 (January 1865).

Goldhammer, Arthur. "Remarks on the Mansfield-Winthrop Translation." *French Politics, Culture & Society* 21:1 (2003).

"Translating Tocqueville: the Constraints of Classicism." *Tocqueville Review* 25, no. 1 (2004).

Grandmaison, Charles de. "Séjour d'Alexis de Tocqueville en Touraine, préparation du livre sur l'ancien régime, juin 1853–avril 1854." *Le Correspondant* 114, n.s. 78 (January–March 1879).

Guellec, Laurence. *Tocqueville et les langages de la démocratie.* Paris: Champion, 2004.

Ed. *Tocqueville et l'esprit de la démocratie: The Tocqueville Review/La Revue Tocqueville.* Paris: Presses de la Fondation Nationale des Sciences Politiques, 2005.

Guizot, François. *Histoire de la civilisation en Europe depuis la chute de l'Empire romain jusqu'à la Révolution française.* Paris: Hachette, 1985 [1828].

Histoire de la civilisation en France depuis la chute de l'Empire Romain. (Paris: Didier, 1859 [1829–32]).

The History of Civilization in Europe. Translated by William Hazlitt. London: Penguin, 1997.

Gutmann, Amy, ed. *Freedom of Association.* Princeton, NJ: Princeton University Press, 1998.

Habermas, Jurgen. *The Structural Transformation of the Public Sphere.* Translated by Thomas Burger. Cambridge, MA: MIT Press, 1989.

Hadari, Saguiv A. *Theory in Practice: Tocqueville's New Science of Politics.* Stanford, CA: Stanford University Press, 1989.

Hamilton, Alexander, James Madison, and John Jay. *The Federalist Papers.* New York: NAL Penguin, 1999.

Hancock, Ralph. "The Uses and Hazards of Christianity." In *Interpreting Tocqueville's Democracy in America,* edited by Ken Masugi. Savage, MD: Rowman & Littlefield Publishers, 1991.

Hartz, Louis. *The Liberal Tradition in America: An Interpretation of American Political Thought since the Revolution.* New York: Harcourt Brace, 1955.

Hatcher, William B. *Edward Livingston, Jeffersonian Republican and Jacksonian Democrat.* Baton Rouge: Louisiana University Press, 1940.

Hegel, G. W. F. *Elements of the Philosophy of Right.* Translated by Hugh Barr Nisbet. Cambridge: Cambridge University Press, 1991.

Phenomenology of Spirit. Translated by A. V. Miller. New York: Oxford University Press, 1977.

The Philosophy of Right. Translated by T. M. Knox. Oxford: Oxford University Press, 1967.

The Phenomenology of Mind. Translated by J. B. Baillie. New York: Harper & Row, 1967.

The Philosophy of History. Translated by J. Sibree. New York: Dover Publications, 1956.

Die Vernunft in der Geschichte. Edited by J. Hoffmeister. Hamburg: F. Meiner, 1952.

"Henri Martin's *History of France.*" *Edinburgh Review* 106 (October 1857).

Hereth, Michael. *Alexis de Tocqueville: Threats to Freedom and Democracy.* Translated by George Bogardus. Durham, NC: Duke University Press, 1986.

Herr, Richard. *Tocqueville and the Old Regime.* Princeton: Princeton University Press, 1962.

Hirschman, Albert O. *The Passions and the Interests.* Princeton: Princeton University Press, 1977.

Hobbes, Thomas. *Behemoth*. Edited by Ferdinand Tönnies. Chicago: University of Chicago Press, 1990.
  Leviathan. Edited by Edwin Curley. Indianapolis: Hackett Publishing Co., 1994.
Holbach, Baron d'. *Système de la Nature*. 2 vols. London, 1770.
Holmes, Stephen. *Passions and Constraints: On the Theory of Liberal Democracy*. Chicago: The University of Chicago Press, 1995.
Howe, Daniel Walker. *The Political Culture of the Whigs*. Chicago: University of Chicago Press, 1979.
Howland, Douglas. *Translating the West*. Honolulu: University of Hawaii Press, 2002.
Hunt, Lynn. *The Family Romance of the French Revolution*. Berkeley, CA: University of California Press, 1992.
Inglehart, Ronald. *Culture Shift in Advanced Industrial Society*. Princeton, NJ: Princeton University Press, 1990.
Janara, Laura. "Brothers and Others: U.S. Genealogy, Democracy, and Racism." *Political Theory* 32:6 (December 2004).
  Democracy Growing Up: Authority, Autonomy and Passion in Tocqueville's Democracy in America. Albany, NY: State University of New York Press, 2002.
Janin, Jules. "Manifeste de la jeune littérature: réponse à M. Nisard." *Revue de Paris*, 2nd ser., 1 (1834).
Jardin, André. *Alexis de Tocqueville*. Paris: Hachette, 1984.
  Tocqueville. New York: Farrar, Straus & Giroux, 1984.
  Tocqueville (1805–1859): A Biography. Translated by Lydia Davis with Robert Hemenway. London: Peter Haliban, 1988.
  Tocqueville: A Biography, 1805–1859. Translated by Lydia Davis with Robert Hemenway. New York: Farrar, Straus & Giroux, 1988.
Jaume, Lucien. *L'individu effacé ou le paradoxe du libéralisme français*. Paris: Fayard, 1997.
Jenkins, Philip. *The Next Christendom: the Coming of Global Christianity*. Oxford: Oxford University Press, 2003.
Journal of Democracy 11:1 (2000).
Judt, Tony. *Past Imperfect: French Intellectuals, 1944–1956*. Berkeley, CA: University of California Press, 1992.
Kahan, Alan. *Aristocratic Liberalism*. New Brunswick: Transaction Publishers, 2001.
  Liberalism in Nineteenth-Century Europe: The Political Culture of Limited Suffrage. Basingstoke, UK: Palgrave Macmillan, 2003.
Kant, Immanuel. "An Answer to the Question, 'What is Enlightenment'." In Kant, *Political Writings*, edited by Hans Riess. Cambridge: Cambridge University Press, 1971.

Kelly, George Armstrong. *Hegel's Retreat from Eleusis*. Princeton, NJ: Princeton University Press, 1978.

"Parnassian Liberalism in Nineteenth-Century France." *History of Political Thought* 8 (1987).

Keslassy, Eric. *Le libéralisme de Tocqueville à l'épreuve du pauperisme*. Paris: L'Harmattan, 2000.

Kessler, Sanford. *Tocqueville's Civil Religion: American Christianity and the Prospects for Freedom*. Albany, NY: State University of New York, 1994.

Kobi, Sylvia. "Entre pédagogie politique et démagogie populiste." *Mots*, no. 43 (1995).

Koebner, Richard. "Despot and Despotism: Vicissitudes of a Political Term." *Journal of the Warburg and Courtauld Institute* 14 (1951).

Kohn, Margaret. "Tocqueville and Beaumont on Race and Slavery." *Polity* 35:2 (Winter 2002).

Krauze, Enrique. "La Culture de la démocratie en Amerique Latine: Variations sur un thème de Tocqueville." *The Tocqueville Review* 21:1 (2000).

Lamberti, Jean-Claude. *Tocqueville and the Two Democracies*. Translated by Arthur Goldhammer. Cambridge, MA: Harvard University Press, 1989.

Tocqueville et les deux Démocraties. Paris: Presses Universitaires de France, 1983.

"Two Ways of Conceiving the Republic." In *Interpreting Tocqueville's "Democracy in America,"* edited by Ken Masugi. Savage, MD: Rowman & Littlefield Publishers, Inc., 1991.

Laprade, Victor de. "De la question littéraire." *Revue Indépendante* 10 (10 October 1843).

Lawler, Peter Augustine. *The Restless Mind: Alexis de Tocqueville on the Origin and Perpetuation of Human Liberty*. Lanham, MD: Rowman & Littlefield Publishers, 1993.

Lefebvre, Georges. "A propos de Tocqueville." *Annales Historiques de la Révolution Française* 27, no. 4 (October–December 1955).

Lefort, Claude. *Essais sur le politique: XIXe–XXe siècle*. Paris: Editions du Seuil, 1986.

Lehmann, Hartmut, and Melvin Richter, eds. *The Meaning of Historical Terms and Concepts, New Studies on Begriffsgeschichte*. Washington, DC: German Historical Institute, 1996.

Levallois, Jules. *L'opinion nationale*. 5 May 1861.

Levenson, J. C. *The Mind and Art of Henry Adams*. Stanford, CA: Stanford University Press, 1957.

Lieber, Francis. *Manual of Political Ethics Chiefly for the Use of the Colleges and Students at Law.* 2 vols. Boston: C.C. Little and J. Brown, 1838–39.

On Civil Liberty and Self Government. Philadelphia: JB Lippincott, 1877.

Lilla, Mark. ed., *New French Thought: Political Philosophy.* Princeton: Princeton University Press, 1994.

Lipsey, R. G., and K. Lancaster. "The General Theory of Second Best." *Review of Economic Studies* (1956).

Locke, John. *Two Treatises of Government.* Edited by Peter Laslett. Cambridge: Cambridge University Press, 1988.

Lukacs, John. "Unveiling Tocqueville the Historian." *Historically Speaking* (May/June 2004).

Luste Boulbina, Seloua, ed. *Sur l'Algérie.* Paris: Garnier Flammarion, 2003.

Luther, Martin. "Lectures on Genesis." In *Luther's Works.* Vol. 3. St. Louis: Concordia Publishing House, 1961.

Lectures on Isaiah." In *Luther's Works,* edited by Helmut T. Lehmann. Philadelphia: Fortress Press, 1967.

Macfarlane, Alan. *The Riddle of the Modern World: Of Liberty, Wealth and Equality.* London: Palgrave, 2000.

Machen, J. Gresham. *Christianity and Liberalism.* Grand Rapids, MI: Wm. B. Eerdmans Publishing Co., 1923.

Maistre, Joseph de. *Considérations sur la France, 1797.* Brussels: Editions Complexe, 1988.

Malia, Martin. "Democracy in the World." *Journal of Democracy* 11:1 (January 2000).

Mancini, Matthew. "Political Economy and Cultural Theory in Tocqueville's Abolitionism." *Slavery & Abolition* 10:2 (September 1989).

Mandeville, Bernard. *The Fable of the Bees.* Indianapolis, IN: Liberty Classics, 1988.

Mandt, Hella. "Tyrannis, Despotie." In *Geschichtliche Grundbegriffe,* edited by Brunner, Conze, Koselleck. Stuttgart: Klett-Cotta, 1982.

Manent, Pierre. *An Intellectual History of Liberalism.* Translated by Rebecca Balinski. Princeton: Princeton University Press, 1994.

"Guizot et Tocqueville devant l'ancien et le nouveau." In *Guizot et la culturepolitique de son temps. Colloque de 1987 de la Fondation Guizot-Val Richer.* Paris: Gallimard, 1991.

The City of Man. Princeton: Princeton University Press, 1998.

Tocqueville and the Nature of Democracy. Translated by John Waggoner. Lanham, MD: Rowman & Littlefield, 1996.

Mansfield, Harvey C., and Delba Winthrop. "Editors Introduction." In *Democracy in America.* Chicago: University of Chicago Press, 2000.

Liberalism and Big Government: Tocqueville's Analysis. London: Institute of United States Studies, University of London, 1999.

"Reply to Our Critics." *French Politics, Culture & Society* 21:1 (2003).

"Translating Tocqueville's *Democracy in America.*" *The Tocqueville Review* 21:1 (2000).

Marcuse, Herbert. *One-Dimensional Man.* Boston: Beacon Press, 1964.

Markoff, John. *The Abolition of Feudalism.* University Park, PA: Pennsylvania State University Press, 1996.

Martin, David. *Tongues of Fire.* Oxford: Basil Blackwell, 1990.

Marx, Karl. *La question juive.* Paris: Aubier Montaigne, 1971.

McCarthy, Kathleen D. *American Creed: Philanthropy and the Rise of Civil Society, 1700–1865.* Chicago: University of Chicago Press, 2003.

Meier, Christian. *La naissance du politique.* Paris: Gallimard, 1995.

Mélonio, Françoise. "Nations et Nationalismes." *La Revue Tocqueville/ The Tocqueville Review* 18:1 (1997).

Tocqueville and the French. Translated by Beth G. Raps. Charlottesville, VA: University Press of Virginia, 1998.

"Tocqueville et le despotisme moderne." *Revue Française d'Histoire des Idées Politiques* 6 (1997).

Tocqueville et les Français. Paris: Aubier, 1993.

Milgate, Murray, and Cheryl B. Welch *Critical Issues in Social Thought.* London: Academic Press, 1989.

Mill, J. S. "Tocqueville on Democracy in America (Vol. II)." In *Essays on Politics and Culture,* edited by Gertrude Himmelfarb. Gloucester, MA: Peter Smith, 1973.

Mitchell, Harvey. *America After Tocqueville: Democracy Against Difference.* New York: Cambridge University Press, 2002.

Individual Choice and the Structures of History: Alexis de Tocqueville as Historian Reappraised. New York: Cambridge University Press, 1996.

Mitchell, Joshua. *The Fragility of Freedom: Tocqueville on Religion, Democracy and the American Future.* Chicago: University of Chicago Press, 1995.

Montesquieu, Baron de. *The Spirit of the Laws.* Edited by Anne M. Cohler, Basia Carolyn Miller, and Harold Samuel Stone. Cambridge: Cambridge University Press, 1989.

Naville, Pierre. *D'Holbach et la philosophie scientifique au XVIIIe siècle.* Paris: Gallimard, 1967.

Nicole, Pierre. *Essais de morale.* Paris: 1671–78.

Nietzsche, Friedrich. *Beyond Good and Evil.* Translated by Walter Kaufman. New York: Vintage Books, 1966.

The Genealogy of Morals. Translated by Walter Kaufman. New York: Random House, 1967.

Niles' National Register. Washington City: William Ogden Niles, 1837–1849.

Nisard, Charles. "D'un amendement à la définition de la littérature facile." *Revue de Paris* 2nd ser., vol. 2 (1834).

Nolla, Eduardo, ed. *Liberty, Equality, Democracy.* New York: New York University Press, 1992.

Ozouf, Mona. "Liberty, Equality, Fraternity." In *Realms of Memory, Vol. 3: Symbols.* Translated by Arthur Goldhammer. New York: Columbia University Press, 1992.

Parker, Charles Stuart, ed. *Sir Robert Peel from his Private Papers.* Vol. 2. London, 1899.

Pascal, *Pensées.* Edited by P. Sellier. Paris: Classiques Garnier, 1993.

Pelczynski, Z. A. "The Hegelian Conception of the State." In *Hegel's Political Philosophy: Problems and Perspectives,* edited by Pelczynski. Cambridge: Cambridge University Press, 1971.

Picot, G. *Histoire des États Généraux.* Vols. I–V. New York: Burt Franklin, 1963 [1888].

Pierson, George Wilson. *Tocqueville in America.* Baltimore, MD: Johns Hopkins University Press, 1996 [1938].

Pitney, John J., Jr. "The Tocqueville Fraud." *The Weekly Standard.* (13 November 1995).

Pitts, Jennifer. "Empire and Democracy: Tocqueville and the Algerian Question." *Journal of Political Philosophy* 8:3 (2000).

Introduction to her edition of Tocqueville's *Writings on Empire and Slavery.* Baltimore, MD: The Johns Hopkins University Press, 2001.

Plato. *The Republic.* Translated by Allan Bloom. New York: Basic Books, 1968.

Poole, William Frederick. *Poole's Index to Periodical Literature.* Vol. 1, Part 2, K-Z, 1802–1881. Gloucester, MA: Peter Smith, 1963.

Poussin, Guillaume Tell. *Considérations sur le principe démocratique qui régit l'union Américaine, et de la possibilité de son application à d'autres états.* Paris, 1841.

The United States: Its Power and Progress. Philadelphia, 1851 [1843].

Putnam, Robert D. *Bowling Alone: The Collapse and Revival of American Community.* New York: Simon and Schuster, 2002.

Making Democracy Work: Civic Traditions in Modern Italy. Princeton: Princeton University Press, 1993.

Quandt, William B. *Revolution and Political Leadership: Algeria, 1954–1968.* Cambridge, MA: MIT Press, 1969.

Rawls, John. *Theory of Justice*. Cambridge, MA: Harvard University Press, 1971.

Rédier, Antoine. *Comme disait M. de Tocqueville*. Paris: Perrin, 1925.

Rémusat, Charles de. *Mémoires de ma vie*. 5 vols. Paris: Plon, 1960.

Passé et présent. Paris: Ladrange, 1847.

Ricœur, Paul. *La Métaphore vive*. Paris: Editions du Seuil, 1975.

Richter, Melvin. "A Family of Political Concepts: Tyranny, despotism, Bonapartism, Caesarism, dictatorship, 1750–1917." *European Journal of Political Theory* 4 (July 2005), 221–248.

"Comparative Political analysis in Montesquieu and Tocqueville." *Comparative Politics* 1, no. 2 (1969), 129–160.

"Guizot and Tocqueville on Democracy: From a Type of Society to a Political Regime." *History of European Ideas* 30 (2004).

"Le concept de despotisme et l'abus des mots." *Dix-huitième Siècle 34 (2002)*.

"The History of the Concept of Despotism. "In The *Dictionary of the History of Ideas*. New York: Charles Scribner's Sons, 1973.

The History of Political and Social Concepts: a Critical Introduction. New York: Oxford University Press, 1995.

ed. *The Political Theory of Montesquieu*. Cambridge: New York, Cambridge University Press, 1977.

The Politics of Conscience: T.H. Green and his Age. Cambridge: Harvard University Press, 1964.

"Tocqueville and Nineteenth-Century Conceptualizations of the Two Bonapartes and their Empires." In *The History and Theory of Dictatorship*, edited by Peter Baehr and Melvin Richter. Cambridge: Cambridge University Press, 2004.

"Tocqueville on Algeria." *Review of Politics* 25 (July 1963).

"Tocqueville, Napoleon, and Bonapartism." In *Reconsidering Democracy in America*, edited by E. Eisenstadt. New Brunswick, NJ: Rutgers University Press, 1988.

Ricken, Ulrich. "*Réflexions du XVIIIe siècle sur 'l'abus des mots.'*" *Mots* 4 (1982).

Rosanvallon, Pierre. "The History of the Word 'Democracy' in France." *Journal of Democracy* 6 (1995).

"L'histoire du mot démocratie à l'époque moderne." In *La pensée politique, 1: Situations de la démocratie*. Paris: Gallimard-Seuil, 1993.

Rosenblum, Nancy. *Membership and Morals*. Princeton: Princeton University Press, 1997.

Rosenfeld, Sophia. *A Revolution in Language*. Stanford: Stanford University Press, 2001.

Ross, Dorothy. *The Origins of American Social Science*. New York: Cambridge University Press, 1991.

Rousseau, Jean-Jacques. "Discourse on the Origin of Inequality." In *The First and Second Discourses*. Edited and Translated by Roger Masters. New York: St. Martin's Press, 1964.

The Social Contract in Political Writings. Translated and edited by Frederick Watkins. Madison: University of Wisconsin Press, 1986.

Saez, Lawrence. "Tocqueville's Fragmented Encounter with India." *The Tocqueville Review* 21:2 (2000).

Sainte-Beuve, Charles. *Causeries de lundi*, 3rd ed. Paris: Garnier, 1857–1872.

Nouveaux lundis. 13 vols. Paris: Calmann-Levy, 1865.

Samuels, Ernest. *The Young Henry Adams*. Cambridge: Harvard University Press, 1948.

Schleiermacher, Friedrich. *On Religion: Speeches to Its Cultured Despisers*. Translated by Richard Crouter. Cambridge: Cambridge University Press, 1988.

Schleifer, James T. "Epilogue: How Many Democracies." In *The Making of Tocqueville's Democracy in America*, 2nd ed. Indianapolis: Liberty Fund, 2000.

The Making of Tocqueville's "Democracy in America." Chapel Hill, NC: University of North Carolina Press, 1980.

The Making of Tocqueville's "Democracy in America," 2nd ed. Indianapolis: Liberty Fund, 2000.

"Tocqueville's Reputation in America," Andrew J. Cosentino, ed. *A Passion for Liberty: Alexis de Tocqueville on Democracy and Revolution*. Washington, DC: Library of Congress, 1989.

Schlesinger, Arthur M. "Biography of a Nation of Joiners." *American Historical Review*, 50 (October 1944).

Sennett, Richard. *The Fall of Public Man*. New York: Vintage, 1977.

Sepinwall, Alyssa Goldstein. "Eliminating Race, Eliminating Difference: Blacks, Jews, and the Abbé Grégoire." In *The Color of Liberty: Histories of Race in France*, edited by Sue Peabody and Tyler Stovall. Durham, NC: Duke University, 2003.

Shapiro, Gilbert, and John Markoff. *Revolutionary Demands*. Stanford: Stanford University Press, 1998.

Shklar, Judith. *Freedom and Independence*. Cambridge: Cambridge University Press, 1976.

Siedentop, Larry. *Democracy in Europe*. New York: Columbia University Press, 2000.

Tocqueville. Oxford: Oxford University Press, 1994.

Simmel, Georg. *Soziologie*. Berlin: Duncker and Humblot, 1908.

Skinner, Quentin. *Liberty before Liberalism*. Cambridge: Cambridge University Press, 1998.

Sklar, Kathryn Kish. *Catharine Beecher: A Study in American Domesticity*. New Haven: Yale University Press, 1973.

Smith, Adam. *The Theory of Moral Sentiments*. Edited by D.D. Raphael and A.L. Macfie. Indianapolis, IN: Liberty Classics, 1982.

Wealth of Nations. Chicago: University of Chicago Press, 1976.

St. Augustine. *The Trinity*. Translated by Edmund Hill. New York: New City Press, 1991.

Staël, Germaine de. *De la littérature*. Paris: Garnier-Flammarion, 1991 [1800].

Considérations sur la révolution française. Paris: Tallandier, 2000 [1983] [1818].

Stern, Fritz. "The New Democracies in Crisis in Interwar Europe." In *Democracy's Victory and Crisis: Nobel Symposium no. 93*, edited by Axel Hadenius. New York: Cambridge University Press, 1997.

Stone, Lawrence. *Causes of the English Revolution 1529–1642*. London: Routledge, 1986.

Stevens, Jacqueline. "Beyond Tocqueville, Please!" *American Political Science Review*, 89:4 (1995), 987–990.

Strauss, Leo. *Thoughts on Machiavelli*. Chicago: The University of Chicago Press, 1958.

Sumner, Charles. *Prophetic Voices Concerning America*. Boston: Lee and Shepard, 1874.

Tocqueville, Alexis de. *Democracy in America*. Translated by Henry Reeve, with an original preface and notes by John C. Spencer. New York: Adlard and Saunders, 2003 [1838].

Democracy In America. 2 vols. Translated by Henry Reeve. Revised by Francis Bowen. Cambridge, 1862.

La democracia en América. Edited and translated by Eduardo Nolla. 2 vol. Madrid: Aguilar, 1990.

Textes économiques: anthologie critique. Edited by Jean-Louis Benoît and Éric Keslassy. Paris: Pocket, 2005.

Torrey, R.A. *The Fundamentals: A Testimony to the Truth*. Los Angeles: Bible Institute of Los Angeles, 1917.

Troeltsch, Ernst. *Protestantism and Progress*. Philadelphia: Fortress Press, 1986.

Tucker, Richard, ed. *The Marx Engels Reader*. New York: W.W. Norton & Co., 1978.

Turchetti, Mario. *Tyrannie et tyrannicide de l'antiquité à nos jours*. Paris: Presses Universitaires de France, 2001.

Turner, James. *The Liberal Education of Charles Eliot Norton*. Baltimore, MD: Johns Hopkins University Press, 1999.

Van Delft, Louis. *Le moraliste classique. Essai de définition et de typologie*. Paris: Droz, 1982.

Villa, Dana R. *Arendt and Heidegger: The Fate of the Political*. Princeton: Princeton University Press, 1996.

Politics, Philosophy, Terror. Princeton: Princeton University Press, 1999.

Socratic Citizenship. Princeton: Princeton University Press, 2001.

Ed., *Cambridge Companion to Hannah Arendt*. Cambridge: Cambridge University Press, 2000.

Walzer, Michael. "The Civil Society Argument." In *Theorizing Citizenship*, edited by Ronald Beiner. Albany, NY: State University of New York Press, 1995.

Weber, Max. *The Protestant Ethic and the Spirit of Capitalism*. Translated by Talcott Parsons. London: Allen & Unwin, 1930.

Welch, Cheryl B. "Colonial Violence and the Rhetoric of Evasion: Tocqueville on Algeria." *Political Theory* 31:2 (2003).

De Tocqueville. Oxford: Oxford University Press, 2001.

Liberty and Utility: the French Idéologues and the Transformation of Liberalism. New York: Columbia University Press, 1984.

"Tocqueville's Resistance to the Social." *History of European Ideas* 30 (2004).

White, James Boyd. *When Words Lose Their Meaning*. Chicago: University of Chicago Press, 1984.

Williams, Mary Wilhelmine. "John Middleton Clayton." In *The American Secretaries of State and their Diplomacy*, edited by Samuel Flagg Bemis. New York: Alfred A. Knopf, 1928.

Wills, Garry. "Did Tocqueville 'Get' America?" *New York Review of Books* (April 29, 2004).

Winthrop, Delba. "Tocqueville's American Woman and 'the True Conception of Democratic Progress.'" *Political Theory* 14:2 (1986), 239–61.

Wolin, Sheldon. *Tocqueville Between Two Worlds: The Making of Political and Theoretical Life*. Princeton: Princeton University Press, 2001.

Woloch, Isser. *The New Regime. Transformations of the French Civic Order, 1789–1820s*. New York: W. W. Norton & Co Inc., 1994.

INDEX

Abbé Lesueur (tutor), 139
abolitionism, in England, 30
Académie de Sciences Morales,
    Tocqueville at, 342
l'Académie française, 261, 265, 355
Adams, Henry, 378
Adams, Herbert Baxter, 379
Adams, John Quincy, 361, 365, 378
administrative, centralization of,
    despotism, 230, 269
"administrative" despotism, 230,
    269
African-Americans, 332. *See also*
    race
The African Repository, 377
l'âge classique, 139, 161
Agrégation de Philosophie, 7, 108
Algeria
    European colonization in, 325
    fraternity in, 319–21
    French conquest of, 315–16
    Islam in, 324
    racial integration in, 320
    Tocqueville in, 21–2, 315, 320,
        324
American Episcopal Church, 300
The American Museum of Science,
    Literature, and the Arts, 364
The American Quarterly Review,
    365, 366, 369

Ampère, Jean-Jacques, 190
Ancien Régime. See The Old
    Regime and the Revolution
Anderson, Benedict, 307
Andrieux, François, 53
appendix, 380–9
Arendt, Hannah, 236
aristocracies. *See also* nobility,
    French
    Aristotle on, 114
    closet, 203–7
    democracies v., 100, 114–15, 117
    language utility in, 152–3
    under political science, 83
    social states and, 98, 125
    under "tyranny of the majority,"
        369
"aristocracy of wealth," in
    Democracy in America (1835),
    108
"aristocratic age," liberalism and,
    277–8
"aristocratic man," 114
Aristotle, 81, 101, 114, 115, 119,
    139, 157
    on aristocracy, 114
    disposition for, 157
    political science for, 81–2
    Tocqueville v., on political
        science, 83, 98, 104, 152

413

THE SCOTTISH ENLIGHTENMENT *Edited by*
  ALEXANDER BROADIE
SPINOZA *Edited by* DON GARRETT
THE STOICS *Edited by* BRAD INWOOD
WITTGENSTEIN *Edited by* HANS SLUGA *and*
  DAVID STERN